T3-BSJ-254

Bolesław Leśmian

Bolesław Leśmian
The Poet and His Poetry

by

Rochelle Heller Stone

University of California Press
Berkeley • Los Angeles • London

University of California Press
Berkeley and Los Angeles, California

University of California Press, Ltd.
London, England

ISBN: 0-520-02549-0
Library of Congress Catalog Card Number: 73-84382

Printed in the United States of America

To Mark

and
to the memory
of our parents.

Contents

Contents

Preface

Bolesław Leśmian, banished to a marginal literary existence during his lifetime by the official literary attitude, has been acclaimed in the post-thaw years as one of the greatest of Poland's classic poets and the most prominent poet since the death of Norwid. Although in the period between the wars many poets were fascinated and influenced by his work, few reacted against the "campaign of silence" that led to a misconception of his work and a failure to evaluate it in its proper historical context.

This study traces the convergence of Leśmian's theory and his poetry within the contemporary Polish and Russian literary scene out of which he emerged as a man and as a poet. His metaphysical poetry is presented against the background of the philosophies with which he identified.

No doubt Bolesław Leśmian would have shuddered at the mention of "theory" in the same breath with "poetry." Programs and pronouncements were anathema to him, and antithesis of spontaneous creation. But while Leśmian did, indeed, create "spontaneously," he was a theoretician in spite of himself. In addition to his poetry, he wrote a series of literary essays which may be read as footnotes to his own works, making it possible to view his critical and creative writings together as the basis of a literary theory. In fact, with the passing of time it has become apparent that he was the only writer to emerge from the Young Poland phase of Polish literature with a coherent program for Symbolist poetry. Great writers do not fall into categories easily, but the Symbolism with which I have attempted to associate Leśmian was not only a literary movement, but an attitude of art toward life, both of which move inexorably forward in a process of ceaseless evolution.

Leśmian created poetry whose aim was to fix the fleeting moment eternally, and to make the ephemeral durable by means of concrete symbols—rooted in myths. In an attempt to demonstrate some of the magic of his creative process, I have translated the poetry cited in this study. Translating poetry presents special problems, but translating Leśmian is an almost insurmountable task. With his frequent neologisms and complex, philosophically charged imagery, he is an extremely difficult poet even in Polish.

In translating, one must often regretfully sacrifice a great deal of what makes poetry. I have tried to preserve Leśmian's ideas and imagery at the sacrifice of meter and rhyme, important but, unfortunately, inimitable aspects of his poetics. A sincere attempt has been made to imitate Leśmian's neologisms, but where this would have proved ludicrous in English, I have provided explanatory notes.

I have translated all quoted material except where otherwise specified, including the poet's philosophical essays and letters. Leśmian as an epistolary writer is elliptical and often manifests a total disdain for strict grammatical rules. In addition, some words have been deleted in his original manuscript. For the purpose of this work, one of whose central aims has been to analyze and understand Leśmian's aesthetics, I was forced to violate the freedoms he enjoyed in his prose by adding words for clarification and omitting words that do not specifically advance the prime objectives under the reader's scrutiny.

This work is a revised and amplified version of a doctoral dissertation completed in 1970, consequently works on Leśmian written after that date have not been taken into consideration although a number of them are very illuminating.

I wish to express my thanks to Professors Thomas Eekman, Vladimir Markov, and Kenneth Harper, the members of my dissertation committee at the University of California, Los Angeles, and to the Regent's Faculty Fellowship for the Summer Quarter 1974, for their financial assistance for the translation of the poetry and the editing of the manuscript. In the process of writing, I was particularly fortunate to have Professor Aleksander Issatschenko read the sections of this volume dealing with language. I wish to express my thanks to Professor Maria R. Mayenowa and members of the Institute of Literary Research in Warsaw, Poland, who were extremely helpful in my research. I also wish to thank Neil Granoien, my collaborator in translating the poetry. My husband Mark has assisted me in innumerable ways; whatever I might say here cannot do justice to the extent and value of his contribution.

Within the text, I have employed the popular transliteration of Russian names. Otherwise, the method used in the quoted material, the notes, and the bibliography is that prescribed by the Library of Congress. It should also be noted that the use of the initial letter instead of the author's given name is customary in the Soviet Union and the satellite countries.

R. H. S.

1

The Perspective of Time

> . . . If there exists, in worlds beyond, a Land of Poetry unencompassed by the senses—then none other than Leśmian was its ambassador on earth, in *partibus infidelium*. . . . He was a creature in the guise of Absolute Poet.
>
> —Julian Tuwim[1]

It is common knowledge that literary criticism exercises enormous power in deciding the fate of a writer. It can condemn, totally banish to oblivion, or resurrect his work almost at will without due justification. Often it is the result of pettiness, narrow-mindedness, jealousy or the desire to cater to the established tastes of the average reader. At best, it can be explained as the absence of a fair historical perspective.

Bolesław Leśmian's creative fate can serve as an example of how a great poet can be victimized by literary critics and historians over a span of nearly sixty years. For it is little more than a decade since his work received the recognition it deserves. Beginning in the late 1950s, some critics, scholars, and poets have at last come to consider him the greatest Polish poet of the twentieth century, the direct descendant of Cyprian Kamil Norwid, and "unique in world literature."[2] He has even been called by a former ideological opponent of the twenties, the Polish Husserl or Heidegger, always remaining, however, in a class by himself—inimitable.[3] Yet, this is the same poet who, prior to the Second World War, was so little known even by students of literature, that his name appeared in no literary textbooks and his poetry was curiously absent from anthologies. Such prominent critics, as Aleksander Brückner and Manfred Kridl afford him little or no space in their works on contemporary Polish literature.[4] This silent treatment lasted, with a few exceptions, until the late 1950s; yet, here was a poet whose works were published over a span of forty years!

Leśmian's literary debut took place between 1895 and 1896, when some of his sonnets were published in the Warsaw newspaper *Wędrowiec*.[5] A year later, his poem, "Park w śniegu" ("A Park in the Snow"), appeared in the famous Warsaw journal *Życie* ("Life"), then in existence only a few months. In 1898 the young poet won second prize for his sonnet "Pieśniowa słodycz z lasu się wylewa . . ." ("A songlike sweetness pours from the forest . . .") in a contest conducted by the same journal.[6] (First prize was awarded to the foremost Decadent poet, Kazimierz Tetmajer.)

Although not a prolific writer, Leśmian worked in a broad spectrum of genres. His poetry, prose, essays, and literary reviews appeared regularly in various Polish periodicals (with the exception of the prestigious *Wiadomości Literackie* ("Literary News"), which deliberately banned his work until the 1930s). He was a frequent contributor to the excellent Młoda Polska ("Young Poland") journal *Chimera*, edited by his friend Zenon Przesmycki, to whom he had been introduced by the poet Antoni Lange, his father's cousin. Here were published his early poems, as well as a collection of prose works, *Legendy tęsknoty* ("Legends of Longing"), in 1904, which betray a lingering influence of Polish and Russian Romanticism and Decadence. However, some cycles, such as *Aniołowie* ("Angels") and *Oddaleńcy* ("The Distant Ones"), were included later, in 1912, in his first book of poems, *Sad rozstajny* ("Orchard at Crossroads"). He contributed to *Krytyka, Miesięcznik Literacki i Artystyczny,* as well as to other periodicals, especially after *Chimera* ceased publication.

It is curious that Leśmian's work was published and that he received some recognition during his lifetime from a few favorable critics, yet he was completely unknown to the Polish intelligentsia.[7] It is equally puzzling that a seemingly unimportant poet should suddenly, about two decades after his death, attain such a prominent place in Polish belles lettres. That other major figures of the twentieth century, such as Stanisław Ignacy Witkiewicz, Bruno Schulz, or later Witold Gombrowicz, were subjected to somewhat similar treatment is small consolation. It is true that time has brought about a change in taste, yet this is hardly a satisfactory explanation.[8] How could so distorted an opinion of Leśmian's work have prevailed and have been perpetuated for such a long time? There must have been more valid reasons, and it is hoped that a brief glimpse at the poet's biography and the period in which he worked will shed some light on this "tragedy of error." However, it is not my intention to rehabilitate the great poet; this has been done admirably by his first monographer, Jacek Trznadel.[9]

My primary objective is to reassess Leśmian's literary work through a presentation of his poetics in proper historical context, revealing him to have been a consistent Symbolist whose aesthetics correspond most closely to that of the Russian Symbolists of the second generation. In the course of proceeding toward this goal, I shall first describe how adverse literary criticism of his work was instrumental in preventing a sober evaluation of his place on the Polish and Russian literary scenes. I shall also attempt to demonstrate the extreme convergence between Leśmian's theory and his poetic practices.

The total disregard for Leśmian's ties with Russian literature and culture, vital to his formative years, the lack of interest in his poetic creed and in his biography, made it impossible for the majority of critics to understand his work. This neglect was apparently intentional, for a hatred of everything Russian must have been combined, in Leśmian's case, with deep-rooted anti-Semitism. These and other factors, ideological and technical in nature, resulted in the misinterpretation of Leśmian's creative success as failure, of his artistic consistency as irrational blundering, and of his genuine concern for Poland's literary excellence as detachment from reality. Moreover, the uniqueness of his poetic language was dubbed a "strange" concoction, foreign to the Polish ear. Yet, he was a poet thoroughly acquainted with the sorcery of Poland's legendary past[10] who dreamed of creating something uniquely Polish—a kind of Polish *bylina.* (This dream was realized in the *Klechdy polskie* ["Old Polish Tales"], written between 1913 and 1914, and published posthumously.)

Little is known of Bolesław Stanisław Leśmian's formative years. He was born in Warsaw in 1877,[11] the son of Józef Lesman and Emma née Sunderland, whose ancestors—expert porcelain painters—were brought to Poland from England in the eighteenth century by none other than Stanisław Staszic, the father of the Polish Enlightenment. The family was given a large estate in Iłża where it established the porcelain industry in Poland in 1823.[12] Leśmian's ancestors were of Jewish descent but had converted to Catholicism, although it is not clear exactly when this conversion took place. The fact remains that his family was well integrated into the mainstream of Polish intelligentsia and that some of its members fought in the insurrection of 1863. Made up entirely of either professionals or artists, the family contributed three outstanding poets to Polish cultural and literary wealth: Antoni Lange, B. Leśmian, and Jan Brzechwa (Lesman).

Leśmian's parents separated when he was still a small child. The situation was complicated by a fight over the children, and the father—an economist and the director of the Retirement Department of the Southwestern Kiev Railways—spirited them away from Warsaw to Kiev. Shortly afterward, Leśmian's mother died of pneumonia and the father married a Polish noblewoman, Helena Dobrowolska, whose family owned estates in the Ukraine where the poet spent his summers in childhood and adolescence. The lush scenery of the Ukraine became a vital source of Leśmian's poetic inspiration. Leśmian was distrustful of his stepmother, which might have caused him to withdraw into a world of his own. He was a sensitive and precocious child, and extremely superstitious (this remained a part of his mature character). Afraid of ghosts, he would cover himself with rosaries before retiring and draw a line around his bed to ward off evil spirits.[13] He loved nature and animals. The loss of his younger brother who, at four, spoke only in verse, was a great blow to him.

Leśmian started writing poetry at the age of eight. As a student in high school, he already had copybooks filled with verse, a secret treasure shared occasionally with his schoolmates, Henryk Hertz-Barwiński, an actor and Malinowski, a biologist. He was even then a spontaneous poet with an extraordinary memory and a gift for improvisation. He could compose a poem and recite it soon afterward from memory. One of his most famous improvisations occurred at the festivities occasioned by the removal of the remains of the greatest Polish poet Adam Mickiewicz from Paris to the Wawel. Leśmian was the only Pole in Kiev chosen to recite the poetry of the great bard, in Polish. While declaiming Mickiewicz's "Great Improvisation" (from *Dziady*, "The Forefathers"), he got carried away and continued with his own improvisation, to the delight of the audience. Following this no doubt inflammatory recitation, he was arrested and sentenced to life imprisonment, a sentence later commuted to a half-year stay in the Łukianówka penitentiary.[14]

His high school and university friends remember the young Leśmian fondly as a brilliant and eager student of extensive interests, to whom studies came easily and who excelled in all subjects. He finished high school at the age of sixteen and graduated from law school at the University of St. Vladimir in 1901. He had a sunny disposition and a keen sense of humor. He was tactful, humble, but outspoken in matters pertaining to art and politics. He was not at all the detached and frightened "little notary public" of later years. Stanisław Zieliński, a Polish consul in Berlin, recalls his colleague from Kiev as the founder of a conspiratory circle of the academic "Polonia" in 1901, and as an active and courageous young man, always to be found in the forefront of the political unrest in Kiev in 1902. (Zieliński relates an incident in which the diminutive Leśmian struck the notorious undercover agent, Maxim, a man twice his size.) The leader of a literary circle, Leśmian was by then already recognized as an outstanding poet, having supposedly published a book of verse during his student years.[15] His home was a cultural gathering place for many literary and artistic notables and he often appeared himself at recitals to help needy families with money collected at the artistic soirées.

In the mid-1890s, Kiev was an important center of the new Russian literary movement. Hertz-Barwiński recalls meeting a young Russian poet in Leśmian's home, about 1897, who had translated Juliusz Słowacki into Russian and who recited *Lilla Weneda.* He assumes that this must have been Konstantin Balmont.[16] He also speaks of Leśmian's interest in Russian literary criticism, philology, psychology, and folklore, and of his admiration for Poe and Baudelaire. The poet's schoolfriend mentions, too, the origin of Leśmian's pseudonym—Lange's invention—which he supposedly began using in 1894.[17] He loved Russian poetry, and the two friends amused themselves by reciting Fet, Tiutchev, and Lermontov, and by translating nonsense verse (apparently Kozma Prutkov's) into Polish. The Kiev period is the most serene and carefree of Leśmian's life. Judging from his correspondence with Z. Przesmycki, it was only toward the end that he experienced poverty and disillusionment. About 1902, when he left Kiev for Warsaw, the poet was making a new beginning in his personal and creative life leaving behind the country which had given him his start as a man and as a poet.

Following a temporary position in Warsaw with the Warsaw-Vienna Railways, in 1903 Leśmian realized a life-long dream of travel abroad. He went to Vienna and Munich, which proved inspirational for his work, but he later destroyed everything he wrote there. In the fall of 1903 he bicycled to Paris, arriving penniless. The retirement of his father, from whom he had been receiving a modest allowance, made even that modest support impossible. Now began a long period of want.

He arrived in Paris, the center of French Symbolism, to experience, literally, the fate of a *poète maudit.* He lived in the Latin Quarter in a tenement called "Maison Roger," which was reminiscent of the *pensions* in Balzac. While in Paris, he was befriended by Wacław Berent and Jan Lemański and also met Władysław Reymont. Badly in need of funds, he would have applied to M. Tyszkiewicz for a stipend, but he rejected the thought for fear of refusal because of his Jewish origin.[18] Despite his desperation and illness, he retained his dignity and sense of humor. Przesmycki frequently lent him money. In 1904 he wrote *Legendy tęsknoty*, and one of the short stories included in it, "Baśń o rycerzu pańskim" ("The Tale of the Lord's Knight"), reveals already at that time his longing for the primordial past.

The year 1904 was a decisive one in Leśmian's life, for it marked the beginning of the protracted literary campaign against him. It was also the year he had the great good fortune to meet Zofia Chylińska, a beautiful and talented nineteen-year-old painter, whom he married in 1905. They had two daughters, Maria Ludwika and Wanda. His wife had an extremely beneficial influence on Leśmian, helping him regain his health and return to his writing. Her energy and cheerful disposition changed his life despite their continued poverty.

News of his wife's pregnancy led Leśmian to contemplate suicide, for they were without means of support. It was while in this frame of mind that Leśmian met Balmont in the Luxembourg gardens. The two became friends. Balmont's third "mate," Elena C., was wealthy, and they lived in luxury. The Russian poet offered to pay Leśmian a ruble per verse and encouraged him to write in Russian. This resulted in his writing two cycles, *Pesni Vasilisy Premudroi* ("Songs of Vasilisa the Wisest"), published in *Zolotoe Runo* in 1906, and *Lunnoe pokhmel'e* ("Lunar Hangover"), that appeared in *Vesy*, 1907.[19] Balmont introduced Leśmian to French as well as Russian poets. The two families spent the summer of 1906 in Brittany.

The years in Paris, after 1905, may be considered the period of Leśmian's poetic maturation. They were also the most creative years of his life. His translations of Verlaine's poetry appeared in the last issue of *Chimera* in 1907. The poet spent 1911 in Warsaw, where with Kazimierz Wroczyński, a literary critic, and Janusz

Orliński, an actor, he founded the Teatr Artystyczny, a theater of which he became the director. In the capacity of director and playwright he proved to be a great innovator and, to a large extent, a forerunner of Beckett and Ionesco. He returned to Paris after the theater closed.

Leśmian's first volume of poetry, *Sad rozstajny*, appeared in 1912, when half of the second volume, *Łąka* ("The Meadow") was already written. Shortly afterward, in 1913, *Klechdy sezamowe* ("Old Tales of Sesame") and *Przygody Sindbada Żeglarza* ("The Adventures of Sindbad the Sailor"), two beautifully stylized versions of Arabic fairy tales, were published by Mortkowicz. Leśmian also wrote a farce for the stage, *Bajka o złotym grzebyku* ("The Tale of the Golden Comb"), which he took with him to Warsaw, in 1913, to arrange for its staging in the Nowości theater. (This work still exists in manuscript form and is in the possession of Leśmian's daughter, Maria Mazurowa.)

Leśmian also translated two volumes of Poe during this period.[20] His article, "Kilka słów o teatrze" ("A Few Words on the Theater"), appeared in the literary weekly *Złoty Róg* (1913). The attempt at a Polish *bylina*, *Klechdy polskie*, was also written at this time.[21]

In 1913 the Leśmians returned from France to take up permanent residence in Poland. The atmosphere in Warsaw became even more depressing for the poet than it had been before. Judging from his correspondence, anti-Semitism was the issue which overshadowed everything else. It even gave rise to an organized economic boycott. This, combined with the belief in literary circles that Leśmian was an epigone of Young Poland (Młoda Polska),[22] made it almost impossible for his contributions to be accepted by literary periodicals. Meanwhile, his wife, stricken with tuberculosis, was in desperate need of treatment. He managed to send her to Otwock, and later they left for the French Riviera. They returned to Warsaw in July, 1914, on the eve of the war. The years between 1914 and 1917 were lean ones, as most of his articles and feuilletons were rejected by the press. A feuilleton dealing with the state of Warsaw theater, "Życie snem" ("Living by Dreams"), was refused and remained, with a ballad, "Satyr i nimfa" ("The Satyr and the Nymph"), in manuscript form.[23]

In 1917 Leśmian was literary director of the Teatr Miejski in Łódź where he staged a variety of plays from Oscar Wilde's *Salomé*, to Ibsen's *Nora*, Gorky's *The Lower Depths*, and Gogol's *The Inspector General*. He also attempted to stage Słowacki's *Ksiądz Marek* ("The Priest Marek") and Stanisław Wyspiański's *Warszawianka*.[24] As director, he maintained a level of theatrical excellence; as playwright, he created *Dziejba leśna* ("Forest Happenings"), a drama that was published posthumously in 1938, in a volume of poems under the same title.[25] He also wrote a drama in Russian. *Skrzypek opętany* ("The Frenzied Fiddler") is apparently based on the Russian *bylina*, *Vasilii Buslaev*. However, there are conflicting accounts of the source of *Skrzypek*. Brzechwa claims to have read a play titled *Vasilii Buslaev*, which seems to have been lost, while the manuscript of *Skrzypek opętany* is a scenario recently acquired by Aleksander Janta from M. Mazurowa.

The poet wrote numerous reviews and articles on the drama, which he considered the highest expression of poetry. However, his career as a director was shortlived. In 1917 he met and fell in love with Dora Lebenthal, a beautiful divorcee and a doctor by profession. Their relationship was the inspiration for the cycle of erotics, *W malinowym chruśniaku* ("In a Raspberry Thicket").[26]

In 1918 Leśmian was at last able to put his law-school training to use, when he received a position as notary public in Hrubieszów. For the first time in his life he was financially secure. However, he was totally unsuited for the task which he delegated to assistants, while he continued to work on his second book of poems, *Łąka* (published in 1920). His creative method was sporadic, spontaneous. He wrote at night, and would withdraw completely into his world of fantasy for months at a time, to reappear only when the work was finished. His enchantment with nature, which dates back to his childhood in the Ukraine, found its fullest expression in the poems of *Łąka*. This volume treated nature as it had never been depicted before in Polish literature.

From Hrubieszów, Leśmian was transferred in 1922 to Zamość, where he lived until 1935. Both cities are situated in an area rich in folklore, a fact of great consequence to the poet's work. These relatively stable seven years gave him an opportunity to write. However, he was again plagued by misfortune. An assistant to whom he had entrusted his law practice embezzled 20,000 złoty, for which the poet was held responsible. Only through Dora Lebenthal, who sacrificed all her possessions and her practice to settle his debts, and through the help of the secretary of justice was he able to escape imprisonment.

Leśmian's health was fragile; a heart ailment now made it necessary for him to leave his position and move to Warsaw. In addition, and apart from his love affair with Dora Lebenthal, he was still preoccupied with the theater and was hoping to try his luck there again.

In Warsaw he led a dual life—that of lover and husband. These were hard years for the poet, whose sole means of support was derived from his literary work and, although he continued to write and discuss philosophy and literature with his friends in the Café Ziemiańska, he remained always on the fringes of literary life.[27] A few favorable reviews of *Łąka* by such important critics as Karol Irzykowski and Ostap Ortwin failed to penetrate the wall of silence surrounding the poet during the 1920s. Ironically, in 1931, largely as an afterthought, he was given "The Award of the Young." Then, to everyone's surprise—including his own—Leśmian was made a member of the Academy of Literature in 1933![28] Only then did the persecution lessen somewhat and the interest in his work grow. He was elated, but also embarrassed by the honor. There is a drawing which captures this mood, showing the diminutive poet, a gnomelike figure, resplendent in evening dress with the medal of an Academician, sitting uncomfortably on his hands, lost in an oversized chair. The small pension he received from the Academy was to be his basic income.

In 1936 Leśmian's third volume of poetry, *Napój cienisty* ("The Shadowy Potion"), appeared. According to J. Brzechwa, it was hailed as a "literary event" only by some critics; the majority heaped invective upon it. He also wrote "A Treatise on Poetry," which was to have been his acceptance speech at the Academy. The speech was never delivered, as Leśmian died three days earlier, his death in 1937 alleged to have been caused by an incident associated with anti-Semitism.[29] The persecution continued even after his death. His body lay unburied for weeks because the head of the Academy denied him the funeral honors befitting one of its members.[30] The news of his death appeared on the last page of the *Wiadomości Literackie*.

In the conclusion of his latest work on Leśmian, J. Trznadel stresses that the poet does not fit into any programs or literary trends:

> . . . neither modernity [Modernism] nor Symbolism. . . . In all of this historical context, Leśmian remains alone. . . . The artistic structure of his poems is consciously many-layered and opens the way to various interpretations.[31]

This type of structure has the same elusive power as rhythm, according to Trznadel. Yet it is precisely allusion and insinuation that are the essential aspects of Symbolist aesthetics, for they help poetry express the multifaceted meaning of life and, in so doing, they enable it to approximate reality. All the important features of Leśmian's poetics, such as the concreteness of the word, his theory of rhythm, his relationship to theism, to the philosophy of Henri Bergson, to folklore, and even his regression to primordiality—all of which prompted Trznadel to consider him an Existentialist—are in fact the strongest arguments in favor of his ties with Symbolism. However, this was a Symbolism foreign to Polish soil which found expression rather among the Russian Symbolists of the second generation.

Leśmian was never a true representative of the Decadence which was a part of Young Poland, but the error in judgment which branded him as such has been perpetuated for decades. In order to correct this error and properly to evaluate his place in literary history, we must first attempt a brief explanation of what Young Poland was.

Symbolism as a literary movement continues to be a controversial subject among literary historians. Not even in France has there appeared an absolutely unified program which would apply to all literary practices or that would indicate a clear-cut line between so-called Decadence and Symbolism proper. Until the 1880s literature in the West had evolved in much the same orderly fashion as history. Yet, despite an apparent political normality and industrial prosperity, there came a sudden rejection of literary traditions at the end of the nineteenth century.

Poland could not escape the new trends in art emanating from the three countries under whose domination she lay, but absorbed these changes in varying degrees, depending upon the political climate in the different occupied regions. However, as a country without sovereignty for a century, Poland could ill afford the luxury of a "socially uncommitted" Decadent literature. There was a need for a literature which would serve nationalistic ideals and lead the way to freedom; thus, it had to be didactic. While the West lay under the spell of "art for art's sake," the Positivists, the Polish Realists, wrote their most important works. Bolesław Prus, Henryk Sienkiewicz, and others adhered to tradition, but were now even more attentive to the national demands of Polish reality.

However, the generation which matured around 1890 eagerly followed developments in France and grew painfully aware of a void in their own literature—especially in poetry which had been neglected since Romanticism by the Positivists. As a result, Western Parnassian, Naturalist, and Decadent works reached Poland almost simultaneously. Although Z. Przesmycki (Miriam), the editor of the Warsaw *Życie* from 1887 to 1888, had introduced Western literature a few years earlier, the first wave of Symbolism did not make its real appearance in Poland until after 1890. This is also the date usually cited as the beginning of Young Poland, the dominant trend in Polish literature from 1890 to 1918. Symbolism found its way to Poland in translations of contemporary French, Belgian and German poets, and in the great number of articles written by the poet, critic, and translator, A. Lange.[32]

The modern literary scene in Poland, founded on Positivism (especially in Warsaw) and Romanticism (especially in Cracow), became a melting pot of various literary trends in which Parnassianism, Impressionism, Naturalism, and neo-Romanticism vied for supremacy and were frequently subordinated to nationalistic tendencies. Although the French *école symboliste* and its predecessors were known already in the nineties, Symbolism did not really exist as a movement in Poland, in spite of the "Symbolist" program formulated by Przesmycki in his "Introduction to *A Selection of Dramatic Works by Maurice Maeterlinck,*" written in 1894.[33] As we shall see, a very decisive role in promulgating Symbolism was played by the three leading literary periodicals, *Życie* (Warsaw, 1887-1888), *Chimera* (Warsaw, 1901-1907)—both edited by Przesmycki—and *Życie* (Cracow, 1897-1900).

In 1887-1900, under the more lenient Austrian regime, Cracow became the center of Polish Modernism. Its focal point was the journal *Życie,* which in 1898 came under the editorship of *der geniale Pole* Stanisław Przybyszewski. In 1899 he published his famous manifesto "Confiteor" in that journal. To the Bohemian circles of Cracow he brought the ideas of Young Germany and Young Scandinavia (led by his friend Ola Hanson). His zeal, dynamism and charisma united artists of various persuasions into Young Poland. An erstwhile Socialist, Przybyszewski was one of the few admired both by Stanisław Brzozowski (1878-1911), the foremost thinker of the period, and also by the Russian Symbolists. The influence of the most notorious "Satanist" in Polish literature upon the minds of young artists cannot be underestimated.

But the unity Przybyszewski achieved was deceptive. Leading litterateurs such as Stanisław Szczepanowski and Artur Górski were suspicious of the foreign terms "Decadence," "Modernism" and "Pre-Expressionism," used in succession by the Cracow group. Actually, Cracow Modernism was based primarily on tradition and on nationalism of the Romantic variety, with an admixture of foreign trends, in particular German and Scandinavian Naturalism, French Parnassianism and early French Symbolism. Even Przybyszewski, in his *Zur Psychologie des Individuums,* followed positivistic and naturalistic tenets to a certain extent since he propagated scientific, physiological, and philosophical naturalism side by side with artistic naturalism.

The term "Young Poland" was not adopted until 1899. Its victory and its association with modern literature were realized in the pages of the Cracow *Życie* in a manifesto "Young Poland," written by A. Górski (Quasimodo). He demanded that modern Polish literature be truly Polish, that is, nationalist. Yet, many young admirers of the journal associated the term with the program and the person of Przybyszewski, its editor and inspiration. Thus, Young Poland gathered around the Cracow *Życie.* There was the outstanding poet-playwright Wyspiański, who most successfully depicted the effects of the lack of freedom upon the people's psychology resulting in their inactivity. The play, *Wesele* ("The Wedding") alone earned him the title of the fourth Bard of the Nation and, consequently, that of a neo-Romantic.

According to some recent scholars, the nineties cannot be considered the period of true Polish Modernism, as it was in those years that the best Positivist work appeared. This was especially true of Russian-occupied Warsaw, where Positivism and Naturalism prevailed. Later, Cracow Modernists and Warsaw Positivists and Naturalists united, due to a shift in the center of gravity of literary activities from Cracow to Warsaw. Around Przesmycki's journal, *Chimera,* there gathered a group of writers all of whom were born about the year 1870. These included men of such diverse trends as Stefan Żeromski, Władysław Reymont, Leopold Staff, and Leśmian. Thus, many of the writers might have agreed with literary historians Ignacy Matuszewski and Julian Krzyżanowski that the term neo-Romanticism applied (especially after 1905) to the entire Young Poland period.[34] Although this assessment might not be wholly accurate, it still indicates that the majority of writers were ideologically committed to collectivity. Not until 1911 was there a reaction against the term neo-Romanticism.

The importance of Przesmycki as the initiator of Young Poland was diminished by the dynamic personality of Przybyszewski; yet, it was he who, with Lange, was the first to introduce Poland to the new literary trends of the West. (The merits of Przesmycki's manifesto will be discussed in chapter 2.) However, it is important to note that in *Chimera*, which published works by Western Symbolists, there was almost a total absence of Russian literature, especially of Russian Symbolists, which was true of most Polish journals. Consequently, there was a lack of understanding of Symbolism, in general, on the part of both the proponents and the detractors of Young Poland. A proper perspective could be attained only by comparing the different modern literary scenes. Therefore, under close scrutiny the apparent influence of French Symbolism on Young Poland is only hypothetical.

In Russia, as in the West, there was a much more gradual crystallization of ideas, a more distinct transition from traditional literature to the Decadence of the *fin de siècle*. But unlike France or Poland, in Russia the literary trend of the last decade of the nineteenth century and the beginning of the twentieth grew out of a terrorist anarchism and an extreme, destructive individualism, first into Decadence, then, later, into a social, but mystical, Symbolist literature, oriented toward the future. Thus, it was a socially committed literature of broad scope. It was lack of understanding of these trends in literature that promoted the mistaken evaluation of Leśmian's mature poetry, which, in fact, was close to the later Russian variant of Symbolism. Even Brzozowski, who insisted on cooperation with Russian literature, recognized the strength of the Russian Symbolists' commitment to improve society only shortly before his death in Florence.

Due largely to the extreme popularity of Maurice Maeterlinck, Symbolism was understood in Poland as a mystical art. Maeterlinck's works not only served as the basis of Przesmycki's manifesto, but his creed was taken up by the leader of Polish Modernism, Przybyszewski, and by the literary historian, Matuszewski. This early variant of Symbolism has been termed "mythological" by the author of a recent study of Young Poland.[35] It favored Symbolists like Villiers de l'Isle-Adam and Maeterlinck, and embraced a Symbolism found in the works of the English pre-Raphaelites and in Richard Wagner, in which the Symbol leaned toward mythology, mysticism, and occultism.

A study of the translations of foreign poetry—especially French—yields an interesting insight into the nature of the Polish variant of Symbolism. From these translations, one might conclude that all of French poetry at the turn of the century was Symbolist. Translated by Brzozowski, Przesmycki, and Lange, the works of Baudelaire, Verlaine, or Hérédia all sound alike, with no attempt made to distinguish among them as to their diction or style. At times the translators disregarded the clear outline of a work, adding to it an element of mystification.[36] To the Polish reader, Baudelaire, Verlaine, Hérédia, and Maeterlinck were all Symbolists of the same stamp; moreover, because of the undiscriminating adaptation of Western Symbolists, all differences between Parnassianism and Symbolism vanished. As Mieczysław Jastrun points out:

> There was no delimitation between literary trends. All the new poetry was simply called Modernistic, without any special concern taken about the theory of Symbolism, combining and mixing the various trends and currents of Modernism.[37]

The Symbolism which appeared on the Polish literary horizon was deformed and little understood even by those who considered themselves its representatives and propagators.

In poetry, symbols were often used in a manner that made them indistinguishable from allegories. The Symbolist tendencies which found their expression in Poland closely resembled the program of Jean Moréas (the author of the manifesto of the principles of Symbolism, published in the September 1886 issue of *Figaro*) and his collaborators. It was this variety of Symbolism, and not that of Stéphane Mallarmé, which constituted—with neo-Romanticism, Impressionism, Parnassianism, and, after 1910, neo-Classicism—the complex phenomenon known as Young Poland.[38]

Although the Young Poland period was usually viewed as lasting from 1890 to 1918, it is, in actuality, possible to distinguish two phases in Polish Modernism: the time of the new literature, between 1890 and 1900, can be considered generally as a revolt of the younger generation against established ideologies—specifically against the Polish variant of Positivism as a literature serving utilitarian and didactic purposes. Characteristic of the poetry of this period, is the tendency to graft new contents and ideas onto forms established by poets of the preceding generation such as Adam Asnyk and Maria Konopnicka.

This "passive" attitude of Polish Decadence was often expressed formally in a direct confessional lyric or in the form of stylized song. The lyrical content continued to be understood literally, as before, except for the added new element of Impressionism. This led to a tendency toward disruption of the continuity of expression and toward the creation of an elusive atmosphere of mystification that blurred the compositional outline. The poetry of Tetmajer is the foremost example of this Impressionistic style which became the dominant style of the very prolific, average Young Poland poetry. This phase of Young Poland has no direct bearing on Leśmian or his work.

The period of Leśmian's poetic maturation and interest in philosophies coincides with the more directional, more crystallized, second phase of Young Poland, although he hardly exerted any influence on its development. This phase represents an essential change of form in most literary genres. In drama, it was achieved by Wyspiański; in prose fiction, it was realized in exemplary fashion by Żeromski, Wacław Berent, and Karol Irzykowski in the innovative tendencies of their style, culminating later in Witkiewicz, the foremost proponent of "Pure Form." In poetry, there was a tendency to become dissociated from Impressionism and to adopt a more concrete, dramatic poetic idiom and more concrete themes. This is apparent in the work of the outstanding poets who are representative of the Young Poland period precisely because of the great differentiation between their works. While Jan Kasprowicz forsook the pathos of his earlier work for a more classical, somewhat Expressionistic and, finally, for a simpler Franciscan style (cf., his *Księga ubogich* ["The Book of the Poor"]), his work stands apart from any coterie and differs decidedly from the Nietzschean poetry of Staff (cf., *Sny o potędze* ["Dreams of Might"]), and from the works of Tadeusz Miciński (cf., *W mroku gwiazd* ["In Darkness of the Stars"]), the precursor of Polish Expressionism.

The stereotype poetic idiom of Young Poland is apparent only in Leśmian's earliest works—which he did not include in his collections himself, but which were compiled and edited by J. Trznadel in *Utwory rozproszone* and in some of the poems of the first volume *Sad rozstajny*. Despite the fact that he freed himself rather early from the approaches to language, folklore stylization, and other mannerisms considered characteristic of Young Poland, he was known—ironically—mostly for his early and least original works published in the journal *Chimera,* then the champion of "art for art's sake" that favored themes detached from contemporary issues. As he was a steady contributor to *Chimera,* and a personal friend of its editor and publisher Przesmycki, he was to remain, in the eyes of the literary critics of opposing factions, one of the most representative poets of the *Chimera* aesthetics.

The fact that his work, which was original, philosophical, and the preeminent Symbolist poetry of Young Poland, was published late and his theoretical and critical works were completely overlooked, may account, in part, for the opinion held about him throughout his lifetime as an epigon of Young Poland. Due to the prevailing anti-Modernistic attitude during the period between the wars (from 1918 to 1939), his poetry was considered an anachronism; this helps explain Leśmian's finding himself, once again, on the fringes of the literary life. The lack of interest, and hence the lack of knowledge and the absence of a historical perspective on the entire scope of his work, accounts for its unquestioning placement in the context of Young Poland although his mature work was not published in book form until after Young Poland had become a closed chapter in Polish literature.

It is easy to understand the ambiguity of Leśmian's position as a Symbolist poet. Although the consistent Symbolism expressed in his programmatic essays and his mature poetry did not fit Young Poland practices, it was not in complete opposition to it. Symbolism was but one of the possibilities open to Young Poland.

Leśmian's realization of this possibility to its fullest extent is one of the elements of his originality. He put greater emphasis on the problem of poetic language than did other Polish Symbolists. He also treated more profoundly the philosophical motifs of poetry and was almost the only one to emphasize its cognitive value. For Przesmycki, the basic concept of the symbol approximated allegory,[39] whereas for Leśmian the basic principle of Symbolism was *rhythm.* Other theoreticians and practitioners of Polish Symbolism, such as Staff, did not distinguish it from Parnassianism—a trend wholly alien to Leśmian's poetics.

This brief examination of the Polish literary scene explains, in part, why Leśmian's creative work did not receive its due evaluation from either his contemporaries or from those present-day critics who, linking Leśmian with Young Poland and its variant of Symbolism, realize that his work does not fit this literary context. They therefore feel compelled to follow an *ex post facto* approach in establishing his place in Polish literature. However, those for whom he is unquestionably a Symbolist, such as Zbigniew Bieńkowski and others, recognize that Young Poland

Symbolism was too limited to accommodate Leśmian's poetic flights. This is, perhaps, the reason why Bieńkowski turns to the chefs d'oeuvre of European Symbolism for purposes of comparison. Janusz Sławiński goes a step further and suggests that Young Poland and Symbolism ought to be considered different phenomena, even, to a certain degree, opposite ones. According to him, an opinion has become very popular of late that

> in Poland, the term Symbolism played the role of the verbal fetish—which found little poetic expression and few poetic facts.[40]

It has been my impression from the start that Leśmian did not fit the spirit of Young Poland. Even his earliest poetry (not included in any of his collections), although showing some similarities to the established trends of Young Poland, differed from it decidedly. Evidently, his sensuality guarded him from the undefined "spirituality" of that Symbolism which was a part of Young Poland. His poetry did not merely evoke a Romantic atmosphere and impressionistic mood, but, even in its initial stages, it demonstrated the conflict of the poetic "I," an inner drama which in his later poetry achieved universal significance by abandoning the "I" and its negation, for the drama of existence and nonexistence. It was a poetry of drama right from the very beginning.

Leśmian expressed his low regard for Polish Modernism as early as 1897 in a letter to Przesmycki from Kiev, in which he regrets that "we do not have *true* Polish Modernism. . . ."[41] His anti-Modernistic attitude is also felt in another letter to Przesmycki, where he writes:

> I can guess more or less the program (what a horrible word!) of *Chimera*, or, I can even say—I know it perfectly. . . . Generally, every program for poetry is the same as a cage for a nightingale. That is why the periodicals *Życie* and *Strumień* [The Stream] remind me of two cages looking desperately for a nightingale.[42]

Programs inhibit the freedom of intuitive poetic expression; the resultant poetry becomes conceptual and loses its spontaneity, freshness, and originality. Elsewhere, writing of his contribution to the periodical *Sztuka* ("Art"), he complains of its low literary level and that "its main objective will be to preserve *Polish nationalistic traits* and a *chummy atmosphere,* which will again (!) become timely."[43] Leśmian considered *Chimera* an excellent periodical, because he found that it "has an irresistible influence on all kinds of views."[44] Precisely what he found valuable in it was that it did not represent an exclusive forum for the works of Young Poland (although some critics, such as Brzozowski, considered that it did).

A letter which Trznadel cites as his strongest argument for Leśmian's anti-Symbolist aesthetics may well be the poet's most emphatic expression of his disapproval of Young Poland, but not of Symbolism as he understood it. Ironically, it is addressed to Przesmycki, the author of the earliest manifesto of Young Poland Symbolism:

> I have grown weary of the *conceptual, opinionated, rational treatment* of things [italics mine] which, in our poetry, have long since ceased to be themselves. A flower is not a flower, but presumably the longing of the author for his mistress. An oak is not an oak, but the reaching of the superman toward the sun, and so on. In short, our poetry has become connected with people's outlook on life. Instead of a world, we have an opinion, a Weltanschauung. I have been seized with a longing to enter the world, to merge irresistibly with nature . . . with the stars, in order to express the above words without ideological justifications, without an ideological *motto*.[45]

Polish poetry could not be considered true Symbolist poetry, for it was too contrived, continuing the conceptual approach of Classicism or Parnassianism under the guise of allegory.

> Fashion bestows upon all such *mottos* as allegory a certain charm, but that which is created within the limits of that *motto* vanishes with time, as something understood historically but requiring a commentary for a generation with other ideals.[46]

Leśmian yearned for a poetry that would aid man to perceive the world with all his senses, that would facilitate a vision encompassing the world's dimensions, but that would not become primarily a Weltanschauung. This kind of poetry can be created only by a poet who merges with nature, who is in close communion with the universe and has at his disposal a symbol which has a concrete meaning. In his "Treatise on Poetry," Leśmian states that *"a symbol is concrete as long as it gives concrete results."*[47] [Italics mine.] For him Symbolist poetry is poetry which expresses in concrete images the constant changes of life beyond us, around us, and within us. Miłosz has called Leśmian

> the purest Symbolist—yet his symbols are not as much correspondences as autonomous, myth-creating images.[48]

The literary harassment that haunted Leśmian throughout his life and after his death was, like everything pertaining to him, of a complex nature. It was directed at him from various factions and may be described simplistically as motivated by ideology, professional jealousy, and anti-Semitism.

The first important attack upon him came in 1904 from the most powerful and influential literary critic of the time, S. Brzozowski, a philosopher with Socialist leanings. Attacking the ideological position of Przesmycki, Young Poland's foremost theoretician, Brzozowski lashed out against Leśmian, assuming that the poet, a frequent contributor to *Chimera,* shared his patron's views. Thus, Leśmian was mistakenly linked permanently with Young Poland and became the scapegoat of the ideological struggle between the two most important literary adversaries of the period: Brzozowski, who propagated a socially committed literature, a literature of action, and Przesmycki, who advanced literature as the expression of individual aesthetics. Leftist or pseudoleftist thought and nationalism were prevalent throughout Poland, especially in the first decade of the twentieth century. (The first of these was common to nearly all countries, while nationalism was found largely in those countries where there was hope of winning freedom with the help of didactic literature.)

Brzozowski reproached Leśmian because, while important things were taking place, ". . . civil wars, marching armies . . .

Leśmian writes in *Chimera, Legendy tęsknoty,* [in which] Mrs. Komornicka expresses her visions of lions, panthers and tigers."[49] He also attacked Leśmian for his excellent poem "Prolog" (1902), a profound work of universal meaning which, according to Brzozowski, betrayed an art totally devoid of a belief in life, and which, therefore, was artificiality personified.[50] This was indeed a misconception of a poem which, on the contrary, is an apotheosis of the eternal values of human creation. Only from the perspective of time does it become clear that Brzozowski, a proponent of Bergson and the foremost propagator in Poland of action and deed, had much in common with Leśmian, whose poetry is filled with action and deed, though of a different purpose. Leśmian's poetic language attests to it, as does his poetic creed. Another point that the poet holds in common with the author of *Legenda Młodej Polski* ("The Legend of Young Poland") is his belief that life is a brave, persistent struggle with an imperfect world. Man may be limited, pathetic, and ridiculous, but by his laughter he shows his strength. Thus, Brzozowski's belief in the imperfection of man in an imperfect world corresponds to Leśmian's faith in his maimed people, and even to the slapdash manner of his poetic (maimed) language.

Brzozowski's attacks were echoed by many others and, eventually, grew into a critical campaign.[51] Its effect was apparent, for even Jan Lorentowicz, an admirer of Leśmian's poetry, was misled. Although he praised Leśmian, he found in him a true representative of Young Poland as envisioned by Przesmycki. He considered that in Leśmian's work "the voices of the soul" predominate over "the voices of life,"[52] (as though the voices of the soul were *not* an aspect of life!).

The second type of harassment, and perhaps the most painful for the poet, came in the twenties, especially from the "Skamander" poets. This group owed a great deal to Leśmian's poetics. Julian Tuwim's "Sokrates tańczący" ("Dancing Socrates") was very much influenced by the technique of the older poet. Konstanty Gałczyński, a member of the "Kwadryga" group, also openly admitted his debt to Leśmian. *Łąka* (1920) turned out to be a great success among many poets and litterateurs, and it could have posed a threat to the younger group that was extremely popular with the public.[53] Its members were the "Hollywood stars" of that era, and loved to bask in the limelight. One may argue that Leśmian's poetry was too esoteric to present such a problem to poets who catered to the tastes of the public. Nonetheless, an admiration for his poetry, mixed with a feeling of indebtedness to him on the part of some poets, apparently led to some personal jealousies. Therefore, they embarked upon a campaign of silence.[54] As a result, in a popularity poll conducted in 1931 by *Wiadomości Literackie,* the propaganda organ of the Skamandrites, Leśmian received the lowest rating (he appeared in 46th place!), which indicates that he was unknown to its readers. His detractors had achieved their goal. Anatol Stern and Leopold Lewin, who described the strange treatment accorded Leśmian by his fellow poets, are by no means the only voices attesting to it.

Leśmian's unacceptability to his contemporaries was partly due to the linguistic conventions he so successfully employed, but which were thought, at the time, to be obsolete or on the way to being discarded. This could have been a valid argument if one were to judge by Jarosław Iwaszkiewicz's article, in which he ridiculed Leśmian's "proto-Slavic" neologisms, calling them "a mere artificiality of poor macabre taste."[55] The poetic language of Leśmian's first creative period which drew to some extent upon Young Poland and Romantic traditions, could have been justifiably considered dated by the Skamandrites and especially by their successors the Vanguard poets, since the word creations of Young Poland were considered by them primarily as embellishments. However, the language of his mature period was definitely not outmoded as, in accordance with his aesthetics, it was a language created to disregard and defy any period, and to be as close as possible in approximating linguistic processes reminiscent of primordial man. Iwaszkiewicz's statement shows that the uniqueness of Leśmian's poetic language which represents the universality of his creed, was misunderstood, and that what was held to be out of tune with literary contemporaneity, was precisely Leśmian's goal! He created a language rooted in the past but oriented toward the future, disregarding any literary conventions in vogue. Again, it should be pointed out that the Skamander group, whose members were mostly leftist in their views, were attuned to the current Polish sociopolitical scene. The same can be said of the Vanguardists. Therefore, even after Poland attained independence her literature was one of social commitment.

The first protest—and a cry of "Shame!"—is to be found in an article written by Wojciech Wyganowski, who believed it was high time that Leśmian be given proper recognition equal to Tetmajer and Staff. He cautioned that future generations would discover Leśmian's greatness, as had been the case with Norwid, and would accuse contemporary critics of injustice.[56] It is noteworthy that when *Wiadomości Literackie* finally acted upon Wyganowski's plea, the article published by Stefan Napierski discussed Leśmian's first book of poetry *Sad rozstajny*, in spite of the eleven years that had passed since the publication of his masterpiece *Łąka*.

The first among the Skamandrites to break the wall of silence was Kazimierz Wierzyński, who, in 1932, published Leśmian's work in *Kultura*. He was also the poet who occupied the chair vacated by Leśmian in the Academy. Privately, all the members of "Skamander" revered Leśmian. Tuwim, the most popular among them, always kissed his hand upon meeting him, a gesture the older poet found embarrassing.

The lack of interest in Leśmian's work shown by most critics and poets of the Young Poland period was explained away as having been a result of his "strange" language and a poetry detached from life. Yet, in the twenties, he was considered an epigone of Young Poland whose language was dated and poetry socially uncommitted. It seems obvious that even the few interested critics of both periods gave little thought to Leśmian's biography, to the sources of his inspiration and, finally, to his poetic creed. Otherwise, they would have recognized that Leśmian drew his first poetic inspirations to a great extent from Russian literature. Like the younger generation of Russian Symbolists, he was enamored of Fedor Tiutchev and shared the Russian's idea that man emanates from nature. He also believed, as they did, that art is the only means of overcoming chaos. Like them, he saw poetry, not as a way of reflecting life's phenomena, but as a way of transforming them. The idea of the autonomy of the word was propagated equally by the younger Russian Symbolists. The mellifluousness and the great variety of rhythm which characterize Russian poetry from Zhukovsky to Balmont, although transformed by Leśmian and utilized by him to serve different ends, were basically rooted in the Russian literary tradition. Thus, his "dated" language turned out to be the most suitable tool for creating a very "non-dated" universal poetry.

The third type of harassment came from the anti-Semitic, extreme-right-wing press. *Prosto z mostu* did not even mention the poet's death. In 1939, after *Dziejba leśna* was published, an article in this very newspaper, entitled "Dziejba Lesmanów" ("The Happenings of Lesmans"), stated:

> Polish poems written by Jews do not belong to a generic, purely Polish poetry. . . . They are—such is the creativity of Leśmian—a product of assimilating the secondary characteristics of Polish culture.[57]

After this follows the enumeration of Lange, Wittlin, Tuwim, and others.

Another example of racial hatred was an article written by Feliks Zahora-Ibiański in 1936 on the subject of Leśmian's poem "Nocą" ("At Night"):

> Today when we are in need of spiritual strength . . . the intrusive vermin spreads decay, "the immortal ones" help the Soviets. . . . Put the . . . spiritual impotents (into the sanitarium), the agents of the enemies (into prison). . . . We must cure ourselves more effectively of this impotence, eliminate Asiatic dirt, burn the parasites without delay, for Europe does not wait for us.[58]

A colleague from Leśmian's university days, Z. Zieliński, the Consul General to Berlin in 1948, felt compelled to offer biographical information on Leśmian's formative years in Kiev to dispel the misconceptions about him. While abroad in the twenties and thirties he had heard about the racist campaign being waged against the poet.[59] Although anti-Semitism was not a decisive force, especially before the thirties, and was condoned by few writers of worth, its ugly tactics contributed to the picture of Leśmian as a Decadent poet. Julian Przyboś states that because the poet was branded a Decadent, "the *fantast* Leśmian was denied, until recently, the right of even a mention in the history of Polish literature for high schools."[60]

All this harassment undoubtedly contributed to the distortion of the image of Leśmian the man and the poet, thus preventing an accurate evaluation of his work and his place in the context of literary history. This poet who, according to Brzozowski, did not have a "belief in life," turned out to be the only one who undertook, "in the face of nothingness, the most desperate, reckless . . . heroic fight to rescue *his belief* in life."[61] The man who was considered to be on the fringes of literary life turned out to be far ahead of his time. For his was a true syncretic Symbolist poetry of an ever changing attitude toward an ever changing life. It was all oriented to the future.

Leśmian was ethereal, small, fair-haired, and birdlike. His characters, like himself, led a dual existence: One existence was in their deformity (which represented for Leśmian the earthly life—a life he did not understand), and the other was the life of the spirit, which is free and which mocks or remains indifferent to infinity and God.

His life, like his work, was filled with contrasts. He was outwardly reticent and diminutive, yet he was a powerful Promethean poet of heroic strength. He extolled man's fusion with nature, but retained compassion for all human suffering. He was at once a traditional poet and yet a poet who fervently believed in change and in the obsolescence of reality. Although an elemental poet, he was the conscious architect of a poetry of almost mathematical precision. Ethereal, he loved everything human. Superstitious, he was an unbeliever. Utterly impractical, with no material desires, he had a passion for gambling, always dreaming of winning money. Very humble, he was also vain and fascinated by Voronov's theory of rejuvenation. He was a diminutive man and a great poet.

Some of Leśmian's remarks on Tolstoy, written on the occasion of the great Russian's death, apply to the poet himself:

> . . . He was so unlike everything *he saw* on this earth, himself not excluded; as though he saw everything for *the first time* and could not reconcile himself to it. A split personality, he did not know exactly, to the very end of his days on earth, which of the two people hiding within him was himself, and which was his double.
>
> . . . A great spirit not of this world, in his flight over it will barely have time to sketch on its surface his destined existence. This sketch will suffice for an exact image. Let us be grateful to the eagle for his incidental traces, which he has marked with his wings on our paths; let us not expect these traces to fit exactly into the same worn paths.[62]

We ought to be grateful that Leśmian, a great birdlike spirit from beyond, has left us as a trace the most unforgettable gift of poetry which does not fit the expected, traditional path.

2

Leśmian as a Theoretician of Poetry

THE IRRATIONAL POET WITH DIRECTION

The majority of the literary critics who were Leśmian's contemporaries saw in him a poet whose creative work was totally detached from the realities of life, totally irrational. This view, expressed as early as 1904 by Stanisław Brzozowski (Adam Czepiel), persisted throughout the poet's life and even after his death. In each period this reproach acquired a somewhat different terminology to suit the current trends. With few exceptions this curious unanimity has been the basis of critical discussion for the last sixty years.

While there were few critics and writers who understood Leśmian's poetry, there were even fewer who knew his poetic credo. And why? Because the historians and critics who sentenced Leśmian's work to banishment and were deliberately silent about it, were oblivious to Leśmian's contribution as a literary critic, essayist, and theoretician of poetry.

Strangely enough, even his admirers were indifferent to many facets of Leśmian's genius. An example is his friend Adam Szczerbowski, who, after the poet's death, wrote a lengthy study that encompassed his total poetic output to that time.[1] He drew a very inspiring impressionistic sketch, commenting with penetrating insight on some important aspects of Leśmian's poetry, but he never touched upon certain essential metaphysical questions of existence and man's relationship to it that are the core of Leśmian's poetry. In failing to discuss these questions and demonstrate their artistic function in the works of the poet, he was unable to find the key to the mystery of that complex and amazing phenomenon—Leśmian's poetic creativity.[2]

It was for this very reason that Szczerbowski's study was a disappointment to such prewar critics as Hieronim Michalski, one of the few who appraised Leśmian's poetry favorably before the war, and who recognized Leśmian as precisely the type of poet whose creative mystery could be explained only in terms of the individuality of his work. Thus, he anticipated finding in Szczerbowski's work an evaluation of "the theory of Leśmian's poetic vision," which he considered a key, not only to the understanding of Leśmian's work, but indispensable for shedding light on the entire contemporary literary scene:

> In some literary periods a creative work of a certain writer acquires a special significance. . . . At the present time . . . it is especially the work of Leśmian. . . . Staff and Leśmian are not only the most outstanding . . . representatives of the poetry of the post-war period, but they also represent two basically opposed elements, the Apollonian and the Dionysian. . . . From the attrition of these comes the chaos which reigns in the poetry of our times. This is why the voice of criticism of these two poets . . . could contribute to the elucidation of this chaos, as well as emphasize some developing trends in contemporary poetry.[3]

Michalski was very perceptive, for ideally Leśmian's theory of poetry should and could be deduced from his poetic works. However, for this the distance of time was needed, and Szczerbowski did not have the benefit of such distance.

The key Michalski looked for emerged only with the passing of time, in the form of a volume of Leśmian's collected *Szkice literackie* ("Literary Sketches") and a volume of his *Utwory rozproszone, Listy* ("Scattered Works, Letters"), both edited and annotated by Jacek Trznadel. These works made it possible to view the total man, the thinker and the poet, and to set his writing in its proper perspective.

The appearanze of *Szkice literackie* astonished even such an admirer of Leśmian as Julian Przyboś, who, as a leader of the first Vanguard in the late twenties, was a fierce adversary of Leśmian's poetics:

An exhilarating surprise! A new Leśmian, an unknown Leśmian, an essayist appeared; the author of philosophical and aesthetic treatises, a reviewer of theatrical performances and collections of poetry from half a century ago. . . . Leśmian, whom, to my regret, I never met although I exchanged a few letters with him, was for me almost a mythical figure, a creature from his own poetry. The life of this notary public from Zamość seemed somewhat unreal, until Leśmian appeared as a member of the Academy of Literature. But—next to Staff he was overshadowed. . . . They [the critics] did not notice then the basic difference between an excellently composed derivative poetry, carrying over the thrills and moods from foreign poetry, and *first-born* [italics mine] original creativity derived from one's own vision: between talent [Staff] and a genius [Leśmian].[4]

The critics and members of the Academy considered Leopold Staff the best poet of the era. The acknowledgment of Leśmian's superiority over Staff by one of the best present Polish poets has been cited in order to emphasize the gross misjudgment and injustice on the part of the influential critics. It also shows their disregard for that "original" poetic vision, which Michalski considered an indispensable key to both Leśmian's poetry and the Polish literary scene. Not only were these original works derived from Leśmian's own theoretical vision, but they also proved to be *synchronous* with his poetic expression of it, a phenomenon rarely found in literary history. He was able to express each new manifestation of the world with a correspondingly unique poetic word.

Some literary trends and schools, especially in twentieth-century literature, were initiated by manifestos of artistic creeds, which usually opened the gates to schism, revolt, or failure almost immediately. For the most part, these manifestos were a collective expression of theoretically formulated views. However, many of them failed in their function to inspire and guide the writers to the realization of the theoretical views they advanced. As a result, their views either did not find literary expression, or found some expression in literary works of dubious value. The fate of the manifestos of the literary period known as Young Poland—out of which Leśmian supposedly grew—did not differ from those found elsewhere. Przesmycki, Leśmian's patron and lifelong friend, drew up a "Symbolist" manifesto declaring that the goal of poetry lies

> in the opening of a little window to the deeply hidden elements of transcendentalism. For in it lies the eternal indestructibility of the creative genius . . . because it hides the unchangeable, . . . immortal element in itself and does not give in to the evolutionary meanderings of the sensual world [and] . . . because only in such an infinity can the spirit and imagination spread their eagle's wings. . . .[5]

Although the manifesto was vague it was considered a most radically formulated program of aesthetics. Correspondence with Zenon Przesmycki, as well as his early poetry, will demonstrate subsequently how far Leśmian was actually removed from his patron and from the mainstream of Young Poland. Not until years later, did Kazimierz Wyka point out the many contradictions in the lengthy manifesto, observing that Przesmycki had propagated a monistic mysticism based on that of Maeterlinck and supported by an

> inherited readiness of scientific proof, uncompromising trust in the authority of science, which arouses strong doubts as to whether he was at all . . . aware of the attributes of a metaphysical experience.[6]

For Przesmycki spiritual "mysticism" was a naive derivative of positivistic convictions that life and art could be bettered only through science. It was not mysticism that revealed truth and gave birth to art, but the broad scope of modern science which allowed for the existence of mysticism. Symbolism, as understood by Przesmycki, was an unchangeable "cognitive" system, a means of perceiving something which, in essence, can never be fully understood. This he explained and accepted as a sign of certain metaphysics or as the mystery of existence. Thus, Przesmycki's concept of Symbolism reveals the vagueness of his understanding of what it really represented. Therefore, the purely poetic and artistic theory he advanced somehow remained suspended in a vacuum. The examples he presented and the style he cultivated contradicted his intellectual elaborations. The inconsistencies in Przesmycki's views, expressed often in the periodical, *Chimera*, were pointed out by Karol Irzykowski in a work fittingly entitled: *Czyn i słowo* ("Deed and Word"), which shows the discrepancy between deed and word in Przesmycki's manifesto and in his creative practices.[7] It was not surprising that his manifesto was a total failure. It could not be accepted as a program for his followers, who deeply and painfully felt its lack of direction, the delusion of progress, and the tragic dissonance between the creative individual and the social system. Not only did the young poets reject his theories, but he himself failed to produce a single "Symbolist" work.[8]

Stanisław Przybyszewski's manifesto, published in the first issue of his periodical *Życie* (1899) and entitled "Confiteor," was a manifesto of art as the "absolute:"

> as an expression of what is eternal, independent of time and space, as the essence of existence, which is the soul in all its good and bad, beautiful and ugly manifestations. . . . Art is the highest source from which life flows.[9]

He went on to say that every manifestation of soul is pure and holy, and mysterious to us as long as it is powerful. Przybyszewski's aesthetics could be defined as expressive. For him art fulfilled aesthetic functions because it was an expression of the artist's personality; it was "sincere" and "authentic." For Przybyszewski this was the *sine qua non* of true art. Of course this theory was no longer original. Judging from Przybyszewski's other utterances and from his practices as an editor, he did not in reality set such limits to the nature of art. He thus exposed himself to attacks and was, in turn, responsible for the attacks by his followers on several sacred cows. Misinterpretations were also occasioned by Przybyszewski's own original work of that period, which was imbued with a metaphysics of sex and concentrated on the conflict between "sex" and "brain." It is not surprising that he failed to create a new literary school in Poland, despite the charismatic effect he had on the Cracow artistic community.

It could be assumed that partly because of the failure of the leadership and its manifestos Polish literature went in various directions in the beginning of the twentieth century. In an attempt to construct a consistent, monolithic system of ideas, the writers of the above manifestos avoided elements which would disrupt the unity of such a system or be in disagreement with their theory. They used lofty words, often contradictory in meaning, with little regard for their applicability to poetic practice. The poets confronted with these manifestos, were confused by their contradictions and vagueness and had no clear idea of what Symbolism really stood for. As a result, they thought that almost anything could somehow fit this trend, when in fact, Symbolism is a complex phenomenon about which much is yet to be learned. Hence, this curious literary period called Young Poland, which allowed for the coexistence of a variety of literary trends.[10]

Against this backdrop of confusion between "monolithic" literary programs and heterogenous literary works, Leśmian's theoretical and philosophical essays stand out as a revelation and are a singular achievement. They serve as the key to the magic of his metaphysical poetry as well as an understanding of the literary period in the context of which Leśmian must be studied in order to be appreciated fully. His newly discovered works have made literary historians suddenly aware of the system of "checks and balances" that had always existed between Leśmian's form and idea, between his theory and poetry. Thus, it became clear to them (unfortunately, decades after his death) that this seemingly irrational poet, "detached from life and reality," was uniquely aware, from the start, of the guiding principles by which he would proceed and of the way in which he would exteriorize his poetic self. Admiration for this rare achievement of concurrence between

Leśmian's poetic vision (i.e., theory) and his creative practice was expressed in the following words of the eminent critic Artur Sandauer:

In general, this seemingly elemental poet amazes us by the intensive degree of his self-awareness.[11]

Similar ideas are expressed by J. Trznadel, who knows that one's own theories "hardly ever fit the artistic practice of a writer or poet. *In the case of Leśmian, the convergence between his theories and his practices are exceptionally far-reaching* [italics mine]."[12]

Leśmian's vision of his poetic self-expression was vast. He wanted to sing of the macroscopic world as well as of the world beyond. He wanted to make his readers look at, and understand the "Incomprehensiveness of Verdure" ("Niepojętość zieloności"), to capture the elusive. For in the world of this poet nothing was in a state of rest, everything was in a state of flux, in the ongoing process of constant incarnations and metamorphoses. He wanted people to see all of it, to embrace the unembraceable. Most of these feelings were expressed already in his earliest poems.[13]

On "embracing the unembraceable:"

. . . Wcielone czary ziemi—myśli serca poją . . .
Idę—lecę, na widzeń rozanielon szczycie,
Jeno wszystkie te cuda zmieścić w oczach żądam!
Czuję w sobie prawdziwe i jedyne życie,
Gdy przez okno mej duszy na ziemię poglądam! . . .
Bo gdyby rzeczywistość stworzyła mi oczy—
Nie usłyszałbym piosnek śród wszechświata głosów,
Nie trysnęłyby farby z bezdennych pomroczy, . . .
("Z cyklu *Sny* " [From the cycle, *Dreams*] I. p. 8)

The earth's incarnate magic fills my heart's thoughts . . . / I walk—I fly atop the blissful summit of visions, / Naught but all these wonders will I hold in my eyes! / I feel within myself the true, the only life, / When I gaze at the world through the window of my soul! . . . / For if reality should create my eyes for me— / I would not hear songs among the voices of the universe, / Nor would colors stream from the bottomless dark, / . . . /

On a new look at life and its metamorphoses:

. . . Staram się na świat biedny innym patrzeć okiem . . .
Z nocy gwiezdnej—słoneczne biorę snów świtanie,
A z piosnek świata—nutę co w obłokach dźwięczy,
A z szumu wichrów—siłę co leci w otchłanie,
A ze słońca złotego biorę blaski tęczy! . . .
I w kwiatach czuję serca ludzi, w listkach drżące,
I w ludziach—pięknych kwiatów nieskażone tchnienie,
I w ptakach—jakieś myśli, w skrzydłach się kryjące,
I w myślach—skrzydeł ptaszych bezbrzeżne dążenie! . . .
("Fragment," p. 16)

I try to look at the world with a different eye . . . / From the starry night—I take a sunlit dawn of dreams / And from the world's songs—a note resounding in the clouds, / And from the roar of the winds—the force that flies into the abyss, / And from the golden sun I take the rainbow's brilliance! . . . / And in flowers I feel men's hearts fluttering in the petals, / And in men—the undefiled breath of beautiful flowers, / And in birds—some thoughts hidden in their wings, / And in thoughts—the unbounded yearning of birds' wings! . . .

On the obsolescence of reality and on capturing various elusive phenomena in the nature of existence:

Kiedy do nieba jakiś dźwięk wypłynie,
To zabrzmi światu i w przestrzeni kona! . . .
Gdy się woń cudna wyrwie z kwiatów łona—
Zadrży w powietrzu—i zaraz zaginie! . . . / . . . /

A wszystkie dźwięki, i światła, i wonie,
Nim ziemia wyda, wszechświat wnet pochłonie,
I skrywa w głębi swego serca—na dnie! . . .

Wielki, kto w życia nieuchwytnym pędzie
Choćby dźwięk jeden stamtąd wydobędzie
Lub woń, lub jeden promień światła skradnie! . . .
("Sonet" ["Sonnet"], p. 7)

When a sound soars heavenward, / It rings out to the world and dies away in space! . . . / When a wondrous fragrance escapes a flower's womb— / It quivers on the air—and perishes at once! . . . / . . . /

And all the sounds and lights and smells / The earth no sooner yields up, than the universe swallows / And hides them deep in its heart—at the very bottom! . . . /

Great is he who in life's elusive flight / Takes from there at least one sound / Or smell, or steals a single ray of light! . . .

The process illustrated in the first example can be only achieved by "thoughts of the heart," by flights of poetic visions, hence only by the intuitive, which allows glimpses into true life. Daily reality based on the rational hinders the all-embracing poetic perception. As the poet looks through the window of his soul at this "vale of tears," a spark taken from reveries facilitates metamorphoses of reality by fusing the best in all elements of the universe.

The transformed flow of images in the second example is achieved formally by means of "correspondences," synesthesia and a polysyndetic structure. The sweep of poetic vision and the style remind one particularly of Słowacki, except that Leśmian's sensuality is closer to Tiutchev's. In the onward rush of life it is only the Promethean poet who, stealing a ray of light from the soul of the universe, can capture some of its elusive beauty. Unlike the two preceding examples which were written as an *Ich-Lyrik*, in the third example the poet uses the genre of the sonnet, in which the narrative lends objectivity to his pronouncements, while the last tercet serves as a *pointe*. In these early poems we can already find Leśmian's belief in the autonomy of all phenomena (e.g., the soul of the universe), while the language, devices, and imagery of these verses are reminiscent of Romantic and early Symbolist poets.

The "alchemy" of Leśmian's poetic creativity did not arise suddenly, in all its perfection; it was the culmination of much preliminary work, many hesitations, defeats, and renewed efforts. Concurrent with his poetry was the development of his poetic theory, which, with the philosophy of early Bergson as a catalyst, crystallized into the philosophical and theoretical essays found in his *Szkice literackie*.

This unique artist, unlike most of the poets who were his contemporaries, was nurtured in a bilingual poetic tradition, both Russian and Polish. It was, no doubt, from Russian literature that he drew his first impressions, for he obtained his primary, high-school, and university education in Kiev.[14] Although he was brought up at home in a Polish atmosphere and Kiev had a large Polish community, the official language, the schools and the geographical environment were still Russian. He was a bilingual poet in the early days of his career.

His knowledge of Russian literary criticism, thought, prose, poetry, and folklore was astonishing. Several acquaintances (Henryk Hertz-Barwiński, Zygfryd Krauze, the poets Julian Tuwim and Jan Brzechwa) mention his passion for Russian folklore. His friend Krauze recalls Leśmian's beautiful recitations of *byliny* (a full collection of which he owned) and of his favorite poets, Afanasi Fet, Aleksandr Blok, and Sergei Esenin.[15] Brzechwa speaks of Leśmian's extensive and intensive studies, especially of the works of the Russian folklorist Afanas'ev, *Vozzreniia drevnikh slavian na prirodu,* and his collection of folk tales. He also studied books of proverbs. Of nineteenth-century Russian poets, according to Jan Brzechwa, Leśmian particularly adored Pushkin and esteemed Fet and Fedor Tiutchev. He was personally acquainted with Konstantin Balmont, Andrei Bely, Dmitri Merezhkovsky, Z. Gippius, Zaitsev, and Khodasevich, and corresponded with Valeri Briusov and the folklorist Y. M. Sokolov. This is also acknowledged by the poet's daughter Maria L. Mazurowa and by Leśmian's Kievan friend Włodzimierz Słobodnik.[16] The poet speaks about some of his interests in Russian thought and folklore in an interview:

> . . . A long time ago I took a fancy to Losev, a Russian writer, whose views are expounded in his book, *The Dialectics of the Artistic Form.* He looks upon poetry as the expression of the inexpressible, the utterance of the ineffable. . . .
>
> In times of over-refinement and exoticism, I was influenced solely by the Polish folk song . . . and Russian *byliny.*[17]

Yet, curiously enough, the Russian influences were overlooked by his contemporary critics who recognized only that he differed from Polish Modernism and from the Polish literary tradition, in general, but would not look for the reasons. Some keen critics of the thirties however, such as Stefan Napierski, who justly evaluated Leśmian's work against the contemporary literary scene, at least drew a parallel between his work and contemporary Russian poetry:

> . . . He alone, in spite of a late debut, has introduced a tone which enriches the mute harp of the epigones of the prematurely decayed Young Poland. . . . He pointed out the possibility of new ways, achieved with a great deal of difficulty. He alone, steadfast and uncompromising in his artistry, has perfected the means of expression to the point . . . that they could measure up to his contemporary Russian poetry, which flourished so magnificently, towering infinitely over Young Poland (which until now has been constantly and shamefully passed over in silence).[18]

This statement indicates that the silence about Russian poetic achievements and Leśmian's possible ties with the Russian literary scene was conscious or could be ascribed to collective pressures and a collective "ethos"; for another critic, Michalski, who relates to Leśmian sympathetically and who fully agrees with Napierski's view, notes:

> Very interesting details were brought up by Wiesław Gorecki about the kinship of Leśmian with French poetry, in *Czas* ["Time"] . . . of this year, and about his kinship with Russian poetry in the unprinted (what a pity!) lecture delivered at the eulogistic ceremony [for Leśmian] by Jarosław Iwaszkiewicz.[19]

Keeping in mind Leśmian's complex background, we can fully appreciate the extraordinary insight and lucidity of his mind which made him select those aspects from both Slavic sources which best suited his own poetic vision.

We can follow the development of his aesthetic self-awareness from scant but important sketches in the form of a commentary to his own poems, and much can be gleaned as well from random sentences in his correspondence. Serving as one of the keys to the understanding of his poetry, they reveal that his poetic vision was developing in a direction where early Bergsonism was a reassuring confirmation of ideas already bearing fruit in Leśmian's poetry, as well as in his various other works.

Almost from the beginning, he regarded his creativity as a negation of the existing dominant trend in Polish Modernism which was a residue of Positivism and Parnassianism. A letter written from Kiev to Przesmycki as early as 1897 reveals Leśmian's critical attitude in evaluating the periodical *Życie* ("Life")[20] as well as the low esteem in which he held Young Poland:

> When I saw for the first time the propectus of *Życie* I felt immediately that it was a coin not made of pure gold. For a *modern* journal it has too little modernity; as for a social one—it has too much of it. . . . It is a pity that we still don't have a true Polish Modernism.[21]

Hoping that the literary journal *Chimera* would soon be established and that it would bring with it a change in Polish Modernism as well as the possibility of his participation in it, he acknowledged his disenchantment with the early Russian Symbolists, complaining in a letter that, in Kiev, he was in "a current, which is not the best."[22] Characteristic, also, is his belief in a modernistic genre—the long poem:

> . . . I ceased to believe in today's generation and in the future of the poor Symbolist Muse. . . . I lost the capacity for writing small poems . . . and for that volatile composition (which is in vogue). I began to write long poems.
>
> . . . Can one write today an epico-lyric, poetical novel, not a Symbolist short story, but a psychological one with realistic action? I have exactly this kind in mind. I want to create a child of the century.[23]

It is obvious from the above quotation that the young poet had by 1897 already found the composition of small genres, as used at the time, an unsuitable form for manifesting his broad vision of life and his poetic creed. The poets of early Russian Symbolism and of Young Poland limited the use of description and narration at the expense of the pure form of lyrical expression via the "confessional," lyrical "I." The volatility and the elliptic devices inherent in this poetry diminished the visual and sensual experience of the reader. Instead of a clear image, he was presented with a chain of associations. Even nature, as depicted by some of the so-called Decadent poets, was narrowed down from the Romantics' vision of cosmos to the artificiality of a hothouse garden or even to the nature of one's own *paysage*. The latter was propagated by Paul Verlaine in "Votre âme est un paysage choisi. . ."[24]

Leśmian showed a predilection even then for clear-cut, concrete, visual, and profound poetic expression (subsequently the hallmark of his art), rejected the established form, and chose large genres and the narrative style in order to attain greater objectivity and dynamism. These were the formal means which he considered necessary to create a daring "child of the century."

In spite of his grandiose plans and the encouragement of second prize for his sonnet published in *Życie*, Leśmian's self-criticism and dissatisfaction with himself were expressed in a subsequent letter:

> I have the following doubt: I know and feel that I have a talent, that I am a poet, for I possess a certain "spiritual wealth" in which I dwell constantly. I am afraid that my talent is mediocre, . . . in short, its place is somewhere beneath Tetmajer. Is it worth to write? Besides, I hear words ringing in my ears: *Today's bards are* tired of *serving the world!* To this I will add my constant dissatisfaction with my own work. Everything I write is "not it," "not it," and again "not it."[25]

Leśmian did not condone the approach of the *fin de siècle* decadent poets, who were determined to glorify themselves, totally immersed as they were in their inner self in the manner of Maurice Barrès's *culte du moi*. Further, by ironically using the term "bards," he revealed his disdain for poets who, in his view, *were expected* to serve the world.[26] Leśmian's comment shows that he was a committed poet, concerned about the world and not *out of touch with life.* It further indicates that his views on the role of the "bard" bring him closer to the belief shared by the second generation of Russian Symbolists.

Further in the same letter, we get the first insight into his poetic vision and into the creative process as a stage of incarnation, of becoming:

> . . . My creative work is twofold: not only to create an image, but also the impression—not only to strike the strings of the lyre, but to incubate in the soul the *very process of the striking.* I feel that in other conditions I could sing better, more powerfully and more broadly, "I know what an eagle must suffer, when his wings cannot gain full momentum in flight!" I lack that very swing. I poison myself with revery, as with vapid but necessary nourishment—and I understand how God suffered when he had to create the world from nothing! The result of this "inter-existence" . . . is . . . if I may say so—"the neuralgia of a starved soul." [Italics mine][27]

These doubts of the nineteen-year-old poet are a consequence of having reached an impasse in his creativity, which was, in reality, a new plateau, from which he yearned to leap into the world of poetry he envisioned:

> . . . I would like to publish my work, for the first period of my creativity is coming to an end . . . I feel it acutely. But I decided not to publish it without consulting you [Przesmycki] personally.[28]

> . . . Everything I have created lately has this title: "Meantime"; the whole of Kiev is the abject materialization of this dastardly and at the same time painful word.[29]

This period of Leśmian's creativity has some affinity with Russian and Polish Romanticism as well as with certain aspects of the poetry of the Decadent *fin-de siècle* school (which I shall discuss later). It is evident that the poet experienced a feeling of suffocation, for neither the Russian literary scene of the nineties, with which he was in contact, nor the Young Poland school provided him with any direction suitable for his inner needs.

Although Przesmycki was his highly respected mentor, he did

not take kindly to his program. In a letter from Kiev, written in 1900, Leśmian confided to Przesmycki the enormous changes which had taken place within him. From this account emerges a reflection of the mentality of a poet who far from being detached from life, far from being irrational, and quite unlike "the bards" of early Symbolism, does not turn away from the world, but, on the contrary, turns to the people for inspiration and discloses the qualities of a committed humanist:

> . . . Craving impressions I set out for spiritual begging among people and (I must boast) I have filled my beggar's wallet with the most diamond-like scraps of human souls. Human stupidity, wisdom, meanness and kind-heartedness, fraud and honesty, crime and love—all of it I put among diamonds. I have learned to forgive, to love, to hate, to search, and to find . . . I have come to the conclusion that the greatest genius of man is that this wretched worm dug himself out from the mire of nothingness into the sun, lifted up his head and—behold! a veritable miracle—he talks, moves, dreams, complains, yearns, crucifies gods on crosses, confesses sins. . . . *Thus each man is for me great.* The difference of talents is the difference of one ant in two anthills. The first has only 1000, and the second 1001. For this reason the first is only "an average mortal and the other—a Newton." . . . Truly a dying Yakut (if I will inspire him with an immortal soul) is greater for me than Zeus . . . and all of the Hindu and non-Hindu idols.) [Italics mine.][30]

This realization of man's greatness boosted Leśmian's self-confidence. It spurred him on to search for new paths beyond even the sun itself.

In this attempt he was greatly aided by Cezary Popławski, a man who was forced, according to Leśmian, "to search for love, ideals, knowledge, and the Lord God in a radius of fifteen kilometers," a man whose soul remained unsoiled by even a speck of banality. Though he never published, he was an artist and a poet in his outlook on life and searched constantly for new paths in art. Popławski had a great critical and literary talent, a terse style of concrete imagery, and steadfast expressiveness.

The qualities both of the man and the artist which the young Leśmian admired in Popławski, provide an insight into the poet's predilections and tastes and serve as a useful guide to the early development of Leśmian's poetic vision. Such information seems of particular value in the study of an artist who was not often given to discussing his views.

So indelible was the impact on Leśmian of some aspects of Popławski's style and approach to poetry that he remained true to them throughout his creative life. This is attested by an interview the poet granted toward the end of his life to Edward Boyé, who remarked:

> The library dust remained within the limits of your notary-public office. Not a single layer of it penetrated to the outside or got stuck to your words which, forged in the dark smithy of the folk language, act always effectively, like incantations, like a "mantra" . . . [a sacred dictum in the Sanskrit language indicating various prayers and forms of magic spells]. They are terse, pithy, concrete, colorful, never gray or dull.[31]

"The close-fitting, the contiguity, of the words to the object they describe, the denseness of the language" were a source of amazement to the young Julian Przyboś, upon his first encounter with Leśmian's poetry.[32]

Leśmian's early disenchantment with the "Symbolist Muse" led the searching poet to free himself from any formal considerations important in the aesthetics of the so-called school of Decadence. The crystallization of his own concepts of artistic form, the artist's creative process, and the reality of the existence of man and the universe occurred, as I shall demonstrate, at a very early stage in his career. Form, previously understood as genre (external form), composition, and style had now become for Leśmian an "organic" whole. It represented a unity of idea and content, a synthesis of matter and idea. This concept of form was indispensable to the young poet, who by 1900 already believed in a changing reality and in creative evolution. Therefore, the form had to be a quick synthesis expressed in the image.[33] His ideas about poetic form were formulated later, in his *Szkice literackie*, and were propagated throughout his creative life. The essays also constitute substantial proof that Leśmian's aesthetic direction was developed early and that his basic creative tenets were consistent throughout his creative life.

His ideas about form and his predilection for the intuitive, spontaneous approach to art rather than the rational approach are expressed in a letter:

Inasmuch as I thought earlier about *form*—so, today, I don't think about it at all. Generally, I do not differentiate form, or rather an image, from a thought, an image from a feeling, and so on. I know of no scalpel capable of dissecting a truly poetic work into substance and form. I have come close to my own soul to such an extent that I feel in myself some kind of a twofold totality, . . . a kind of a planetary system. . . . My dreams are meanwhile mightier than myself. But this does not matter! I merge with them slowly like a shadow with the light, and after each such fusion I feel a joy and ecstacy . . . and although life is bleak, yet I draw . . . all the pulsating veins out of it.[34]

Leśmian's awareness of the supremacy of intuition over rationality simultaneously found expression in a long poem, *Pari-Banu,* sent by the youthful poet to Przesmycki for evaluation and possible publication in the periodical *Chimera.* The poet had apparently found himself at last, for he considered it

. . . the first work, which I wrote with great calm and often with a smile of my soul. That is why I fell in love with it.[35]

The excellent fragment of the poem published in 1901 under the title *Ze wspomnień dziecińśtwa* ("From Recollections of Childhood") starts out appropriately:

. . . Przyjemnie czasem zgnieść w sobie rozsądek,
Jak pasożyta, co niszczy marzenie,. . .[36]

. . . It is pleasant at times to crush reason in oneself, / Which, like a parasite, destroys reverie, / . . . /

The importance Leśmian attached to the poem, and the argument he used to elucidate its aesthetic values in a subsequent letter to his maître, necessitate the closest scrutiny of this early period in his career. It can be assumed that this poem serves as a link in the evolutionary process of Leśmian's creative work. Perhaps it would be more accurate to say that it is a testimony to the continuity and consistency of his poetic self-awareness.

Anticipating objections to *Pari-Banu* on the part of Przesmycki he writes:

> . . . Apparently I have committed in it some kind of sin against art which unduly caused your displeasure. I can guess the nature of it. . . . It apparently concerns the lack of greater depth of an ideological plan, of extremity in conclusions and of vacillation in reasoning. . . . But all of these ostensible shortcomings were intentional, were the basis of my artistic goal for the given poem. *The period of childhood* which I chose as the background *is exactly the time when, in spite of consciousness, one feels the supremacy of feeling.* . . . In it I also find—among others—elements of beauty, in which even a smile, involuntary humor, . . . unwillingly enters the realm of perceiving things from the world beyond.
>
> Besides, my goal was to treat things lightly, which is so typical for human thought, when going through a series of efforts, of immersions, of throwing off the shroud of mystery, . . . [Italics mine.][37]

Long before we learn about Leśmian's views of the existence of the universe and man's relationship to it from his *Szkice literackie*, he has expressed them, perhaps in a less finished form, as follows:

> The full relationship of the soul to the universe ought to contain in itself everything human—not only sadness, longing, belief, doubt, but also laughter, humor, and even jest.[38]

Bergson's postulate of creative evolution which is based on the existence of two opposing elements, matter and the *élan vital*, the unharnessed current of life stemming from intuition, discussed by Leśmian in his essay "Z rozmyślań o Bergsonie" ("From Meditations on Bergson," published in 1910),[39] merely supported and helped to form his own ideas, expressed as early as 1901 in a letter:

> . . . This smile of the soul evolves slowly, through a series of evolutionary strain, strife, ecstasy, distortion, injury, etc.—into irony, sarcasm, hearty laughter, and death. Between a smile and death there is the same relationship as between a tear and death. Heraclitus and Democritus equally explore the mysteries of the universe.[40]

The idea of the evolutionary process of life, in which the new reality is created in the wake of obsolescent reality, and thus everything is in a constant state of becoming, finds its poetic expression in another long poem *Niedopita czara* ("The Undrained Cup") written in the same year as the letter above. Even Leśmian's terms, *Wicher życiowy* and *Duch Wichrowy*, used later instead of Bergson's *élan vital* in Leśmian's philosophical essay, have already appeared in this poem:

. . . I wszystko wtedy zatraca różnicę!
I nie ma w sobie końca ni początku,
I oko stwierdza ową tajemnicę,
Że nawet motyl, i nawet to kwiecie,
Które jesienią trwać nie chcą na świecie,
Ma w sobie coś, co nie jest kwiatem,
Ani motylem—lecz snem, mgłą, zaświatem,
I swą pozornie doczesną istotą
Łączy się w jedność z wieczystą Tęsknotą,
Co nie umiera nigdy, zawsze bliska
Śmierci, a zawsze ku życiu wytryska! / . . . /

I zdało mi się, że to *Duch Wichrowy*
Gra na ust twoich lutni koralowej / . . . /
Tę pieśń bez jutra. . . . / . . . / [Italics mine.][41]

And then everything loses its distinctness! / And has within itself neither beginning nor end, / And the eye confirms this mystery, / That even the butterfly and even the bloom / Which in autumn do not wish to linger in the world, / Have something in themselves that is neither bloom / Nor butterfly—but dream, mist, the world beyond, / And with its apparent worldly presence / Becomes as one with eternal Longing, / Which shall never die—always close to / Death, yet it shall always spring to life! / . . . /

And it seemed to me that the Spirit of the Whirlwind / *Played on the coral lute of your lips / . . . / This song without tomorrow, / . . . /*

The existence of all phenomena knows neither beginning nor end; it has an ingredient of mystery, of the *élan vital* which propels it into eternal flux, erasing all boundaries and therefore producing ephemeral songs. The dramatization of the process of equalization is expressed formally by polysyndetons, a structural device which will become characteristic of his poetry.

In the essay "Znaczenie pośrednictwa . . ." Leśmian expresses his view against causality which, he believes, fetters creativity and does not allow the effect to be a total surprise.[42] The poem *Pari-Banu* was a specific and an early attempt to free his creativity from this "deadening" causality:

In addition, I was concerned in the poem, not to come to conclusions, . . . but only to give . . . *effects*, and also not to poison feelings with thoughts; that is why I *love* this work as an only son, for it seems to me that it is the first and the last of my works not poisoned by reason.[43]

The poet somewhat sarcastically adds, by way of appeasement, that perhaps his other long poem *Cień* ("Shadow") would be more fortunate since it contained many profundities, all kinds of "thoughts, extra-thoughts, over-thoughts, etc." He noted with irony that he did not love the second poem as an only son, but as a brother.[44]

Just as the theme of childhood led the poet to the clarification of his poetic creed and to simplicity achieved, according to him, through the supremacy of intuition, so was he now in search of creative devices that would best express his poetic vision. In a letter of 1904 he informed his *maître* that he had rid himself of the declamatory style which prevailed throughout the land and had achieved simplicity of style.[45] With his usual sense of humor he added:

Lately immersed in a superb solitude I have forgotten everything . . . about the existence of any literary trends—Expressionism, Impressionism, Modernism, Ecstatism, Highfalutinism, Intensivism and other *modes et robes.* I tried only to extract, to draw upon my own layers of impressions, *upon first-hand* impressions and not upon those handed over from a second, third, or tenth paw.

Besides, I strove for a unique artistry, to which everything is accessible, that is unafraid of anything, and does not give a thought to what is and what is not permissible or proper. I also strove for denseness, coherence, imperviousness of those impressions. . . . Each image of mine is created and is called into being by *narration,* which (I see it now clearly) is the kind of writing by means of which the author relates that which he might or might not be able otherwise to bring out of his inner self into the light. The rest is—delusion [italics mine].[46]

He pointed out the many stages of evolution he had gone through and was going through, all of which, unfortunately, he was unable to relate adequately in a letter. His entire Weltanschauung was in a state of Becoming. He was going through a terrible *Sturm-und-Drang* period, as he called it. Like the world surrounding him, so he, as a part of it, was in constant inner flux. He confided to his *maître:*

> . . . I have such a nature, that no sooner do I think about a new work than I immediately lose the capacity of criticism for the preceding one. If someone were to ask me now, what *Pani Atamanowa* [a novelette, written in prose] is all about, I would blush and be unable to say a word about it![47]

Yesterday's reality was no longer today's, since what stimulated the poet to create a particular work in the past became obsolescent, and could no longer be a stimulus in the present. The poet, looking back from a newly arrived at plateau, is not only unable to evaluate his previous work properly, but, perhaps, cannot even recall the now irrelevant stimuli.

This constant whirlwind of the evolutionary process continues apparently throughout Leśmian's career. In a letter from Paris written years later (1912), he informed his patron that he was changing from day to day so extensively that it was hard for him to evaluate his first book of poetry or even to choose a proper title for it. Consequently, he decided to accept the title suggested by Przesmycki: *Sad rozstajny.* Writing about his new experiences he noted:

> I do not know whether these are crossroads or an impetus in different directions, all due to a multitude of elements which have suddenly stirred up inside of me.[48]

These ongoing changes in Leśmian's poetic awareness resulted in a collection of new works, differing entirely from the first volume of his poetry (*Sad rozstajny*) in atmosphere, in the broadening of the scope of genres (even including epics) that, again, were departures from traditional concepts. "Each cycle is from another barrel, another country, almost from another planet." It also contained a long poem, most original in tone, language, and content.[49]

Although described by many literary critics, with some justification, as a man of contradictions, a man with a dual nature, Leśmian, nonetheless, apparently possessed a homogeneity similar to that sawfish which he gives as a model of intuitive action in his philosophical essay "Z rozmyślań o Bergsonie." The sawfish displays no dichotomy between intuition and intellect, between mind and matter, and is thus an example of the indivisible action that results in intuitive creativity. Since the creative part of the fish is an extension of its mouth—a part of its body (i.e., of matter)—the action of sawing is a direct action, as are the acts of hearing and seeing. There is no division into rationality and intuition between the desire to act and the action itself. The action, the creativity, is part of its being alive—as the saw, the instrument, is a part of its body. To live is—to saw—to act intuitively.[50]

The above comparison was meant to describe the process of Leśmian's creativity. On several occasions he commented on the same subject in correspondence with his mentor:

> . . . I have noticed one thing in myself, rather early—that I create precipitately (blindly)—and only after I have created a work, do I ponder on what I have done and what I have achieved.[51]

This observation indicates an acute self-criticism and a spontaneous talent that allowed the poetry to form plastic images despite its spontaneity—a phenomenon not unlike that of a flower which emits a fragrance the instant it opens.

On another occasion, requesting an evaluation of the cycle of poems entitled *Pieśni przelotne* ("Fleeting Songs"), Leśmian wrote:

> . . . You know how merciless I am toward my own works. . . . I have not dedicated myself as a poet *to any ideal*—I write, floundering through

these or other worlds, almost gropingly by way of fascination, rapture, bewilderment, but rarely by way of reflection or meditation. I feel in myself a tremendous impetus and I feel that I am reaching worlds to which a wide road is hidden. However, in this phase of constant metamorphosis in which I find myself, I have psychologically no time for self-criticism. . . . Your sudden entrance into the moment of the creative process, already passed . . . and your opinion is indispensable for me.[52]

I have never felt so good spiritually and physically as at the present. Never before had I had such a clear vision of things and such an ability to sing fully and to breathe freely. [Italics mine.][53]

This effusion of feeling, as well as all the preceding statements made by the poet, explain the process of his creative evolution as the effect of pure intuition. Not attached consciously to any literary trend or accepted ideals which would make him follow conventionality and introduce reason into the stream of his creative process, the poet strove to spin his poetic myth following consistently the path of intuition. This *consistency* in Leśmian, the acclaimed "irrational" poet, accounts for the paradox that he is also the most "rational" one—a word Leśmian would frown at. For there was no dichotomy, nor could there be any, between his ideas of the poetic creative process, and its exteriorization.

The process of Leśmian's creativity is in itself the true incarnation of that *Wicher życiowy* ("the impetus of life"). His poetic vision and his poetic works are an expression of the authentic human persistence of constant Becoming which, after all, is part of the cosmic whirlwind that Henri Bergson calls the *élan vital.*

The early Bergson suited the twenty-three-year-old poet. In Bergson he recognized and almost discovered himself (i.e., in the idea of creative evolution, the belief in myth and the importance of rhythm). Leśmian found in Bergson that much needed assurance which he sought in vain in Young Poland and in early Russian Symbolism. In order to overcome the stifling atmosphere he felt around him and to achieve originality, he needed sound support and aid in defining his own wisdom. As we shall see, Bergson's philosophy enabled him to crystallize his poetic vision.

FORMULATED POETICS

Leśmian's most essential theoretical and critical reviews were contained in the *Szkice literackie* and were written in a relatively short span of time, roughly between 1909 and 1915.[54] This was a period of literary depression in Poland, especially in respect to poetry. It was, relatively speaking, a time of modest intellectual ferment (except for a few men like Irzykowski and Brzozowski), and of meager cultural atmosphere in general. In view of the existing literary climate, it is surprising that Leśmian's works, which appeared in *Prawda*, in *Literatura i Sztuka*, in *Kurier Warszawski*[55] and in other important periodicals, went largely unnoticed by the literary critics. No one bothered to assess their importance or to draw necessary conclusions from them, even in regard to Leśmian's own poetic works.

Leśmian expresses his poetic creed in various forms: in philosophical treatises, theoretical essays, and in critical reviews dealing primarily with the current Polish literary output. These versatile theoretical works are an exposition of the poet's philosophy as they speak directly about his vision of the world and, what is more important, they reveal Leśmian's relationship to poetry. All of his pronouncements constitute an invaluable commentary and guide to his own poetic work. His inquiries as a literary theoretician and practicing poet are concurrent, and therefore consistent with his earlier thoughts expressed in his letters to Przesmycki. The spontaneous creative art left him with afterthoughts that were no less creative, as evidenced by the *Szkice literackie*.

One may conclude that the theoretical essays were written by the author of *Sad rozstajny*[56] with the primary intention of defining his own stand on aesthetics, rather than to represent a poetic program that would influence literary opinion directly.[57] Viewed as a commentary, the *Szkice literackie* allow us "to capture the dialectics of the interdependence between what Bruno

Markwardt would call 'formulated poetics' and 'immanent poetics',"[58] and alter decidely the evaluation of Leśmian's creative work. Not only do the *Szkice literackie* point towards a new possibility, i.e., a parallel investigation of Leśmian's theoretical and poetic works (an attempt not yet fully realized)[59] but they also represent a new dimension in the complex studies of so-called "Leśmianology."

The diverse nature of Leśmian's expositions makes it possible to examine them on different levels. On the primary level they represent a lucid study of historiosophic, sociological, and even psychological problems confronting art and the creative individual in the complex structure of modern society. On the literary level, they serve as a document expressing a variety of aesthetic views on the contemporary Polish literary scene. This subject, discussed fragmentarily over the last fifty years, has nowhere received such a many-sided elucidation as in the *Szkice literackie.* The uniqueness of the essays lies in that they were written during a period when Young Poland was already an established convention, having passed "from the realm of style . . . into the realm of literary grammar."[60] As Leśmian lived mostly abroad in those years, his physical distance very likely lent objectivity to his judgments.

The *Szkice literackie* discuss not only the trends of the period, but also the style of Young Poland, "which originated in the storeroom of accepted poetic prescriptions, compositions of words . . . and images."[61] Leśmian gained his insight into the epoch by reviewing primarily the works of second-rate poets, writers of peripheral importance, who usually adhere to the prescribed rules of a program and thus provide the best examples of a literary trend. J. Trznadel writes:

> Having read the *Szkice literackie,* I understood precisely what the anonymous spirit of the times was, which is impossible to capture in the works of outstanding individual writers.[62]

Similar observations are to be found in the review of Janusz Sławiński, who attributes this great achievement to the poet's peculiar sensitivity to some of the characteristics of the poetic code of Young Poland, namely, its static, mediocre realizations.[63] Leśmian's sensitivity enabled him to detect deviations from the code and see in them the forecast of a new kind of poetics.[64] He appears, therefore, to be a more worthy literary critic than his contemporaries.

Whether Leśmian applied his "formulated poetics" to the works of important poets like Staff and Miciński, or to that of lesser poets, he always remained consistent in his frankness, excellent style, and deep aesthetic insight. A sensitive critic, Leśmian appreciated more profound literary subjects, but when confronted with graphomania, he indulgently compared the results to weeds that also have the right to live under the fence of poetry.[65] As a literary reviewer Leśmian must be considered an important contributor to the development of Polish literary criticism.

If one has in mind any traditional poetic program, then it is difficult to conceive of the *Szkice literackie* as a "formulated poetics." It was not Leśmian's intent to create a program, for he did not believe in programs. Its structure as well as the multi-leveled, diversified nature of the *Szkice literackie* defy such labeling. However, it would be wrong to assume, judging by the titles of some of the theoretical essays alone (i.e., "Z rozmyślań o Bergsonie," or "Znaczenie pośrednictwa. . . .") that they do not deal with poetic problems. They do contain instructions of a literary nature. Viewed in their totality, the *Szkice literackie* definitely represent a theoretical body of poetics, multifarious and far-reaching in its significance. This is acknowledged by many contemporary literary historians, as well as by the eminent literary critic A. Sandauer:

> . . . In the *Szkice literackie,* recovered lately from obscurity by J. Trznadel, we find . . . a theoretical program of *Łąka* ["Meadow"]. It is [expressed primarily in] the article, "Znaczenie pośrednictwa. . . ."[66]

Leśmian's theoretical essays are an exposition of a profound thinker, an erudite man who conceived of and thoroughly digested various philosophical ideas based on such opposites as nature and culture, intuition and intellect, the individual versus institution, and "primary reality" versus "secondary reality." He gave the same considerations to different literary schools in order to arrive at the "essense" of poetic creation. His "formulated poetics" is a theory of a poetic language oriented and devoid of strict metalingual pronouncements, transgressing the limits of literature and expanding into considerations of a philosophical, sociological, and psychological nature. But all these considerations, including the marginal pronouncements in his critical works, lead to one essential question: that of creative work, especially poetry. The poet's intent is to show every aspect of the "essense" of the poetic phenomenon and to explore the metaphysical as well as the sociological situations from which poetry emerges. Through this unusual approach we learn "about the true nature of art, about the basis of the creative process and about the 'vital' context of poetry."[67] These characteristics have prompted some critics to consider Leśmian's "formulated poetics" an anticipation of the aims of the between-wars Vanguard.

Leśmian formulates his theory of cognition especially in the essays, "Z rozmyślań o Bergsonie" and "Znaczenie pośrednictwa. . . ." The basic principle of his theory is a critique of rationalism which does not allow man to understand the real essence of the world and stifles artistic creation. Leśmian advocates the kind of cognition in which intuition and imagination dominate. These he considers to be superior to logical cognition. In the metaphysics of most philosophers reason also plays a major role (cf., Kant and Schopenhauer); in Bergson's metaphysics (similar to Leśmian's), myth is given the primary consideration.[68]

Myth as a product of intuition and imagination expresses and also symbolizes certain deep-rooted aspects of human and superhuman existence, which explains why metaphysics, religion, and even the exact and logical sciences have their roots in myth. Leśmian reminds us how

science drew upon the sources of myth which exists in the land of metalogic. . . . Let us recall the illogical myth about the ether, as about a substance *solid and weightless* at the same time. . . .[69]

Myth, according to Leśmian, is not merely a transfer of past philosophies or folk narrations, but is constantly created anew. It is an authentic expression of creative life and of human persistence in the cosmic onward rush.[70] Leśmian believes that

each philosophical system has its own mythology . . . which is unavoidable and indispensable for human thought, as air is for breathing. . . .

In each metaphysical system, that which constitutes its core, its main principle, its revelation—is never proven, it is a mystery. . . . The mystery (truth) is exposed to the same creative changes as is life itself.[71]

In the mystery which is unproven, Leśmian sees the source of creative originality. Just as Bergson builds his philosophical system upon the antagonism between two forces, matter and the *élan vital* (which results in creative evolution) so Leśmian considers myth as the basic concept of poetic cognition, because myth enables the poet to establish a "dialogue" with nature, with the realm of reality, obscured in modern times by the power of rationality. Myth helps to understand the true essence of creative life.

Leśmian asserted that poetry has cognitive functions. According to Trznadel:

For . . . Leśmian, the poetic word and the structure of a poem are specific means of cognition, of fixing and capturing the fleeting moment; a means by which the cognition of reality is achieved to the fullest extent.[72]

The proposition of the cognitive functions of poetry distinguishes Leśmian's poetic theory from the theory of Young Poland (as seen in the manifestos of Przesmycki and Przybyszewski) and from that of early Russian Symbolism, which primarily stressed the expressive and aesthetic values of poetry.

Leśmian's theory asserts that poetry allows us to perceive the world directly, in its actual form, and not in a schematic or abstract form perceived by means of syllogism (verified reasoning) or the power of tangibility. Because poetry is primarily an intuitive process, it overcomes abstraction, in effect, by rejecting causality which establishes a false order in creative life. Leśmian believes that ". . . the main characteristic feature of creative life is its unpredictable, limitless possibilities." In his poetics, consequently, causality is replaced by a "fantastic necessity."[73] This enables one to capture the world in its flux and dynamism.

The negation of causality is closely connected with the acknowledgment of anthropomorphism as an essential means of poetic cognition. Anthropomorphism changes the rationally oriented world, in which creative art is predictive, static, and statistically oriented. The animation of inanimate objects brings about a leveling process in poetry, through which man merges with nature and his surrounding objects. The resultant poetry reveals the world as a dynamic, animated entity, set into a state of motion and metamorphosis. Poetic creation can no longer be predictable, and thus it approximates life. Anthropomorphism, according to Leśmian, enables poetry to express the true reality of life.[74] By means of anthropomorphism, Leśmian's poetry attempts

> to penetrate into the depth of objects, . . . in which matter becomes energy, and to observe them internally, to see their inner motion.[75]

Leśmian's "formulated poetics" attempts also to explain a basic characteristic of man's predicament, i.e., his ambiguity, which comes of living under the pressure of a dual existence in which he is but

> a trace, resulting from the blow of the creative spirit against static matter. . . . He is at the same time the conqueror and the conquered; an impetus into the future, and motionless. He is that dent in matter, which is a sign

> of its resistance to the spirit. He is the place where the creative work of life is brought to a halt. There is as much confirmation in him as there is negation.[76]

This is an excellent example of that spiritual dialectic which is the main principle of Leśmian's poetic expression. It also demonstrates the ontological character of his poetics. The essential function of poetry is to free man from the predicament imposed upon him by the social order of modern culture and to bring him into close contact with nature. Each creative act arising from man's contact with spiritual realms, each poem, is *ipso facto* a negation of "established" reality. Poetry is the most effective medium for exposing the falsehood of schematized reality. *Poetry is also the only "dialogue"* with the "forgotten" world.

> This "dialogue," or the return to nature, to the [state] of liberated man, to the "direct life," takes place in the creative process.[77]

It is true that these "dialogues," the contacts with the "direct life," are not permanent phenomena. Leśmian sees them only as

> moments of inspired ecstasy, . . . which cannot be considered fates, or principles, . . . or durable foundations for a continuous building of a collective society. These inspired moments . . . are a source of new treasures of unforeseen creation, of new specimens, captured by *natura naturata* for its "museum in the universe."[78]

Through these inspired moments poetry assumes a mythogenic function. Leśmian compares these ephemeral miracles of creation to the miracle of the burning bush on Mount Sinai. Although these are only moments, they prove that intellect, which is a means of orientation in the superficial world surrounding man, cannot compete with its dramatic opponent—intuition. In spite of being stifled by the intellect's various forms of "mediations in the collective life" (such as poetry created to suit the tastes of consumers and critics), intuition is the only means of man's direct association with nature. Poetry as the product of intuition has an important function to fulfill in society. This view constitutes the focal point of Leśmian's poetics. Poetry represents an active association with primordial nature, a return to the lost paradise, to the free state of man when he was still a part of nature and not alienated from his fellow man. Therefore, only poetry, which represents the repressed, yet true, reality of life, can liberate man by mediating between the world of tangible values and the world inaccessible to cognition.

Although this is the most important, it does not exhaust all of the functions which Leśmian attributes to poetry. In the modern world religion is unable to satisfy the need, the hunger, of that part of the human psyche which cannot be controlled by logic, which yearns for revelation and ecstasy. The "gods," no longer the property of the church

> . . . obtain freedom and the right of citizenship in secular life, and go into the world in order to become means of cognition, . . . instruments of inspired creation. . . . We find them today in artistic life.[79]

The "gods," as appropriately pointed out by Jan Błoński, "are the fleeting incarnations of the vital power, if not *the* [italics mine] *Power* [itself], as mentioned in Leśmian's poem, 'W locie' ['In Flight']."[80] Thus, poetry becomes the key to the gates of the mystery of Being, and assumes the function of religion. Poets, in particular, are instruments of inspired creation because they have the Word of revelation. They are the "guardians" of man's dwelling in the true Being. In this context, poets play the role of demiurges who veto the domination of the mechanized "average man" in the modern society. The poets are the initiated, because they are in contact with the "beyond," as well as with the elemental (primordial) state of man. This, according to Leśmian, is the true spiritual dwelling place from which modern man is completely uprooted.

The core of Leśmian's poetics makes it evident that the perceptive, creative man occupies the central place in his poetry. The way man perceives things decides what reality is for him.

Realilty is neither constant, nor eternal. For Leśmian, the reality of an object is the identity of its idea with itself; the reality of a poem is its indivisible entity of form and idea. The same applies to man, who,

> . . . in view of the mystery of life, is an indivisible entity, elusive for the intellect. The creative man is different every moment, not only every moment, but changes constantly . . . and continuously.[81]

Each age, each person, possesses a different and unique reality. The more complex the world around us, the less accessible to our perception are the limits of the world. Leśmian presents a comprehensive review of the evolutionary process in man's perception of reality, ranging from that, for example, of the Flemish school of painters—with their indiscriminate perception of reality in which each detail shared reality equally with man—to a perception narrowed down to a scrutiny of types, and, later, to psychologically rounded characters as representative of man's reality. In modern times man's conflict with the world has become a conflict with himself. Man's belief in his ego has further narrowed the scope of his reality. Looking deeper into it, he persists in a ceaseless pursuit of "the least discernible and the most realistic."[82] Leśmian believes that the most realistic thing in man's soul is

> a certain primordial *song without words,* a certain tone. . . . This tone does not originate in the realm of logic, . . . but in those realms, . . . in which the concept of existence is liberated from the fetters of grammar and syntax. . . .
>
> Man . . . knows, . . . that in order to become real he must emit his own tone. . . . For *this is his only and most faithful reality.* . . . It differentiates him from others and assures him immortality. [Italics mine.][83]

This is a prototype of reality which is least submissive to the criticism of logic. Thus, the creative man had moved his reality out of reach of its possible enemy.

Changing reality is a subjective phenomenon. Every creator, every poet, has his own. This theory is closely connected with the differentiation between the indirect intellectualized reality, *natura naturata,* and the direct, intuitive reality, *natura naturans,*[84] propagated by Leśmian, especially in the key essay, "Znaczenie pośrednictwa. . . ." This differentiation, which has both a philosophical and a social character, applies to poetics as well. It is primarily a counterpart of the antinomy existing between contemporary society and the creative individual living apart from that society. *Natura naturata* is an abstract, derivative, "secondary" reality, ruled by schematization and conventionality, and created artificially by the evolutions of society. It represents the reality of the modern contemporary world ruled by conformity, by stable, unchanging and already proven principles which curtail the activities of a truly creative individual. On the other hand, *natura naturans* is the realm of creation; it is a reality in constant movement, not schematized and not subordinated to the laws of causality; it does not present a threat to man's individuality.

> The domain of *natura naturans* is the creative realm of existence, its basic source, its limitless possibility. In short, it is what is not yet embodied, what has yet to reveal itself, but which is constantly and eternally being incarnated and visible. . . . Each concrete thing revealed in this realm *is synonymous with itself.* For it possesses only one and its own meaning . . . not imposed . . . by the requirements of social coexistence.[85]

According to Leśmian *natura naturans* is a metaphysical state of all direct feelings, elemental and creative. Thus a creative individual is able to identify with it, while *natura naturata* represents a state alien to the creative individual, because it reflects the features of the contemporary social organism. This antinomy is explained as follows:

> Inasmuch as a creative individual, the ever active biological entity, can and must dwell in the realm of *natura naturans,* living by that which is

> being momentarily created . . . eternally hungry for the new in himself—*like a crane with its neck stretched into the future*—so, conversely, the collective life, in which *the number* [italics mine], having achieved real essense, concreteness, demands for its mathematical activities a slowed-down, . . . arrested time. . . . Collective life must be based on unchanging, verified principles of utmost stability, . . .—on those already created. Precisely this realm of a slowed-down or arrested time is *natura naturata*.[86]

Anonymous mathematical laws have created in modern society a type of alienated man who is removed from true reality and doomed to live in a system of social connections. "This type, . . . the 'gray, average man,' whose soul consists of statistical data, [whose reality is based on] recurring facts as the only real principles . . . raised to the rank of eternal laws"[87] is the mediator in modern society. Due to his mediation, *natura naturata* extends into the realm of literature as well, where it finds expression in the works of second- and third-rate poets. Leśmian thought poetic conventions alienated the poet from "primary" reality, depriving his artistic creations of sincerity and truth. Consequently, he stood opposed to literary schools. "Socially committed" poetry was anathema to him and, therefore, ideologically, he was worlds apart from most of his contemporaries. Leśmian's critical work was a "consequent dispute with the world of poetic platitudes, which feeds on current values."[88] As he dealt primarily with the works of little-known writers, his critical works acquire the attributes of a poetic program, in which poetry performs two kinds of mediation and has two opposing functions: On one hand, it participates in the system of "derivative" reality; it is the literary equivalent of other manifestations of this reality, such as becoming a treasure of libraries, museums, and catering to the demands of consumers and literary critics. On the other hand, poetry represents the *élan vital,* which forces the entropy of stagnant social life into action. The function of poetry is to expose the status quo, to establish a "dialogue" with the "true" reality

> hidden beneath the surface of the outward appearances of existence . . . of a social scheme; . . . to show the "true" face of poetry, turned to the world and to that reality which was given to primitive man directly.[89]

However, this reality which the primitive man possessed is not given directly to the modern poet. He must first conquer it, and capture it by fictitiously resembling primitive man.

This assimilation is the basis of Leśmian's poetic theory. It does not mean that Leśmian is fascinated by "primitivism," or "the savage." Primitive man was understood by him to be an individual in direct contact with the universe, for whom reality was a constant process of creation, of becoming. Moreover, incapable of abstract thinking, he understood the world anthropomorphically—as a likeness of himself. Anthropomorphism was a creative condition in his existence, because every act, every vision born of his outlook on life, touched upon the ceaseless dynamism of the world. There was little distinction between his creative idea and god, who represented man's expansion into infinity. In a sense, primitive man, in Leśmian's mind, was a mixture of heaven and earth, "an antediluvian dragon, whose torso, half human and still half divine, allowed him to dwell simultaneously in two worlds."[90] One might say that he was a natural poet: whatever he said had, in a sense, a poetic quality.[91] He expressed his "poetic wisdom" in myths, which he created elementally and intuitively in the process of perceiving the phenomena of the world about him. He was also a born metaphysician, whose concepts, however, were not subjugated to the schemes of logic. Myth, as the basis of his cognition and as the only truth, was the expression of his metaphysics.[92]

Like Herder, Leśmian points out the differences between the thinking of this primitive metaphysician and modern man:

> He—the primitive man, strove to assure that the images he perceived should become his thoughts. We, on the other hand,—endeavor to translate our thoughts into images. . . . We depict thoughts. He contemplated images.[93]

This kind of thinking in images was possible for primitive man because

> his concepts were not yet sufficiently separated from his total being to exist independently, . . . outside of himself. The abyss of pretense did not yet exist between him and his notion of himself. That is why he was not

forced to *find himself, to strive toward himself.* He was himself from the start. . . . In this then lies his elemental power, his spontaneity, his concreteness, his totality. In this finally rests his anthropomorphism, as the principle of indivisibility of spirit and body, thought and man, who creates this thought as an extension of his physical being.[94]

This concept of primordiality does not necessarily apply to primitive man in a historical sense. Leśmian recreated an image of primitive man, stressing in him the characteristics he valued in a poet. The close relationship between the state of primordiality and poetry is especially apparent in his considerations of the nature of man's reality. Leśmian attributes to the man of the mythical epoch a very extensive reality, saying:

The lower the spiritual level of man—the wider the scope of his reality.[95]

The attribute "lower" has no pejorative meaning here being understood as a state uncontaminated by civilization. The return to such a wide scope of reality that can only be achieved through creative power, has the most positive value for the poet. It becomes the hallmark of creation. Poetry is meant to be an escape to the limitless heaven of possibilities.

This "primitive" state of the modern poet is, of course, only a manifestation of his aesthetic awareness. It should be understood metaphorically. Leśmian's notion of the primitive poet's anthropomorphism can be applied equally well to the creative individual of our times—to that kind of poet who must have at his disposal all the characteristic features inherent in primitive man. However, as has been pointed out by Herder, this kind of poet will have to possess a rare poetic genius. He will be *the one* whose poetry will assure continuation of true poetry in human literary history.[96]

This high standard set by Herder seems to have been met by Leśmian himself,[97] beginning especially with his second volume of poetry, *Łąka.* The theory of the poet as primitive man became the underlying factor of his creative work, both in his poetry and in his programmatic essays dealing with the subject. Moreover:

> It is safe to say that the myth [of the poet as a primitive man] which, since the beginning of the XVIII c. has appeared in various poetic theories, has at last achieved its full incarnation in the poetic creation of Leśmian, . . . becoming also . . . the essential motivating power of his poetics.[98]

The resemblance and the process of assimilation of the poet to the state of primitive man are especially apparent in his attitude toward language.

Leśmian believed that language based on stiff and arbitrary definitions represents an obstacle to poetic creation; it deprives it of its directness. He shared this belief with Bergson as well as with many avant-garde literary groups of the first decades of the twentieth century, including the leading proponents of the second generation of Russian Symbolists such as Bely, Viacheslav Ivanov, et al. Language had to be transformed from its state of detachment from the creative process into a dynamic instrument suitable of expressing true poetic reality.

Unlike some Futurists, he did not find the solution in rejecting most of the existing linguistic conventions. Consistent in his poetic creed, he retained those traditional aspects of language which fitted into the scheme of his poetics. He believed that "destruction" of the existing language and its replacement with a transrational language,[99] as used by some Russian Futurists, especially such interpreters of *zaum'* as Aleksei Kruchenykh or Vasili Kamensky,[100] would not yield the results toward which he was striving.

Leśmian's convictions and approaches regarding language proved to be more enduring than the extreme ones. He believed that the transformation of the poetic "substance" could be achieved through a dynamic rejuvenation of habitually used cognitive language, which would be capable of producing new effects if presented in a new way.[101] Through dynamism, the poet would be able to overcome the obstacle of language considered as an object, and transform it into language understood as action.

This change could only be attained through man's direct contact with nature and his inner self. Each poetic expression should be the result of a kind of "return" to the primordial formative stages of the language. It should be "an escape from the words which became terms to words—living organisms—created in the beginning stages, which can endure continuously."[102] Language in its formative stages carried the seeds of poetry in it.

Just as for primitive man, so for the poet too, language did not represent a ready-made and permanently established reality. It had to accommodate changes in external and internal realities in man's perception. Therefore, for Leśmian as well as for primitive man, language was the embodiment of ceaseless creation, as was poetry—the continuous creative process. To use the classic terminology of Wilhelm von Humboldt, language is *energeia* and not *ergon,* it represents activity and not a static entity. Language, understood as eternal rebirth and rejuvenation demands continuous effort on the part of the creative man. According to Aleksandr Potebnia, the Russian (Ukrainian) continuator of von Humboldt:

> Language is an effort . . . of the spirit repeating itself eternally—in order to create out of the articulated sound an expression of thought.[103]

Potebnia saw in poetry the emancipation of the word from the tyranny of the idea. He considered

> poetry . . . a powerful defense mechanism used by the "word" in order to vindicate its autonomy in face of "hostile" pressures. . . . Poetry . . . was language *par excellence,* language at its most creative. Conversely, each manifestation of speech activity, such as the coining of new words, may be conceived of as a poetic act.[104]

Leśmian's abiding interest in folklore, linguistics, poetic theory, and literary criticism goes back to his student years in the philogical *gymnasium* (high school) in Kiev. They must have been furthered by his acquaintance with the works of the Ukrainian linguist as well as that of other Russian scholars.[105]

Ideas similar to those expressed by Potebnia appeared in Leśmian's early theoretical essays (1909-1910) and, more specifically, in his latest treatise:

The newest scholars in linguistics divide language into two categories, namely: into an individual, and into a social language. We call the first the liberating word, the second, the conceptual word.[106]

Aleksandr Veselovsky (1838-1906), a leading Russian authority on comparative literary history, was a probable influence on Leśmian's attitude toward literary criticism, but especially toward language. Veselovsky, too, was interested in tracing the poetic word "to the epic past, or even farther back to the myth-making stage."[107]

Bearing in mind the likely influence of these two great Russian scholars upon Leśmian's poetics, we could say that to some extent he combined their ideas with his own "fiction of absolute genesis"[108] created by projecting language into the realm of primordiality, where it was just coming into existence. This regression to the roots of the language is the basis upon which Leśmian formulated his theory of linguistic practices which acquire a distinct and extremely expressive character. Thus, according to Sandauer:

Reading Leśmian, one has the illusion that he is forcing his will upon the language. . . . Leśmian's poem seems to emerge at those metaphysical roots of language where everything is permissible, because that is where everything begins, where there are still no rules, because that is where they will be proclaimed. Having been only a poet, in other words, a servant of the language, he could easily pass for *the creator* of it. [Italics mine][109]

His departure from the linguistic practices commonly used in the Polish language as a means of social communication, in fact, his theory and his poetry, are a conscious negation even of those functions which language fulfills in some contemporary Polish literature. Leśmian was acutely aware of the tragic dichotomy of language. He therefore thrusts into semantics in order to defend the autonomy and the magic quality of the poetic word.

Leśmian's novel attitude toward language is not limited to the invention of neologisms. He succeeded in combining the concept of language as an instrument of "dialogue" with the primitive past with the concept of language that plays the dominant role in poetry. The latter brings Leśmian close to the concepts of such Russian Symbolists as Andrei Bely and Viacheslav Ivanov, and, in certain aspects, even close to Russian Formalism.[110] This combination, however, finds expression in the poetry he wrote simultaneously with his theoretical essays, as early as 1910, long before the Russian school of Formalism came into being. The theory of the dominance of the word over content and form in poetry is also stressed by Leśmian in one of his critical reviews:

The content, the concept of a work, . . . i.e., *what* the author writes, is important to us. Also important is the form, . . . *how* he writes. But perhaps the most important is . . . the poetic substance, the word *with which* he writes. . . . The content (the synthesis) depends on acts of our will . . . form (the analysis) depends on our consciousness, . . . the word the substance does not depend on either of the two. . . . The content and form can . . . fall into oblivion . . . due to the feverish rush of time, but that which is *the substance* of a given work endures forever as a concrete, lasting, unique achievement. [Italics mine.][111]

He apparently kept in touch with the field of linguistics to the end of his life, for he speaks about recent developments in linguistics, via philosophy, in his interview with E. Boyé. Although admittedly not acquainted with the works of Husserl and Cassirer, he says:

Philosophy has arrived at a new linguistics. We start to speak about the word as about an "eidos" [i.e., a form, a being, the essence, the prototype of a concept], as about a symbol, and a myth.[112]

The combination of the two concepts of language discussed before accounts for "one of the dramatic tensions which organize [Leśmian's] poetics internally."[113] "The fiction of genesis" allows the poet to use the existing language dialectically. It gives him the freedom to create neologisms, drawing largely upon existing words used by society. This process of "rejuvenation" of words extends to phrases as well. Actually, Leśmian was just as interested in the new interrelation between words, as in the new word per se. *The word* becomes the "hero," the essential autonomous linguistic unit in poetry.

Leśmian's solutions differ decidedly from those of the theoreticians of the so-called "pure poetry" (except for his youthful period of creation). Contrary to some proponents of this school (e.g., Henri Brémond, who believed that the unspoken word best expresses man's association with the extra-empirical world), Leśmian maintains that the word must stand out, must have an independent value of its own, a distinctive prominence which can be regained only when

an . . . elemental whirlwind of creation—i.e., the *élan vital*—blows off . . . the "czapka niewidimka" ["The Invisible Cap"] from the humble word devoid of color, . . . and exposes once again its real form, its forbidden splendor.[114]

The freshness of the original color, lost in the frequency of spoken usage, would be restored. Leśmian said:

Words shall rejoice at being able . . . to meet again after a long separation instead of continuing in their everyday life, . . . deprived by accepted usage of any kind of independent cognition.[115]

Hackneyed language was Leśmian's *bête noire.* The poets of Young Poland, the group from which he supposedly emerged, concocted a language of Romanticism, Positivism, Parnassianism, and Impressionism suitable for a passé Decadent poetry of atmosphere, abstraction, and ornament. The Skamandrites, heady with the atmosphere of Poland's springtime, were aware of the need for a new idiom appropriate to the celebration, with the common man, of freedom and the here and now. For this they turned to untapped sources of city jargon (cf., Tuwim), rural dialect and foreign exoticism. More radical in their approach to poetic forms were the Vanguardists. For them language was to be depoeticized to correspond to the stark realities of modern life. Few metaphors are found in their rigorous poetry which describes in the barest of terms, the dreariness of city life and, later, imminent upheaval. With the Vanguard, the poetic word becomes totally subservient to content. In his "Treatise on Poetry," Leśmian carries on a polemic with representatives of the Cracow avant-garde school of the period between the wars (Tadeusz Peiper and J. Przyboś), who believed that the sentence is of primary importance in poetry, since it focuses attention on the intellectual content. Leśmian, however, was of the opinion that this matters little to poetry, which owes its effect to the magic of the word image. He was alarmed by poetry

> which has contempt for the magic inherent in the word. . . . The Cracow School considers it even . . . a threadbare artistic device. . . . In the verse of these poets words lose their . . . independence, their creative . . . unpredictability. . . . Instead of striving toward . . . unrepeated originality in art, the poet strives toward contemporaneousness, . . . to resemble the surroundings.[116]

For Leśmian, the poetry of the Vanguard ceases to be poetry; he compares it to birds whose wings have been clipped and addresses himself to the poets of the Cracow School:

> Either a bird is a bird or it is not! There are no half-birds! A partial wing ceases to be a wing. Either the word liberates itself from conceptual fetters, or it puts them on voluntarily.[117]

In the latter case, the word ceases to be, for Leśmian, a poetic substance. In accordance with the Symbolist tradition, he understands the poetic word in a specific way. It differs from the dry and rigid definition of an object which cannot be considered a creative art. In poetry, the word permits a penetration to the essence of things, an intuitive capture of their hidden attributes.

Leśmian's "fiction of the genesis" of language fulfills still another basic function in his poetics. The word possesses the ability of inventing. The act of naming an object for the first time creates the object. In fact, even a renamed object gives the impression of being created anew. In this concept of the word we find, perhaps, the closest analogy of poetic language to the language of the primitive man, the so-called "natural poet," who in the process of naming an object discovered its existence at the same time. J. Przyboś, paraphrasing Lévi-Strauss whose theory of the genesis of language he considers the simplest and the most convincing, says this about primeval language:

> In the beginning, the word was a given object. There was no difference between the sign and the designate; the word was instantly realized, it was visible and tangible. In this primordial Eden, one picked words as one would pick ripe fruit of the tree.[118]

In his efforts to overcome the obstacle presented by conventional poetic language, Leśmian passed the limits of "natural" poetry, advancing the process of "objectifying" the language to a far greater degree than any other poet before him. Przyboś writes that Leśmian,

> in a sense, . . . creates words out of things. These word formations hit straight into the heart of the matter, and are as firmly rooted in it as an unremoved arrow. They stand out like creatures of nature.[119]

As for primitive man, so for Leśmian too, the meaning of the word is linked with the very existence of a thing. "It contains the revelation of it in its innermost nature. To know the word is to have power over the object."[120] Therefore, for primitive man, as well as for Leśmian, language itself is an ontological conception.

This conception of language attains its full realization in Leśmian's lyrics, in which it becomes the organizing principle of his poetic world. This is already apparent in his early poetry (cf., the poem *Sad,* written in 1902), however, it is particularly evident in his long poem *Pan Błyszczyński,*[121] in which the hero, symbolizing the poet-magus, creates a garden out of nothingness by the sheer power of the glitter in his sparkling eyes. This poem is, according to J. Przyboś, the best example of how poetic language can capture the elusive and achieve the impossible.

It would have been a purely formalistic play of rhyme and rhythm if not for the pithiness of each word, which makes the poem a thing beyond belief.[122]

Everything in that garden, writes Szczerbowski

has clearly drawn forms and has a very concrete reality of its own. Everything is endowed with the magic of a new consciousness forced on it by the powerful will of the creator.[123]

The word, however powerful, cannot solve all the problems confronting poetic creation, for the word always represents a relationship to something undefined and elusive, existing outside its domain. It is the function of poetry to capture this element which resists capture, to express the inexpressible, to utter the ineffable.[124] The poet calls this elemental power "the extralingual current,"[125] and, "a song without words."[126] This song is an earlier phenomenon than words, and is not subject to the laws of logic. The task of the poet is to find the proper words for the song. (Cf., the title of his metapoetic poem, "Słowa do pieśni bez słów" ["Words to a Song Without Words"].

The most important factor in the search for such liberated words is *rhythm*. According to his theory, rhythm is the basic organizing element of poetry; it imposes a certain internal order in the interrelation of words, an order purely natural and not rational.[127] It is more than just a metric device; it represents that "extralingual current" which transforms the poetic text, and establishes a dynamic interrelation between the words, resisting schematization. Its main essence is freedom. Imposing its order upon words, it liberates them at the same time. In a sense, it establishes a relationship between poetry and the universal, cosmic rhythm.

According to Leśmian, rhythm is the dialectical

partner of the word in poetry. . . . The word is turned toward the world of established pattern, rhythm—toward the primordial world. Poetry is the terrain of friction between these two attitudes. In addition, the ability of the rhythm to "allude" to presentiment of reality, predetermines, in advance, the outcome of this conflict.[128]

Rhythm is the irrational element; like other elements in Leśmian's "formulated poetics," it fulfills a double function: poetic, as well as extrapoetic. On the primary, poetic level it is, first of all, a means of transforming mundane words into poetic ones. It returns to words their magic quality and the freedom they enjoyed in the primordial era, before they became codified as a "mediator" of social communication. Secondly, when rhythm replaces conventional syntax, it becomes a catalyst of these liberated words, the organizing factor within the poetic fabric. The new interrelation of words results in poetic images which are a synthesis of words representing the "true reality" of life. Submitting to the dictates of rhythm,

> words gather unconsciously around . . . elusive and melodious lure. They lose the definite character and abstract limitation of their content, escaping the permanently established laws of logic and grammar, regaining their primordial freedom of their ceaseless creative changes, . . . and their ability of constant adaptation to the . . . elusive content of existence.
>
> Some . . . universal association . . . allows words . . . to unite into a new sentence. . . . Words regain the disturbed harmony, the lost paradise, in which each analogy, each metaphor reminds them of a secret bond, of an eternal kinship . . . and identity. Conscious of this kinship and identity, word unite eagerly—the hue with the form, the form with the scent, the scent with the sound, restoring its unity to the whole world.[129]

Rhythm is the creative, guiding force behind Leśmian's principle of "correspondence,"[130] which presupposes a semantic analogy between different sense perceptions. It implies that the human mind may reach the same revelations through a pattern of words as through a pattern of colors or sounds. This kind of a new interrelation of words enables the poet to crystallize his visions, to summarize his observations into one integral unit immediately and at every moment. For, as Przyboś says, "thinking in images is a creation of synthesis as quick as lightning."[131] Leśmian succeeds in expressing, through a poetic image, this synthesis of "the sudden 'fraternization' of the most extreme hues, shapes and sounds existing in the universe."[132] In this, he closely resembles primitive man whose thinking, according to Ernst Kretschmer, was primarily "a syntactical series of images,"[133] governed by rhythm. For Vico "image and rhythm constituted the essence of this first, . . . poetic language,"[134] in which primitive man expressed the unity and harmony of his world.

Like "a mysterious magnet, rhythm attracts the unique, the infallible and most suitable words, which merge into a melodious unit."[135] Through rhythm, poetry becomes the symbol of a lost paradise, reclaiming from music the native gift which (according to French Symbolists, too) belonged originally to poetry alone.[136] Through rhythm, poetry becomes a primeval language, which, in its rhythmicality and melodiousness, was close to music, sharing with it the same source.[137] One understands Leśmian's affinity for folklore where this closeness of poetry and music is perpetuated.

The preeminence of rhythm in Leśmian's poetics is especially stressed in his "Treatise on Poetry" (written in 1937). In it he polemicized with the Vanguard poets, as when he defended the merits of the poetic word, claiming that rhythm is superior to syntax which assures only a rational order of words. Furthermore, the breach which the new poetics established with the traditional metrical system, was a source of concern to Leśmian (who used the two traditional Polish systems of versification, the syllabic and the syllabotonic verse).[138] He pointed out the latent possibilities of syllabic verse and maintained that "it is difficult to erect an altar to poetry on the ruins of rhythm."[139] Every creative work is first of all a rhythmic work, and only rhythm is capable of introducing a variety of possibilities into poetic creation. Not only does it gather in the poem the elusive flow within and outside of the word, but records it as a repetitive melody with the capacity

> . . . to regain its existence and to endure, . . . retaining in each death the same rhythmical capacity of rebirth.[140]

It is through the repetitiveness of melody that one recognizes a poem because it imprints itself in human memory. As it was in primeval times and still is for some primitive cultures, poetry existed in symbiosis with music and, in the form of a song or recitation, accompanied the events of human life. Dwelling in the memory of the people, it became the expression of traditional and historical events. Ernest Grosse, a scholar of primitive art and Leśmian's contemporary, stressed the importance of rhythm in primitive poetry:

A verbal expression of feeling, in order to become lyric poetry, ought to put on an aesthetic vestment, i.e., to assume a form of rhythmic repetition. . . . Songs, by means of which the primitive peoples extol their joys and sorrows, are usually . . . an arrangement of the simplest sentences—based on rhythmicality and repetition. . . .[141]

Rhythm with the help of mnemonic art established the literary tradition. Oral poetry, expressed in lyrical and epic songs, became the first literary form long before poetry was recorded in writing.

Leśmian bases his poetic practices, such as rhythmicality and melodiousness, on the need for poetry to become established in human memory, to be recited, to further human communication. He clearly points out the analogies to primeval folk poetry:

Rhythm fulfills yet another traditionally and historically noble task, namely: it helps the poems in their inherent capacity to establish themselves in human memory. The poem likes to dwell in human memory, not in books. . . . The singer entrusted his songs to the memory of rhapsods. . . . That is why a poet, whose past is the past of all the worlds and the beyonds, and whose eyes are fixed on primitive times, ought to create his poems as though there were no print in existence.[142]

It is easy to understand why "rhythmicality," or, more correctly, metrics, was considered by Leśmian the *sine qua non* of poetics. He, therefore, rejected the phrase-intonational verse of the Cracow Vanguard school, that, with its broken rhythm and lack of melodiousness, could not fit Leśmian's conception of poetry. In his estimation, their verse was closer to the graphic arts (it had "to dwell in books"). Leśmian considered it prose—the realm of *natura naturata* (the expression of the practical intellect of society), and for him, according to K. Irzykowski:

Prose—was his Satan; to differentiate poetry from prose, to feel poetry, to write poetry—[was] the truest meaning of life.[143]

For Leśmian, poetry, as the act of unlimited creative freedom, as a dialogue with the past, springs directly from *rhythm—the creative impetus* which corresponds to the *élan vital.* It sets lethargic matter (the conceptual language) into motion, transferring it into the realm of *natura naturans.* Rhythm represents not only the liberating, organizing force of words, but the individualization of poetic language as well. As such, it is the most essential factor in poetic language. It fulfills a normative function. Leśmian expressed this very clearly, especially in the "Treatise on Poetry."

In the twenties, criticism of the Vanguard poets by such scholars of versification as Franciszek Siedlecki and Karol Zawodziński was based solely on a normative approach, stemming from an identification of "poetics" with "metrics."[144] Leśmian's ideas, although they included similar attitudes, are strongly rooted in a metaphysical context.[145] For Leśmian, rhythm is not only a criterion that differentiates poetry from prose, it also defines the essence of poetry with regard to extrapoetic categories. Rhythm enables poetry to overcome "the metaphysics of collective life" in modern society, and returns the poet to the free existence of primitive man, another realm of metaphysics. Rhythm, which guides and establishes order in poetic pronouncements, corresponds to the rhythm accompanying all processes of existence in the universe—the organic processes as well as elementary cultural processes such as work, play, and revery. Even man himself is guided in each era by a different internal and external rhythm.[146] Rhythm represents a philosophy of life.

> The rhythmic [Weltanschauung] outlook on life ceases to be dogma, a conviction, a principle or a dead code of a recognized movement. The thought set in motion by rhythm . . . acquires . . . an elemental change, which is tied to life itself. . . .[147]

Every epoch has its own rhythm and rhythm is a cyclic phenomenon. Facts and incidents of life are finite and nonrepetitive (and this constitutes the tragedy of human life) rhythm, on the contrary, is an indestructible, recurrent force, and in this lies its joyfulness.[148] Everything caught in the creative current of rhythm escapes the earthly law and becomes immortal. This is especially true of poetic creation:

> A song once more repeated, a poem reread once again, reoccur from the beginning to the end and, dying on the lips, retain the capacity of resuscitation. *Due to rhythm* we repeat not only *their sounds and words, but the entire process of their hidden existence* [italics mine].[149]

Thus, a creative work subjected to rhythm attains immortality, becomes absorbed by the cosmic laws of eternally recurrent movement, while the creator, weaker than his work and subject to the laws of life, is but mortal and must die.

The recurrence of rhythm brings about the reproduction of the time vested in immortalized poetic works and the reality contained in them. Poetic creation is

> this melody, this elusive flow of words which is a reflection of *time saved up in a given poem,* and indispensable for the development of this very poem. . . . Creativeness is the recording of this growth [and consequently of time absorbed by it]. [Italics mine.][150]

A recent critic, J. Błoński, sees in this statement the clearest example of Leśmian's concept of rhythm as a sign of equality between the poet's metaphysical aspiration, which is the penetration into creative duration (involving time), and poetic aspiration (the very act of composing a poem).

Rhythm fulfills concurrently a cosmic as well as a literary function.[151] Due to its recurrence, rhythm becomes, in Leśmian's poetics, a form of intuitive cognition as well as a link with the primordial past. Rhythm is also the element that enables Leśmian, as Ludwik Fryde observed, "to reach, by means of poetry, the beyond." Fryde also concludes that Leśmian's highly original concept of poetry is derived from cognitive premises rather than from artistic ones.[152]

For Leśmian rhythm was a means of attaining a specific aesthetic reality which would give his poetry the semblance of a philosophical theory of cognition. This phenomenon was already noticed in Leśmian by the critic H. Michalski, who wrote:

> This musical vibration of the soul, which served other Symbolists to evoke a mood, he subjugates to the laws of a process of reading into the mysterious and uninvestigated beyond. . . . Leśmian does not stop at evoking a mood, but goes further, giving poetry a meaning analogous to a philosophical theory of cognition.[153]

The diverse nature of rhythm, and the contrast it presents to the word, exemplify in a sense, all the contrasts on which Leśmian's theory of poetic language is based. Respecting the universal principle of rhythm, poetry joins the order of the universe.

This concept of associating poetic rhythm of the world, especially of the primitive world, did not originate with Leśmian. Rhythm was one of the basic elements of early French and Russian Symbolist poetry, where it was used for formal effects. However, for the second generation of Russian Symbolists (i.e., Blok, Bely, and Ivanov) rhythm assumed a cognitive role which gave poetry a new dimension. In many ways this approximates Leśmian's concept of rhythm.

The emphasis on rhythm in Symbolist poetry reflected scientific, psychological, and philosophical considerations of its role as the element which governs the universe. According to Leśmian, rhythm guards creative individuality, the independence of a poet, and his exclusive right to a rhythmically profound communion with the universe. Rhythm thus enables him to create poetry that is a microcosm of the true reality of life.

What kind of poet is capable, in Leśmian's opinion, of expressing this true reality of life? It is not one who turns to contemporaneity for inspiration, for this kind of poet subordinates his creative individuality to the demands of the "average man" and to the approval of institutionalized literary criticism. Joined by their concern for the mundane demands of society, poet, critic, and reader comprise the powerful clique that Leśmian calls "King Rat."[154] In his polemic against the Vanguard poets, he tried to examine the historical and psychological "merits" of the complex and periodical phenomenon "contemporaneity" [*współczesność*]:

> And what does the pet notion of young poets, *modernity,* really mean? What does it . . . consist, of what contents and gestures! Perhaps only of gestures. . . . It is difficult to establish exactly when the concept of modernity appeared in the civilized world. . . . *As a source of inspiration, is modernity really enough?* After all, it is something that ceases to be the moment you perceive it. . . . As to myself, that splendid modernity reminds me of a woman concealing her age. [Italics mine.][155]

With the attitude of a poet-moralist, Leśmian scorns the relationship of the writers and the critics based "on mutual help and exchange of favors."[156] Leśmian could not, and would not, formulate his poetics or create poetry to suit the demands of contemporaneity. As he once stated in an interview: "I do not look for anything in contemporariness. I am, what I am!"[157]

A true poet must be far removed from contemporaneity which holds no mystery for him. Great art can only be born within the soul of a poet who is true to himself. Leśmian was a *poète maudit* in that he stood apart from society and literary coteries. He believed the role of a poet requires that he speak out against stifling literary conditions imposed by fashionable modernity. Even those traditional aspects of poetry to which he remained faithful (e.g., versification, genres), acquired a new, a rejuvenated meaning which, in the given historical context, neither the critics nor the reading public were ready to accept, fully appreciate, or approve.

Perhaps the best description of Leśmian as a poet can be derived from his own words, intended for such poets as the author of the *Slovo o polku Igoreve* and James Macpherson, who created and who decoded the mystery of their own being by

> transferring it into a mythical fairyland, into a land inaccessible to the human eye, which allows these creators to reach supreme solitude and total freedom of creation. In this kind of creation one can detect a split of

the human being: into one that is earthly, mundane, . . . and another that is unusual, creative, gazing towards immortality, liberating itself from the laws of gray existence by the lawlessness of free and unsubmissive wings.[158]

Regarding his own creative work, Leśmian seldom expressed his feelings directly in his *Szkice literackie.* This is consistent with his aversion to definitions, although it could also stem from his modesty as well as his hyperdeveloped self-critical sense, already apparent in his earlier correspondence with Przesmycki. We get some insight into his intimate feelings and poetic aspirations from his critical reviews of the works of other writers, usually by way of deduction and digression. His essay on Edgar Allen Poe—a poet by whom he was influenced—can serve as an example. We can deduce from it what it was that Leśmian considered to be the true process of his own poetic creation and the worthy function he would like his poetry to fulfill. He sees this as possible, of course, when the poet's dreams are fulfilled artistically, and when the creative realization of his dreams—poetry—finds a right to exist in society. Thus, in speaking of the works of Poe, he says:

Dreams border on reality, reality on dreams. Besides—the difference between them disappears joyfully at the moment when it is consumed by the eternally puzzling and indivisible unity. The object and its reflection attain the same rights on earth . . . and in the heavens. And there are here no trivial and subordinate objects: everything is equally important and eternal. . . . To dream and see your own dream, to bring it under the absolute control of an absolute artistry, and to attain for it the miraculous right of existence in its environment—this is the only feat which a poet ought to carry into effect.[159]

In this way poetry may enable modern man to get a glimpse of the existence denied him, and it may help him to perceive the true reality of life. Poetry can liberate man from predicaments confronting him in a highly stratified social system based on materialism, mediations, and false values.[160]

The *Szkice literackie* contains formulations made with a suggestiveness which few pronouncements in the Polish theory of poetry can match. These essays are also an authentic and credible proof of Symbolist tendencies in Leśmian's poetics. These tendencies are presented in such a manner that by differentiating Symbolism from Young Poland they enable us to get a realistic picture of the era. It is easy to understand why Sławiński considers the *Szkice literackie* a true Symbolist manifesto.

> . . . they can be considered close to a program, a second Symbolist text, in spite of the fact . . . that they did not play the role of a program in its time.[161]

In comparison with the first, vague manifesto formulated by Przesmycki, Leśmian's mature program can be evaluated as a manifesto closing an era, and an original form of Symbolist theory. This view has been attested by Polish poets and literary historians. For such poet-critics as Mieczysław Jastrun and Zbigniew Bieńkowski, Leśmian is "the only Polish Symbolist of consequence."[162] His entire poetics constitutes "the sum total . . . *the one and only aggregate of Symbolism* on a worldwide scale, encompassing everything which Symbolism represented. [Italics mine]."[163]

The diversified nature of Leśmian's program must have prompted the interpretations of those critics for whom the poet has lately become like a magic bag containing all kinds of the initial and later inspirations of the twentieth century. The very fact that Leśmian's poetics are considered to be such a magic bag and a treasure not likely ever to be fully explored, reveals their truly Symbolist nature. For Symbolism, as understood by the poet, was an attitude toward art and a continuing process oriented toward the future.

These varied interpretations of Leśmian's poetics require that they be placed in the proper literary historical context out of which Leśmian emerged as a poet. Therefore, it is my intent to conduct this investigation in a dual context, that is, in the Polish (discussed earlier), and the European: the French, and especially, the Russian literary scene.

3

Leśmian's Poetics and the Philosophical Ambience

"Towards my goal I struggle, mine own way I go."
—Friedrich Nietzsche, *Thus Spake Zarathustra*

INTRODUCTION

Springing from various literary sources, Symbolism, at the turn of the twentieth century, represented various trends as well as a change of values. It was, primarily, a new approach toward such long existing themes as civilization, life, the everyday existence of man, expressed heretofore in half-measures, largely because of the limitation of poetic language. Owing to this new approach, lyrics reached a fuller self-knowledge than ever before. Poetry became a form of action incited by the poet's fascination with the vitality and dynamism of the surrounding world and by his adulation for the primitive past and for pagan mythology. It was an indication of the longing for a vitalism which was to free the individual from the limiting Christian ideals. This vitalism was expressed in literature primarily by the motif of Dionysus, the embodiment of intoxication with life. The poet believed that his creation touched upon mystery and opened new vistas to the comprehension of reality. More than ever before, poets wrote philosophical essays in order to understand themselves and to explain their viewpoints.

For the Symbolists of the second generation, perhaps more than for any other poets before them, poetry became an integral part of the "true" reality of life as well as a metaphysical experience. Poetry was trying to capture mercurial reality by means of a transformed, autonomous language and rhythm. Symbolism representing such a broad approach was much more than a threshhold for Leśmian to pass over. It was a beginning for all contemporary poetry, for all its basic concepts including those concepts which fit Leśmian the poet and Leśmian the theoretician of his art.

In order to assess Leśmian's poetics properly in the literary context of Symbolism, it seems appropriate to examine the philosophical concepts which had the greatest impact on the development of this literary trend. In the search for his own poetics, any artist, regardless of how original he may ultimately become, usually absorbs some inherited conventions even in the process of creating his own vision of the world. Therefore, a cursory review of philosophers and poets who helped to shape the French *école symboliste* (the most influential variant), will give us an idea of the extent to which Leśmian's poetics were influenced by them in the formative stages of his poetic career.

Cognitive subjectivity in art started with Kant, and was further developed under the influence of Schopenhauer. According to this theory, a work of art represents part of nature as seen by the artist. In poetry, such a concept of art led to an extreme kind of Impressionism, for the emphasis shifted now from the picture of nature to the artist himself. Now the poet's inner world became the focal point of the work of art. The new poetic goal was to transmit to the reader the elusive states of the human psyche. In this art, the double meaning of poetic reality becomes increasingly pronounced. The external world, as seen through the eyes of the poet, is presented as a symbol of spiritual reality.

These changes in poetry were wrought mainly under the influence of the idealistic philosophers whose doctrines represented a strong reaction against materialism. In the words of a famous Frenchman:

> After passing the period in which, according to Auguste Comte, reason rebelled against the power of the heart, we are entering a different period in which the heart rebels against the power of reason.[1]

These tendencies were furthered by the works of Thomas Carlyle, who proclaimed that "all things seen are symbols,"[2] and by John Ruskin's theories stressing artistic creation as the reflection of transcendental reality. Ruskin also maintained that creative power leads to cognition by means of intuition. To these ideas we ought to add Schopenhauer's concept of contemplative art as a relief from suffering as well as the attainment of highest cognition. An important influence was also the great attention given the subconscious in the work of Karl Hartmann, who argued that logical thought and illogical will merge to create the one, the universal unconscious mind which animates the world.[3]

Changes in poetry were further encouraged by works of the artists themselves, such as Baudelaire's doctrine of *correspondances*—that impressions received by one of the senses could be transmitted through any of the other senses, and Wagner's "Lettre sur la Musique," in which the composer saw the goal of art as the capture of reality slumbering deep in the human soul. All these concepts ushered in the age of Modernism and served as a foundation for the complex Symbolist poetry.[4] Later (in the nineties), under the influence of Poe, the Parnassian slogan, "l'art pour l'art" ultimately evolved into "l'art pour la poésie,"[5] signifying a more profound approach to poetry than a mere preoccupation with form. The new aesthetics in poetry, born of complex Romantic influences, the ideas of Nietzsche, and the concepts of certain French theoreticians, led to an esoteric poetry.

Baudelaire had already warned the poet to isolate himself and not to lower the standard of poetry before the crowd. Charles

Morice expressed the sentiments of the majority of French poets when he wrote:

> To write for simple people. . . . Try it! One does not write for them, one speaks to them; this is an act of mercy, which has nothing to do with art, this is the function of a country pastor and a suburban teacher, this is not the vocation of a poet.[6]

The flight of the poet from the "herd" resulted in "hermetic" poetry and coteries. Isolating themselves from the everyday world and its problems as well as from a burgeoning technology, the poets—no longer the bards of the people—had to look for other compensations. These they found in the mystical and the intuitive metaphysical concept of art which, raising their "special mission" in life to a cult, led to their excessive preoccupation with their own egos.

These then, in brief, were the aesthetics of French Symbolism as embraced by Russian poets in the early nineties. A student in Kiev until 1901, the young Leśmian could not have escaped these influences; therefore the evolution of his philosophy more closely parallels the aesthetic development of early Russian Symbolism, rather than that of Young Poland. Also the Positivistic inspirations and Parnassian tendencies that still dominated the early phases of Polish Modernism were totally alien to the young poet. He did share, however, with both literary contexts the influences of the philosophies of German Romanticism, especially that of Schelling and Schopenhauer, and, of course, Nietzsche, as well as the evolutionary thought of the nineteenth century. The influences of German philosophers are especially apparent in Leśmian's earliest poetry.

While Schelling's influence upon Leśmian was probably indirect, absorbed via Russian Romantic poetry and early French Symbolism, Schopenhauer exerted a direct influence on the young poet during the period of the philosopher's greatest popularity in Europe. Schopenhauerism, which emanated from the split personality of the Romantic hero and propagated the doctrine of will, suffering, and Nirvana, suited the pessimistic sensitivity of the *fin de siècle*. The multifarious and symbolic structure of *the will* in Schopenhauer's system lent itself to many interpretations. Its foremost concern was the representation in a modern setting of alienation and *Langweile*, of "an old tragedy of duality in the new tragedy of experiencing time and death by human existence."[7] Schopenhauer's system combined philosophical tenets with their adaptation in literature, art, aesthetics, psychology, and historiosophy. It suited well the rapid transformations and the conflicts besetting modern man. His philosophy was considered to be, to its very core, a Brahmanist synthesis, while he was looked upon as a prophet and a Buddha (which, incidentally, he called himself). Tolstoy, who himself was the epitome of man's inner conflict, wrote a letter to his friend Afanasi Fet:

> Do you know what this summer was for me? Ceaseless rapture over Schopenhauer, and one continuous spiritual bliss, such as I never experienced until now. . . . I am convinced that Schopenhauer is the greatest genius among all people.[8]

Tolstoy's appraisal of Schopenhauer's genius was shared by many—his philosophy was the subject of discussion on many levels: it was taught in the universities of Europe and, in Russia, even in gymnasiums.[9]

Thus, Leśmian found himself exposed to the direct influence of Schopenhauer's doctrines. Judging by the young poet's pessimism in his ceaseless groping for a poetic identity, seen especially in his earliest correspondence, it is easy to understand the attraction of Schopenhauer. These early influences—especially as seen in his works collected in *UR*—would have a strong revival, particularly in some of the later poems of *Napój cienisty* and *Dziejba leśna* in which the poet enters the world "through the gates of sadness."

NIETZSCHE'S ICONOCLASM

Schopenhauer was not the only German philosopher to influence Leśmian directly. With Schopenhauer on the one hand, and

Bergson and Freud on the other, Nietzsche exerted the greatest pressure on the aesthetics of the *fin de siècle* and the beginning of the twentieth century in Europe. In Russia, an early interest in Nietzschean doctrines may have been stimulated by parallel doctrines in the works of Dostoevsky, continued by propagators of Symbolism (e.g., Minsky, Merezhkovsky), as well as by the early Symbolists (the so-called Decadents), and by Lev Shestov. They found in Nietzsche's later works[10] an apotheosis of an ideology that especially appealed to them, i.e., the extreme individualism of his Beyond-Man and Superman, immortality and atheism, the aloofness of the poet from the "herd," the will for power, and a critique on modern society.

Nietzsche's influence on Young Poland was the most dominant, together with that of Bergson. However, Nietzsche's work only reached Poland about 1900 and Bergson's influence dates only from 1905, whereas Leśmian's exposure to Nietzscheanism as attested by his correspondence, goes back to his student years in Kiev.[11] For a young poet in his *Sturm-und-Drang* period, believing from the start in creative evolution, in constant flux, and in the good and bad of all existence, Schopenhauer's pessimism, which resulted in passiveness, was becoming unacceptable. Schopenhauer's rejection of the inevitability of progress, his complete departure from the strain of optimism—a holdover from Renaissance thought—his acceptance of unhappiness and pessimism as the universal condition of human life, were alien to the youthful Leśmian, a Renaissance man by nature.[12]

On the other hand, Nietzsche's stress on sensuality, joyfulness, suffering, strife, metamorphosis, and, foremost, on exaltation resulting from contact with the transcendental spheres of the beyond—were, for the time being, reassuring to the poet's fluctuating state of mind. The many doubts expressed in his letters to Zenon Przesmycki echo some of Zarathustra's words: "How ashamed I am of mine ascending and stumbling! How I mock at my vehement panting and puffing!"[13] Nietzsche's Dionysian spirit of exaltation and suffering resulting from an excess of experiences appealed to a poet suffocating in the provincial atmosphere of

Kiev. The following letter, written in 1900, expresses well the longing for adventures that would shake him to the core. With the naiveté of a novice he turns to Przesmycki:

My sadness is as follows: I long for impressions—and have none. . . . If, for argument's sake, I shall not be able to visit both Italy and Switzerland due to meager funds, which of these should I choose? Which of the two would rouse me more easily, frighten me, impress me more, and finally infect me forever with a tremendous and an incurable feeling, a mood, or something of that nature?[14]

The Nietzschean "breath of infinity" helped him spread his eagle's wings and opened endless horizons for the searching poet. The lure of infinity entices him and probably inspired one of his earliest poems, in which he actually uses Nietzsche's expression:

/ . . . / Ja idę—i czuję sercem,
Jak w ziemi rodzą się czary,
Ja idę—i wierzę senny,
Że step—bez końca bez miary! . . .

I piję *tchy nieskończenia*,
I radość w piersi mi płacze,
I strach mnie jeno zdejmuje
Że koniec stepu zobaczę! . . .
("Na stepie" ["In the Steppe"]) [Italics mine.][15]

/ . . . / I go—and I feel in my heart / How magic is born in the earth / I go—and dreamful, I believe / The steppe is endless and immeasurable! . . . /

And I drink in the breath of infinity, */ And joy weeps in my breast, / And I am seized by the fear / That I shall see the end of the steppe! . . .*

A telling feature of this early poem is Leśmian's use of the traditional Russian iambic tetrameter. Adding to its mellifluousness, are the internal and external structural parallelism of the verses and the use of the device of polysyndeton (the repetition of the conjunction "and") reminiscent of Russian and Polish folk songs and Ukrainian *dumki*. Both figures suggest a passionate bursting forth, a headlong rush into infinity, which here, characteristically for the poet, is represented by the Ukrainian steppe. All of these devices will become a part of Leśmian's mature poetry.

The Nietzschean doctrine of the *Übermensch* must also have reinforced Leśmian's confidence in himself as a man and as a poet. The following words, written to Przesmycki, express much more than just confidence:

. . . besides (please forgive my presumptuousness), I feel within myself such strength and might that I would fling into the face of the Lord God himself these words—that I am powerful![16]

This betrays in Leśmian a touch of the "Superman" virus (which, incidentally, was very much apparent in Rimbaud, whom he admired). Evidently, he attempted for a while to adapt this idea to himself, to make it his reality. However, it neither suited his character nor his ultimate poetic creed, and turned out to be a passing state.

Yet, the remarks in this letter regarding man's relationship to God seem to have endured:

Before (during Classicism) people trained their sensual nature to resemble gods, and today they train gods to suit their spirit and they are able to see Christ in a wretched worm entangled in the crown of thorns. . . . *The gods are asleep!* Let them sleep (who cares), as long as the trees keep rustling for us, and our hearts (sic!) keep beating! The gods have too little sangui, and truthfully, a dying Yakut (*if I inspire him with an immortal soul*) is greater for me than Zeus. . . . [Second italics mine.][17]

This statement expresses well the sentiments of the young poet who considers his poetic inspiration much more effective than God's might. It calls to mind Zarathustra's idea about gods:

All gods are a simile of poets, an imposition by poets! Verily, we are always drawn upwards—namely into the kingdom of clouds. On these we place our coloured dolls and call them Gods and beyond-men.

Dead are all Gods. . . .[18]

The poet's initial and essential stand regarding God as a superfluous entity, expressed in the letter above, could be viewed as a commentary of sorts to a sonnet written about two years earlier, for which he received a reward from the periodical *Życie* in Cracow.

Pieśniowa słodycz z lasu się wylewa
Z wilgotną wonią dyszących konarów,
Echami pieśni drży omglony parów.
Nie widać ptaków—to powietrze śpiewa! . . .

Znojnych całunków przelata ulewa,
A dusza moja śród błękitnych żarów,
Zda się szeleści pod dotknięciem czarów,
Nie widać duszy—to szeleszczą drzewa! . . .

O, śnie—olbrzymie! Pieść mnie w takiej chwili!
Kwiaty, pijące ze źródeł bezdeni,
Pozwólcie dotknąć mym ustom korzeni!

Niech sen mój złoty nagle się przesili!
Co to?—Szept bóstwa słyszę, w niebo wzbity,
Nie widać bóstwa—to szepczą błekity. . . .
—"Sonet" ["Sonnet"][19]

A songlike sweetness pours from the forest / With humid smell of breathing boughs, / The mist-shrouded ravine trembles with echoes of songs. / There's not a bird to be seen—that's the air singing! . . . /

A shower of sweltering mists flies past, / While my soul amidst azure embers / Seems to rustle at the touch of magic, / There's not a soul to be seen—those are trees rustling! . . . /

O dream—o giant! Caress me at this moment! / O flowers drinking from the springs of abysses, / Let me touch my lips to your roots! /

May my golden dream pass its crisis! / What's that?—It's the whisper of deity I hear soaring into the sky, / There's no deity to be seen —that's the whisper of the heavens. . . .

The poet hears the whisper of the azure. He has reached the heavens on his own, independent and in the absence of God. He has achieved this by means of revery which allows him to come in touch with the primordial sources of the creation of beautiful things, such as flowers and poems.

Leśmian's "iconoclasm," apparent in his early correspondence and poetry, may be attributed to Nietzschean influences. In a soul-searching poem called "Ideały" ("Ideals") he admits to the fact that God is dead within him: "bóg we mnie zabity."[20] The notion that man is the truly divine phenomenon in the universe is a source of amazement and exhilaration to the young poet. This marveling at man who, not long ago, was a mere worm emerging from the mire of nothingness but is now capable of performing fantastic feats of superseding God and even of crucifying him, echoes some aphorisms of Zarathustra:

> Ye have made your way from worm to man, and much within you is still worm. . . .
>
> Behold! I teach you beyond-man; he is that lightning, he is that insanity! . . . One must have chaos within to enable one to give birth to a dancing star! . . . Hath not the oddest of all things been proved even best of all?
>
> Man is a . . . bridge connecting animal and beyond-man—a rope over the precipice. . . . He is a *transition* and *destruction*. . . . I love the great despisers because they . . . are arrows of longing for the other shore.[21]

Chaos, irrationality, and "insanity" are what Leśmian considers the unpredictable, "the fantastic necessity" and, therefore, the most creative element. This is the sudden lightning, the revelation which comes unexpectedly in man's creative moments. It is the exact opposite to the notions of the past when "intoxication of reason was likeness unto God, and doubt was sin."[22] Time and again Leśmian stresses that flashes of intuition are the basis of all creation and therefore of the divine. We find it mentioned in his early correspondence as well as in most of his theoretical essays (cf., especially, "Znaczenie pośrednictwa . . .") and, of course, in his poetry. The same is true of the idea of man as a bridge over the precipice, numerous examples of which we find in his poetry. However, most important are earliest examples reflecting some Nietzschean echoes:

Lecimy modrym rzeki pokostem, / . . . /

Niby błękitnym lecimy mostem,
Co tylko jeden brzeg ma za sobą . . .
("W noc księżycową" ["On a Moonlit Night"])[23]

We fly a river's blue veneer, / . . . /

We fly like an azure bridge / That has but one shore behind it . . .

Man is represented as the meeting place, as the bridge connecting the lower spheres of the universe with the divine:

Czylim światów tajemnych zjawionym przedmurzem,
Na które drzewa cień swój kładą nieprzytomnie?
Ciało moje—na brzegu, reszta—w mroku den.

Jam jest miejsce spotkania łez ze złotym kurzem
Słońca, ptakom widnego! . . .
(From *Zielona godzina* ["The Green Hour"])[24]

Am I the bulwark of mysterious worlds revealed, / Across which trees senselessly cast their shadow? / My body—on the shore, the rest—in the darkness of the depths. /

I am the place where tears meet the golden dust / Of a sun birds see! . . .

The material part of man, his body, is on this shore, while his spirit is in the realm of the beyond, in the darkness of abysses which for Leśmian represent God—divinity. Thus, man forms a bridge between the two realms.

The desire of the creative man's search for truth, by means of reaching the beyond, manifested already in Leśmian's earliest work, is inseparable from his assertion of the creative *man's independence from God,* and even *God's dependence on man.* Showing disdain for the passive, ineffective gods is not just an empty challenge of youthful daring, nor is it merely an expression of prevailing aesthetics. It is the result of Leśmian's genuine and profound belief that creative art must fill the void left by the bankruptcy of the gods.

The underlying and essential factor that persists from the very beginning of his poetic creativity is his opposition to a God whose ineffectiveness is evident in the tortured world He created.[25] Therefore, God is dead and art must come to the rescue of man:

/ . . . / "Nikt nie wie—i nikt dzisiaj nie odpowie tobie."
A gdzie Bóg? Już od dawna pochowany w grobie. / . . . /
("Betleem" ["Bethlehem"])[26]

/ . . . / "No one knows—and today no one shall answer you." / And where is God? He lies long since buried in the grave, / . . . /

If poets are to replace gods, they must first free themselves from gods' shadows. The poets must overcome themselves, they must go through stages of purification and metamorphosis. This Nietzschean belief, expressed via Zarathustra's experiences

I overcome myself, the sufferer, and carrying mine own ashes unto the mountains invented for myself a brighter flame. And lo! The ghost *departed* from me![27]

is echoed in Leśmian's lines:

/ . . . / To—ostatnie cierpień przesilenie
Jutro po nim przyjdzie wyzdrowienie!
Spopieliłem wszystkich łez atomy,
Spopieliłem wszystkie piersi gromy—
Nowe gwiazdy ujrzę na błękicie
I od jutra—nowe zacznę życie! / . . . /
(From *Motywy jesienne*, "Pieśń o cierpieniu"
["Autumn Motifs," 'Song of Suffering'])[28]

/ . . . / This is suffering's final crisis, / After it tomorrow shall health return! / I have burned to ashes the atoms of all my tears, / I have burned to ashes the thunderings of my breast— / New stars shall I behold in the heavens / And tomorrow I shall begin a new life. / . . . /

Another early poem illustrates how the soul goes through stages of decomposition in the land of *Götterdämmerung*.

/ . . . / Z wolna, z wolna się rozkłada
Na sny jakieś nieskończone.
Na westchnienia rozemglone,

Na wieczności tkanki złote, . . .
Na cierpienie, na tęsknotę,
Na purpury i błękity,
I na tęcze i na świty,
Tak rozkłada się powoli,
Że mnie każda chwila boli,
Każda chwila co przelata
Nad rozpaczą tego świata! / . . . /
("W państwie zmierzchów" ["In the Realm of Dusks"])[29]

Bit by bit, it crumbles / Into some kind of unfinished dreams. / Into sighs of unclouded illusions, / Into golden tissues of eternity. / . . . / Into suffering, into longing, / Into purples and azures, / And into rainbows and dawns, / So slowly does it crumble, / That each moment causes me pain, / Each moment that flies / Over the despair of this world! / . . . /

Though the poem formally represents a poor specimen of decadence, it, nevertheless (by means of the polysyndeton, the anaphora "into") conveys the sequential agony that results from the changes of the soul, as well as the narrator's impatience with every moment of despair over this world that separates him from the new dawn and the rainbow in the azure beyond. The rainbow symbolizes poetic creation that unites the worlds of dream and reality. In the same way as the dispersed color spectrum, the fragmented spirit in the poem above awaits the integration of the soul, similar to the fusion of the spectrum that produces a rainbow. This process is depicted in a later poem "Tęcza" ("The Rainbow"):

Aż luźne znikąd jednocząc migoty,
Nagłą zawisa ponad światem bramą,
By ci przypomnieć, że zawsze tak samo
Trwasz w każdym miejscu u wnijścia tęsknoty.

By ci przypomnieć, żeś z duszą, snem zżartą,
Wpatrzony w bezmiar, wsłuchany w swe dreszcze,
Wszedł do tych światów przez bramę rozwartą,
Co się za tobą nie zamknęła jeszcze.[30]

Until from nowhere, uniting loose glitters, / It hangs like a sudden gate over the world, / To remind you that always in the same way / In every place you linger at the entrance to longing. /

To remind you that, with your soul corroded by dreams, / With your eyes fixed upon infinity, with your attention riveted upon your thrills, / You have entered these worlds through an open gate, / That has not yet closed behind you. /

The dream-glitters merge into a sudden rainbow which represents a gate to magic new worlds. Reaching the beyond, the poet finds his own flame, he is the light, he sets the world aflame with his divine spirit. The flame engulfing him causes him to call out in exaltation:

/ . . . / Kochajcie mnie, kochajcie, bom miłością groźny!
Nie znam granic ni kresów! Pożądam i płonę!
Płonący wołam światu: Razem ze mną płoń!
(From *Zielona godzina* ["The Green Hour"])[31]

/ . . . / Love me, love me, for I am awesome with love! / I know neither limits nor ends! I desire and I burn! / Burning, I call to the world: Burn with me! /

The poet has finally rid himself of God's shadow. In fact it is now he who casts an enormous shadow of God.

/ . . . / A od mojej postaci, widnej mi w marzeniu,
Znienacka u stóp legły—upada na kwiaty
Cień Boga—ponadmierny, niespokojny cień![32]

/ . . . / And from this form of mine I see in revery, / Suddenly there falls across the flowers at my feet / The shadow of God—an immeasurable and restless shadow! /

Yet to reach the beyond, the creative man must still wander and continuously seek and, if necessary, even die in quest of the divine truth articulated by Zarathustra.[33] The poet expresses this as follows:

/ . . . / płyń, moja łodzi! Płyń, koczownico! / . . . /

Czym ja się zrodził na oceanie,
Że mi są domem—czarne otchłanie?
Że mi do ziemi tak jest daleko,
Jakby nie było tam dla mnie schronu?
Płyń, moja łodzi! Płyń—aż do zgonu!
My się kochamy z falą i rzeką! . . .
("W noc księżycową" ["On a Moonlit Night"])[34]

/ . . . / Sail on, my boat! Sail on, o wanderer! / . . . / Could I have been born on the ocean, / That black abysses are my home? / That the earth is so far away, / As though there were no shelter for me there? / Sail on, my boat! Sail on—till death! / We are in love with the wave and the river! / . . . / . . . /

The poet is compelled to continue wandering, for he cannot find a shelter on the hostile, inhospitable earth. He must shun his fellowman who is alien to him. However, he feels at home over the dark precipices. He loves the ebb and flow of the wave, the everlasting stream of life, the eternal flux, but he is a stranger on earth.

Szmer wioseł dwojga w gęstwinie fal—
I szmer—i słońce—i śpiew—i dal!

Tak właśnie trzeba i tylko tak:
Płynąć wbrew ziemi—niebu na wspak!

Perły, korale skradzione dnu
Rzucać w głębinę własnego snu— / . . . /

Dwoistą łodzią w bezmiary płyń!
Podwójnie kochaj, podwójnie giń! / . . . /

(From *Pieśni mimowolne*, "Szmer wioseł" ["Unintended Poems, 'The Plashing of Oars'"])[35]

The plashing of two oars in the thicket of waves— / The plashing—the sun—the singing—the distance! /

This is just the way and the only way: / To sail against the earth—bottomside up to the heavens! /

Pearls, corals stolen from the bottom / To cast into the depths of one's own dream— / . . . /

Sail into infinity in a double boat! / Doubly love, doubly die! / . . . /

Here, the water reflection, an image popular with the Symbolists, acquires an added dimension. The poet must wander through life in both worlds. By using internal rhyme and a trochaic meter,

Leśmian is able to reproduce the relentless, hurried beat of the oars. The structural parallelisms within the couplets and the fixed caesura after the fifth syllable emphasize the dividing line between the two realms, bringing into focus the twin image of the duality in the poet's existence. To find one's own self and one's creative truth, one must swim against the earthly tide, defying God. One must swim forth into an infinite duality. The poet develops the idea of twin, reflected worlds and the traveler in the boat suspended between them. Thus his body and spirit symbolically experience loving, suffering, and perishing with double intensity in a half-human, half-divine way.[36]

Swimming against the earthly tide, the poet is not understood by the sterile and dead philistine "herd," and must separate himself from "the much too many."[37] The Romantic theme of *odi profanum vulgus,* revived in *fin-de-siècle* aesthetics, is given particular emphasis in the later works of Nietzsche. Zarathustra's aphorisms are the best example:

They understand me not. I am not the mouth of these ears![38]

In one of his earliest poems, written in 1897, Leśmian echoes the sentiments of this Romantic theme exactly:

Niechaj się serce z milczenia nie budzi,
Bo gdy ma dusza skrzydłem w świat uderzy,
Ściga ją mara babelowej wieży,
Powieką cieniów dzieląc mię od ludzi! . . .

Głosy mej piersi—bezechowość studzi!
Wkoło mnie tłuszcza głuchoniema bieży!
Odkąd przekleństwo na ludzkości leży,
Darmo się człowiek marzeniami łudzi! . . .

Osamotniony potomek Babelu
Uczuć i myśli nie znajdzie słownika!
Chce się spowiadać—nie ma spowiednika! . . .

Woła—nie słyszą! Sam—idzie do celu
I przejdzie smutny w braci swoich tłumie,
I nikt go z braci nigdy nie zrozumie! . . .
("Sonet II" ["Sonnet"])[39]

Let not my heart awaken from its silence, / For when my soul smites the world with its wings, / It is haunted by the nightmare of Babel's tower / Dividing me from people with the eyelids of shadows! . . . /

The voices of my breast—echolessness chills! / The rabble, deaf and dumb, hurries by me! / Ever since that curse befell humanity / Has man in vain deluded himself with revery! . . . /

Left to himself, the descendant of Babel / Shall find no words for feelings and thoughts! / Should he want to confess—there shall be no confessor! . . . /

Should he cry out—no one shall hear! Alone—he shall move toward the goal / And sadly shall he pass through the herd of his brothers, / And none of his brothers shall ever understand him! . . .

The exalted words of the poet fall on no friendly ears among the deaf and mute "rabble" rushing past him. He is alienated, his voice freezes from lack of response and indifference. Lonely, not understood, he reaches his goal never having shared his prophecies with his fellowmen.

This "antiphilistine" theme reaches its climax in a cycle of poems entitled *Oddaleńcy* ("The Distant Ones") written in 1905, which Leśmian felt was a direct result of the influence of *Thus Spake Zarathustra.* It is very likely that this influence was exerted through a Russian source, for in a letter from Paris to Przesmycki we read the following:

I read with great interest Berent's *Źródła i ujścia.* It is one of the best articles that has yet appeared about Zarathustra. However, I consider the article written by a certain Russian—Ivanov—the best.[40]

The affinity of *Oddaleńcy* with the literary stand of the philosopher as expressed mainly through Zarathustra, is manifested in most of the cycle's poems. The very title implies the cult of the chosen ones whose separation from the "rabble" and withdrawal into a "land of beyond" is essential for their lofty, spiritual experiences.[41] The ideal land is depicted in an early programmatic poem, "Metafizyka," which contains many of

Zarathustra's postulates and is an apotheosis of the divine, philosophical, and aesthetic experience, represented—as in Nietzsche's work—as a cult of laughter and dance:

Kraina, gdzie żyć łatwiej i konać mniej trudno—
Gdzie wieczność już nie tajnie wystawa na straży
Trosk doczesnych—gdzie bardziej jest bosko, niż ludno—
I gdzie każdy za wszystkich nie cierpi—lecz marzy! / . . . /

I jest tu owa cisza błękitna, ostatnia
Z tych, co jeszcze na uśmiech zdobywać się mogą. / . . . /

Lecz się nigdy nie strwoży, rozumnie zbłąkany,
Bezkrólewiem w niebiosach lub własnego cienia
Zgubą w jarach—lub zbytnią łatwością zamiany
Jednych cudów na drugie. . . . Niech cud się też zmienia! / . . . /

On tu przyszedł sam przez się, by własne szaleństwo
Karmić strawą najlepszą na ziemi i niebie—
I nad brzegiem przepaści wytańczyć dla siebie
Jeden lęk drogocenny lub niebezpieczeństwo! . . .[42]

A land where it is easier to live and less troublesome to die— / Where eternity no longer stands furtively on guard / Over everyday concerns—where it is much more divine than human— / And where each does not suffer for all—but dreams! / . . . /

And there is that azure stillness here, the last / Of those who still can force a smile. / . . . /

But one gone sensibly astray shall never take fright / At an interregnum in the heavens or at his own shadow's / Loss in ravines—or at the excessive ease of exchange / Of certain miracles for others. . . . May even miracle change! / . . . /

He came here on his own, his own madness / To nourish with the best food on earth and in heaven— / And on the brink of an abyss to dance up for himself / One precious fear or peril! . . .

It is easy to understand Leśmian's affinity for the realm of metaphysics, for it allows him a ready exchange of miracles and facilitates creative evolution.

Laughter and dance in the midst of fright and danger is a starting point of the aesthetics which will persist in various degrees throughout Leśmian's poetic career, fitting its creative evolution. Leśmian is precisely the kind of poet about whom Zarathustra says:

Free from the happiness of slaves; saved from Gods and adorations; fearless; . . . great and lonely this is the will of the truthful one.

I love him who willeth the creating of something beyond himself and thus perisheth.[43]

Especially in his mature period will Leśmian dare to create at the edge of the precipice, challenging and defying the precipice, which for him will be God (cf., the poems "W locie" ["In Flight"] and *Eliasz* ["Elijah"]). This Nietzschean element can therefore be considered as having had a lasting influence on Leśmian's mature work. Although the extent of the influence is difficult to evaluate in view of the fact that the aesthetics, especially of laughter, was also propagated by Bergson (his *Laughter* had already been translated into Polish in 1902), there is no doubt that the cycle *Oddaleńcy* represents the first strong manifestation of this aesthetics and that the credit for this clearly belongs to Nietzsche.

For the philosopher, the aesthetics of laughter and dance is connected with the rejection of the existence of the sad God and the promulgation of the Dionysian myth.[44] Creation is the foremost result of joy, exhilaration. Therefore, according to Nietzsche, godliness must include the capacity for laughter and dance. Zarathustra would be willing to "believe in a God who would know how to dance," and he considers "false . . . any truth which did not bestow upon us a single smile." He also adds elsewhere:

If there hath ever come unto me a breath of creative breath and of heavenly necessity that compelleth chance itself to dance star dances; if ever laughed with laughter of creative lightning that is followed by the long thunder of the deed—it is because Zarathustra has reached beyond.[45]

He has become a member of "a new *nobility* . . . opposed unto all mob." "This nobility, . . . that is exactly godliness, [means] that *there are Gods, but no God* [italics mine]."[46]

The chosen ones, the new nobility, the beyond-men cognizant of the illusory existence, pampered excessively by the fates speak out:

/ . . . / Marny ten, co przypływów chłonąc niewyśpiewność,
Wierzy, iż sieć jest siecią, a połów—połowem! . . .
My zbadawszy istnienia dwuznaczność i zwiewność,
Z sieci namiot uczynim pod niebem jałowem! / . . . /

Oddaleńcy! Raz jeden zbłąkani wśród szlaków,
Już się nigdy nie zbliżą do własnej oddali!
Nikt w nich teraz nie pozna wesołych rybaków,
Zwinnych nurków, rabusiów pereł i korali!

Jak pieszczochy przeznaczeń, których nic nie cieszy,
Drwią z gwiazd morskich purpury, z mew bielszych od mleka,
Żagiel, burzą wydęty, tylko ich rozśmieszy,
A szum fali przypomni że czas się przewleka.

(From *Oddaleńcy*, "Wobec morza" ["The Distant Ones, 'Toward the Sea' "])[47]

/ . . . / Wretched is he who, drinking in the flood of unsingable song, / Believes that a net is a net, and a catch—a catch / . . . / We, having delved into the ambiguity and etherealness of being, / Shall make a tent of nets under the barren sky! . . . / . . . /

Distant Ones! Once lost among the ways, / Shall never again come close to their own distance! / Now none shall see in them the merry fishermen, / Agile divers, plunderers of pearls and corals! /

Like darlings of the fates, whom nothing pleases, / They mock the purple of the sea's stars, the sea gulls whiter than milk / A sail bellied by a storm, shall only make them laugh, / And the roar of the wave shall remind them that time drags on.

Only storm and danger will make these superhumans laugh, and only new adventures and momentary dreams will make it possible for God to dance through them—to create—rare pearls of poetry.

The cycle *Oddaleńcy* represents also a climactic stage of the "iconoclasm" evident in Leśmian's earlier poetry, but much more pronounced under the indisputable influence of Nietzsche. Aside from the apparent parallel in the atheistic stand of Zarathustra and *Oddaleńcy*, there is even a stylistic parallel. Many verses bring to mind Zarathustra's rich, colorful aphorisms, exclamations, and apostrophes, as exemplified in the following poem addressed to the chosen brethren, the demiurges:

/ . . . / Tu—wybucha z witrażów tak tęczowy płomień,
Że ty—bogu, a tobie—bóg wyda się tęczą,
I obydwaj, zarówno pełni oszołomień,
Posłyszycie, jak wasze westchnienia współdźwięczą. / . . . /

Więc gdy mi takie wino uderza do głowy
Mocą nieba całego aż do nieboskłonu—
Czyż nie jestem—o, bracia, nieufni do zgonu—
Opojem znad lazurów i sam—lazurowy?

Czyliż teraz mój okręt, szalony beztroską,
Dość się hardo na zdradnej nie załamie rafie?
I czyż—bóstwem pijany—do was nie potrafię,
Znawcy znawstwa samego, przemówić dość bosko? . . . / . . . /

Za ich żywot pokrętny i śmierć niespokojną
Wznoszę kielich, po brzegi pieniący się bogiem! . . .

(From *Oddaleńcy*, "Toast świętokradzki"
["The Sacrilegious Toast"])[48]

/ . . . / There bursts now from the stained-glass window such a rainbow-flame, / That you—to God, and God—to you shall appear as rainbows, / And both, each filled with like bewilderment, / Shall hear your sighs fall in concert. / . . . /

So while such wine goes straight to my head / With the might of all heaven to the horizon— / Am I not—o brothers, mistrustful to the end— / A drunkard from above the azures, and myself—azure? /

Can it be now that my boat, mad with recklessness, / Shall not smash itself on a treacherous reef arrogantly enough? / And can it be that—drunk with divinity—I shall not be able / To address you, experts of expertness itself, divinely enough? / . . . / . . . /

To their twisted life and restless death / I raise a chalice foaming at the brim with God! . . .

This "Sacrilegious Toast" is made to the new "nobility." One, however, detects a note of sarcasm directed at the poet, drunk with godlike power, and at the literary critics who underestimate his divine, creative powers. Parts of the poem sound like a paraphrased Zarathustra, especially the last two verses:

Bless the cup, which is about to overflow, so . . . it may carry everywhere the reflection of thy rapture. . . .[49]

In some poems, the sacrilegious theme represents a mixture of the influence of Baudelaire and Nietzsche in that satanic pathos is attributed to the psyche of the creator. An example of this is the poem, "Nieznanemu Bogu" ("To the Unknown God"), and, to an even greater extent, "Ich szatan" ("Their Satan"):

Ich szatan, utraciwszy święty zapał grzechu,
Lekceważy swe ognie trawiące i czary.
Niespodziane wybuchy nadziei lub wiary
Psują mu doskonałość szatańskiego śmiechu. / . . . /

/ . . . / —ten truteń obłoczny, / . . . /
Resztki nieba rad wyssać z kałuży pomrocznej! . . .

Bo w zmierzch piekieł zużytych wzierając niechętnie,
Śni idylle niebiańskie, a chytrze swe lice
Odmładzając w błękitach—pradawną różnicę
Między sobą a bogiem niweczy doszczętnie! . . .[50]

Their satan, having lost the sacred zeal of sin, / Makes light of his consuming flames and magic. / Sudden outbreaks of hope or of faith / Spoil for him the perfection of satanic laughter. / . . . /

/ . . . / —this drone of the clouds, / . . . / Is glad to suck bits of sky from a benighted puddle! . . . /

For peering into the twilight of burnt-out infernos, reluctantly, / He dreams of heavenly idyls, and slyly making his visage / Young in the heavens—the age-old difference / Between himself and god erases completely! . . .

In this poem the satanic and the godly, coexisting in the chosen ones, evince the morbidity of self-torture. The satan, represented by the lack of inspiration,[51] rejoices at the fall of the divine in the chosen one. This cloud-enveloped drone is his own tormentor; he occasionally rejuvenates his face by a touch of heaven and becomes indistinguishable from God. In this poem one feels again the poet's slight disdain and mockery of the "chosen ones" who, in their pursuit of equality with God, do not discriminate in their means. They will even utilize a mere reflection of heaven in the murky puddle of earthly existence to maintain that equality. Hence, they are poseurs. Much stronger is the "iconoclastic" statement in "Ta oto godzina" ("This Very Hour"):

/ . . . / Twój wybraniec, dbający o cześć swej korony,
Na miecz ją w swoich ogniach przetopił samotnie,
I miecz, ostrzem ku światu tak długo zwrócony,
Zwróci teraz ku sobie—natychmiast, bezzwrotnie! . . . / . . . /

Bo może w tej godzinie, w tej najmniej zwodniczej,
Znajdzie w sobie godnego swej napaści wroga,
I rażąc siebie mieczem, spragnionym zdobyczy,
W piersi własnej—własnego dorąbie się boga![52]

/ . . . / Thy chosen one, anxious for the honor of his crown, / Recast of it a sword in his fires, lonely, / And the sword, its blade turned so long against the world, / He will now turn against himself—instantly, without regret! . . . / . . . /

For perhaps at this hour, at this least beguiling hour, / He shall find in himself an enemy worthy of his assault, / And smiting himself with his sword thirsty for conquest, / Hacking at his own breast—he shall strike his own god!

In the least deceptive moment, striking at an enemy worthy of his sword, the "chosen one" finds God within himself. This can happen only when his wrath is directed against himself and when he persists in the assault on his inner world. Only when he suffers and strives for self-perfection, can his sword chance upon his own divinity. Yet, we find the most predatory iconoclasm in a poem thematically reminiscent of one of Zarathustra's metamorphoses into a lion and tiger. The daring plunderer, the superman turned animal, yearning for revenge, challenges his creator to a bloody duel:

/ . . . / Kimkolwiek jesteś—czy Lwem niewidzialnym,
Czy wszechobecnym raczej Jaguarem—
Węszę twe tropy w błękicie upalnym
I kuszę ciała wonnego wyparem! . . .

Wyjdź na swe żery z jaskini lazurów!
Otom—gotowa! . . . śnij uczty weselne!
Chcę być radością dla twoich pazurów,
Chcę krwią upoić twe kły nieśmiertelne—

I chcę cię zdradzić, gdy przywrzesz do łona,
Pokąsać w strzępy twą wieczność, twe moce,
By chłonąć nozdrzem ten szał, że Bóg kona
W chwili gdy ja się słońcu przeciwzłocę!
(From *Poematy zazdrosne* "Pantera" ["Jealous Poems: 'The Panther' "])[53]

/ . . . / Whoever you may be—the invisible Lion, / Or the ever-present Jaguar— / I scent your traces in the sweltering blue / And lure you with my fragrant body's vapor! . . . /

Come from the cave of azure for your prey! / Here I am—ready! . . . dream of wedding rites! / I want to be a pleasure to your claws, / I want to gorge your immortal fangs with my blood— /

And I want to deceive you, as you cleave to my womb, / To bite to shreds your eternity, your powers, / So that I may breathe in through my nostrils this madness that God shall be dying / At the instant that I shall turn gold against the sun!

The poem is the incarnation of the Dionysian dance and joy which results from excess of brutal bloodthirstiness in anticipation of destruction. Abounding in apostrophes, the poem can almost be considered an extended metaphor of Zarathustra's single apostrophe: "Do you want to tear apart God within man?"[54]

The cycle *Oddaleńcy*, representing the peak of Nietzsche's influence on Leśmian's early poetry, focuses primarily on the two tenets expounded by the philosopher in *Thus Spake Zarathustra:* the idea of the creative man's "pathos of distance"[55] from the "rabble," and his "iconoclasm," accentuated through the aesthetics of laughter and dance. It can be said that the cycle *Oddaleńcy* represents at once the peak as well as the decline of these Nietzschean influences upon Leśmian's early poetics. This conclusion, derived from studies of the subject, was also confirmed by the poet himself in a letter to Z. Przesmycki (mentioned in connection with Wacław Berent's article about Zarathustra):

. . . As for myself, I arrived only today at a proper understanding of Zarathustra, but about this later. By the way, you were right to reproach me for not being "true to myself" in my cycle *Oddaleńcy!* But my procrastinating spirit went through much worse trials, tribulations, errors and fervors. However, now only a thin veil separates me from my world.[56]

The Nietzschean idea of "the pathos of distance" adapted by Leśmian verges on adulation in such poems as "Metafizyka." It represents the poet's approval of the daring superman and of the need for distance from the "herd" even if it means experiencing but a single moment of the divine dancing through him in the process of creation. However, in some poems one detects, beneath the veneer of Dionysian intoxication and bravado, the poet's contempt for the pampered new gods (cf., "Ich szatan," or "Wobec morza") who are more like their satan, the "cloud-enveloped drone," than divinely inspired demiurges. It seems, therefore, that at first the responsiveness to the idea of "the pathos of distance" was a daring adventure, a boost to the poet's ego, a pose; but perhaps most of all it was a trial-and-error experiment encouraged by his literary and philosophical ambience. It expressed a temporary zeal for the superman—in the essentially antiaristocratic and very humane poet—later discarded in the selective process.

Trials, tribulations, and constant change—acknowledged in the poet's letters—were, from the start, characteristic of Leśmian's formative years. In a sonnet of 1897, the theme and style of which reflected Decadent aesthetics (i.e., the poet's alienation from the "herd"), and in a letter of the same year he declared that he had ceased to believe in the aesthetics of the present generation and the Symbolist muse and, a year later, he criticized the contemporary "bards" for adhering to Nietzsche's "pathos of distance," for being "tired of serving the world." Likewise, while expressing in poetry his yearning for a voyage into the unknown "sea of beyond" away from the people, he confesses to Przesmycki in a letter of 1900 that he had turned towards the sea of people, in which his fishing rod caught many a "diamondlike scrap of human soul," as a result of which he had grown spiritually and discovered man's greatness.[57]

The same pattern of vacillation can be observed in Leśmian's poetic awareness during the period in which *Oddaleńcy* was composed. Having reached the spheres of beyond, having shared with the "new nobility" (the beyond-men) the exalted, but brief, aesthetic experience, Leśmian paid a final tribute to late Nietzsche-ism in this cycle of poems. Thereafter, rejecting Zarathustra's main objective, the Superman, as deceptive and unacceptable to his poetic ideology, the poet leaves the exalted heights of beyond. He does follow Zarathustra in one respect—in trying to find himself. This time, however, the poet rushes back to earth, to his inner sanctum, to the world of his own resources. This new awareness the poet shares with his mentor Przesmycki, in a letter written approximately at the same time as *Oddaleńcy*. Indicating his disillusionment with all "isms," the poet resolves to arrive at a unique artistry by drawing upon his "own layers of impressions."

The need to rush away from the "chosen ones" towards his own self is expressed in a poem belonging to the cycle *Oddaleńcy*, entitled appropriately "Pośpiech" ("Haste"), the last stanza of which may be considered a continuation of the letter mentioned above:

/ . . . / Nie! On niegdyś, snów pierwszych złudzony jałmużną,
Ujrzał siebie gdzieś—w ledwo stworzonym zaświecie,
I teraz niespokojny, raz jeszcze, na próżno
Sam do siebie się śpieszy! Wy mnie rozumiecie? . . .[58]

/ . . . / No! Once, deceived by the alms of early dreams, / He saw himself somewhere—in a beyond barely created, / And now, restless, once more, in vain / He hurries by himself! Do you understand me? . . .

Judging by the above quotation, it becomes clear that the poet's infatuation with the Nietzschean idea of the Superman was a brief one, since its transient stage is already evident in the *Oddaleńcy* cycle. Even "the land" of metaphysics, the ideal habitat for the "Distant Ones," proved equally to be a temporary retreat. For the author of *Łąka* metaphysics would acquire an entirely different meaning as a basis for his poetic creativity.

While the concept of the Superman is a short-lived influence in Leśmian's poetics terminating with *Oddaleńcy*, "iconoclasm" (the second dominant Nietzschean influence) presents a more complex phenomenon. In the traditional sense, Leśmian was to remain a consistent iconoclast, but the Nietzschean iconoclasm characteristic of the times was the end of a particular phase of his poetic career. Historically, Leśmian belongs to a literary milieu in which religion and mythology are essential, although unidentifiable with any institutionalized dogmas. Leśmian's relationship to God is a complex syncretic system which lends itself (like his poetry) to various interpretations.[59]

The dual orientation of Leśmian's "formulated poetics" can also be applied to the question of his relationship to God. Leśmian's iconoclasm, interdependent in his ontology with the concept of artistic creation, remains as constant as his belief in the essential role of poetry and the poet in literature. For Leśmian, creative evolution and the art it inspires constitute at all times the true manifestation of divinity, that is, of God. While the basic idea of iconoclasm is the same, one can distinguish various phases superimposed upon it. In my opinion, these phases are best analyzed by following the evolutionary stages of Leśmian's poetics, which point, by means of regression, to primordiality, and especially to pantheism, for it is this which lies at the base of his mature poetics.[60]

SPINOZA'S PANTHEISM

This simplified approach allows us to distinguish three main phases in the poet's relationship to God. The first phase is of the least duration and, in a sense, gives rise to the subsequent two. The overrefinement and excessive consciousness of Decadent aesthetics widened the gulf between man and God. Then too,

Nietzschean iconoclasm was aimed at a conventional God, an institutionalized entity which represented a single Aristotelian synthesis of all divine concepts. Such a God was considered abstract and limited in creative power. In contrast, man inspired by intuition possessed limitless creative potential. Hence, the poet, following Nietzsche, stresses the Superman's independence of a God he disdains and whose existence he denies.

It seems that Leśmian had this particular phase in mind, contrasting it to the state of consciousness in primitive man who knew no separation between heaven and earth, God and man, when he wrote:

> When, in the course of time, a division of consciousness shall occur within man . . . when he shall lose his heaven on earth, he will often long for this form of a dragon with a double torso, for the god-man, for God's descent to earth, adoring himself in the context of past existence.[61]

The poet knows that hypertrophy of his consciousness has brought about the loss of paradise on earth and he longs for its return. He attempts to regain it through fictitious regressions to primordiality and enters the second phase of his relationship to God—pantheism.

However, the transition from the phase of Nietzschean "iconoclasm" to pantheism is not immediate. The notion of the superiority of man's creative imagination over God's is apparent in the initial stages of the poet's regression to primordiality. God descending to earth is still portrayed as the fallen God, "the panic-stricken God of forest lunacy."[62] Even then, in the period of man's greatest familiarity with God, having created "an interregnum in the heavens," God evokes scorn in man, as before. This is well illustrated in the following poem:

W parowie, pod leszczyzny rozchełstanym cieniem,
Spadły z nieba bezwolnie wraz z poranną rosą—
Drzemie Bóg, w macierzankach poległy na wznak.

Dno parowu rozkwita pod jego brzemieniem.
Biegnę tam, mokre trawy czesząc stopą bosą,
Schylam się nad drzemiącym i mówię doń tak:

"Zbudź się, ty—ptaku senny! Ty—ćmo wielkanocna,
Co zmartwychwstajesz pilnie, by lecieć w ślepotę
Świateł gwiezdnych, gdzie w mroku spala się twój czar! / . . . /

Pójdziem razem! Ramieniem własnym cię wspomogę!
Pokażę ci sny nasze i nasze moczary—
I słońce w oczach ptaków, zapatrzonych w sad! . . ."

Tak doń mówię—i dłonią wyciągnięta *mężnie*
Nad nim, jak nad *zwaloną* od uderzeń *bramą*,
Trafiam na jego ku mnie wyciagnietą dłoń!

I zgaduję—oczyma wodząc widnokręgnie—
Że on do mnie z parowu modlił się tak samo,
Jak i ja—nad parowem—modliłem się doń! . . .
(From *Zielona godzina* ["The Green Hour"]) [Italics mine.][63]

In a ravine, in the tattered shade of a hazel grove, / Fallen passively from the sky with the morning dew— / God dozes stricken, lying on his back in wild thyme. /

The ravine's bottom blossoms under his weight. / I run there, barefoot combing the wet grasses, / I bend over the dozing one and talk to him thus: /

"Wake up, you—sleepy bird! You—Easter moth, / That rises readily from the dead to fly into the blindness / Of starry lights where in the dark your magic burns out! / . . . /

We'll go together! By my arm alone I shall sustain you! / I shall show you our dreams and our morasses— / And the sun in the eyes of birds staring into an orchard! . . ." /

Thus I speak to him—and with my palm outstretched manfully / Over him, *as over* a gate knocked flat *by blows, / I meet his palm outstretched to me! /*

And I guess—scanning the horizon with my eyes— / That he had prayed to me from the ravine the same / As I—above the ravine—had prayed to him! . . . /

The creative man exudes vitality and optimism as he stretches out his hand to God, who is likened to an overturned gate. The disdain for the weak, ineffectual God whose only labor is his resurrection on Easter, will reappear in a much more intense form, in the third phase of the poet's relationship to God. This phase, represented in *Napój cienisty* and *Dziejba Leśna*, will be discussed below in connection with Bergsonian influences.

The oscillations, the transitional stages discussed above, do not reflect a lack of conviction on the part of the poet. On the contrary, they reflect a consistency of belief in an obsolescent reality and a creative evolution. Rather than reject different philosophical and literary aesthetics at their face value, the poet's thirst for exploration and for experimentation dictated the use of different ideas, the discarding of some and the selection of those advancing him toward his own poetic goal. His thirsting spirit is typical of his generation; what is not typical is his gift of selectivity and his masterful control and channeling of all the accumulated spiritual treasures.[64]

The extensive discussion of the ideological influences of late Nietzscheism upon the formative stages of Leśmian's poetics serves as an example of the poet's sense of selectivity. Succumbing to this powerful influence that represented the spirit of the time, he was able to curtail the extent of its influence, but only after having convinced himself empirically of its unsuitability, especially in its antihumanistic aspects. This rejection marks the actual end of an aesthetics that will not reoccur in his later poetic creation.

Leśmian benefited from late Nietzscheism in some respects. It boosted his confidence in the might and the limitless possibilities of the creative man, and it strengthened both his belief in man's independence from God and his negation of promises of a life hereafter. He retained the Nietzschean intoxication with life which would intensify as the poet turned toward nature. Occasionally, the author of *Łąka* would express his exuberance, desiring:

/ . . . / słońce witać krzykiem i wrzaskiem i wyciem,
Żyć na oślep, nie wiedząc, że to zwie się życiem—
("Pragnienie" ["A Wish"])[65]

/ . . . / to greet the sun with cries and screams and with a howl /
To live blindly, not knowing that this is called life—

However, this orgiastic, excessive joy with just being alive would prove rare and would give way to an active intoxication, to an obsession with an intensified, crowded, creative existence. Thus, transforming the Nietzschean influences and combining them later with Bergsonism, the poet arrived at a dominant principle of his poetics: to be truly alive means *to create.* The adaptation of the Dionysian aesthetics of laughter and dance with an apparent intent to augment the expression of biological vitality was likewise utilized by the author of *Łąka* in a unique way, seldom leading "in the direction of joyous optimism."[66] This fact provides us with insight into Leśmian's mature poetry in which he transformed principles selected from different sources to suit his own aesthetics.

Consequently, the parallel between Leśmian's earliest poetry (cf., *UR* and parts of *Sad rozstajny*) and the prevailing aesthetics proves superficial and limited. Adapting and reflecting certain sensibilities of the period did not hinder him from expressing different ideas (as gleaned from his correspondence), spurred as he was by his disappointment in the early Symbolism of both Russia and Poland. Therefore, one can assume that this was a temporary affiliation utilized primarily to perfect his poetic craft while his own poetic ideology crystallized, thereby hastening the break with the prevailing aesthetics. In this he was aided by various philosophers, not necessarily the most popular ones of the era.

Conscious of the fact that eternal creativity and constant evolution represent the true reality of life, he found reassurance for his convictions in Heraclitus's tenet of *Panta rei* long before he was acquainted with the works of Bergson.[67] This "weeping" philosopher as well as the "laughing" Democritus represented for Leśmian two opposing elements: the Dionysian and Apollonian elements inherent in the human soul which constitute a unity indispensable for a full relationship of the soul with the universe.

(Cf. quotations nn. 38 and 39 in chapter 2.) According to the poet, the soul must encompass everything human: both the sad and the joyous. Leśmian considered Decadent aesthetics responsible for the hypertrophy of self-consciousness, which resulted in a rift in the creative man's inner self and in his separation from nature. He was opposed to dualism of soul, of body and mind, because to him it represented an obstacle to dynamism, to a direct contact with reality, the kind of reality which he called, after Erigena and Spinoza, *natura naturans.* In retrospect, one can assume that the aesthetics of the *fin de siècle* belonged, in Leśmian's definition, to the realm of *natura naturata.*

It is highly possible that Leśmian adapted from Spinoza more than just these terms which he modified and combined later with the Bergsonian *élan vital.* He could have been influenced by Spinoza's opposition to dualism, extending it to the opposition of the dualism of God and the created world. Spinoza tried to prove that "an infinite . . . divine being could not exist alongside a finite and contingent nature external to the divine being."[68] The concept that could have attracted Leśmian most in Spinoza's philosophy was, *Deus sive natura,* according to which:

"God" is the name of the one substance whose other name is "Nature," the contrast between God and the world, a contrast which is at the heart of Judaism and Christianity, is obliterated. The one substance can have nothing outside itself to limit it.[69]

It is hard to establish to what extent Spinoza's pantheism influenced the young poet who admitted to an acquaintance with the works of the philosopher[70] and who saw in the fictitious regression to primordiality the only salvation of the creative man. Leśmian longed to merge with nature, with which he was enamoured. He defines his relationship to nature as follows:

I long to perceive nature, as a thing in itself. In all of this there is definitely some kind of metaphysics, which I am unable to define, but speaking about nature I treat it in such a manner as though it is not only I who long for it, but it, too, longs for me.[71]

This would correspond in many ways to the ideas expressed by Spinoza, except that the obliteration of the contrast between God and the world is much more extreme in Leśmian. He wants to return to the womb of nature from which man originated and lose the human *Gestalt* as well as the accursed self-consciousness, enabling him to obliterate all ties with the conceptual God. For, in Leśmian's view, not God created man,[72] but nature; therefore, nature is God. The poet wants to enter into a mystical union with nature in an "impersonal" way (expression used by Ostap Ortwin).

One of his first attempts at attaining this state is expressed in a jubilant poem of a cycle which marks the evolutionary path in Leśmian's poetics. In a state of exaltation from his journey to earth and his close contact with nature, the hero realizes that nature has taken note of his arrival; the flowers have seen him. He greets nature as a long-lost friend:

Bog się zmieszał w mych oczach z brzaskiem słońc, na śniegi
Wbiegłych złotem—i z szmerem jaszczurek w pokrzywie,
I z wonią bzu i z słodką krwią dziewczęcych ust!

Dzwoń, Zielona Godzino! Miłością bezwstydny
Płomień się, wonny świecie, pozbyty żałoby
Po mnie, com długo krył się przed tobą w mój żal!

Idę oto na słońce, wiedząc, żem wskroś widny
Drzewom, w drodze spotkanym, i ptakom, co dzioby
Zanurzają w me usta, odbite wśród fal.

Żem się przyśnił i zwidział tym kwiatom i ziołom,
Żem się pokładł na życiu, jak żuraw na łące—
Ponad siebie rozkwitam, ponad siebie trwam!

O, ruczaje, skąd niebo przygląda się siołom!
O, gąszcze dziwów leśnych! O, *kwiaty, widzące*
Mój na ziemi zjaw nagły—sen i chwała wam!
(From *Zielona Godzina* ["The Green Hour"]) [Italics mine.][73]

God became confused in my eyes with the dawn of suns / Running up the snow like gold—and with the rustle of lizards in poison ivy, / And with the scent of lilac and the sweet blood of a maiden's lips! /

Ring out, o Green Hour! Brazen with love / Burn, o fragrant world, freed of mourning / For me, long hidden from you in my sorrow! /

Thus I go to the sun, knowing that I am transparent / To the trees I meet on the way and to the birds that beaks / Plunge into my mouth reflected among the waves. /

That I came in a dream and revealed myself to these flowers and herbs, / That I lay down on life like a crane on a meadow— / Beyond myself I bloom, beyond myself I endure! /

O brooks, whence heaven contemplates the villages! / O thickets of forest wonders! O flowers that see / *My sudden appearance on earth—dream and glory to you! /*

Here, in the process of approaching the domain of flora and fauna, the image of God is erased and the sorrow is gone usually connected in Leśmian's poetry with the presence of God. An orgiastic exuberance replaces it now. The urgency of this act and the ebullient state of expressed by imperatives, apostrophes, syntactical parallelisms, and by trochees at the beginning of each verse.

A letter dealing with the title for the first volume, written in the same year as this poem, can be considered an addendum to it. It confirms the fact, expressed poetically, that Leśmian is a "*homo adorans* in perpetual need of contact with"[74] nature, conceived of as a divine autonomous entity. We read the following:

Because nature is the essential, the main (and perhaps the only) territory of my creation, . . . because nature has . . . the ability of "seeing," I therefore wanted to name the volume: "The Seeing Flowers."[75]

It is a nature endowed with supernatural powers with which the poet yearns to merge. This somatic, sensual act is expressed most powerfully in the initial poem of *Łąka:*

W zwiewnych nurtach kostrzewy, na leśnej polanie,
Gdzie się las upodobnia łące niespodzianie,
Leżą zwłoki wędrowca, zbędne sobie zwłoki.
Przewędrował świat cały z obłoków w obłoki,
Aż nagle w niecierpliwej *zapragnął* żałobie
Zwiedzić duchem na przełaj *zieleń samą w sobie.*

Wówczas demon zieleni wszechleśnym powiewem
Ogarnął go, gdy w drodze przystanął pod drzewem,
I wabił nieustannych rozkwitów pośpiechem,
I nęcił ust zdyszanych tajemnym bezśmiechem,
I czarował zniszczotą wonnych niedowcieleń,
I kusił coraz głębiej—w tę zieleń, w tę zieleń!
A on biegł wybrzeżami coraz innych światów,
Odczłowieczając duszę i oddech wśród kwiatów,
Aż zabrnął w takich jagód rozdzwonione dzbany,
W taką zamrocz paproci, w takich cisz kurhany,
W taki bezświat zarośli, w taki bezbrzask głuchy,
W takich szumów ostatnie kędyś zawieruchy,
Że leży oto martwy w stu wiosen bezdeni,
Cienisty, jak bór w borze—topielec zieleni.
("Topielec" ["The Drowned One"]) [Italics mine.][76]

In blowing billows of fescue, in a forest glade, / Where the forest grows suddenly to meadow, / Lie the mortal remains of a wanderer, rather useless remains. / He had roamed the whole world from cloud to cloud, / Until suddenly in his restless mourning he was seized with a desire / In spirit to explore *at one fell swoop* the verdure in itself. / *At that instant the verdure demon in the breath of all forests / Engulfed him as he paused along the way beneath a tree, / And enticed him with a rush of endless blooming, / And tempted him with panting lips mysteriously laughless, / And bewitched him with the decay of fragrant, yet-unembodied things, / And lured him ever deeper—into that verdure, into that verdure! / And he ran along the shores of ever-different worlds, / Unmanning his soul and breath amidst flowers, / Until he waded into ringing jugs of such berries, / Into such a dazzling dark of ferns, into grave mounds of such quiet, / Into such an unworld of thickets, into such a still undawn, / Into the last storms somewhere of such sounds, / That he lies dead here in the abyss of a hundred springtimes, / Shadowy, as a forest in a forest—the drowned one in verdure. /*

In this poem, Leśmian's wanderer has a sudden urge to "explore . . . the verdure in itself," to merge with it, as did primitive man. Using the Kantian term *an sich selbst*[77] and following the philosopher's reasoning, Leśmian implies the inscrutability of this autonomous entity for modern man's level of consciousness, in part a product of his alienation from nature. Yet, this gulf between man and the universe can be overcome only by intuitive cognition, exploration "in spirit." A reckless onward rush into the unknown brings the protagonist into direct contact with the material realm and consequently with its spirit, for, as Leśmian believes, "one gets to know life straightaway *in its given totality,* in its flight . . . in its unrestrained current."[78] The spirit, an elemental force which appears real in the image of the verdure demon, lures the wanderer by revealing to him the beauty of the existing and nonexisting green. Penetrating deeper and deeper into the mysteries of nature, the hero forfeits his existence as a man, but when he drowns, he merges with the infinite abyss of verdure. Thus, he is "at the same time the conqueror and the conquered, the onward rush and the immobility. . . . There is in him as much existence as nonexistence."[79]

The precipitous process of the hero's penetration, dehumanization, and final fusion with nature is presented gradually, yet dramatically. The slow pace of narration at the beginning gains momentum in the ninth verse by means of polysyndeton. The agitation comes to an almost sudden halt in the two last verses. The hero lied dead, yet merged with nature. The parallel imagery fuses into one final summarizing *pointe.* Thus, the form and the idea represent an indivisible unity. The poem "Topielec," is an apotheosis of Bergsonism and a poetic extension of Leśmian's philosophical discourse with Kant. Here he created a poetic language, using prefixes of negation such as *bez* ("un" or "non") as well as *za* ("beyond"). This language enabled him to depict, in concrete images, both existing and nonexisting phenomena—the matter and the spirit of nature as a whole—fused with the self of the protagonist.

The return to nature is a part of a uniquely perceived motif of return to primordiality which became the basis of Leśmian's poetry and of his philosophy. It represents the second stage in Leśmian's relationship to God—an extreme kind of pantheism[80] which is not only the organizing principle of his poetic world, beginning with the cycle *Zielona godzina* and especially in *Łąka,* but is *"also a poetic fact."*[81] Leśmian himself gives us a clue to the complex problem of this relationship in the essay "Znaczenie pośrednictwa. . . ." He considers the true primitive man a "theist in body and soul,"[82] who longed for deeds requiring self-denial and who was, therefore, able to remain an integral part of nature, whereas the fictitious primitive man is more of a pantheist.

> Due to a prolonged study of nature, we are emotionally much more pantheistic than primitive man, turning away from the kind of *pantheistic deeds,* which would . . . force us to . . . self-denial.[83]

This statement attests to Leśmian's fascination with the conscious states of primitive man. It also explains the reason for the conflicts in the poet's metaphorical stand regarding his desire to merge with nature. The different levels of consciousness in primitive man and the fictitious primitive have a limiting effect on the totality of this union.

The fictitious primitive man—the poet—is only capable of perceiving nature and man on an equal basis as two autonomous entities complementing each other and communicating with each other. The poet decides "to shake its [nature's] hand as that of an equal."[84] In view of this reality the poet is forced to adopt a "poetic compromise," consisting of a synthesis of the two entities, of two actions; an "action" of nature is closely tied to the lyrical "action" and resembles the dialogue of primitive man's relationship with nature found in folklore. In folk mythology there exist close mystical ties between nature and man, which nevertheless allow man to retain his independence. This coexistence is maintained and finds artistic expression in the juxtaposition of the fantastic with the real, and in the constant metamorphosis of nature in Leśmian's poetry. It allows for the momentary obliteration of limits between man, nature, and other species considered in folklore an expression of supernatural power: Kazimierz Moszyński, a contemporary of Leśmian, discussed the motif of metamorphosis in folk literature:

> . . . the deep, intimate mixing of people, animals and other objects or phenomena, can be noted (ascertained) at every step, while studying the religious life of primitive people and listening to their fairy tales or stories. . . .[85]

Russian folk literature especially abounds in these examples.

The poetic attempt of total union with nature expressed in "Topielec" results in failure for man, who, unable to find out anything about the mystery of nature, is drowned in its amorphous state. This poem, the introduction to the volume, *Łąka*, shows man plunging into the mystery of the universe with all his vital exuberance.

Aware of the fact that unlike the primitive man (the natural poet), the fictitious primitive man (the poet) can never attain total fusion with nature because of the difference in the level of their consciousness, Leśmian resorts to a kind of poetic "compromise" which allows each autonomous entity to retain its independence and a soul of its own.

This phenomenon is best expressed in the long poem, *Łąka* (which symbolically closes the second volume of poetry by the same title), where the meadow comes to visit the man and enters into a dialogue with him as an equal. Thus we see how the synthesis of the two "actions" come to life in poetic expression. At the same time, due to the element of metamorphosis, man loses his "lamentable" human image and resembles, temporarily, the weeds that surround him:

Przeto Bóg, co mnie stworzył, zbladł podziwem zdjęty,
Żem uszedł jego dłoniom w tych pokus odmęty!
W kształt mię ludzki rozżałobnił,
A jam znów się upodobnił,
Kwiatom i wszelkim trawom i źdźbłom gorzkiej mięty.[86]

/ . . . / Therefore God, who created me, grew pale and astonished, / That I had escaped his hands into the depths of these temptations! / He gave me a lamentable human form, / But again I became like / The flowers and all kinds of grasses and blades of bitter mint. / . . . /

This poem represents the strongest affirmation not only of nature, but of man as well. Man is finally liberated from the "mournful" relationship with God by his deep ties with nature. "In the eyes of Leśmian nature was for the world what poetry was for him: the fundamental truth of existence."[87]

This poetic synthesis, achieved by means of folk tradition, is the most viable solution to the realization of Leśmian's fictitious regression to primordiality. This is why the poet gravitates towards genres characteristic of folk literature. As we shall see in the discussion of the long poem, *Łąka,* and of other of his works, the poetry of Leśmian's mature period cannot be considered mere folk stylization. It is rather an original creation combining various folkloric aspects, but in an entirely novel way. The form and the lexical texture are new, as though each occurrence, each object, were being created for the first time.

Although the concept of pantheism was not formulated by the poet (who hated conceptualizations), his fascination with primitive cultures and with the conscious states of the primitive man, to which he tried to adapt in order to merge with nature, point toward pantheism as the basis of his relationship to God. In particular, the analogy of the poet's relationship to nature with the one represented in folklore is the most effective way in which Leśmian's variety of pantheism can be explained. Agreeing with Miłosz *et al.*, that it is a central problem of Leśmian's poetics,[88] I give it more than cursory attention here. How much Spinoza's *Deus sive natura* had to do with Leśmian's pantheism is not a matter of conjecture.[89] The complexity of Leśmian's relationship to God suggests Voltaire's remark:

> Theism . . . ought to be called not so much a religion, as a philosophical system.[90]

Leśmian's philosophical evolutions parallel, to a certain extent, the ideological development of Young Poland, especially in its second phase. This period did not limit itself to the wisdom of Western philosophies, and represents a period of great interest in the East, especially in the culture and literature of India. In Poland, the main popularizer—primarily as a translator—of Hindu philosophy, motifs, and the oldest epic, *Ramayana*[91] was Antoni Lange. Manifestations of interest in Hindu culture are evident in the periodical *Chimera,* in which Lange's translation of the Upanishad appeared. The popularity of Hindu motifs was not only due to a fascination with the exotic, it was also bound up with the philosophical aspirations of the epoch. Schopenhauerism was very likely acting as a mirror of the Veda doctrines, and also as an incentive for their dissemination. Interest in Hindu culture is evident in Kazimierz Tetmajer's "Hymn do Nirvany" ("Hymn to Nirvana") and in the Hindu stylizations in the works of Jan Kasprowicz and others.

Leśmian was introduced to Hindu culture rather early by Lange (a cousin of Leśmian's father). During Leśmian's student years in Kiev, he belonged to a "bohemian" artistic circle nicknamed "The Drunken Boat,"[92] an indication of the *voyant* atmosphere prevailing in it. Kazimierz Wierzyński, a poet of the Skamander group, writes of the members of this circle:

> Baudelaire and Poe were their patrons and "Mahabharata" and "Sakuntala"—the voyage to the truth of the world beyond, towards which the Kievan Argonauts strove with the phantasy of youth.[93]

The influence of the Veda doctrines can be detected in the dialectic nature of Leśmian's poetics. They suited his ideology and, at this point, his pantheism, as is apparent in his article on the epos *Ramayana.* The influences are of various types and of various intensities, depending on the different stages in Leśmian's poetic evolution.

The pantheistic stage, starting with *Zielona godzina,* represents, according to Adam Szczerbowski, the "first meeting of the poet's soul with the soul of the world . . . which equals the soul of nature."[94] It is as if the poet stepped forward to a great God who cannot be distinguished from the forest:

> . . . who symbolized here [in this cycle], as later through the meadow, the verdure, the mists, . . . an eternally primordial, infinite space, an unknown thing in itself, an existence, the absolute—Brahma.[95]

In order to communicate with the "soul of nature" (i.e., God), the poet must transgress the limits of human thought, disregarding any notion of space and time, entering a dreamlike state. This oneness of his soul with Brahma, the divine spirit (representing the doctrines of Vedas) enables the poet to perceive things in an entirely different perspective, and see how

W pobok dęba—w ukośnym majaczy skróceniu
Cień rozwartej na słońce, niewiadomej chaty,
Która kiedyś powstanie, burząc jego pień.
(From *Zielona godzina* ["The Green Hour"])[96]

Beside the oak—at an angular shortcut there looms / The shadow of an unknown hut facing full to the sun, / Which shall someday arise, destroying its trunk.

This way of seeing things approximates in the poet's mind the perception of the soul of nature which he tries to emulate in order to merge with it. Such a capacity of observation has an unlimited range. It enables the poet to extend his seeing far ahead; it enables him to see a future reality built on the destruction of a present reality. Thus, erasing the limits between man and nature, between form, space, and time, the poet strives to arrive at a constantly shifting poetic world which becomes a Heraclitean river, where everything is in a state of becoming (*in statu nascendi*), of registering this brief state of incarnation just long enough to endure momentarily, only to disappear in the constant flux of existence.

To attain this poetic goal which would best reflect his perception of the world, Leśmian resorts to a variety of ideological approaches and literary devices. The first step is toward merging with nature by utilizing folklore as a mediator. The poet reaches this stage in the volume, *Łąka.* It is a communion with Atma, "the soul of nature," or God dwelling in the "Incomprehensible Verdure," understood according to Szczerbowski,

as Rig-Veda understands him; as the One who created this world, or perhaps did not create it; who knows the origin of omniscience, and perhaps does not know it.[97]

The enigmatic style, fitting the fluctuation between belief and doubt, and expressed in a riddlelike form, represents, to a large extent, Leśmian's aesthetics, his attempt to resolve the puzzling essence of nature, and his lack of assurance. The negative definition of God is part of a mystical tradition. (In Russian poetry it had been used by Derzhavin in his ode "God.")[98] Negation, especially used in the form of a riddle, is the oldest form of folkloric tradition and, according to Hegel, it is an invention of the Eastern world.[99] This tradition has also influenced Russian folklore, where negation serves to ascertain, to strengthen an occurrence. Thus, we find the frequent use of negative parallelism in folksongs, for example:

To ne veter vetku klonit,
Ne dubravushka shumit.

It ain't the wind that bends the twig, / Nor the oaken grove that rustles.

Similarly we observe this antithesis in other genres of folk literature, especially in byliny or in the epic *Slovo o polku Igoreve* ("The Lay of Igor's Raid"):

Boian zhe bratia, ne desiat' sokolov
   na stado lebedei puskal,
No svoi veshchie persty
   na zhivye struny voskladal.[100]

For it was not, my brothers, ten falcons / That Boyan loosed upon a flock of swans, / But his magic fingers / That he set to the living strings. / . . . /

Negation was also a device frequently used by the Russian Symbolists, who believed that by negating a phenomenon one is closer to expressing what it really represents.

This is also true of Leśmian, but, in his case, negation represents the basis for the dialectics of his poetry. Duality, changing existence, "denied existence," are themes which run like a thread through all of Leśmian's poetry. They stem primarily from his uncertainty of the present existence, and through negating it, he intends to reach a higher level of unity with the universe (partially by means of regressing to primordiality) which would assure a more stable existence (either by merging with nature and attaining a state of Nirvana, or via myth to construct fictitious existences of "highest degree"). This attempt reflects Hindu influences. However, the constant negation of existence has other motivations as well. It is primarily due to his belief in evolution, in changing reality (cf., Bergson). This is why there is at times only a slight separation in Leśmian's poetry between existing and nonexisting things.

In Leśmian's poetry, negation is solidly grounded in the poetic form and is not limited only to syntactical, stylistic devices, such as negative parallelism and genres discussed above. It is primarily the expression of the creative lexical power. The negation of existence, the acknowledged nonexistence, is set in space and time, and materialized by means of concrete images. The best poetic example of the dialectics of existence is "Ballada bezludna" ("The Desolate Ballad"). It must have prompted Artur Sandauer to arrive at an interpretation of Leśmian's philosophy, using, in formal analysis, the Hegelian triad of dialectics.[101] This approach has been rejected by the eminent critic and literary historian, Wacław Kubacki, who attributes Leśmian's gravitation towards dialectics exclusively to the influences of Orientalism.

According to Kubacki, this influence is manifested in every aspect of Leśmian's poetics. In my estimation, this is somewhat overstated, because the dialectics in Leśmian's poetics are rather firmly tied to Bergson's concept of creative evolution which persists throughout Leśmian's mature creative period. It is true that Eastern influences appear in some ballads based on Hindu themes, e.g., "Pururawa and Urwasi," "Asoka," "Dżananda," the rhapsody "Śmierć Buddy" ("The Death of Buddha"), the long poem *Nieznana podróż Sindbada-Żeglarza* ("The Unknown Journey of Sindbad the Sailor"), and also his fairy tales based on Hindu motifs, e.g., *Klechdy Sezamowe* ("Old Tales of Sesame") and

Przygody Sindbada-Żeglarza ("The Adventures of Sindbad the Sailor"). Likewise, I do agree that some Hindu influence can be noted in his choice of motifs. Thus, the motif of life and death, for instance, represents "in Leśmian a modernistic variant tinged with Hindu philosophy,"[102] combining certain elements of Schopenhauerism. In *Napój cienisty,* in which the questioning of any kind of existence becomes the poet's obsession, one detects a much more inensified Hindu influence in the negation of existence.

Śniło mi się że znika treść kwiatów wątpliwa,
I że ogród istnienia zlistwionego syt—
Ginie, szepcąc twe imię, dziewczyno wróżb chciwa—
A śmierć szarpie na strzępy twój spieszczony byt. / . . . /

Znikło miasto gdzie wrzała bezzasadna praca
I gdzie się rozbudował śmiech, niebyt i żal.
Nadaremnie się obłok—słońcu przypodzłaca:
Znikł obłok—żywot wieczny—bóstw kilka—i dal.
("Sen" ["The Dream"])[103]

I dreamt that the dubious substance of flowers disappears, / And that the garden, sated by its leafened existence— / Perishes whispering your name, o maiden greedy for omens— / And death tears to shreds your pampered existence. / . . . /

A city disappeared where useless work was in full swing / And where there flourished laughter, nonbeing and sorrow. / In vain did a cloud sidle up to the sun's gold: / The cloud vanished—so did eternal life—some idols—and the distance. /

Death deals a blow to all existence—even to the myth-creating power (the maiden), all of which becomes a dream.

The absurdity of existence becomes even more pronounced when the questioning of its meaning, the explanation or the justification of man's tragic existence is expressed by allegorical characters—figments of the poet's imagination. This is particularly evident in the cycle "Postacie" ("Characters") in *Napój cienisty*. Perhaps the most effective examples can be found in the poem "Srebroń," where a question is posed and answered in the same stanza:

/ . . . / Gdzie jest bezdroże? A gdzie—droga?
Gdzie—dech po śmierci? Ból—po zgonie?
Więc nie ma tchu i nie ma Boga?
I nie ma nic—a księżyc płonie? / . . . /[104]

/ . . . / Where is the trackless wilderness? And where—the track? / Where is breath after death? Pain after the end? / So there is no breath and there is no God? / And there is nothing—and the moon is aflame? / . . . /

There is no answer to the question which is answered in the form of a question, an astonished realization that there is no breath, no God, and yet the moon still shines. In this same poem, existence as well as creation are questioned. The perplexed Srebroń whispers, "Lecz po co srebrnieć?—Nie wiadomo. . . ." ("But why this silver flurry?—Nobody knows. . . .")[105] The absurdity of existence is acknowledged by the last stanza:

/ . . . / I gdy tak mówi—nicość właśnie
Kłami połyska—zła i szczera—
I jeszcze jedna gwiazda gaśnie—
I jeszcze jeden Bóg umiera.[106]

/ . . . / And while thus he speaks—nothingness precisely at this moment / Flashes its fangs—evil and bold— / And yet another star goes out— / And yet another God is dying.

Leśmian's neologism "srebrnieć" is startling. It alludes not only to stellar existence and the assimilation to it but, foremost, to poetic creation. His expansive visions are an amalgam of metaphors. "Srebroń" ("The Silvery Sparkler") is the poet himself catching "silvery mice in the net of his rhymes." While he questions the purpose of his creative "silver flurry," death and nothingness turn it to ashes, and "Srebroń," the poet-god himself, ceases to exist.

The climactic stage of Hindu influences is reached in the last volume, *Dziejba leśna* ("Forest Happening"). It abounds in Hindu phraseology and motifs. Especially apparent are paraphrases of the Upanishad doctrines of identity:

Zewsząd idę ku sobie; wszędzie na się czekam,
Tu się spieszę dośpiewnie, tam—docisznie zwlekam.
("Tu jestem" ["Here I Am"])

I go toward myself from everywhere; I await myself everywhere, / Here I rush to the end of my song, there I linger quietly. /

Już mnie nigdzie nie ma i nigdy nie będzie!—
Nie ma ciebie nigdzie, bo już jesteś wszędzie!
("Puściła po stole swawolący wianek" ["She flung her playful chaplet on the table"])

Already I am nowhere and shall never be!— / You are nowhere because you are already everywhere! /

By iść do tamtych stron, odzyskać trzeba zgon,
Zagubiony w tym bycie, co narzucił się światu.
("Zachód" ["Sunset"])[107]

To go to those regions, one must regain death, / Lost in this existence that has worked its will upon the world. /

In the final, third phase of Leśmian's poetic creation, the preoccupation with nature and existence (of which he is unsure), gives way to an intense crowding of events, occurrences, deeds (i.e., "happenings"—as indicated by the title of the last volume of poetry). This, in my judgment, is an expression of the poet's attempt to hang on to life, to existence, assuring himself of its continuity by means of intensified actions. Psychologically, the poet, threatened by nothingness, holds onto anything he can. "Wiem, że muszę wypatrzeć w nicość śniącą się drogę." "I know I must explore a road that dreams into nothingness").[108] Not sure anymore of the soul of the universe, of nature—i.e., Atma—he tries to cling to the material, tangible side of existence, to "a blade of grass." One of the poems of *Dziejba leśna* has the refrain:

/ . . . / Pokochaj zboże! Nic nie ma, prócz zboża! . . . / . . . /
Więc las pokochaj! Nic nie ma, prócz lasu!
("Miłość stroskana" ["Worried Love"])[109]

/ . . . / Fall in love with rye! There is nothing but rye! . . ./ / . . . / Therefore fall in love with the forest! There is nothing but forest!

Having always believed (as did Bergson) that existence can be measured only by creation, the poet now intensifies this aspect.

His keen observation of all the minutiae of every manifestation of occurrence—be it sound, motion, or deed—is also intensified. The following verses attest to it:

/ . . . / "Czemu dziś we wspomnieniu tak *pilnie je śledzę?*
Ruch każdy, snem sprawdzony *odtwarzam zawzięcie* . . . / . . . /
[Italics mine.]

("Krajobraz utracony" ["The Lost Landscape"])

/ . . . / "*Why today in my memories* do I watch them so intently? / Each movement, *verified in dream, I obstinately recreate.* . . ." / . . . /

/ . . . / "Byłem w miazgach mdłych mroków w tumanach bez treści—
Lecz i tam się coś krząta, szemrze i szeleści!"

("Śmierć Buddy" ["The Death of Buddha"])[110]

/ . . . / "I was in the pulp of blurred darks, in mists without meaning— / But even there something stirs, murmurs and rustles!"

The crowded occurrences and confused actions are often performed by creatures taken from folklore, by ghostly creatures of the imagination, or by some, whose names cannot be found in any dictionary. Yet, their sudden movements reveal the poet's philosophy:

Skrzeble biegną, skrzeble przez lasy, przez błonie,
Drapieżne żywczyki, upiorne gryzonie!
Biegną szumnie, tłumnie powikłaną zgrają / . . . /

Biegną tylko po to, *aby śnić istnienie.*
Świat im śni się w biegu—daleki i bliski. / . . . / [Italics mine.]

("Skrzeble biegną . . ." ["Forest creatures run . . ."])[111]

Forest creatures run, through the forest, through the fields, / Predatory little creatures, ghostly rodents! / They run squealing, swarming in a tangled pack / . . . /

They run only to dream of existence. / On the run they dream of the world—the distant and the near, / . . . /

Whether such creatures exist in life is unimportant to Leśmian. Their actions are the only necessary proof of their existence. The rodents run to "dream of existence." Only when in motion are they able to perceive the world. These hurried actions are accompanied by whirlwinds:

Zaroiło się w sadach od tęcz i zawieruch—
Z drogi!—Idzie poeta—niebieski wycieruch! / . . . /
("Poeta" ["The Poet"])[112]

The orchards teemed with rainbows and gales— / Make way!—
Here comes the poet—a heavenly wiper! / . . . /

All the poet's senses are alerted to action. This dynamism of various kinds and stages is expressed poetically by unique lexical means. Wacław Kubacki considers the crowded, confused intensity of the action

a more precise definition of "existence," because it reflects the fluidity, changeability, the instantaneousness of the manifestations of life, the mysterious, illusory, puzzling, therefore the deceptive character of existence. In short, "happenings" [deeds, actions] are the equivalent of "Mâyâ."[113]

Thus, at the end, the poet finds the only manifestation of life in Mâyâ, representing the material and deceptive feature of existence. The crowded, confused actions, the equivalent of Mâyâ may also symbolize (as implied by the word "dziejba" ["happening"]) an upheaval and an ominous cataclysm.

BERGSON

Perhaps no other philosopher, with the exception of Heraclitus, shared more profoundly the belief that existence represents a fluidity and changeability of life than did Bergson. This is perhaps one of the main reasons his philosophy attracted Leśmian most.

For him, Bergson was the greatest philosophical authority, the strongest support in crystallizing his own poetic ideology during the formative stages of his career.[114] Therefore, adding Bergson to the influences discussed previously, we are able to strengthen still further Leśmian's affiliation with the philosophical ambience representing the beginning of the twentieth century.

As mentioned earlier, Bergson exerted an extremely strong influence upon Polish intellectual life prior to the First World War (beginning about 1905). Much was written about him in scholarly philosophical journals as well as in the literary press. Most of his important works were translated into Polish.[115] The enthusiastic reception of Bergson in Poland coincides chronologically with his widespread popularity in the entire European cultural world. In Poland, Leśmian's philosophical essays represent the most outstanding manifestation of Bergson's literary acceptance.

Judging by the late dates of the translations of Bergson's works (except for *Laughter*) and by the publication dates of the poet's essays dealing with Bergson's philosophy (1910), one would assume that Leśmian must have been acquainted with these works somewhat earlier, apparently during his stay in Paris, when his poetics reached maturity. It is, however, impossible to establish the exact date, since Leśmian's only mention of Bergsonism appears in a humorous letter written in verse to Przesmycki in 1912:

/ . . . / Ilem czekał, ilem wyczuł—
Sny wypiszą mi na twarzy,
Tedy stanie snom na straży
Wiatr od mórz i górskich przyczół.

A za wiatrem stanie społem
Chór aniołów—bergsonistów;— / . . . /[116]

How long I've waited, how much I've felt— / Dreams shall etch on my visage, / Then the wind from the seas and mountain faces / Shall stand watch over my revery. /

And after the wind shall gather / A choir of angels—Bergsonists— /

This, however, was two years after the poet had written the philosophical essays expounding his views on Bergsonism. As mentioned before, Leśmian's letter from about 1900 speaks of the correlation of his ideas with those of the philosopher.

The first essay, "Z rozmyślań o Bergsonie," proves how thoroughly the poet understood and digested the philosophy of "creative evolution." It also indicates the reason for the poet's strong attraction to Bergson, whose philosophy freed him, once and for all, from the oppressive atmosphere of early Symbolism. Bergsonism was to him a philosophy of promise, future-oriented, and the incarnation of dynamism. Above all, it was rooted in myth, which Leśmian liked to compare to a rainbow and a bridge connecting man with the intuitive, with the unproven realm of being, considering it the most valuable source of creation.[117]

According to Bergson, science and metaphysics meet in the intuitive. Therefore, he urges both disciplines to turn towards myth (the product of intuition), representing the only proof of attaining the absolute. Intuition enables man to penetrate into the interior of another entity (man or object), to coincide with that part of it which comprises the unique, the ineffable, and the mysterious. The attaining of such a state, of such a union, Bergson considers the absolute. He expresses it as follows:

> Only by coinciding with the person [or thing] itself, would I possess the absolute.
>
> An absolute can only be given by *intuition*, while all the rest has to do with *analysis*.[118]

These concepts reaffirmed Leśmian's earlier belief that only through intuition can one reach a totality within oneself which, according to him, is indispensable for creating myths—poetry and art in general.

Intuition as a creative factor differs from intellect because it represents an ephemeral part of the human psyche capable of adapting itself to the constant flux of existence. The intellect, on the other hand, deals with analyses of static ideas. This conviction the poet shares with the philosopher, who maintains that the "philosophy of ideas" (belonging to the realm of intellect) is an illusion, because, in analyzing reality, the intellect uses an approach of a cinematographical mind.[119] He believes that, in contrast,

> . . . intuitive knowledge which establishes itself in the moving reality and adopts the *life itself of things* . . . attains the absolute.
>
> . . . Analysis operates in immobility, while intuition is located in mobility or, what amounts to the same thing, in duration.[120]

Therefore, it can be assumed that the "absolute," attributed to instinct, represents instinct's ability to capture pure duration by means of creative evolution. For Leśmian, the "absolute" is ahead of us, as something yet to be created. For him intensive creativity is existence in duration.

The Weltanschauung of the philosopher and the poet, as observed by Jan Błoński, is "oriented towards a creative current, towards a single, unrepeated unity of a thing in itself."[121] In Bergson's view, the duration of the universe is, of course, also identified with the creative process. Leśmian believed that creative moments in man occur only when there is a total unity of body and spirit, intuition and intellect. It is a state in which man feels most intimately bound with his own self and with the forces that created him. Bergson describes these rare creative moments as follows:

> It is into pure duration that we plunged back, a duration in which the past, always moving on, is swelling unceasingly with a present which is absolutely new. . . . We must, by a strong recoil of our personality on itself, gather up our past which is slipping away, in order to thrust it, compact and undivided, into a present which it will create by entering. Rare indeed are the moments when we are self-possessed to this extent: it is then that our actions are truly free.[122]

This quotation also reveals the convergence in Bergson and Leśmian regarding the concept of the actual process of creativity.

In his second philosophical essay, "Znaczenie pośrednictwa w metafizyce życia zbiorowego," Leśmian calls these truly free actions creative direct reality—*natura naturans.* The poet utilizes the Bergsonian philosophy of creative evolution in conjunction with his modified concept of Erigena and Spinoza—defined as *natura naturans* and *natura naturata.* Thus, Bergson became a point of departure in Leśmian's own deliberations. The poet shifts the emphasis from an opposition of matter and *élan vital* situated in the cosmic reaches of the metaphysics of social life. Just as for Bergson matter (and intellect) is the obstacle to *élan vital,* so in Leśmian's metaphysics the *homo faber* ruling over the material world in social life is the obstacle to the creative life of that society. The poet contrasts the creative state representing "direct reality" (*natura naturans*) with the state of things already created which have become "secondary reality" (*natura naturata*) by serving as a mediator in social life.[123] The objects of "the secondary reality" enter the realm of intellect and analysis as they become the mediator between the creative man and *homo faber,* who acquires them to enrich his material domain. Thus, agreeing with Błoński, one can conclude that the opposition of two entities, originally representing an ontological contrast, become in Leśmian's metaphysics rather an epistemological contrast.[124] The essay, "Znaczenie pośrednictwa, . . ." represents a summation of Leśmian's own ideology. It also demonstrates the extent to which Bergson's philosophy was utilized—what the poet retained of it, and how he deviated from it.

In his quest for the truly free creative action the poet resorts to a fictitious regression to primordiality (discussed earlier), grafting it onto the philosophy of creative evolution. For Leśmian, primitive man is the epitome of totality within himself, because in this stage there is no division between man's body and soul. Primitive man creates intuitively, his actions are free, he achieves the absolute; he is a natural poet. Leśmian considers primitive man most metaphysical because he is least intellectual, and therefore possesses an extensive perception of reality. Leśmian's turning toward nature, as toward an autonomous entity (a thing in itself), is likewise motivated by the desire to attain a unity within himself and with the power which created him—that is, nature. He believes that by reaching such an "absolute" state he can create poetry in the manner of primitive man. In his concept of the "metaphysical" state of primitive man, as well as in adopting "the myth of genesis" (a return to primordiality and nature), he deviates entirely from Bergson and arrives at his own philosophy.

However, the philosopher's supporting ideas and influence left a lasting impression upon Leśmian's creative processes. The kind of poetry he envisioned and subsequently composed, is the ultimate expression of creative evolution. It resulted from the interaction of two contrasting entities: the *élan vital*—i.e., rhythm, and matter —i.e., language. The concept of rhythm (as discussed in chapter 2) was part of the French and Russian Symbolist theories prior to the appearance of Bergsonism on the literary horizon. However, the author of *Matière et Mémoire* greatly strengthened the role of rhythm, as the immaterial, essential, moving force liberating the conceptual word. In an early work, *Essai sur les données immédiates de la conscience,* Bergson points out the importance of rhythm as an aesthetic phenomenon.[125]

It seems that Leśmian's conception of rhythm corresponds in many ways to Bergson's definition:

> The rhythm of the word does not have . . . any other objective than to reproduce the rhythm of thought.[126]

Rhythm is a phenomenon linked also to the elements of time and duration. According to Bergson, pure duration is mobility, and can be measured only by the creative act.[127] This belief is shared by Leśmian, for whom it is rhythm (the prime mover of words in creating poetry), which

> allows one to gather in the poem something that is developed and flows within and outside of the words; something which either substitutes the essence of time, or is time itself, of course understood as duration. . . [128]

Other functions of rhythm pertaining to Leśmian's poetics have been discussed earlier. The same applies to the extrapoetic attributes of rhythm.

The matter with which rhythm is confronted in the process of poetic creation is language. The convergence of Leśmian's ideas with Bergson's is especially felt in this area. Leśmian, aware of the duality inherent in language, tried to combat this problem even prior to his acquaintance with the author of *Creative Evolution.* Bergson's philosophy was instrumental in solving this complex problem. Bergson (as well as the poet) considered the word free and transferable by nature, "an external thing which the intelligence can catch hold of and cling to."[129] He realized that such a conceptualized word is unsuitable for expressing ever-changing reality. It is unable to express

> an action which is making itself across an action of the same kind which is unmaking itself, like the fiery path torn by . . . a rocket of a fireworks display.[130]

Only by coinciding with the object can the word really express the "momentary mythology"[131] of the created work.

A few quotes from Bergson will show the extent to which Leśmian's poetic language converges with the ideas of the philosopher:

> One recognizes the real, the actual, *the concrete* by the fact that it is variability itself. . . .
>
> Will not philosophy consist simply in watching oneself live, as a dozing shepherd watches the running water?
>
> This would mean getting to know the unique nature of duration, and the . . . very active . . . almost impetuous nature of metaphysical intuition. [Italics mine.][132]

Bergson's concepts of an extremely active intuition at work in an ever-changing reality are exactly what Leśmian's poetry expressed by means of poetic language.

Intensive existence, dynamism, constant becoming, flux are expressed in a unique and complex lexical way. Leśmian's neologisms and tautologies are also a poetic realization of Bergsonian intuitive observation. It represents the identification of a thing with itself, e.g., "stodoła się stodoli," "a barn barns itself" —one of many examples. (Such derivative words based on identical roots Roman Jakobson has termed "etymological figures."[133]) Leśmian is constantly observing and watching himself live, as the shepherd mentioned above. "The words covering an object convert it again into a thing"[134] and bring it from the darkness of nonexistence into existence, as was the case with language invented by the primordial man.

The dynamization of Leśmian's language was also influenced by Bergson's *Laughter*. Likewise, the drama of nonexistence, or "denied existence," expressed by means of various lexical negations, has its partial roots in Bergson's philosophy of nonexistence. Leśmian utilized Bergson's philosophy by creating his own theory of language as a means of expression in the narrow sense; his language has primarily philosophical and cognitive functions. Kazimierz Wyka's perceptive remark demonstrates the extent of the poetic realization of Bergson's ideas.

> In Leśmian it is as though the *élan vital* has penetrated into the very core of semantic categories, has stirred them and put them into motion.[135]

One can agree with the opinions expressed by numerous critics that Leśmian "poeticized" Bergson's philosophy to a large degree. This certainly applies to the concepts of the creative process, of myth, and, foremost, of language. Leśmian did not write versified tracts, but expressed his philosophical ideas by transforming the substance of poetry—language.

Accepting (at least simplistically) the premise that Leśmian's poetic ideology—especially as expressed in *Łąka*—revolves basically around a philosophical triangle (Man, God and Nature) in a manner somewhat reminiscent of Spinoza and of the Russian poet Derzhavin, we can say that Bergson acted as a catalyst in the crystallization of these ideas. In the evolutionary process, Man and Nature are at once constructive and destructive powers. This is especially true of Nature, which represents, in the process of evolution, both vitality and self-destruction; hence its transient existence. In this context God also represents a transient entity, since God is equated with Nature.

However, in the third phase of Leśmian's poetic creation his convictions concerning God remain, on the primary level, a constant—that is poetry is the true manifestation of God. Supported by the philosophy of creative evolution, they become even firmer. In a reality which represents an unceasing state of Becoming, the concept of a finite God is unacceptable. Such a God can only be an obstacle in the evolutionary current. In Bergson's definition

> God . . . has nothing of the already made. He is unceasing life, action, freedom. Creation, so conceived, is no mystery; we experience it ourselves when we act freely.[136]

This idea confirms Leśmian's belief that the creative act is diverse; the philosophy of action absorbs religion, molding it into new means of cognition to explore the mysteries of the universe. "With regard to religion [this philosophy] represents the last rapacious act."[137] Furthermore, Leśmian believes that life belongs to creative man and not to God. God has done his deed, having created this *mare tenebrarum,* and therefore is now obsolete, dead. Thus, Bergson was the final influence freeing him from any temptation of religion. (This despite the realization that Bergson's philosophy may lead to religion eventually.)

Leśmian's "iconoclasm" of the third phase, supported by Bergson's philosophy, is combined with Hinduism. In its final phase, this "iconoclasm" can be defined as agnosticism which arises as a consequence of the poet's tragic realization that each entity is unknown to the next. Furthermore, having lost all ties with nature and unable to perceive its mystery, the poet also loses his equilibrium. He is unsure of himself. He feels threatened by the chaos surrounding him. He does not know which reality to believe in:

W cienistym bezładzie Znikomek błąka się skocznie,
Jedno ma oko błękitne, a drugie—piwne, więc raczej
Nie widzi świata tak samo, lecz każdym okiem—inaczej—
I nie wie, który z tych światów jest rzeczywisty—zaocznie? / . . . /
("Znikomek" ["The Evanescent One"])[138]

In the shadowy chaos of existences the Evanescent One wanders along hobbling, / One blue eye has he—the other brown, so that he rather / Doesn't see the world the same, but differently with each eye / And doesn't know which is the real world—is it beyond seeing? / . . . /

"Znikomek" is the insignificant, evanescent man (perhaps symbolizing the poet himself). The world is a riddle and man's life an absurdity. All his actions are nonsensical. It does not really matter how "Znikomek" sees the world, or whether he sees it at all. The structure of the stanza is reminiscent of a riddle, especially the last two verses. The futility of human existence and its paradox are accentuated in the last word, which stands as a *pointe*, "Znikomek" exists in all worlds as though in absentia?—"zaocznie?" Even of this the narrator is uncertain—hence the puzzling question mark. The play on etymological figures (*oko*—"eye" and *zaocznie*—"in absentia") may also imply the *circulus viciosus* of man's existence.

The third phase of Leśmian's "iconoclasm" differs decidedly from the first, which was supported by Nietzschean ideas. In *Oddaleńcy* the "iconoclasm" was expressed by a Superman's attitude in asserting his independence of God. Although the "Distant Ones" were demiurges, in a sense they, too, were lost and recluses by choice. (Cf., the poem, *Nieznana podróż Sindbada Żeglarza* ["The Unknown Voyage of Sindbad the Sailor"]). Forced "to drag their hunger across the seas,"[139] they nonetheless exuded a vitality and a bold optimism. Their experiences were expressed in a major key. Finding the Superman's aesthetics unsuitable, the poet descends to earth to create a new existence for himself. To a certain extent he enters a second, or pantheistic, phase of "iconoclasm" in his fictitious regression to primordiality and his communion with nature. However, in the third stage of his creativity, nature becomes enigmatic to him. He feels a discord between man and nature. Longing for his own identity, he returns this time to man's "sorrowful" existence on earth and to a "private" primordiality (i.e., to the reminiscences of childhood), questioning even more than before the existence of God.

Thus, Bergson's doctrine of "the circle of divine thought [i.e., creative thought]"[140] has been fully realized in Leśmian's creative evolution. Disillusioned in his previous grandiose attempts, the poet realizes that Horace's *carpe diem* is the only reality left for man. That is why the poetry of the third phase, in contrast to the other, is expressed in a minor key—it epitomizes extreme pessimism. It should be pointed out that Leśmian's mature poetics and, especially, the last phase of his deliberations, represent, for the most part, a departure from Bergsonism proper and are the expression of the poet's own philosophy.

Now the poet turns his attention from nature to the human predicament, the new reality. Now his "distant ones" are the weak, the downtrodden, the deformed human beings, or simply "characters," grotesque creatures of his imagination.[141] (Cf., "Zmierzchun," "Śnigrobek," "Kocmołuch," *et al.*) As observed by Ludwik Fryde:

> The folk motifs subside. There is a tendency toward grotesque, dissonant effects. . . . *Napój cienisty* represents the third stage in the development of Leśmian's poetic world; *the third and last.* The creative principle constituting the basis of this [poetic] world was shaken to its foundation. [Italics mine.][142]

The new reality is "the vale of tears," which Leśmian defines in the poem, "Zły jar."

In "Zły jar," as in most of the later poems, we find a poet seeking justification for the tragedy of human fate. Few writers have expressed so powerfully the cry of anguish of suffering man:[143]

A ja wiersz ten dla świerszczy i aniołów piszę—
I tak mi źle na świecie—tak mi strasznie źle!
("Sen" ["Dream"])

And this poem I write for crickets and angels— / And things are bad for me in this world—so awfully bad!

W złym jarze człowiek blady krtań nożem przecina . . .
Więc cóż?
Sam przez się! . . . Własnoręcznie! . . .Mówią, że—Przyczyna!
Że—Nóż!
("Zły jar" ["The Evil Ravine"])[144]

In this evil ravine a man is cutting his throat with a knife . . . / So what? / Cutting his own throat . . . With his own hands . . . They say that's the Cause! / That's the Knife!

The last example leads from expressing facts of the human predicament to the events which presumably caused these facts to happen. The poet is unable to find the justification he sought, and any attempt to do so leads to absurdity. "Zły jar" is the creation of a merciless God, whom the poet reproaches. The attitude of reproach is already apparent in the latter part of the volume *Łąka:*

Rzekł Bajdała do Boga:
"O rety—olaboga!
Nie dość ci, żeś potworzył mnie, szkapę, i wołka.
Jeszcześ musiał takiego zmajstrować Dusiołka?"
("Dusiołek" ["A Choking Nightmare"])[145]

Said Bajdala to God: / "Help—for God's sake! / Isn't it enough that Thou hast monstrously created the nag, the little ox and me, / Didst Thou have to contrive such a Choking Nightmare?"

As is usually the case in Leśmian's poetry, the form expresses the idea. In order to intensify the absurdity of the situation, the poet resorts to all sorts of artistic devices. A philosophical and ethical dilemma regarding God has been expressed by the protagonist, a half-witted peasant Bajdała ("Prattler"). The problem has been set in a semifantastic plot and a stylized folkloric form. Most effective in conveying the reproach of God is the lexical aspect. One neologism *potworzyć,* originating out of a semantic duality (i.e.,—*stwarzać*—"to create," and *potworny*—"monstrous") expresses Leśmian's concept of the duality of God's creative powers. For the poet, God's creations are always associated with evil and suffering. Speaking about Leśmian's language, Kazimierz Wyka remarks:

> . . . His words [Bajdały]—("prattlers") do nothing more than lead to *absurdity the argument of* [God's] *creations* . . . God, says Leśmian, is the creator of Dusiołki ["monsters, petty demons"], if one persists, stubbornly, in the belief that *he is* a Creator.[146]

At this early stage the poet's reproach to God for man's tragic fate is still mild and in this example bears humorous overtones. The grotesque in this poem is remarkably close to Bergson's ideas on that subject as presented in *Laughter*.

This attitude will change subsequently to a bitter indictment of God, expressed in the form of theodicy, which is especially pronounced when the poetry becomes more personal, as in *Napój cienisty*. One of the many examples is the poem "Do siostry" ("To My Sister"):

Boże, odlatujacy w obce dla nas strony,
  Powstrzymaj odlot swój—
I tul z płaczem do piersi ten wiecznie krzywdzony,
  Wierzący w Ciebie gnój![147]

O God, Who flyest off to lands alien to us, / Stay Thy flight— / And clutch weeping to Thy breast this eternally wronged one, / This dungheap who believes in Thee!

God is indicted for not caring about those who believe in him and who are forever maltreated and oppressed. Where is God when man needs his support?

Recognizing that man stands alone with no eternity and no God to turn to, he squarely meets his cruel and painful destiny unafraid, and with his moral stature intact. The evil Mâyâ has destroyed his dream and he is surrounded by nothingness and illusion.

/ . . . / A już stało za drzwiami to Złe, co niweczy.
Szumy mego ogrodu nad gęstwą wszechrzeczy. / . . . /
("Modlitwa" ["A Prayer"])[148]

/ . . . / And behind the doors already stood that Evil, which annihilates / The sounds from my garden over the thicket of the universe. / . . . /

The poet does not surrender to passivity, but even challenges "nothingness":

/ . . . / A jeśli Bóg, cudaczną urażony pychą,
Wzgardzi mną, jak nicością, obutą zbyt licho,
Ja—gniewny, nim się duch mój z prochem utożsami,
Będę tupał na Niego tymi trupięgami!
("Trupięgi" ["Bast Shoes"])[149]

/ . . . / And if God, offended by my whimsical haughtiness, / Should feel contempt for me, a poorly shod nothing, / I—enraged, before my spirit should become as dust, / I would stamp these bast shoes at Him!

Wearing the bast shoes symbolizing his poverty and suffering on earth, he appears in heaven stamping his feet in defiance. The use of the defiance of the bast shoes is a folk stylization. In the *skazka* (Russian folk tale) *lapti* ("bast shoes") are not only a symbol, even their confrontation with the tsar is traditional. Here, Leśmian replaces the figure of the tsar with God.

Left with nothing but life on this earth, the self-reliant man is capable of enduring a great deal:

/ . . . / Uderzaj bezlitośnie, uderzaj dość silnie,
Bom—człowiek! Zniosę wszystko! Pomocuj się ze mną!

Kto potrafi żal dłońmi tak tłumić obiema!
Kto zdoła, gdy mu z oczu nicość jawę zmiecie,
Tak nic nie mieć, naprawdę nic nie mieć na świecie,
Jak człowiek, co nic nie ma, naprawdę nic nie ma!
("Ubóstwo" ["Poverty"])[150]

/ . . . / Strike mercilessly, strike hard enough, / For I am—man! I will endure everything! Wrestle with me! / Who can suppress such sorrow with the palms of both hands! / Who can cope, when nothingness shall sweep reality from his eyes, / Having nothing, truly nothing in the world, / Like man who has nothing, truly nothing!

Only man confronted with nothingness and poverty is able to bear it and suppress his overwhelming grief because he is stronger than God. The poet, an "incorrigible Existor" (niepoprawny Istnieniowiec")[151] clings to life in spite of its harshness. Yet, in his final act of the defiance of God, he will again challenge God and search for a third existence, which exceeds God's imagination and capabilities. This attempt is expressed in "W locie" ("In Flight") and especially in *Eliasz* ("Elijah"), poems which are apocalyptic and visionary in scope.

Realizing that everything is illusory, the poet believes that only myth is immortal. However, if myth is also an illusion, then at least the creative effort justifies human existence. The best example of this realization is his philosophical ballad "Dziewczyna," in which illusory cognition ends in catastrophe. To Wyka, the ballad represents "a praise of effort and the tragedy of existence."[152] In my opinion "Dziewczyna" can be also interpreted as the symbol of an unfulfilled myth (i.e., poetry) originating in the reveries of the twelve brothers. Even in his dedication Leśmian hints at "poetic magic." "Dziewczyna" can be also considered a continuation of the Russian cycle of Leśmian's poems: *Pesni Vasilisy Premudroi* ("Songs of Vasilisa the Wisest"). Vasilisa, the wisdom of the people, declares that she is the one who does not exist, but that her dreams exist and inspire all the giants of the world:

Dwunastu braci, wierząc w sny, zbadało mur od marzeń strony,
A poza murem płakał głos, dziewczęcy głos zaprzepaszczony.
I pokochali głosu dźwięk i chętny domysł o Dziewczynie,
I zgadywali kształty ust po tym, jak śpiew od żalu ginie . . .
Mówili o niej: "Łka, więc jest!"—I nic innego nie mówili, / . . . /

"O, prędzej skruszmy zimny głaz, nim śmierć Dziewczynę rdzą
powlecze!"—
Tak, waląc w mur, dwunasty brat do jedenastu innych rzecze.
Ale daremny był ich trud, daremny ramion sprzęg i usił!
Oddali ciała swe na strwon owemu snowi, co je kusił! / . . . /
("Dziewczyna" ["The Maiden"])[153]

Twelve brothers who believed in dreams explored the dream side of a wall, / And beyond the wall there cried a voice, a maiden's voice spent in vain, / And they fell in love with the sound of her voice and with their eager image of the girl, / And they reckoned the shape of her lips by the way her song died away in grief . . . / They said of her: "She weeps, therefore she is!"—And nothing else they said, / . . . /

"O let us swiftly crush the cold stone before death covers the Maiden with rust!— / Thus, striking the wall, the twelfth brother speaks to the other eleven. / But in vain was their labor, in vain their shoulders' link and strain! / They squandered their bodies for the dream that lured them! / . . . /

Here the brothers—believers in reveries—can be seen as twelve poet-apostles who, lured by the Maiden's voice, set out to examine the dream side of an existence they are certain of. "She weeps, therefore she is!" they say, confirming Leśmian's and Bergson's idea that where there is action there is existence. Her dying song entices them to rescue the source of their imagination. Yet, the twelve brothers fail in their effort and die. When the wall is finally demolished by the shadows of their hammers, there is nothing behind it. The Maiden was an illusion, an unfulfilled myth. The only reality left is their valorous deed, the attempt to free "poetic magic."

The only solace in this unbearable reality of life on earth are the poet's reminiscences of childhood. This theme is a link in Leśmian's creative evolution—it begins with the poem "Ze wspomnień dzieciństwa" ("From Recollections of Childhood") in *UR,* recurs in "Wspomnienie" ("Reminiscence") in the volume *Łąka* and is again taken up on *Napój cienisty* in the poem "Z lat dziecięcych" ("From Childhood Years"). It is the only compensation left him, the only reminder of the happiness, the fullness of life he experienced in the earlier stages of his work, when he communed with nature. This private primordiality is Leśmian's only means of perceiving life anew, in all its freshness. (Cf., the philosophical essay "Przemiany rzeczywistosci" "The Metamorphoses of Reality.") The realia surrounding him in childhood are described in minutest detail, thereby expanding the range of reality in the manner of the primitive man. This realism gives the poet a feeling of security, of stability. It evokes the feeling of an "intensive, limitless existence with all the fibers of his body."[154] Childhood and the minutiae of its reminiscences are the last tangible refuge in a world of nothingness!

Man, having performed his duty, must die in the world of external flux. Just as God, having created the world, becomes obsolete, so must also the poet perish, leaving behind the myth he created. But the poet has made peace with this idea and prefers a finite death to immortality. This is expressed in "Dwaj Macieje," a kind of stylized folk epic poem (bylina). Having acquired the herb of immortality, the "Dwaj Macieje" ("The Two Matthews") prove to be much more magnanimous than God, and truly humane. They give the herb to the *Płaczybóg*, "weeping God" who is much more in need of immortality, saying to him:

/ . . . / Pewniejsze dwie wieczności, niżli wieczność—jedna.
Dość Ci, Boże, źdźbło małe tego ziela spożyć,
By do drugiej wieczności bez uszczerbku dożyć. / . . . /
("Dwaj Macieje" ["The Two Matthews"])[155]

/ . . . / Two eternities are more certain than one eternity—one only. / You, God, have only to consume a bit of this herb / To reach the second eternity unscathed. / . . . /

Sandauer's interpretation of this poem is extremely fitting:

From the ruins of gods and God, visions, dreams, and incarnations—emerges—as the expression of Leśmian's final wisdom, the godless humanism of the two Matthews—who, having acquired the herb of immortality, present it to God so that they may die—finally and irrevocably—in a human way. Mortal man, having created values more lasting than the one he himself represents, attains the highest value.[156]

In his relationship to God, Leśmian utilizes Bergson's concept of duty as a support and a point of departure, arriving at a complex system of his own. God, to whom he constantly keeps returning though he denies his existence, is a much needed stimulus for the ceaseless evolutionary process of his polemics. Negation and contrast are, especially in the third phase of his creativity, the basis of his poetics, and apply almost to every aspect of it. In his negation of God's existence Leśmian, the agnostic or atheist, reasons very much in the manner defined by Jean Jacques Rousseau:

> Whereas a theist bases his reasoning only on probabilities, the atheist . . . seems to base his [reasoning] on contrasting probabilities.[157]

4

Leśmian and the Russian Contemporary Literary Scene

BACKGROUND

It is impossible, of course, to deal exhaustively with the subject of the similarities between the work of Leśmian and that of the major Russian Symbolist poets of the second generation, but it is important to indicate, however superficially, that to a certain degree Leśmian was concerned with the same themes and poetic problems that fascinated his Russian counterparts. What follows will be an attempt to describe these similarities. It is likewise impossible to name all the Russian poets with whom Leśmian shared poetic concerns. In order to demonstrate Leśmian's ties with the Russian poetic community, I have selected Andrei Bely and Viacheslav Ivanov, as they are the most representative of the Russian poets and theoreticians of the second generation.

Leśmian's whole literary Weltanschauung was closer to the Russian variant of Symbolism than to anything then existing in Poland. It had its roots in the education Leśmian received in Kiev and in the poet's natural tendencies. He was nurtured on Russian literature and culture, imbued with a deep feeling for the Russian language, and even expressed concern in a letter about the "Russicisms" in his Polish poems sent to Warsaw for publication.[1] The influence of Russian is apparent in many of his Polish neologisms. Leśmian's deep understanding of Russian culture and thought is demonstrated in his articles on Tolstoy and Konstantin Balmont. He shows a remarkable insight into the Russian soul in his letter to Stefan Żeromski about the works of Saltykov-Shchedrin, in his review of Władysław Jabłonowski's work about Russia, "Dookoła Sfinksa" ("Around the Sphinx"), and in his remarks on Dostoevsky, Turgenev, *et al.* It is pertinent to recall that the Symbolist movement in Russia was in a sense launched by Nikolai Minsky (N.M. Vilenkin) and I. Jasinsky in Kiev.[2]

Czesław Miłosz is indeed correct in his assertion that *Orchard at Crossroads* and *Meadow* revealed Leśmian as "a poet whom it was difficult to compare to any of his contemporaries."[3] I would add that it was difficult to make such comparison within the Polish literary context (especially with regard to *Łąka* ("Meadow"). Leśmian's ideas and attitudes could be expected to fit much more congenially into the Russian scene.

A definite influence exerted on young Leśmian during his residence in Kiev was that of Ivan Chelpanov (1862-1936), a famous Russian psychologist and philosopher, and a professor at the University of St. Vladimir in Kiev. As mentioned in chapter 2, while he was still a high school student, young Leśmian attended Professor Chelpanov's lectures. In his lectures, as well as in his doctoral dissertation, *Problema vosprijatiia prostranstva v sviazi s ucheniem ob apriornosti i vrozhdennosti* (written between 1896 and 1904), Chelpanov propagated the intuitive perception of time and space. He also questioned the accepted notion of causality as a cognitive form of consciousness. He believed that causality, understood as an a priori phenomenon, stifles the creative process. Speaking about symbolistic prerequisites of criticism, he contended that we ought to transfer ourselves into a realm far removed from scientific psychology, into a realm approximating the creative artistic intuition. Chelpanov's most important contribution to literary criticism is the teleological principle which he considers to be an indispensable prerequisite of criticism. In *Mozg i dusha* ("*The Brain and the Soul*"), 1900, he speaks out against the materialistic explanations of psychic phenomena. According to Bely, criticism via teleology is strongly connected with Symbolism.[4] The influence of Chelpanov's ideas on the youthful poet are already apparent in the earliest poetry, as well as in his early correspondence with Zenon Przesmycki.[5] Time and again he speaks out against causality and points to intuition as the only source of a free creative process.

Young Leśmian probably knew the works of Aleksandr Potebnia (1835-1891) already as a student of the philological *gymnasium* in Kiev, since they were an important part of the "cultural background" of that period. His early interests in philology, in Russian folklore and poetics lend credence to the assumption that the poet's ideas parallel those of Potebnia. His book *O nekotorykh simvolakh v slavianskoi poezii* (Kharkov, 1860) contained a discussion of the symbolism in Slavic folk poetry. Leśmian was probably also acquainted with such works as the first edition of *Mysl' i iazyk* (Kharkov, 1862) and there can be a strong possibility that Potebnia's book, *Iz lektsii po teorii slovesnosti* (Kharkov, 1894), and especially the chapter on myth had an impact on the poet's thinking. Furthermore, Potebnia's disciples popularized his theories by publishing them in a collection of eight volumes, *Voprosy teorii i psikhologii tvorchestva* (Petrograd-Kharkov), the early volumes of which came out in 1907. Finally, Potebnia's theories were popular with the Russian Symbolists of the second generation, especially with Bely. In his articles published in the journals *Vesy* and *Zolotoe runo,* to which Leśmian also contributed, Bely refers to various works of Potebnia, e.g., indirectly in "Printsip formy v èstetike"[6] (*Zolotoe runo,* 1906), and directly in "Lirika i èksperiment" (*Zolotoe runo,* 1909) as well as in "Magiia slov"[7] (*Simvolizm,* 1910, passim).

In view of the books owned by Leśmian that indicate the fields of his interest, a reasonable conjecture can be made that Aleksandr Veselovsky (1838-1906), Russia's foremost authority on comparative literary history and criticism who had an acknowledged influence on Bely (cf., "Magiia slov"), also influenced Leśmian's thinking (see n. 6, p. 320). In his *Istoricheskaia poètika* he speaks about the relationship of mythology to the word.

According to Veselovsky, "legends . . . are connected with metaphoric language. The creation of symbols unites knowledge, cognition, and incantation *in one word* [italics mine]."[8] He traces his concept of the magical word to the Eastern schools of esoteric wisdom. For him, natural song led to the creation of literary ballads; "the song-incantation has power over gods. . . . The incantation creates images, the word creates flesh."[9] One can discern the source of some of Bely's ideas (cf., also Veselovsky's concept of *troichnost'*, deriving from Hindu Vedantas, and ultimately adapted by Bely to the system of triads (*triedinstvo*) in his "Ėmblematika smysla").[10] Veselovsky's idea about poetic language finds an echo in Leśmian. It appears that Leśmian's predilection for the natural song and the ballad (the two predominant genres of his poetry), shows again how closely the poet approximates the ideas of the scholar.

Leśmian, whose mature poetry was a strange phenomenon on the Polish literary scene, fitted the Russian literary context as a poet and as a man. He was personally acquainted with leading figures of Russian Symbolism both of the first and the second generations. He was a close friend of K. Balmont, whom he met in Paris in 1905 and with whom he kept in close touch. Leśmian confided to the poet Jan Brzechwa, not without pride, that sending his cycle of Russian poems *Lunnoe pokhmel'e* to the journal *Vesy* (1907), he was given priority over Balmont's poems.[11] Balmont was aware of Leśmian's appreciation of his poetry,[12] and, as attested by Balmont's favorable appraisal of Leśmian's poetry in one of his later articles, the appreciation was mutual.[13] At a celebration of Balmont's departure for Mexico (1905), Leśmian met Dmitri Merezhkovsky and Zinaida Gippius, Boris Zaitsev, N. Minsky, Aleksandr Benua, and Bely.[14] In 1912, at a surprise party given at a Parisian café in honor of the twenty-fifth anniversary of Balmont's literary debut, Leśmian was present together with notable French poets.[15]

Leśmian knew Vladyslav Khodasevich and corresponded with Sergei Sokolov, the editor of *Pereval*. He also corresponded with

V. Briusov, with whom he probably was acquainted in 1901-1903, and whom he met later in Warsaw in 1914 as a war correspondent.[16] He was obviously in his own element when studying the works of such writers as Viacheslav Ivanov whose essay on *Zarathustra* he especially admired.

Russian poets considered him almost as one of their own. He was included in the well-known anthology *Chtets i deklamator* (1909 and 1913) as a Russian poet. His poetry appeared in Russian periodicals, such as *Pesni Vasilisy Premudroi* in *Zolotoe Runo,* (1906, nos. 11-12), *Lunnoe pokhmel'e* in *Vesy* (1907, no. 10), and *Volny zhivye* in *Pereval* (1907, no. 11, p. 17), where Leśmian's name was on the list of contributors.[17] It is important to note that the Russian cycle of poems *Pesni Vasilisy Premudroi,* written in 1905, is a metapoetic work expressing Leśmian's mature poetic creed while in his Polish poetry of the same period he is still groping for direction (as in the cycle *Oddaleńcy* ("The Distant Ones" written at the same time.) This would indicate that it was perhaps easier for the poet to crystallize his ideas in Russian than in Polish. A drama *Vasilii Buslaev,* written in 1907, the manuscript of which was supposedly sent or brought personally by Leśmian to Briusov, was never published. Another proof that Leśmian's poetry was known to Russian poets and readers is the following announcement:

> The Polish poet Bolesław Leśmian *known also in Russian Literature* [italics mine], is preparing a translation of K. Balmont's poems, which will be published together with critical essays on his creative work.[18]

Later specialists in Russian poetics have likewise indicated that Leśmian is properly placed among Russian poets, e.g., Chizhevsky in his article, "Bolesław Leśmian als russischer Dichter"[19] and Johannes Holthusen, who includes Leśmian in the anthology of Russian Symbolist poetry as a Symbolist of the second generation.[20]

Perhaps the most prominent Russian literary ties detectible in Leśmian's poetry should begin with the poetry of Fedor Tiutchev and Afanasi Fet, the poets most admired by the young Russian Symbolists. Particularly amenable to Leśmian's poetic views were the pantheistic concept of nature, the juxtaposition of the state of the human soul and natural phenomena, the discovery of a second, extrarealistic world which Tiutchev drew from the philosophy of Schelling. Ideas originating in his work which were of particular attraction to young Leśmian included Tiutchev's notions on man's duality and his illusory existence. Echoes of these concepts are not hard to detect in various and later works by Leśmian, as in the introductory remark to his "Z rozmyślań o poezji" ("Treatise on Poetry"), where he notes (paraphrasing Nietzsche): "Whatever one would say about poetry is a mistake."[21]

This aphorism echoes Tiutchev's much-quoted verse from his poem "Silentium": "Mysl' izrechennaia est' lozh" ("A thought once uttered is a lie"), indicating the limitation of the word to express the mystery of the soul. This concept is shared by Leśmian in an early poem "Niedopita czara" ("An Undrained Cup"): "O! wszyscy o tym wiedzą aniołowie, / Jak trudno duszę wypowiedzieć w słowie!"[22] ("O well, all angels know, / How difficult it is to express the soul in a word!"). This is a sudden, somewhat helpless confession within a poem oversaturated with lofty words originating in Polish and Russian Romanticism and the excessive lyricism of Decadence. Tiutchev starts and ends his poem with an apostrophe:

Molchi, skryvaisia i tai
I chuvstva i mechty svoi— / . . . /
Est' tselyi mir v dushe tvoei
Tainstvenno—volshebnykh dum; / . . . /
Vnimai ikh pen'iu—i molchi! . . .[23]

Be silent, conceal thyself and hide / Thy feeling and thy dreams / . . . / There is in thy soul a whole world / Of mysterious and enchanted thoughts; / . . . / Harken to their singing and be silent!

We find much the same idea in Leśmian's later, programmatic poem "Rozmowa" ("A Conversation") between the body and the soul (presumably that of the poet):

/ . . . / Milcz! Nie mówi się prawdy, lecz bez słów się śpiewa.
Kłamie ten, co zna słowa, a nut nie pamięta. / . . . /[24]

Be silent! One does not tell the truth but one sings without words. /
He lies, who knows the words but remembers not the tune. / . . . /

Here the flesh tries to convince the spirit that they share the same path. The magical thoughts of the soul were understood by Tiutchev as "songs," as *true* poetry. This notion is expressed by Leśmian, in whose aesthetics to sing is synonymous with inspired poetic creation. That is why he shall forever invent words capable of expressing *the song without words.*

The two fateful themes in the poetry of the Russian master, the *Abgrund* and the *Urgrund* (inspired by Schelling's *Identitätsphilosophie* are basic for Leśmian's poetic world. The "abyss" lurking beneath the colorful rug of the cosmos creates *Angst* in Tiutchev's soul. In Leśmian's poetry the ever-present "abyss" associated with the image of God evokes equally torturous anxiety. The *Urgrund* however has in Leśmian a positive value. Primordiality becomes the basis for Leśmian's aesthetics. The theme of nature and love is expressed by Leśmian, as in Tiutchev in a highly intensified method.[25] Tiutchev's desire to merge with nature, as with a revitalizing, divine and universal entity, represents also for Leśmian "the communion of the perishable with the eternal, the time-ridden with the timeless."[26] Leśmian's poetic evolution is also analogous with that of Tiutchev.

In the poetry of Fet, which Leśmian could not recite without tears, he found the Russian's concentration on the elusive "moments" of existence, his musicality, his fluid spontaneity, lucidity, and stark plasticity particularly attractive. Leśmian believed that a poet mush chisel his words to the exact dimensions and requirements of the elusive, unrepeatable moment. Leśmian's intuitive apprehension of elusive reality was in fact identical to Fet's (much admired by Tolstoy). "When I speak I stop thinking"[27] Leśmian once said to Tuwim. As in Fet's poetry, we find in Leśmian the rare phenomenon where the poetic material (the components) and the finished product express the quintessence of the poet's creed. This must be particularly due to the quality of the word, its vivid concreteness and musicality. Because of the latter, Leśmian (like Tolstoy) considered Tiutchev's and Fet's poetry, in some ways even above Pushkin's.[28] There is also a certain similarity in the personal, emotional lives of Tiutchev, Fet, and Leśmian, which inspired all three poets to create the most memorable cycles of erotics ever written by men in an advanced age.

Leśmian was influenced by Celtic and Slavic folklore, but especially by Russian *byliny* (epic poetry) and fairy tales (*skazki*).[29] The source of much of this material was Afanas'ev's *Vozzreniia drevnikh slavian na prirodu.* Folkloric devices common to the *byliny* and *skazki* appear regularly throughout Leśmian's poetry; nature is the nature depicted in folklore. It is an autonomous, animated entity, not representing any particular native *paysage.* This also explains why his poetry did not fit traditional Polish poetry in which nature usually served as a background.

Leśmian was a Symbolist. Like the Russian Symbolists of the second generation he did not consider Symbolism a literary school but an attitude toward past literatures and a means of improving the future of mankind. This view was espoused by both Ivanov and Bely; the latter writes:

> Symbolism is at once Classicism, Romanticism, and Realism. It is Realism insofar as it reflects reality. . . . It is Romanticism, insofar as it is a vision corrected by experience . . . it is Classicism for unifying form and content.[30]

There is ample evidence that Ivanov, Bely, and Leśmian all probably relied, in this view, on the ideas expressed by Tancrède De Visan in his introduction to "Paysages introspectifs, poèmes, avec un Essai sur le Symbolisme" which Ivanov reviewed in 1904 (*Vesy,* no. 10). René Ghil also provided a lengthy commentary on De Visan's article for the third issue of *Vesy* in 1905.[31]

De Visan presented his radical views on Symbolism, which, in poetry, had previously been associated with an entirely different meaning. He considered Symbolism, not as a literary school, but as a lyrical attitude corresponding to contemporary thought, encompassing all its levels: the scientific, the philosophical, the religious, and the artistic. At the same time, Symbolism was, in his opinion, deeply rooted in the past:

> The Symbolist poet unveiling the ideas hidden behind forms feels naturally attracted toward ancient myth and the old national legends. . . . For the Symbolist mythology contains more truth than our history textbooks.[32]

Discussing the importance of myth, the French poet quotes Novalis: "Alles poetische muss märchenhaft sein."

De Visan considers the Symbolist poet a metaphysician because of his concern with the immediate data of consciousness, with the reality of the living, intuitive content of experience. The role of the Symbolist poet, according to De Visan, lies in disseminating sublime truth. The poet possesses the secret of teaching the masses, and he ought to raise the level of their cultural and ethical standards. The Frenchman warns, however, against sacrificing the demands of true art to fulfill this noble social task. Yet, to him it is far "greater than the works of philosophers, and of fanatics of *pure reason* [knowing that such a noble act] will satisfy Tolstoy. . . ."[33] The Symbolist poets have, in his opinion, the capacity for

> communion with nature. They desire to express the inexpressible . . . to fuse their soul with the universal conscience, in order to feel . . . the pulsation of the matter, the respiration of the world.[34]

Like Ferdinand Brunetière, De Visan considers the symbol as a means of communicating the abstract by materializing it. The sole purpose of a symbol is, in fact, to manifest to the masses physically that which is accessible only to a chosen few. "Its object is to incarnate the idea."[35] The poetic word is more than a mode of expression, it represents a goal in itself.

De Visan's views on Symbolism are echoed by Leśmian, who was in essential agreement with Ivanov and Bely. In the interview with Edward Boyé, when asked whether he was an active Symbolist during his stay in Paris, the center of the movement, Leśmian replied:

I was fascinated by Symbolism that was none other than Romanticism, which was, in turn, none other than Greek tragedy in many cases. One of the Russian authors says [Via. Ivanov, in "Dve stikhii v sovremennom simvolizme"] that each century draws upon its own cosmos which after a while to following generations appears to be a fantastic reverie, as the Greek cosmos, let us say, is for us. Meanwhile, the characters drawn from this cosmos, such as the Prometheuses, the Herculeses, the Theseuses were just as real for the Greeks as Madame Bovary, Père Goriot, and Anna Karenina are for us. Today's cosmos demands a different reality than the cosmos of the Greeks.[36]

Leśmian, realizing that a given man and a given truth are realities only to given epochs, thought it possible to return intellectually to the past, to discover there the original truth of that time, and to refurbish it for application to contemporary situations. The subsequent discussion of Leśmian's ties with Bely and Ivanov will demonstrate that the views of the three regarding the role of the Symbolist poet and of the function of the Symbol are the same as those of De Visan.

ANDREI BELY

It is amazing that Leśmian and Bely were similar in poetic attitudes, themes, and even resembled one another somewhat in outward appearance and inner characteristics, a fact which may help to understand certain aspects of their work. Both were small, blond, blue-eyed, ethereal, cerebral, and aristocratic. Fedor Stepun saw in Bely a "spirit flying over Moscow."[37] Both were hyperactive, charismatic, excellent raconteurs, birdlike, and child-like in the charming sense. Both gesticulated with their expressive hands. Nikolai Valentinov described Bely as having "a head of a cherub, wings of an angel, and nothing more."[38] Aleksandr Blok's image of Bely, according to Oleg Maslenikov, was that he was the least physical of all Russian poets. Marina Tsvetaeva identified Bely with the spiritual rather than with the physical world, and D. S. Mirsky compared him to "an undisciplined and erratic Ariel."[39] According to Zaitsev, Konstantin Mochulsky, and Valentinov, he was like Prince Myshkin (in *The Idiot*), or a *iurodivyi.* Leśmian's friend, the philosopher Franz Fiszer called him "an idiot," to which the poet replied: "Yes, but by the grace of God."[40]

Perhaps because of their respective home environments, both precociously manifested a split personality. Finding in daydreams their only escape from unacceptable reality, both fled as juveniles to art. Both confronted the dilemma of living in a society which mystified and disgusted them; both began working in their own dream world, which became their true reality. Both were torn between a scientific apprehension of the world and their artistic responses to the world; rational and irrational impulses dueled continually in the poets' minds. Both were obsessed with the desire to examine nature and the cause of everything empirically and minutely. They were baffled in their search for a purpose to man's existence and consequently steeped themselves in philosophy, hoping to fashion an answer to life's enigmas from different philosophies. Both Bely and Leśmian were beset by the desire to know and to believe.[41] Yet, both realized (Leśmian at the end of the second creative stage of his life, and Bely by 1903) the futility of their transcendental belief and concluded that no absolute exists. Nevertheless, they continued to search for an absolute. Leśmian shared with Bely the belief that the modern age had deprived man of individuality; both consequently rebelled against "modernity," hoping to reestablish the importance of the individual in the Renaissance sense.[42]

Maslenikov has noted that Bely wanted to reassert "the validity of intuitive revelation and mystery, to give the value of imagination its due"[43] which could, with equal justification, be said of Leśmian. Like Bely, Leśmian began first with the assertion of his own individuality; he returned to himself in order to rise above the Philistines. In order to reestablish the validity of their intuitive knowledge, both poets determined to build their philosophies on irrational bases, on myth born of intuition. (Bely, however, was, in the beginning, a neo-Kantian.) Both found themselves suspended over a "precipice" where the will to believe clashed with skepticism.

I have enumerated a number of close similarities between Bely and Leśmian without pretending to have provided an exhaustive summary. In the interest of accuracy, approximate similarities should be noted. Both poets, as did others of their epochs, saw in mystery the source of all creativity, both wanted to interpret art as a religion. In this instance a crucial difference in religious interpretation of art should be noted: Bely viewed art as a religion, a sacrament, as theurgy; Leśmian was predominantly a pantheist, an agnostic who viewed God as manifested through ceaseless creation. For Leśmian (as expressed in "Z rozmyślań o Bergsonie") God was, in fact, art.

In their retreat from civilization and its presumed accomplishments (which they felt were in actuality stifling) there were discernible differences in the avenues of retreat taken by the two poets. With ephemeral deviations (e.g., Bely's excursion ca. 1904 into neoprimitivism) Bely immersed himself in philosophy after his ideological and personal crisis to find solace as well as answers to the persistent questions concerning the human predicament. Leśmian, who always felt exceptionally consistent affinities with nature, steadily followed an artistic path back into primordiality. The primordial existence conceived in poetry offered the poet an artistic state of Nirvana which did not carry over into his material life. Ultimately, this Nirvana failed when the poet realized that such imagined assimilation cannot provide an answer to the question of why men live.

We can observe a similarity of influences in the creative processes of the two poets. Bely's first "Symphony" was created under the influence of Nietzsche's *Thus Spake Zarathustra* and the Upanishads, the same influences are apparent in the formative years of Leśmian's poetics. In the early poems, *Sad rozstajny,* we discern the Eastern influences, and Nietzsche's in the cycle of *Oddaleńcy.* A chronological parallel can be drawn between Bely's ascent to the beyond, expressed poetically in the ecstatic tones (both in mood and in hue) of *Zoloto v lazuri,* and Leśmian's similar flights described in the cycle *Oddaleńcy* (ca. 1904). This is a period of myth-creating for Bely. The poet is enraptured by nature. This exuberance is mixed with religious ecstasy, resulting in dynamic "crystallized myths," accompanied by tempestuous elements, the thunders and the brilliance of the sun. Bely attains a prophetic pathos, when he describes the fateful theme of the end. Carried by the spirit over millenia, he sees through the "mist of the centuries, the light of common resurrection."[44] The prophet soars in the azure calling others to join in the feast on the summit:

/ . . . / V svetlyi mig uslyshym zvuki
Otkhodiashchykh bur',
Molcha sviazhem v pesne ruki,
Otletim v lazur'!
(From "Nash Arno" ["Our Arno"])[45]

/ . . . / At that radiant moment we shall hear the sounds / Of retreating storms, / Silently we shall join our hands in song, / We shall soar into the azure!

Yet the prophet and creator of cosmic symbols gets dizzy at these heights. In *Vozvrat* ("The Return," the third symphony), disgusted with the greed of the oppressed who have come to share in his feast, he turns into a Lucifer suspended over the precipice.

In Leśmian's *Oddaleńcy* the myth creating and the exalted mood are not religiously inspired. The *Oddaleńcy* like Zarathustra are Supermen, "iconoclasts," demiurges who gather to feast in the azure, toasting each other with a goblet filled up to the brim with God whom they replaced:

/ . . . / Za tę całą drużynę zgiełkliwą i rojną,
Co otuchę donośnym wezwałaby rogiem—
Za ich żywot pokrętny i śmierć niespokogną
Wznoszę kielich, po brzegi pieniący się bogiem! . . .
("Toast świętokradzki" ["The Sacrilegious Toast"])[46]

/ . . . / To that whole noisy and animated band, / That would muster their hopes with a resounding horn— / To their twisted life and restless death / I raise a chalice foaming at the brim with God! . . .

The Supermen, like Bely's magus, become disenchanted with their lonely heavens, and the satanic mood takes over. After their exuberant flights, like Icarus, both poets plunge precipitously back into the *mare tenebrarum.*

Both poets were united in their artistic relationship to the literary heritage of Gogol. Bely and Leśmian, like the great Russian master, viewed life as a grotesque play of absurdities, filled with puppetlike, wax-masked, figurants, as a theater in which the inanimate is miraculously animated and where the natural yields without opposition to the supernatural. Gogol's extended metaphors, his subcurrents of negations, his puns—means of reflective absurdities—continually echo in the two poets' works. Thus, generally speaking, Gogol's animate "Nose," for instance, is not essentially different from Leśmian's animate "Palm" or Bely's red, animate Dominoes. Using a synecdoche or a metonymy these writers, by taking a shortcut, are able to express the absurdity, the suffering, the chaos of human life.

Although it is not my intention to discuss Leśmian's prose, it is perhaps in his prose that Gogol's influence is most prominently visible. This influence is especially evident in *Klechdy polskie* ("Old Polish Fairy Tales," 1914), where the structure and subject matter are like that of *Vechera na khutore bliz Dikan'ki.* In Leśmian's correspondence he expresses not only his admiration of Gogol's subject matter and narrative techniques, but also of Gogol's linguistic peculiarities. He also considers that in writing the *Klechdy* he has achieved an artistic conquest of the Ukraine.[47] Some aspects of Gogol's art are of considerable significance in Leśmian's creative evolution. (However, this topic requires a separate study.) The folkloric sources, the mixture of the natural with the supernatural in the *Klechdy polskie* act as a link and an overture to the realization of his poetic creed in *Łąka* ("The

Meadow"). Bely's appreciation of Gogol is well known. His prose, especially *Serebrianyi golub'*, evokes the Gogolian atmosphere. Mirgorod is like Celebeevo. He also recreates the pathetic rhythm of the great master's tirades reminiscent of *Strashnaia mest'*. (Cf., also for the same reason early Leśmian's "Baśń o rycerzu Pańskim" ["The Tale of the Lord's Knight"], *Legendy tęsknoty*, *UR*.)

Leśmian's views on rhythm, not as mere metric device, but as world-view were not completely matched by Bely's notions. Bely initially experimented with formal objectives in mind (e.g., finding more effective vehicles for his ideas) but later his formal investigations were paradoxically placed in the service of cosmic speculations. Especially during the period of his interest in occultism and anthroposophism. Ultimately he returned to a more formalistic stance. Both poets regarded themselves as "bearers of rhythm."[48]

As pointed out during the discussion of the "cultural background" of the period, matters concerning language and *the word* were central to the Weltanschauung of the second-generation Russian Symbolists. Doubtless under the influence of Potebnia as well as Veselovsky, both Bely and Leśmian realized the duality of the word which was to serve both everyday and poetic functions. For Leśmian as well as for Bely, words were "the flesh"[49] of art, the magic which calls objects into existence by the process of naming alone. Regarding this concept, both poets behave as though endowed with supernatural powers. As with primitive man who, by naming an object "created it," so Leśmian, too, acts as the natural poet, for in creating a word he creates a natural myth. In "Magiia slov" Bely affirms this very principle:

> By means of a word I subjugate a phenomenon; the creation of living speech is always a struggle of man with hostile elements. . . . Living speech preconditions the existence of humanity itself. . . . Poetry, cognition, music, and speech represent a unity. . . . Living speech was magic and the people . . . using it were beings who bore the stamp of communion with the deity.[50]

In the process of naming, the collective consciousness of man unites with nature's consciousness. In the view of both poets, this unity is only possible for a creator, for only he is capable of naming. The creation of each word is accompanied by a sound expressing the temporal and spatial relationship between man's inner self and the outer world. Words have other functions, for in creating a neologism man is able to give a new existence to an object. Like Leśmian, Bely considered language a natural myth, a concept central to the theories of Veselovsky and Potebnia. Language is therefore endowed with "an ontological existence."[51] The "magic" of a neologism, for example, lies in the fact that by rejuvenating or transforming a word and applying it to an object or experience we create, in fact, a new entity. Thus Bely and Leśmian insisted on concrete symbols (nonallegorical) for application to only one phenomenon, because in the evolutionary process everything is in a state of flux and therefore every phenomenon is unique and unrepeatable (cf., Ivanov's concept of two kinds of Symbolists—the Idealist-Symbolist and the Realist-Symbolist—would of course embrace such poets as Leśmian, Blok, etc.).

Concrete symbols, in Leśmian's view, could be discovered only through intuition.[52] Bely and Leśmian believed the symbol to be an indivisible unit of form and content; they thought of it as imperative to the artist's efforts to combine life and creative work. In fact they believed that life ought to resemble art. Bely said:

> For me the world is a fairy tale; the childish "I" subjugates itself to an unknown command, it creates mythology; thus the world appears . . . created by art.[53]

For Leśmian rhythm was an outlook on life: rhythm preceded the word and constitutes the main nerve of all manifestations of life. It was for Leśmian a means of attaining a specific aesthetic reality which gave his poetry the semblance of a philosophical theory of cognition. According to Bely, the truth of literature grew out of vital elemental rhythm. In this concept Bely seems to have been influenced to a certain degree by Bergson's idea of *élan vital,* for it is rhythm that is the force behind the material (the word) allowing the poet to express the musical rhythm of his own, unique soul. Creative art is a manifestation of the soul's unique rhythm according to Nietzsche, Novalis, and, ultimately, Bely; consequently we can distinguish one poet from the other. (Noteworthy in this respect are Bely's "symphonies," not only for their novelty of genre, but for their symphonic variations of rhythm.)

Closely related to the concept of rhythm, and inherent in language, is music. Nietzsche's "spirit of music" was adhered to by the second generation of Symbolists, but with a different connotation; it was not the empty mellifluence thought to be characteristic of the works of Decadents. Music and rhythm had a mystical meaning for both Bely and Leśmian. Bely said that music symbolizes what later becomes incarnate in life.

> By means of music one invites or calls upon the heavenly and dark powers to become totally incarnated. This is why music is magic and why every magic is musical.[54]

Bely applied his theories on music and rhythm in his reevaluation of Russian literature of the nineteenth century, which he thought patently religious. He called Gogol, Tolstoy, Dostoevsky, and Nekrasov "musicians of words" and "preachers." All of these great writers, according to Bely, demanded a transformation of life. They demonstrated that form and content are indivisible.[55] Leśmian's views were more modest. Music, combined with rhythm, was the elemental part of poetry. It is not unlikely that the sonorities of the Russian language may have influenced Leśmian, who was extremely attentive to rhythm and sensitive to musicality of verse. Leśmian, like Bely, believed that music expresses the constant Becoming, because it represents the noumenal world. Consistent with his aesthetics based on folkloric stylization, he considered verse devoid of musicality to be merely prose, because for him "The world perceived through music is closer to truth than when perceived by means of dry logic."[56]

For Leśmian, as well as for what he envisioned as the natural, primitive man-poet, rhythm and music had to be incantation, it had to appeal to the mnemonic faculties of the most primitive listener. Like Bely, he thought that art should aim at becoming the means of transforming the future.

Leśmian would agree with Bely that the decline of old cultures is accompanied by "the cult of the word." The living word (neologisms in art), according to Bely, is able to revitalize the dead words of the past in order to accommodate the new era. He urged, therefore, the return to "healthy barbarism." He says, in fact, "We ought to be barbarians."[57] Leśmian thought of words as a rainbow bridge uniting the past with the future.[58]

In general, all of the two poet's concepts pertaining to artistic devices correspond closely. This is largely true for themes and motifs (especially of Leśmian's early period), not discussed here. Both poets saw in art the only salvation of mankind in the future. Though they recognized that this notion was naively idealistic, they felt sure that naïveté and idealism bring man happiness; that future happiness was to be brought about by intuition, and not by cognition.

As we have seen, the earliest philosophical influences on Bely were Nietzsche's *Thus Spake Zarathustra*,[59] the Upanishads, and Gogol. The same can be said for the influences on the early works of Leśmian; however, just like Leśmian, Bely had drawn upon many philosophical sources. But perhaps unlike Leśmian, Bely is generally considered primarily a neo-Kantian in the formative stages of his career. (The Western poets who influenced them both were Poe and Baudelaire.)

Leśmian did not share Bely's inclinations toward Vladimir Solov'ev's theories of Sophia, that medieval and Goethean, feminine embodiment of the earth-soul. For him, the soul of the earth was overshadowed by the wisdom of the people which he embodied in the figure of Vasilisa Premudraia, a positive character in Russian *skazki* ("fairy tales"). Bely attempted to fuse a mystical revelation with the theory of cognition and Solov'ev's philosophy, but he found that all of this led to tragedy and failure. The Russian demiurge was forced to return to earth and devote his energies to Russia's primitive people. Sophia was replaced ultimately by Mother Russia. He turned toward that Dostoevskian notion that the essence of Mother Russia lay in suffering. (Cf., with similar ideas about suffering as a source of purification in Leśmian's views.) Bely's return to earth from his transcendentalism can be compared in certain aspects to Leśmian's ultimate return to earth from his myth of primordiality. Like Blok, however, Leśmian was much more sincerely concerned with the actual fate of downtrodden oppressed people than were those Symbolists who expressed merely theoretical concern for the disinherited. This was manifested in his way of life, in his poetry, and in his theories. He considered modern society inhuman, detached from true reality, and empty, yet he makes the following remark:

> This will seem a painful paradox, filled with sarcasm, that only the complaints of the moaning beggars . . . the sound coming from their chests hollowed by starvation are directly connected with real life. Only their tortured voices, and shaky movements are capable of filling that emptiness of society, of reviving it, of making it bearable, and of justifying its existence.[60]

The consistency of Leśmian's philosophical pronouncements and his art (cf., "Pieśni kalekujące" "Maimed Songs" *et al.*) is evident even in the way he expressed his humanism; in referring to physically maimed people he creates a correspondingly "maimed" verbal texture of puns, slapdash approximations, etc.

The quest for humaneness actually permeated Leśmian's entire work. His total preoccupation seems to be how to get away from the faceless, heartless mass of "gray men" dominating society, fighting for their own existence and for materialistic acquisitiveness, while forgetting the beauty of human nature and the human soul. This is why Leśmian retreats in his art to primeval times where men were part of the cosmos and nature, where the simple wisdom of ordinary men prepared them far better to cope with the realities and demands of their lives. Consequently, he infused his art with folkloric aspects and elements from ancient Slavic mythology. He believed that the plain folk can, in their simple wisdom, adjust better to life's tragedies, through laughter, the grotesque, and through their close relationship with nature. The maimed and the crippled were not created just to bedevil his imagination. Through physical or psychological deprivations they are demonstrated to have been singled out for torment by a merciless God. They are therefore believed by the folk to be closer to real spirituality, mysticism, and, perhaps, to saintliness. This is a particularly Russian imprint on Leśmian's thinking, deriving from the Russian concept of the *iurodivye*.[61]

This very attitude is well developed, if somewhat messianically and apocalyptically, in Bely's poetry, as, for example, in "Otchaian'e":

Dovol'no: ne zhdi ne nadeisia—
Rasseisia, moi bednyi narod!
V prostranstvo padi i razbeisia
Za godom muchitel'nyi god!

Veka nishchety i bezvol'ia.
Pozvol' zhe, o rodina mat',
V syroe, v pustoe razdol'e,
V razdol'e tvoe prorydat':— / . . . /
(From the cycle, *Rossiia* ["Russia"])[62]

Enough: don't wait, don't hope— / Disperse, my hapless people! / Fall and shatter in space / Year after torturous year! /

Ages of poverty and bondage. / O Motherland, I beg you, / In thy dank, in thy barren expanse, / In thy expanse let me weep. / . . . /

This messianic spirit echoes Tiutchev's poem:

Êti bednye seleniia,
Êta skudnaia priroda—
Krai rodnoi dolgoterpenia,
Krai ty russkogo naroda! / . . . /[63]

These wretched villages, / This meager landscape, / My native land long suffering, / Thou land of the Russian people! /

It also appears in the works of Dostoevsky, Nekrasov, and Ivanov. Bely and Ivanov anticipated that the new dawn (or the "third coming," as they called it) would ultimately come out of the Christlike downtrodden masses. Such Polish literary authorities as Artur Sandauer and Mieczysław Jastrun, Jacek Trznadel, and Marian Pankowski have indicated that they are well aware that the Russians' mystical beliefs provided a basis for Leśmian's humanism.

In his early theoretical articles, many of which have been included in *Simvolizm* (1910), Bely sought support in various philosophies to clarify the nature of the symbol, symbolism, culture, and the role of art. He considers ideal poetry expressed by the incarnated word to be a fusion of the image with the symbol. His most serious and central quest, however, was for an answer to the perplexing problem of justifications for human existence. He was able to establish certain doctrines of Symbolism and ideas about art.[64] He saw Symbolism primarily as an attitude with historiosophic hues, and postulated that by reevaluating the past, mankind would be able to solve its future problems. The transformation of human life, according to Bely, could be realized only through art, which he called "the mystery of life."[65] Art would ultimately replace religion. Art as the new religion would replace philosophy. Initially relying on science and philosophy for answers to his questions, Bely grew disillusioned in their efficacy, for they failed to provide him with clearly defined answers. His belief that intuition and myth ought to be the basis for philosophy and science was shared by Leśmian. The disillusioned Bely returned to earth, his Slavophile tendencies intensified; Russia in its uncontaminated, natural state became his main concern. Now he believed that

The artist finds the authentic incarnation of a symbol in nature. It is nature and not imagination that is the forest of symbols.[66]

This idea was expressed in one of his essays of the collection *Lug zelenyi* ("The Green Meadow"), a collection which shows how well, in many ways, Leśmian fits within the framework of the Russian literary scene. In contrast to Young Poland, the second generation of Russian Symbolists, especially Bely and Ivanov, returns to the past and defines Russian literature as mystically, musically, and historiosophically oriented.

Bely thought of song as the underlying factor of all literature in Russia, as the tie between past and future, the goal of which is the communal sharing of joy and understanding. In *Lug zelenyi* Bely, like Leśmian in "Znaczenie pośrednictwa. . . ." expresses a belief prevalent at that time, that contemporary society and science kill the creative individual,[67] and that Russia's future happiness lay only in the return to the "green meadow," the uncontaminated Russia of the past. (Cf., with Leśmian's *Łąka*—"The Meadow.") Bely, at the time of writing *Lug zelenyi*, was paradoxically crossing the path of Leśmian's final developmental stage, that is, while Leśmian was progressing from nature as primordial Nirvana to a "mortal," down-to-earth life with its "private primordiality" and reminiscences of childhood, Bely was returning from his own ego to Mother Russia.

Having primarily discussed points of positive contact and various parallels between the theories of the two poets, a few words should be addressed to the problem of the divergences of their artistic attitudes. Leśmian's art is a more consistent and accurate mirror of his Weltanschauung, while Bely's sometimes yielded distorted images; it is important to stress that, ultimately, the Russian poet was forced to call himself a "false prophet."

Leśmian's "immanent poetics" (poetic creation) can serve as a testimony to his aesthetics even if he had never written any philosophical essays. Unlike Bely (and Ivanov), he did not consider himself a theoretician and was, in fact, opposed to programs (see his correspondence with Przesmycki). His theoretical formulations were not intended to be programmatic.

Unlike his Russian counterparts he was not a leader, nor was he even acknowledged as a major poet. Although he believed that art has a special place in society, he attributed no special glory to the ego of the poet; he seldom employed the lyrical "I" (and then mostly in his early creative period). Bely, on the other hand, subjectivized his art to the highest degree, making his work largely autobiographical. Relying on objective, narrative techniques, Leśmian often resorted to stylized epics, folksongs, and ballads in which his lyrical "I" neither appeared, nor promoted conclusions. However, the Russian poet did not use folk stylization in his verse as a vehicle for his narrative techniques. Only in his later poetry, beginning with *Napój cienisty* ("Shadowy Potion") did Leśmian develop a more personal note.

The idea that the poet should live Symbolism as proclaimed in Bely's and Ivanov's theoretical essays could not survive application to the poets' actual lives. This is particularly true in the case of Bely. Leśmian put all his beliefs into practice. Unlike Bely, Leśmian never regarded any literary movement as a basis for his art; therefore he could not be as disappointed in the second generation of Russian Symbolism as Bely was. Leśmian chose not to constrict his convictions with names. Symbolism was for Bely, an intuitive revelation of truth, a universal, infallible cognitive principle. Leśmian believed in creative evolution and a changing reality, ("Metamorphoses of Reality") in which he foresaw his evolutionary creative development to the very end.

VIACHESLAV IVANOV

The second most influential and prominent leader of the Russian Symbolists, Ivanov was not a man of such violent extremes as Bely. He was a man of immense erudition, a connoisseur of antiquity, German philosophy, a student of the German historian Theodor Mommsen. His stability, affability, and erudition were recognized by the Symbolist poets, who looked up to him as to their leader. He, in fact, reigned in his "Tower" in St. Petersburg from 1905 to 1911. In contrast to Bely he was more consistent and was able to define his aesthetics in a clear manner. The consistency of convictions, a Renaissancelike erudition can serve as preliminaries for comparing Ivanov and Leśmian. In their attitude towards the first generation of Symbolists they are in unison.

Ivanov considered Decadence merely a literary school preoccupied with the aesthetics of an art expressing both exaltation and *Langweile.* He defined Decadence as "being the last of a series."[68] This definition echoes the ideas expressed by the Italian philosopher of the eighteenth century, Giambattista Vico, and presents further evidence of Ivanov's great philosophical erudition.[69] He deplored ego-oriented Decadent poets. Like the young Nietzsche (his greatest philosophical authority), Ivanov viewed the "egotistic artist not (as) a source of art but a hindrance."[70] Such sentiments closely correspond to the ideas of Leśmian expressed at a very early stage of his career, appearing with particular prominence in his correspondence. For Ivanov, as for Leśmian (and Bely), art was the incentive of life. In this also Ivanov was a disciple of Nietzsche who, rejecting the quietism of Schopenhauer, proclaimed that

> Art is a great stimulus of life. How then can it be understood as a thing devoid of intention and goal, as art for art's sake?[71]

Art, and especially poetry, had consequently to fulfill a great mission. Infused with music it was to become the religion of the future. Zarathustra said: "Heal thy soul with song, for creating . . . is the great salvation from suffering and an alleviation of life."[72] Like Bely and Leśmian, Ivanov strove toward an art-induced transformation of life. Symbolism remained for the three poets a permanent historiosophic attitude. "Symbolism as a conception of life will never cease to exist."[73] For Ivanov it was based on Russian mysticism, on a reevaluation of Russia's literary past, and, in addition, on the Hellenic and Hebraic spirit, as well as ideas drawn from the Middle Ages. Like Leśmian, Ivanov saw

Symbolism not as an "illusion," but as energy which removes the soul from the mundane reality and sets it in the movement of a spiral (which approximates Bergson's ideas, close to Leśmian's heart).

Ivanov considered the symbol to be the only appropriate tool both for the creation of a new art and for bridging the gap between the human and the divine. Ivanov considered the symbol, as all things originating in God, "a contradicting sign."[74] As such it cuts through all spheres of consciousness. The symbol conceived in this mystical symbolistic manner was bound together in a vertical relationship serving as a link between the mundane and the highest spheres of existence. The poet and the reader would thus be able to transcend the duality of the real and the ideal. It was implied that the poet and the reader would ascend a *realibus ad realiora*.[75] Such an idea of the structure of symbols corresponds, in my view, to the medieval concept of reaching the heavens via vertical Gothic architecture. For Ivanov, the symbol was to be a holy word reminiscent of the ancient sages, each invested with a special, secret meaning. Hence the poet was transformed into a prophet or demiurge.[76] (Cf., Leśmian, Bely, Potebnia.)

Ivanov distinguished between two kinds of Symbolism: idealistic and realistic. His preference was for a realistic Symbolism expressed with concrete symbols. In this preference he is akin to both Leśmian and Bely. His reasoning behind such taste for concrete symbols was strongly connected with the idea that "in ancient art, the art of naming and defining was all-powerful and constituted the beginning of realistic art."[77] At the same time, this concrete word was symbolic, for it was used in religious rites and represented divine reality. Unlike Leśmian, however, Ivanov found the goal of Symbolist realism the creation of objects corresponding to sacred objects. Leśmian's notions were restricted simply to improving life. Only a concrete Symbol was seen as a myth-creator, for its goal lay in providing an image to unseen objects. "Realistic Symbolism is a revelation of things that the artist sees as reality. It consists of a crystallization of lower reality."[78] Ivanov found such a mysterious vision in the poetry of Tiutchev whom he considered the greatest realistic Symbolist in Russian literature. We can observe in Leśmian what Ivanov discovered in Tiutchev. Leśmian was able to invest unseen, unknown things with extreme palpability, partially because he believed in their reality and was able to make it the reader's reality. Tiutchev was a master of concise revelations of lower reality. Leśmian, who did not look at the earth from an elevated point of detachment, saw everything with the miraculous clarity and concentration characteristic of a child, curiously watching the movement and existence of nature's minutiae. Furthermore, he was able to describe the very act of creating the human form. (Cf., "Ballada bezludna," "The Desolate Ballad" or "Pan Błyszczyński".) He expressed all phenomena, which could have occurred only at the time of the earth's creation and were therefore never witnessed by any human eye, with such perfect plasticity that doubting their reality became impossible. Both Tiutchev and Leśmian are representative of realistic Symbolists *par excellence.* Leśmian, for whom myth was the basis of his aesthetics, was moreover a myth creator. Ivanov called myth-creating concretes "synthetic," because they combine the perceptions of the "boundless" world and the realization that through the human soul man discovers mysteries.[79]

Ivanov, like Bely and Leśmian, sensed in every work of art a hidden music inseparable from the word and promoting the expression of the mystical and the rational. He believed, like Leśmian, that every poet must create his own true sounds and that music is preeminent.[80] Creative ecstasy, in fact, was called song by Leśmian, Bely, and Ivanov. The very spirit of art was musical for Ivanov, who called music: "the yearning for the inexpressible, the soul and life of aesthetic enjoyment."[81]

Regarding the relationship of the poet to the masses, Ivanov accepted Solov'ev's idea of *sobornost'* ("religion of the community") while rejecting the idea of *keleinost'* ("religion of the cell"). In

"Poèt i chern' " he criticized poets who disassociated themselves from the people, thus failing in their role as prophets. The tragic rift between the modern poet and "the herd" started, according to Ivanov, with Pushkin's "Poèt i tolpa" and culminated in Tiutchev's "Silentium," after which Decadent poets became interested in this problem. To combat the rift, Ivanov attempted to reestablish the communal aspects of Hellenic art. Ivanov discerned the best expression of this art in Greek tragedy which he viewed as a triumph of myth. Leśmian, too, saw in drama the highest expression of verbal art. In all these communal creations the poet was at once the voice of the community, its leader, and a bridge linking contemporary society with its ancestral heritage.

The problem of alienation in modern times disturbed both Leśmian and Ivanov. Ivanov pointed out the advantage enjoyed by the ancient poets who were able to preserve their rapport with their communities. Leśmian, like Ivanov, bewailed some contemporary poets' loss of rapport with their communities, or their facile communication of mediocrity to mediocrities; he realized, consequently, the ephemeral nature of their "art," which he viewed as *natura naturata* (secondary reality).[82] The idea of *sobornost'* corresponded well to the Nietzschean concept of tragedy as a communal creative experience. Unlike the Decadents, who embraced the later Nietzschean ideas, Ivanov was drawn particularly to the early Nietzsche, i.e., the *Geburt der Tragödie aus dem Geiste der Musik,* in which the Dionysian spirit was essentially musical and democratic.

The rejection of life as it is, leads to a search for methods and ideas for improving life. Ivanov, Bely, and Leśmian saw mysticism as an escape from life. According to Ivanov, mysticism is born of "nonacceptance of the world."[83] In Ivanov's case, the acceptance of the Dionysian spirit representing the split in the human psyche and the soul's dark forces and abysses is the apotheosis of acceptable and productive revolt against the Apollonian harmonious forces. The nonacceptance of life was much more extreme in Leśmian. It was expressed in his obsession with theodicy (a term coined by Leibniz). As mentioned earlier, Leśmian rejected the existence of God, yet he maintained a running polemic with the indifferent, cruel deity who habitually fails man when man is in crucial need of aid. Man, for his part, must resist the deity. It is appropriate here to recall that Ivanov, in "O nepriiatii mira," believed "mystical energetism" to have originated in Judaism. He asserted that "the Jews, exclusively among tribes of the earth, demanded and proclaimed the right of man to his free self-awareness. They have placed man as a judge of the world and as a plaintiff before God."[84]

Ivanov quotes from the Old Testament in Hebrew, "Eli, Eli, lama azaftani?" ("God, why hast Thou forsaken me?").[85] Leśmian seemed to follow this path, perhaps unconsciously, for he was independent of God from the very beginning and in the final stage of his career, the voice of the plaintiff assumed tragic overtones. In the essay, "At the Sources of Rhythm," Leśmian wrote (1915):

> Life is man's domain, but it is no evidence of a deity. Światowid . . . turned with his four faces toward the people and realized this fact. Death, which for man was an eternal stranger, stood by the side of God, reminding him with a smile on its lips that he had sung his creative song to the end. Światowid understood both the smile and the reminder. He did not complain that together with the song of life he had to give the people flora and fauna, life itself, leaving only death for himself. . . . He knew that the Twilight of the Gods would be *a triumph for creation, a triumph for man, whose fate and further development—supplemented by freedom—would rest ultimately in his own, human hands* [italics mine].[86]

Here Leśmian metaphorically expressed the ethical superiority of man over God. He affirmed humanism and man as a self-sufficient entity. Yet, this was, at the same time, a climactic stage in the controversy between Leśmian and God; though he hoped to annihilate God, he retained a tragic realization that creative man must die, leaving only myth behind. Leśmian expresses this realization in "Śmierć Buddy" ("Buddha's Death") (published posthumously), which can be considered his poetic testament.

Ivanov defined mystical anarchism as spirit, liberating itself boundlessly. "In this sense mysticism is an expression of contemporary consciousness taken in its dynamic aspects,"[87] wrote

Ivanov. This statement may be applied to some extent to Leśmian's own beliefs, for the Polish poet, believing that everything is in constant motion, the inner experience being also in dynamic flux, affirmed this nonacceptance of the world, at least in its religious, political, and social aspects. One can justifiably contend that Leśmian was in almost complete accord with the second generation of Russian Symbolists. There were, however, a number of issues upon which Leśmian and Ivanov would not have agreed.

The most obvious point of dissimilarity between Ivanov's and Leśmian's artistic and philosophical views is that Ivanov was a theosophist (and a follower of V. Solov'ev's philosophy), basically religious in all his views (ultimately becoming a Catholic). Leśmian was a consistent iconoclast, expressing his reverence for life in agnostic pantheism. His entire poetic creation was an assertion of man's independence of God. Both poets were apocalyptic, visionaries, but Leśmian remained a creatively defiant revolutionary before God, and a creative evolutionist before art. Ivanov, consistent as always, remained a conservative in art and a mystic convinced to the end of the "second coming."

Characteristic of Leśmian's poetry is the kind of theodicity *à rebours.* It serves as a running polemic with God, though denying his existence. Remarkable is the fact that while employing theistic images in his argumentations, the secular tenets emerge victorious. This phenomenon may partly explain the extraordinary, powerful dramatic quality of Leśmian's intellectual and artistic dispute, which (in Jacek Trznadel's observation) "has no equivalent in the poetry of our century."[88] Leśmian intensifies his reproach toward God in direct proportion to the growing awareness that the ultimate reality is life on earth. In contrast to Ivanov's classical notion of theodicy based on that of Ivan Karamazov's nonacceptance of God's creation and acceptance of God, Leśmian accepts the worldly existence, negating both the existence of God and immortality. This is the last desperate and defiant act against God. It is an attempt to show man's freedom in accepting the tragic existence on earth, without the patronage of a religious justification. (Cf., "Jam—nie Osjan" ["I am—not Ossian",]).

Thus, Leśmian eschatology differs decidedly from Ivanov's, who, at the end of his life, anticipated reincarnation, whereas Leśmian rejected immortality. In a gesture of human love, he returned God's immortality in the belief that God needed it more than man. In several poems (*The Two Matthews,* "I Am Not Ossian," *Elijah, Buddha's Death,* "The Cemetary") he developed his variant of theodicy.

Unlike Ivanov, who remained a follower of Nietzsche, Leśmian's fascination for the German was short-lived. Unlike Leśmian, Ivanov did not consider folklore themes valuable in the transformation of man's contemporary soul. Instead, he turned to the "dark roots of existence,"[89] and to Hellenic mythology in search for a solution. Leśmian, on the other hand, never liked Hellenic mythology, drew deeply from the sources of folk mythology (predominantly Slavic), and assimilated folkloric devices, genres, and language, transforming them into the best vehicle for his thoughts. While in Leśmian's poetry the power of nature and the power of human spirit represent a unity, Ivanov rejects, in his art, the unity of these two different entities. He considers tragic art to be almost exclusively a human art.[90]

The idea of *sobornost'* proclaimed by Ivanov could not be realized either in his theories or in his poetry. Ivanov considered Symbolist poetry a catharsis of the soul. In catharsis he saw the goal of art. In his theories there are some contradictions; e.g., he claimed that the hero originates from the chorus and not vice-versa, and yet he denied the importance of folklore.[91] According to the Russian poet, neither folk themes, nor folklore, in general, are important in myth creation: "One can say that the chorus sings a myth, but the gods create it."[92] Yet, in another article he considers

> the true myth to be a postulate of a collective self-determination. . . . An individual myth . . . is impossible, it is a *contradictio in adiecto.*
>
> Art in its leanings toward myth-creation gravitates towards a national folk art.[93]

Further, discussing the mystical nature of future choral activity, Ivanov envisions the creativity of "the prophetic commune" [*obshchina*] based on its inner, collective resources, with theaters, choral tragedies, etc., serving as creative centers of self-determination of the people. He believes that "only then will the fusing of the audience with the actors result in one orgiastic body."[94] In "Poèt i chern' " Ivanov criticized as simply wrong the poet who seeks solitude and seclusion to prepare himself to give the crowd the answers. Only the Symbolist poet, he thought, could resurrect the ancient time of communal creativity through symbols; but if the myth were to be first created by the esoteric few, then handed down to the masses in order to become a true myth, earthly happiness could not logically be expected. The contradictory statements presented in the two essays indicate, in my opinion, that the idea of *sobornost'* does not represent a clearly defined consistent theory capable of yielding practical results.

Compared to his poetry, Ivanov's theories further prove the dichotomy of his thinking, even with regard to his own creativity. He called individualism "intellectual Don Juanism,"[95] yet his magnificent poetry, a great achievement to poetic diction, is highly individualistic. The latter attribute is related to the poet's gravitation toward mysticism. Ivanov believed that individualism can only be achieved via mysticism, which he considered "the genesis of the newest trends in philosophical thought and artistic creation."[96] Besides, he was the propagator of a Symbolism which strongly supported extreme creative individualism. As a result his poetry is unique, written in a grand and complex style combining classical and medieval forms. His language is a rich mixture of Church Slavisms, Hellenisms, and archaisms. One of his favorite genres is the "garland" sonnet. Even his choice of Hellenic poetry tends towards the complex dithyramb and ode. His symbols require decoding. As Vladimir Markov observes, "sometimes a Latin footnote in an obscure book by a German scholar can explain everything."[97] Consequently such a "hermetic" poetry can hardly be a prototype for communal creation.

In opposition to Ivanov, Leśmian had a much simpler and

therefore a much clearer vision of his role as a poet and of his work. He believed that a poet ought to create as though there were no print in existence. He should resemble the singers of ancient Greece who, relying on mnemonic art, entrusted their songs to the rhapsodists. The poet and the listener are brought close together by the rhythm and *melos* of mnemonic poetry. Leśmian's "formulated" and his "immanent" poetics correspond remarkably well, making him unique. Through his unique utilization of folklore and his theories of primordiality, Leśmian came paradoxically much closer to realizing the ideal of *sobornost'* than did the creator of that ideal. The following verses can serve as an example:

/ . . . / Nawołujcie się ludzie, pod jasnym lazurem,
Chórem w światy spojrzyjcie, zatrwóżcie się chórem!
  Miłość, wichrem rozpędzona,
  Wszystko złamie i pokona,
Zaś tych, co się sprzeciwią, w śnie skrępuje sznurem!

A opaszcie świat cały ścisłym korowodem,
Aby wam się nie wymknął, schwytany niewodem . . .
  Zapląsajcie, zaśpiewajcie,
  Pieśnią siebie wspomagajcie,
Toć wejdziemy w świat—próżnią, aby wyjść—ogrodem! / . . . /
("Łąka" ["The Meadow"])[98]

/ . . . / Gather together, o people, beneath the bright blue, / In unison turn your eyes to the worlds, in unison take alarm! / Love, sped by the whirlwind, / Shall break and conquer all, / While those who will resist, it shall bind with a rope in their sleep! /

But encircle the whole world in a closed ring-dance, / So that, caught in your net, it should not slip your grasp . . . / Begin the dance, strike up a song, / Sustain one another with a song, / For we come into the world—through a void, to exit—through a garden! / . . . /

CONCLUSION

The comparison of Leśmian with Bely and Ivanov demonstrates how his poetics corresponds with the syncretic nature of the second-generation Russian Symbolism. The Symbolist aesthetics and ideas contained in the theoretical pronouncements and works of Bely and Ivanov proved to be the best possible means of comparison with Leśmian's poetics. It should be pointed out, however, that a comparison of their poetry would never have yielded the same results. This stems to large degree from the discrepancy between the ideological tenets and the poetic practice of both Russian poets (especially in the case of Bely, the self-acclaimed "false prophet").

In summarizing the main points of comparison among the three poets, they are similar in:

1. Their literary and cultural backgrounds; their conception of Symbolism as an attitude of historiosophical dimensions. The function of Symbolism to express via symbols, that is, concrete images, the true, essential reality, to transgress from the world of the phenomenal into the world of the noumenal; their belief in the genesis of poetic creation (myth-creating) and of the poetic word (i.e., myth); their use of literary and metric devices of Symbolist poetics (symbol, rhythm, music, etc.); and in their theory of the role of Symbolist art, especially of poetry in life and society.

2. The near similarities occur in: some philosophical influences; their mysticism, eschatology, and the Apocalypse; and their use of some themes and motifs.

3. The divergencies among them are: the religiously and theosophically oriented Symbolism of Leśmian's counterparts (the occultism and anthroposophy in Bely's case); the discrepancy between their ideologies as applied to their poetry and lives; the fact that Leśmian was not a leader, not a conscious theoretician of a literary era, and did not belong to any literary coterie; and that Leśmian did not have the influence or recognition that was given either of the two Russian poets.

In addition, striking parallels in the "creative fates" of the poets should be pointed out (especially applicable to Leśmian and Bely). In Bely's case, Russian Symbolism found a perfect representative, its total reflection, and one of its main ideologists. His complex duality-ridden nature epitomizes the complexity of Russian Symbolism. His failure to realize Symbolism as his way of life also represents the failure of the practitioners of Symbolism to put its lofty ideals into practice. Yet his achievement as a Symbolist writer, especially in prose and literary criticism, as a consistent stylist, as an innovator of genres, in linguistics and metrics, puts him among the leading figures of twentieth-century Russian literature. His concern with form as the only meaning of art makes Bely a forerunner of Russian Formalism. Bely, who was popular throughout his life, achieved (according to Maslenikov and Mochulsky) true recognition as the most original and influential writer of the Symbolist movement only after his death.

Ivanov's "tragedy" is also the reflection of the tragedy of Russian Symbolist art. In reality, the artist achieved extreme individuality, yet he propagated rejection of the poet's emancipation in the interest of communal creation. Thus the prognosis of saving the future by communal artistic life proved a failure. "His dreams about myth, tragedy . . . about poetic simplicity, commit suicide one after the other."[99] As for his artistry, it is elevated in style, superb, and consistent, regardless of the medium (prose or poetry). Although his poetry expresses the same ideas as his theoretic prose, it fails in the applicability of those theories to life.

Leśmian alone, as a poet and thoeritician, represents true Symbolism in Poland. He is also considered, posthumously, as the only ideologist of this Symbolism in Poland (cf., J. Sławiński, *et al.*). Leśmian's duality and complexity, like Bely's, fits the many-layered aesthetics of Symbolism. Leśmian's tragedy is the personal, human tragedy of an agnostic.

His negation of God's existence is not for the purpose of aggrandizement of God's power in order to become a demiurge. His transcendentalism and "iconoclasm" are a springboard toward the absolute freedom of man outside of the realm of deity. His relationship to God is not a religious problem but, as it were, an intellectual and philosophical problem. By giving up the immortality for which he strove, he commits "spiritual suicide."[100]

In Leśmian's case recognition was slow in coming. His genius, his great experimentation in combining genres expressed by means of consistent stylistic excellence, his innovation in prose, folk stylization, and drama, word formation, and stanzaic structure, were given due recognition only in the late fifties and sixties. During his lifetime, despite his influence on the "Skamander" group and other poets of the twenties, he was never given due credit. Like Bely he is considered as a forerunner of Formalism. His poetry has been interpreted as representing virtually all the modern literary trends. This makes him a Symbolist *par excellence.* Lately his fame has even penetrated the "iron curtain" of Soviet literature.[101]

The belief of all three poets that life's reality passes as a dream, that only art represents true reality and the essence of life, was proven in their artistic achievement. As Bely and Leśmian[102] said, the *what* does not matter now, but the *how* made them immortal. Their belief in the immortality of myth (i.e., creation) proved to be justified.

5
Leśmian's Immanent Poetics: Poetic Analysis

Niech się pieśni me same ze siebie wygwarzą,
Obym ich nie dobywał, ale w sobie dożył!
A nie chcę im górować ni barwić się twarzą,
Jeno być niewidzialnym jak ten, co mnie stworzył.
—Bolesław Leśmian, "Zamyślenie" ("Meditation")

Let my songs prattle forth on their own, / So that I shouldn't dig for them, but let them grow within me! / And they'd better not put on airs or show a pretty face, / But keep invisible like the one who created me.

Leśmian, unlike his Russian Symbolist counterparts, did not believe in programs or dogmas, nor did he have a desire to be a propagator of any ideas. His desire was to create poetry intuitively in a manner expressed in the stanza of the "programmatic" poem used above as an epigraph. Yet paradoxically, his "formulated poetics" became recognized as *the only program* of a true Symbolism in Poland. The attempt to place Leśmian in a proper historical perspective necessitated a discussion of his development as a poet against a background of various literary and philosophical trends. Borrowing the remark of a Polish literary critic, I should add the following: "All the enemies of tying research on literary history with philosophy ought to be reminded that the author of *Łąka* is perhaps the only poet in Polish literature so exceptionally philosophically oriented."[1] His works often serve as an artistic representation of certain intellectual and philosophical theses. Therefore, in relating Leśmian to various philosophical influences I hoped to provide the scholarly reader with a full dimension of the many-layered treasure that Leśmian's poetry represents.

Yet, despite the fact that his "formulated poetics" represent a formidable achievement as a program summarizing for us all his aims and ideas, it only provides us with an abstract vision of his total poetics. Julian Przyboś, enthusiastic about the discovered *Szkice literackie*, found that they did not do justice to Leśmian's own creative work.

> An attentive critic could easily conclude, comparing the poems written in this period with his thoughts about poetry, that Leśmian the theoretician and Leśmian the aesthete did not encompass, even in the most general way, the wealth of his own poetry.[2]

Therefore, to do justice to the work of "one of the greatest and most outstanding visionaries in . . . [Polish] poetry"[3] the true introduction to his poetics must come via formal analysis. I shall attempt to demonstrate (using Leśmian's own words)

> *what he writes with*—what are the resources of his imagination, feeling, and inherent rhythm, what kind of emotions of body and soul fill his content and form.[4]

In short, I shall juxtapose his "formulated poetics" with his "immanent poetics," attempting to support the statement made at the outset of this work about the extraordinary convergence between Leśmian's theory and his poetic practice.

It should be pointed out that this analysis dealing with form (i.e., poetic devices) will disregard the sequential arrangement of Leśmian's poetry into volumes. There is a very valid reason for this approach: the volumes are not arranged chronologically. In each of them we find works from different periods. As noted with surprise by Kazimierz Wierzyński,[5] *Napój cienisty* (his third volume) includes poems written at a very early stage of his poetic career. A good example is the excellent poem "Wspomnienie"

("Reminiscence"), published in 1913 in *Nowa Gazeta* and included in *Łąka* only seven years later.[6] A similar situation holds true for the title poem, "Łąka," written around 1914 (about the same time as *Klechdy polskie*), not very much later than the publication of his *Sad rozstajny*. Both of these long poems belong to Leśmian's greatest achievements.

Leśmian's disregard for a chronological arrangement of his poetry does not come as a surprise, but is, rather, consistent with his convictions. In the philosophy of creative evolution time was not considered a phenomenon proceeding in a linear way; in fact, time was of little consequence in Leśmian's Weltanschauung, and could only be expressed in the amount of work invested in a poem.

> Arranging his collections in such a fashion, he subconsciously fell victim to the belief which he tried consciously to express in his poetry—namely, the illusoriness of the uniform, unvarying historically empty time, giving the foretaste of eternity [which according to Leśmian meant death]. In the last period the poet created outside of the epoch.[7]

Leśmian's poetry was future-oriented and it dealt with universal problems, therefore for him chronology was immaterial.

A word of caution is in order. Next to Norwid, Leśmian's poetry is the most difficult in Polish literature. Like most Symbolist poetry, it lends itself to many interpretations, depending on the creative reader upon whom the poet relied. Although it is primarily philosophical, his poetry can have the effect of pure incantation for the uninitiated reader. In fact, it was Leśmian's primary aim that the rhythmic and unusual combination of poetic language should have this immediate sensory effect. However, the creative reader, in trying to explore this multilayered poetry and to put together the jigsaw puzzle it represents, will be extremely gratified to discover that each tiny element fits perfectly into its place. The various devices are employed with extreme mastery—hence, some critics' comparison of Leśmian with Marinist Baroque poets.

IMAGERY AND LANGUAGE

The range of themes, tropes, and images evoked in Leśmian's poetry is relatively small. His poetic world is confined primarily to mythological imagery, with Slavic and folk mythologies predominating. Nature in its primitive state is the basic background for the poems. Thus, "nature" prevails over "culture" (with only a few works, such as "The Contemporary Landscape" and others, devoted to culture). The poet related even the most traditional and intimate poetic themes, especially eroticism as well as metaphysical and philosophical reflections, to his vision of nature and mythology. As a rule, the poems take place in the mythological past, a fact which determines the character of their images. Their scope may be enormous, ranging from the cosmos, as in the long poem, *Elijah,* to a meadow and a garden. The protagonists of Leśmian's many narrative poems are generally characters drawn from folk mythology who remain in direct contact with primitive nature. This is most evident in the cycles, *Ballads* and *Characters.* (The ballad, "Gad," has its origin in Scandinavian folk ballad.)[8] The motif representing a reptile (a dragon) turned fairy prince, appears frequently in Slavic folklore (cf., Russian *skazki,* as well as Polish fairy tales):

Szła z mlekiem w piersi w zielony sad,
Aż ją w olszynie zaskoczył gad.

Skrętami dławił, ująwszy wpół,
Od stóp do głowy pieścił i truł. / . . . /

Już me zwyczaje miłosne znasz,
Zwól, że przybiorę królewską twarz.

Skarby dam tobie z podmorskich den,
Zacznie się jawa-skończy się sen! / . . . /
("Gad" ["Reptile"])[9]

With milk in her breast she walked to the green orchard, / When a dragon surprised her in the alder wood. / Catching her about the waist, he squeezed her in his coils, / He fondled her and poisoned her from head to toe. / . . . /

My customs of love thou already knowest, / Allow me to assume a kingly mien. / Treasures will I give thee from the ocean depths, / The dream shall end, and reality begin! / . . . /

The protagonists are sometimes even animals, as "A Horse," "A Springtime Ox," and are treated with great love and respect as man's equals and companions:

/ . . . / A gdy noc już nastanie, pozamykam dźwierze
I wspólnie odmówimy wieczorne pacierze.
("Koń" ["Horse"])[10]

/ . . . / And when night falls, I shall lock the doors, / And together we shall say the evening prayers.

Nature in Leśmian's images is never described conventionally or naturalistically. Most often, it is the subject of a fantastic vision. The poet treats it as if it were a living being, sometimes exactly as he treats man who, to him, is nature's direct partner.

The characteristic trait of images in Leśmian's poetry is their highly developed self-sufficiency. In fact, *images* constitute the basic means of expression. It is in this that his works differ from the so-called Young Poland's ("Młodopolska") poetry, in which, as in the works of Kazimierz Tetmajer, early Jan Kasprowicz, and partly in the pre-1918 works of Leopold Staff, images were of value only insofar as they served to express emotions directly, as, for instance, by means of charged epithets. Examples characteristic of this direct subjugation of the poetic image to the emotional content can be found in Tetmajer:

Serce me spało, a moja myśl
tonęła gdzieś w lazurze,
nagle ujrzałem przy sobie tuż
skromniutką czarną różę.

Wspaniałą krasą jej kwiat i liść
bynajmniej się nie płoni,

a przecież dziwny jakiś czar
przykuwa wzrok mój do niej.
("Czarna róża" ["The Black Rose"])[11]

My heart slept, and my thought / sank somewhere in the azure, / suddenly I saw close by / the most modest little black rose. /

With great beauty its flower and leaf / is not at all aflame, / and yet some strange magic / fixes my gaze upon it. /

Stanisław Korab-Brzozowski:

Na wyciagniętych deszczu strunach
Wiatr wzdycha, jęczy i łka;
Na miękkich pajęczyn całunach
Królewna tka.

Jej ręka leciuchna i żywa,
Szybka jak białych lot chmur,
Układa mych tęsknot przędziwa
W przedziwny wzór.
("Prządka" ["The Spinner"])[12]

On the outstretched strings of the rain / The wind sighs, moans and cries; / On the soft shrouds of cobwebs / The royal Princess weaves. /

Her very light and deft hand, / Fast as a flight of white clouds, / Works the yarn of my longings / Into a most wondrous pattern. /

Leśmian exhibits this tendency only in his juvenilia (collected in *UR*), and in a few poems in *Sad rozstajny*.

These are examples of similar tendencies in Leśmian's earliest lyrics:

Księga mych marzeń—to mój skarb jedyny!
Mam ją przy sobie i zawsze, i wszędzie . . .
Czerpię z niej wiosnę w jesienne godziny,
Com w niej wyczytał—było albo będzie! . . . / . . . /

W mej piersi płomień pięknych snów migota,
Biorąc mi serce za zwątpień narzędzie,
I sam już nie wiem, czy jest to tęsknota
Za tym, co było—czy za tym, co będzie! . . .
(From "Sny" ["Dreams"])[13]

The book of my dreams—that's my only treasure! / I keep it with me always, everywere . . . / I draw springtime from it during autumn hours, / What I read in it—was or shall be! . . . / . . . /

In my breast flickers the flame of beautiful dreams, / Taking my heart as an instrument of doubt, / And I myself don't know if this is longing / For that which was—or for that which is yet to come! . . .

This tendency is expressed by the frequent presence of words describing feelings directly, as well as by using commonly accepted emotionally charged symbols. In the poem "Na stepie" ("On the Steppe"), this Romantic tendency is manifested in the correspondence between the image of nature and the image of personal feelings. (Cf., "The Crimean Sonnets" by Adam Mickiewicz.) The first acts as an introduction for the second image and is closely subordinate to it, as exemplified by the following:

/ . . . / Step dymi modrym płomieniem,
Wiatr to się ocknie to zdrzemnie.
Cienie biegają po ziemi,
Niby się gonią wzajemnie . . .

Ja idę—i czuję sercem
Jak w ziemi rodzą się czary,
Ja idę i wierzę senny,
Że step—bez końca bez miary! . . . / . . . /[14]

/ . . . / The steppe smokes with a blue flame, / the wind now wakes, now dozes off. / Shadows run across the earth, / As though pursuing one another. . . . /

I go—and feel in my heart / How magic is born in the earth, / I go—and dreamful, I believe / The steppe is endless and immeasurable! . . . / . . . /

This tendency is absent in Leśmian's mature works. The poetic "I"—"the lyrical subject"—is usually contained in some element of the image. As a result, his images are extremely concrete. (In this he is a disciple of Poland's greatest bard—Mickiewicz). He presents things and events in their definite and momentary, single dimension, even when they are fantastic and visionary in character (which is usually the case). Works as diverse as the erotic poem, "W polu," on the one hand, and the ballad, "Marcin Swoboda," on the other, can serve as examples. The concreteness of imagery in the poem "W polu" manifests itself in the fact that the poet looks at nature as though through a microscope. In many cases this concreteness leads to the fantastic.

Dwoje nas w ciszy polnego zakątka. / . . . /
Nadbrzeżna trawa, zwisając, potrąca
O swe odbicie zsiwiałą kończyną,
Do której ślimak, pęczniejąc z gorąca,
Przysklepił muszlę swym ciałem i śliną. / . . . /

Tych kilku dębów ponad brzegiem liście,
Podziurawione i przeżarte chciwie
Przez gąsienicę, trwają tak przejrzyście
Nad własnym cieniem, co utkwił w pokrzywie. / . . . /
("W polu" ["In the Field"])[15]

The two of us in a quiet little corner of a field. / . . . / Grass drooping along the shore touches / Its reflection with a hoary tip, / To which a snail, swelling from the heat, / Has arched its shell with body and saliva. / . . . /

The leaves of these few oaks above the shore, / Greedily riddled and gnawed through / By a caterpillar, persist so transparently / Above their own shadows stuck in poison ivy. / . . . /

It is most characteristic that this concreteness and predilection for minutiae does not result in a static image. The poet presents action, motion, transformation in the course of description, thus attaining a ceaseless movement. The ballad "Marcin Swoboda" is a good example of these tendencies in the narrative poems, because each stanza equals a single occurrence, representing a very accurate way of relating the story. Such an approach heightens the poetic effect for this is, in fact, how a macabre and unusual story is presented, as a rule:

Z górskich szczytów lawina, Bogu czyniąc szkodę,
Strąciła w przepaść nizin Marcina Swobodę.

Spadał, czując, jak w ciele kość szaleje krucha,
I uderzył się o ziem ostatnią mgłą ducha.

Poniszczony śmiertelnie, chciał się z bólem wadzić,
Wokół bólu jął miazgę człowieczą gromadzić. / . . . /

I z trudem bezkształtnego ciała rozwłóczyny
Doczołgały się wreszcie aż do stóp dziewczyny. / . . . /
("Marcin Swoboda")[16]

From mountain tops an avalanche, doing God harm, / hurled Martin Swoboda over a lowlands precipice. /

Down he tumbled, feeling the brittle bones rage in his body, / And struck against the earth with the last vapor of his soul. /

A bit fatally injured, he wanted to ward off the pain, / Around his pain he began to gather human pulp. / . . . /

And with great effort the shattered bits of shapeless body / Dragged themselves finally to the feet of a maiden. / . . . /

These poems differ in composition. The first is a monologue in the strict sense of the word as evidenced by its beginning. The second is a narrative work. Yet they both represent the world in its concrete and specific manifestations. One may say that the analytic attitude of the poet to the world is revealed in images (which is reminiscent of the "natural poet," the primitive man). In the poem "W polu," he enumerates the specific elements of the landscape he describes in a sequential manner, and calls attention to details, each of which is distinctly evocative and individualistic. Much like a child, the narrator spies on nature and shares his impressions with the companion—the lover—asking her at the same time about her well-being without interrupting his active observation of the surroundings. In the above-mentioned ballad he assumes the same attitude with respect to the events which comprise the plot, each element of which is told briefly yet expressively. This concreteness coexists with the fantastic which is precisely what constitutes the distinctive feature of Leśmian's poetry. Both poems are very typical of his creation.

The presence of an analytic quality in Leśmian's poetry does not mean that synthetic formulations are foreign to him. They appear from time to time, if only in the endings of poems. Such is the case in the first example where the only evidence of the second person's presence is her white hand which he moves over the grass. However, that is not the manner in which synthetic formulations are chiefly manifested. Leśmian leaves the actual task of synthesis to the reader. Facts and details are put together and shaped in his poems in such a way that the recipient forms a vision of the whole by himself (this is an example of a typical tendency in Symbolism, namely, that an active role is assigned to the reader).

Such concreteness of images is based on Leśmian's Weltanschauung as expressed in his theoretical essays. Things, facts, and events are of interest to him in the form in which they actually occur at a given moment. Since his attention is focused on the phenomena themselves, we can call his attitude *phenomenalism*. It is manifested in not showing the causes of phenomena, a device of particular significance in Leśmian's poetics. His lack of concern for causality allows him to present things in motion and in a state of change without logical order. Phenomenalism is often a basis in constructing plots. Instead of a causal chain, Leśmian juxtaposes events and descriptive elements in a sequence in which they actually occur, without trying to explain them. With respect to events, the ballad, "Śmiercie," can serve as an example of this tendency, in that the events mentioned are arranged without any indication of their cause-and-effect relationship:

Chodzą Śmiercie po słonecznej stronie,
Trzymający się wzajem za dłonie.

Którą z naszej wybierzesz gromady,
By w cmentarne uprowadzić sady?

Nie chciał pierwszej, że nazbyt miniasta,
Grób, gdy hardy, pokrzywą porasta. / . . . /

Blada jesteś, jak to słońce w zimie—
Kędy dom twój i jak ci na imię?

Dom mój stoi na ziemi uboczu,
A na imię nic nie mam, prócz oczu. / . . . /
("Śmiercie" ["The Deaths"])[17]

Deaths walk on the sunny side, / Holding each other by the hand. /

Whom will you choose from our throng / To take away to the cemetary orchard? /

He did not want the first, for she puts on airs too much, / A haughty grave is soon overgrown with poison ivy. / . . . /

You are pale, like the sun in winter— / Where is your home, and what is your name? /

My house stands in a corner of the earth, / And for a name I have nothing, except eyes. / . . . /

In this kind of a ballad with a plot the tendency leads to a parallel enumeration of events and a parallel arrangement of problems expressed by the characters—e.g., the dialogue of Death with the third girl.

The poem "Zwierzyniec" is a good example of the disregard of the causal arrangement of the elements in a plotless poem:

Flamingo, różowiejąc, smukli się nad wodą,
Skrzydłatego jedwabiu zaciszną urodą. / . . . /

Wielbłąd w słońcu zapłowiał stąd o kroków siedem
Jak sprzęt Boży, okryty poniszczonym pledem. / . . . /

Ślepie, z których się słońce nigdy dość nie wylśni,
Patrzą na mnie z plamiście rozwrzaskanej pilśni, / . . . /

Pies mój, kwiat oszczekując, łbem się tuli ku mnie—
By poistnieć w mym świecie trafnie i beztłumnie— / . . . /
("Zwierzyniec" ["The Zoo"])[18]

A flamingo, rosily glowing, slenderly appears above the water / Like the remote loveliness of winged silk. / . . . /

The camel suddenly faded in the sun seven paces away / Like a furnishing of God covered with a threadbare rug. / . . . /

Eyes, from which the sun can never sparkle enough, / Look out at me from a spottily screaming felt. / . . . /

My dog, barking away at a flower, snuggles his head against me /
To exist for a bit in my world—proper and unhurried. / . . . /

This poem is particularly characteristic of Leśmian's poetry in that it represents a composition of juxtaposed elements which, although existing side by side, do not result in a plot; therefore, there is no causal relationship. It is a specific kind of lyric poetry, fantastic in nature, and linked only in that all described elements constitute a component of the zoological garden. Each stanza is devoted to one of its elements, as the flamingo, the camel, the eyes of a wild animal, the dog.

Negation of causality has a considerable impact on the composition of poems and determines the role of parallelism. It is related also to Leśmian's peculiar handling of the time element. He is, basically, not interested in the passage of long periods of time; he is preoccupied with the moments at which a given thing or phenomenon appears, or in the moments he perceives them. Artur Sandauer describes this very aptly as "mythology of the moment,"[19] a term that can, perhaps, be compared with that of James Joyce called "epiphanies." Everything in Leśmian's images appears for a mere moment, only to vanish or yield its place to another element. An example of the instant image can be found in a poem from the cycle *Green Hour,* where the narrator's reflection in the water is superimposed by a wave upon that of birds. The birds appear to be dipping their beaks into the mouth of the man.[20] This instantaneousness is an original achievement of Leśmian and has nothing in common with the poetic Impressionism typical at the turn of the century in which moments were related to a fleeting mood, a characteristic generally foreign to Leśmian's literary work. (As previously noted, Leśmian barely came in contact with Impressionism in his earliest period, in *UR,* and in some of his Russian poems, especially from the cycle *Lunnoe pokhmel'e.*)[21]

The philosophical meaning of Leśmian's concrete images is determined by the way in which they are formed. Sometimes they are presented as they arise in the subject's perception; hence we can speak here of a specific kind of epistemological lyric poetry. In the poem "W śniegu," the process of cognition itself seems to have been fixed. This poem is representative of Leśmian's epistemological attitude. Very often the poet not only presents an event or a vision of nature; he also questions the cognition of the phenomena he is speaking about. Judging by the first three stanzas of the poem, one can assume that it only represents a poetic landscape (which abound in Leśmian). However, the last stanza shows that this does not satisfy the poet, for he questions the means of cognition of this very landscape:

/ . . . / Co za światy przelotne i wędrowne kraje
Spadły razem ze śniegiem na te ścieżki strome?
I czemu tak radośnie oko nie poznaje
Tego, co tak niedawo było mu znajome? . . .
("W Śniegu" ["In the Snow"])[22]

/ . . . / What sort of transitory, wandering worlds / Have fallen with the snow onto these steep paths? / And why does the eye fail so joyously to see / That which it so recently knew? . . .

Here the perceiving man and his cognizant approaches emerge in the foreground. A similar formula pertaining to cognition (especially vision) appears in the poem "Wieczorem":

/ . . . / Staw posrebrniał i widzi inaczej niż my,
Jak księżyc wschodzi nad borem . . . / . . . /
("Wieczorem" ["In the Evening"])[23]

/ . . . / The pond has turned silver and sees differently than we / How the moon rises over the forest . . .

In this example the power of perception is attributed to the pond. The epistemological lyricism is evident in the way in which the images create a certain vision of a world governed by its own laws. This specific philosophical nature of Leśmian's images is the result of his unique attitude toward the word.

In the process of word formation, Leśmian creates his own poetic ontology—his representation of the world. (This is how I shall refer to the grouping of images comprising a certain whole.) It is built of words, according to definite principles. The characteristic feature of this world is its homogeneity, that is, all of its elements are treated in the same way, in keeping with the Symbolist principle that naming a thing brings it into being. Therefore, not only do the designations of things and natural phenomena (such as "a horse," "a meadow," etc.) have an existence of their own, but also those of abstract concepts (e.g., "dream," "time," etc.). In Leśmian's poetic ontology, all these designations are treated on the same level.[24] Such homogeneity is motivated by the "primitive" world outlook peculiar to the poet. This concept that things and subjective images ought to be treated as equal entities (cf., his article, "Przemiany rzeczywistości" ("The Metamorphoses of Reality"), is expressed by means of two basic principles of poetic imagery: *anthropomorphization* and *reification.*

Anthropomorphization is here broadly defined; it includes all those poetic devices that treat things, states of being, and phenomena as living beings. (Animizations and personifications, which are usually differentiated in texts on poetics, are here subsumed under the notion of a superior kind of anthropomorphization.) Reification, in Leśmian's poetry, means ascribing the status of things to abstract concepts and sometimes to living beings. Anthropomorphization and reification thus constitute the basic principle for the structure and association of images. With respect to abstractions, reification is, in certain cases, a stage which makes anthropomorphization possible.

Anthropomorphization manifests itself in ascribing the reactions of living beings, usually of humans, to phenomena and states. This is illustrated in the fourth stanza of the poem "Nocą," where the poet says that there is nothing above:

/ . . . / Jest tylko ta próżnica, w którą czar przelewa
Słońce, ażeby spełnić mgieł wolę daleką . . .
Ta próżnica—te kwiaty—motyle i drzewa—
Drzewa—kwiaty—motyle—i ten dom nad rzeką . . .
("Nocą" ["At Night"])[25]

/ . . . / There is only this futility into which magic spills / The sun to fulfill the distant will of mists . . . / This futility—these flowers—butterflies and trees— / Trees—flowers—butterflies—and this house on the river . . . /

It is worth noting that equal treatment is afforded to all phenomena, be they abstract or concrete, and note also the absence of causal ties between them. Not only is the magic shown here to be as active as a human being, but even the motives for its actions are depicted. Anthropomorphism is one of the most essential devices in Leśmian's poetry. It has a great meaning for his poetics and is also invested with philosophical attributes, as is the case in the verses cited above, where it serves as a means of expressing the poet's pessimism (i.e., his distrust and lack of belief in the existence of the beyond). This life on the earth is useless, "to no purpose"—as expressed by the "strange" word *próżnica*—it is the only reality left. (This noun is only used adverbially with the preposition: *po próżnicy*, meaning "to no purpose.") Another example is the poem "Garbus" ("The Hunchback"), where the personification of the "hump" allows the poet to express his creed. The hump, a synecdoche, at once symbolizes the hardship of life and wants to assert its autonomous existence. Defying the death—the finality—of the hunchback's existence, it represents the lofty, the inspired part of man. While the hunchback lies dying, face down, the hump looks up at the butterflies in the sky and reproaches its "camel" for hindering its dreams.

Anthropomorphism is the device by means of which Leśmian achieves the unity of his poetic world. It enables him to abolish all existing differences and limits: between animate and inanimate objects, between man and other realms of existence. Often anthropomorphism applies to single episodes of a poem, as in the poem "Srebroń," in which there is "noc spragniona wymian," ("the night thirsts for changes"), "światła mrą" ("the lights die"), "nicość kłami połyska" ("nothingness flashes its fangs"). Sometimes it is the decisive factor in the entire composition of a poem. An example of this phenomenon is found in each of the following two poems:

/ . . . / Świat raz jeszcze ustala
Swój stosunek do mgły i korala . . .
Żadna mgła się nie dowie,
Ile było koralowych prób?
Komuż niebyt się uda?
Powiedz słowo.—Toć mówię: "Utruda."—
Powiedz drugie!—"Błędowie."—
Powiedz trzecie!—"Trzecie słowo—grób"—
("W chmur odbiciu" ["In the Reflection of Clouds"])[26]

Once again the world fixes / Its relationship to mist and coral . . . / Shall no mist learn / How many trials of coral there were? / Who shall succeed in non-being? / Say a word.—Well, I say: "Weariness."— / Say another!—"Deviousness."— / Say a third!—"The third word is—grave!"—

Here nature is treated, not as a static object of description, but as a reality in action. Reflecting clouds in the water, the world attempts in a dialogue to examine its relationship to the mists (inspiration) and to the corals (creative achievements). The answers of the second person, prompted by the personified world, present an extremely pessimistic relationship of the world toward the creative forces. The three responses (the first two of which are neologisms) spell doom, death. The following example is different:

/ . . . / Ślepym srebrem zaledwo spojrzyścieje w światy.
Srebru śni się, że szumi i polewa kwiaty.

Woda roi, że mgły się za ręce w blask wiodą,
Lecz ciał zlękłych nie widzi. Co począć z tą wodą?
("Spojrzystość" ["A Way of Looking"])[27]

/ . . . / Like blind silver, it can barely become visible to the worlds. / The silver dreams that it gurgles and waters the flowers. /

The water fancies that mists, hand in hand, lead each other into the radiance, / But it cannot see their frightened bodies. What can one do with such water? / . . . /

Here anthropomorphism applies even to the natural and supernatural realm. In the poem, the water nymphs have emerged from the water onto the moon. They and all the surrounding elements are in the process of becoming incarnated, of existing "somewhat." The water looks on at this transformation with a look that cannot reach into the realm where "reality weeps" ("łka rzeczywistość").

The process of becoming is expressed by neologisms based on the word "spojrzenie" ("a look") which has a static connotation. It acquires a kinetic, emanating quality due to the suffix:—*ość;* in the noun, and the suffix:—*yścieje;* in the verb for action. (The latter form of the verb is more prevalent in Russian.)

The tendency towards this kind of dynamization is characteristic of Leśmian's poetry since the earliest years of his writing. Another example is the poem "Szewczyk" ("The Little Shoemaker"):

W mgłach daleczeje sierp księżyca,
Zatkwiony ostrzem w czub komina,
Latarnia się na palcach wspina
W mrok, gdzie już kónczy się ulica.[28]

The moon's crescent glimmers faintly in the mist, / Its point stuck in a chimney-top, / The street lamp rises up on tiptoes / In the darkness where the street comes to an end.

The metaphor succeeds in creating a vivid concrete image which corresponds in its plasticity to a Chagall-like picture.

Anthropomorphism in Leśmian's poetry has been widely discussed by many literary critics. Most contend that it is different from the traditional variety. The remarks by Irzykowski explain this difference:

. . . Leśmian's favorite vision is the revivification of nature's forms, and even setting them in motion. . . . These are neither personifications nor symbols. The wooden character of these phantoms [Irzykowski has in mind the poems "Dąb" and "Asoka"] is exquisitely well preserved. This was in fact the poet's artistic goal, to create apparitions of an entirely new kind.[29]

Leśmian not only invests the natural phenomena (in this case trees) with human qualities but lets them retain their own. Thus, they represent an autonomous entity, with properties and souls of their own. This variety of anthropomorphism is more than a poetic device—it has philosophical connotations. The best example of natural phenomena set in motion, revived, and transformed, is the poem "Przemiany" ("Metamorphoses"), said to be more fantastic than those of Ovid.[30]

Tej nocy mrok był duszny i od żądzy parny,
I chabry, rozwidnione suchą błyskawicą,
Przedostały się nagle do oczu tej sarny,
Co biegła w las, spłoszona obcą jej źrenicą—
A one, łeb jej modrząc, mknęły po sarniemu,
I chciwie zaglądały w świat po chabrowemu.

Mak, sam siebie w śródpolnym wykrywszy bezbrzeżu,
Z wrzaskiem, który dla ucha nie był żadnym brzmieniem,
Przekrwawił się w koguta w purpurowym pierzu,
I aż do krwi potrząsał szkarłatnym grzebieniem,
I piał w mrok, rozdzierając dziób, trwogą zatruty,
Aż mu zinąd prawdziwe odpiały koguty.

A jęczmień kłos pragnieniem zazłociwszy gęstem,
Nasrożył nagle złością zjątrzone ościory
I w złotego się jeża przemiażdżył ze chrzęstem
I biegł, kłując po drodze ziół nikłe zapory,
I skomlał i na kwiaty boczył się i jeżył,
I nikt nigdy nie zgadnie, co czuł i co przeżył? / . . . /[31]

The gloom that night was close and sultry with lust, / And cornflowers, aglow in summer lightning, / Suddenly thrust themselves into the eyes of the doe, / That had fled into the forest, startled by an alien stare,— / And azuring her head, they darted away like does, / And greedily peered at the world like cornflowers. /

A poppy, uncovering itself in the field's boundlessness, / With a scream that for the ear was no sound at all, / Blood-changed into a scarlet-plumed cock, / And shook its scarlet comb until it bled, / And, splitting its fright-poisoned beak, crowed into the gloom, / Until real cocks took up its cry. /

Gilding its spike with ripe desire, the barley / Bristled its anger-fretted husks / And with a crackle, crunched itself into a golden hedgehog / And ran, piercing tiny weedy barriers on its way, / And whined, and glowered and bristled at flowers, / And no one shall ever guess what it was it felt or lived through? / . . . /

This masterpiece is amazing in its concreteness. The transformation of phenomena has a sensual effect. The image of shifting plasticity—as in a Cubist painting—is accompanied by the voice of the poppy turned rooster. Enjambement is rarely used in Leśmian's mature poetry. However, in the first and fourth verses he uses it precisely where there is a transgression of boundaries and a fusion of one element with another. Thus, the syntactical shift erasing the borderline of the verse, accentuates graphically the image of the shift from flora to fauna. This poem provides support for the statement made by Ostap Ortwin that there is not the slightest trace of traditional anthropomorphism in Leśmian's *Łąka* and no subjective feeling towards nature. It is, rather, a depersonalized poetry devoid of any barriers between man and nature.[32] Ortwin's observation fits this poem perfectly and has merit if anthropomorphism is perceived in a conventional sense. (However, his statement is farfetched when applied to the whole collection of poems. *Łąka* is the expression of a humanism manifested in many ways, but especially through folk humor.) Leśmian's anthropomorphism is an effective means of realizing his theories in poetic practice.

It is characteristic of Leśmian's stylistics that the function of anthropomorphism is achieved primarily by means of verbs, as is evident in "Metamorphoses." Employing verbs enables him to depict actions and deeds even in those instances where another poet would resort to description. The poet utilizes various means to express, in concrete terms, the essence of a "thing in itself," avoiding, however, the purely descriptive, hence static, states of phenomena. He presents things in the dynamic state of *natura naturans.* In the quoted poems, nature has been invested with human attributes, not by means of similes, but by ascribing to it *actions* characteristic almost exclusively of the human world.

Reification as an introductory stage of anthropomorphization is combined in Leśmian's poetry with an enormous number of abstractions. Such abstractions were characteristic of all Młoda Polska poetry. There, however, they were invested with a strong emotional hue, using designations of feelings and experiences (such as "love," "sadness," "regret," etc.). Such words appear relatively rarely in Leśmian. His abstract expressions refer either to psychological phenomena ("dream," "revery" being the most frequent), or else to direct philosophical categories (of which the most frequently used words are "time," "abyss," "nothingness," "infinity"). These are not the object of reflections; rather, the poet includes them in the image itself by means of reification and anthropomorphization. In *Eliasz* ("Elijah"), for example, nonexistence is the property of a thing ("zaraźliwy liszaj niebytu"—"an infectious tetter of nonexistence"); in "Pszczoły" ("The Bees"), nothingness constitutes a concrete feature ("Z wszystkich sił swej nicości"—"With all the might of its nothingness"); in "Schadzka" ("A Rendezvous"), "sen kołacze do wrót" ("The dream knocks at the gate"); in "Pierwsza schadzka" ("First Rendezvous"), "W pajęczynie po kątach zagnieździł się czas" ("On cobwebs in the corner settled time"). Such examples are numerous.

In analyzing these examples of imagery from the point of view of language, the most fundamental phenomenon is the juxtaposition of abstract expressions and concrete words (catachresis). These juxtapositions are the most important aspect of Leśmian's attitude toward language. The simplest form is the juxtaposition of two nouns, one abstract and one concrete; but Leśmian does not limit himself to this. A typical occurrence is the juxtaposition of words heterogeneous in character, such as "bush, maiden, nothingness" in "Zmierzch" ("Dusk"), or "death, grass, oblivion, and dew" in "Cmentarz" ("Cemetery"). Leśmian often creates phrase combinations in which the abstraction must be treated as a concrete (e.g., "W zakątku cmentarza" ["In a corner of the graveyard"]: "Noc spędzać . . . pod wiecznością" ["To spend the night beneath eternity"], "w radość uchodzące ścieżyny" ["paths leading to joy"]).[33] Sometimes the same principle is applied to the use of the combination of epithets with nouns (e.g., in "Meadow": "sen wędrowny" ["a wandering dream"], "szumny od istnienia" ["teaming with existence"]).[34] We find yet another ingenious juxtaposition of epithet and noun, where the usual epithet of an object becomes the attribute of the succeeding one. The shift creates a "sequential" image, indicative of the state of flux. This expressionistic device is used often. In "Zaloty" ("Courtship"), instead of an "aching hand," we find an "aching crank." Most frequently and typically, however, abstractions are combined with verbs which, in principle, should refer to concrete concepts only. We mean here not only those anthropomorphic combinations with a long tradition, such as "Cisza ciszy—nie słyszy . . . czas nie czuje czasu" ("Quiet hears not quiet . . . time feels not time"—"Dżananda").[35] The juxtapositions are sometimes shocking in their originality and unusual quality (e.g., "wieczność warczy" ["eternity growls"], an oxymoron used in the poem *Łąka*).[36] These juxtapositions of the concrete and the abstract are closely related to the topic of metaphor.

Since Leśmian achieved a uniformity of images in all of his poetry by means of these devices, they are an important component of his originality. His solution to the problem of creating concrete images from the abstractions permitted him, not only to impart dynamism to his vision of the world, but also to introduce a hidden philosophical quality, one that does not consist of direct statements but is rather expressed through the images themselves. Leśmian speaks about definite things, only hinting at the deeper, hidden meanings. To find them is the task of the reader. (This approach is reminiscent of the early Pasternak.)

The phenomena discussed above are one of the principal structural devices of the poetic image. Leśmian's system of metaphor is different from the one current in the period of Młoda Polska (Young Poland); it forecasts later solutions, and sometimes even surpasses them. In the poetry of Młoda Polska, the predominant form of metaphor was the so-called "genitive metaphor," consisting of two nouns, one in the nominative and one in the genitive (e.g., "Kropla goryczy" ["A drop of bitterness"], "śpiew duszy" ["a song of the soul"]). These metaphors were diffused to a high degree throughout the total composition of a poem, quite often consisting of loose groupings of such metaphors linked by the dominant position of the lyrical subject (this was one of the manifestations of Impressionism in lyric poetry). Leśmian generally avoids both the "genitive metaphor" and the diffusion of such metaphors throughout a poem. His metaphor often extends into a part of a sentence or even into a complete sentence, and thus fulfills an important compositional function in the poem. (It is in this approach to metaphor that Leśmian anticipates the so-called Cracow avant-guarde of the 1920s, for whom it was part of their literary program.) He also used the "extended metaphor" as did the Russian Symbolists of the second generation and post-Symbolists. Usually, the second "extended" part of the metaphor carried the meaning. Examples can be found in Ivanov and others.[37]

Sometimes the metaphor extends into an entire poem as in the case with the poem "Ręka" ("The Hand"):

Podczas gdy ciało w mękach żebraczego postu
Kurczyło się, jak ochłap wyschłego moczaru,
Ręka ma w samowolnym obłędzie rozrostu
Wszerz i wzwyż potworniała od żądzy bezmiaru.
Wypaczona od skwarów i pusta, jak dzieża,
Miażdżąc stawów hamulce, rosła mi i rosła,
Czując radość zawczasu ciosanego wiosła,
Co już w samym zapłodku śni morskie bezbrzeża!

Ręko, nadmierna Ręko,
W pięść modlitewną się złóż!
Męko, nadmierna Męko,
Zmalej i skurcz się i znuż! / . . . /[38]

While my body in the torment of a beggar's fasting / Shrank like the bowels of a dried-up swamp, / My hand in wilfull madness of growth / In length and breadth assumed a monstrous shape in its greed for immensity. / Heat-warped and empty as a kneading trough, / Mashing its joint-stops, it grew and grew, / Anticipating the joy of a hewn oar, / That even at conception dreams of the sea's boundlessness! /

O Hand, enormous hand, / Clench into a fist for prayer! / O Torment, enormous Torment, / Dwindle, shrink and tire! / . . . /

This poem can be considered a hyperbolized synecdoche. It is a part which, having become autonomous, still represents the whole from which it disassociated itself. The hand symbolizes all human greed and vices, while growing to enormous proportions and assuming an independent existence. It can also be an allusion to the poet's extensive imagination, which reaches out into infinity, challenging God. The images are remarkably similar. Everything has a hollow roundness about it: the warped bowels, the dried-up swamp, the hand, the kneading trough, the hewn oar, and even the fist.

An example of a "realized metaphor," which shows Leśmian to be at once a follower of Gogol (as is also the case with "Ręka") and a forerunner of such Russian poets as Mayakovsky, is the poem "Dąb" ("The Oak"):

Zaszumiało, zawrzało, a to właśnie z dąbrowy
Wbiegł na chóry kościelne krzepki upiór dębowy
I poburzył organy rąk swych zmorą nie zmorą,
Jakby naraz go było wespół z gędźbą kilkoro.
Rozwiewała się, trzeszcząc, gałęzista czupryna,
I szerzyła się w oczach niewiadoma kraina,
A on piersi wszem dudom nastawił po rycersku,
A w organy od ściany uderzał po siekiersku!

Grajże, graju, graj,
Dopomóż ci Maj,
Dopomóż ci miech, duda
I wszelaka ułuda! / . . . /[39]

There came a stir and a roar, and straight from the oak grove / The sturdy specter of an oak ran into the church's choirloft / And smashed the organ with its ghostly, unghostly hands, / As if there were several of him in a gang at once. / A branching thatch of hair flew, crackling, / And before the eyes there stretched an unknown land, / While he applied his lungs to all the pipes in knightly fashion, / And struck at the organ like an ax from the wall! /

Play then, o player, play, / Let May help you, / Let the bellows help you, and the pipe, / And every delusion! / . . . /

The oak, a traditional symbol of divinity and eternity, turned here into apparition, is the creator of songs—the poet. The negating riddlelike attribute of his hands allows him through creation to reach the unknown land. The folkloric stylized refrain built on tautology and the parallelism of the apostrophe, serve as an incantation which enhances the delusion. The poem has metapoetic attributes.

Here the poet employs hyperbole which grows and multiplies as the plot develops, assuming enormous proportions. The oak, turned organ player, wins the homage of God and the saints who gather around him to admire his virtuosity. This type of trope, characteristic in modern poetry (starting with Romanticism), was described by Viktor M. Zhirmunsky:

> Developing . . . the metaphor is transformed into an independent theme of an entire poem. . . . The metaphor becomes almost a poetic truth. The process of the "realization of metaphor" constitutes an essential and unique feature of the Romantic style.[40]

At other times Leśmian employs the method of the vicious circle, which serves as a device of dynamization of the metaphor. As noted by Sandauer, "The compared subject flows into its own likeness,"[41] creating a constant flow from one metaphor into another, a constant circular action. It was on this phenomenon that Leśmian constructed the poem "Przemiany" ("Metamorphoses"), cited previously. The verbs serve as a link in the dynamic flow of action, at the same time maintaining the analogy of the subjects. For example, "mak, . . . przekrwawił się w koguta" ("a poppy . . . blood-changed into a scarlet-plumed cock"); "A jęczmień . . . w złotego się jeża przemiażdżył" ("And the barley . . . crunched itself into a golden hedgehog"). Due to the predicate, each subject (mak—kogut, jęczmień—jeż) represents one stage in a continuous process, thus constituting a metonymic unit.

The poet develops even genitival metaphors into sentences; e.g., "jarzmo wyczekiwań" ("The yoke of expectations"); ". . . jarzma wyczekiwań nie wdzieje na szyję" ("he will not put on his neck the yoke of expectations"), etc. ("Ta oto godzina"—"This Very Hour").[42] The metaphor is always a component in a longer word sequence, and its contents are always a component of a certain system of representations which is being developed dynamically as is the case in the poem "Chałupa" ("The Hut"); "poobciosam niebyt tak, że będzie gładki . . ." ("I shall hew nonexistence so that it shall be smooth"), etc.[43] As a consequence, verbs play an extremely important role in Leśmian's metaphors; and the figure of speech arises from the relationship of the verb to the noun or to another part of speech, as though in progression, in action. This is what enables him to extend the metaphor into a sentence.

As a result of this phenomenon, Leśmian's metaphor is seldom self-explanatory, but is rather dependent on the context of the whole statement to a much greater degree than is true of his contemporaries. In "Asoka," for example, the metaphor "zieleni wlewać się strugą" ("to flow in a stream of green")[44] would not be clear were it not for the whole context which indicates that the poet is speaking about a willow. Thus, the context makes the metaphor understandable and fully explicable in its particular position. This unusually important role assigned to context is related to two features of Leśmian's metaphor. First, is its casual, hasty, seemingly careless character. In Leśmian, the essence and the function of the figure of speech is the creation, not so much of permanent relationships between words and their designates, but rather of relationships that are extemporaneous and momentary. Thus the value of the metaphor lies not in the "beauty" perceived when singling it out, but in the function it plays in the complete poetic vision. The second reason context plays such an important role is that words are juxtaposed in an unusual, original, and sometimes even shocking way, both when viewing them against the background of colloquial Polish and when comparing them with the practices of poets such as Kasprowicz, Tetmajer, Staff, and those of the "Skamander" group. Only in his earliest creative period did Leśmian use conventional metaphors. Later on, he assembled in them words of disparate meanings which had not usually appeared in combination before. It is in such cases that the *context* plays an enormous part. In isolation, certain metaphors may not make sense; their full meaning becomes clear only in the context of the entire poem. Thus, in "Na poddaszu" ("In The Attic"), "trumnisko utkane z wyżyn i z niczego" ("a big coffin woven out of heights and out of nothing").[45] "Wyżyny—"heights" —becomes clear once we see that the notions of the high and the low are counterposed in the poem. The poet speaks of phenomena placed high up, such as an attic, stars, etc. *Wyżyny* here implies everything that is elevated and thus relates to *trumnisko.* Context plays an important part also in those cases where the metaphor is particularly complicated, consisting of numerous heterogeneous elements. A characteristic example is the following:

/ . . . / I dłonią jak sierść zwierza głaszczę mimowolność
Pieśni, których warczenia w sobie się spodziewam. / . . . /
("Zamyślenie" ["Meditation"])[46]

/ . . . / And with my hand I stroke like an animal's fur the instinct
/ Of songs, whose growl I anticipate in myself. / . . . /

The heterogenous elements indicate in this metapoetic work the primitive and involuntary origin of the song (poetry), which the poet anticipates in himself.

The use of the *symbol* in Leśmian's poetry is a separate matter, and a complicated one. If symbol is very broadly defined, we can say that all of Leśmian's creative output is Symbolist, since its meaning is never limited to that rendered directly, but is always suggestive of deeper hidden meanings. The reader must engage in guessing in order to fully understand the meaning of a poem, for it is never completely explicit. Yet, such a broad understanding of the "symbol" seems neither correct nor convenient for the analysis of those general features of poetic language which are certainly related to Symbolism.

We shall speak of the symbol in a more narrowly defined sense than that of concrete representation, developed in such a way that it might suggest a meaning other than the purely denotational, one which cannot be precisely defined. Several of Leśmian's poems such as "Głuchoniema" ("The Deaf and Dumb"), "Wiatrak" ("The Windmill"), "Fala" ("The Wave"), "Otchłań" ("The Abyss"), are of this type. Their symbolism lies in the fact that they consist of descriptions of concrete things, but their meaning goes beyond these descriptions. Yet we cannot say exactly what *fala* or *wiatrak* represent. Leśmian's symbols are as far removed from symbols with a single meaning, used by many Symbolists of Młoda Polska, as they are from allegory. Trznadel's remarks on Leśmian's use of allegory are confusing. His idea regarding allegory was also refuted by Michał Głowinski, who, reviewing his book on Leśmian, maintained that for Symbolists

> the concept of a symbol was precisely a concept of a concrete image which, absorbing different meanings, can become the basic element of poetry. . . . Without the concept of a concrete image, the idea of a symbol is inconceivable.[47]

For Leśmian (as for Bergson and the later Russian Symbolists, (cf., chapter 4), a symbol was concrete, representing the unity of form and content given in an individual experience. The symbols expressing his experience at the time of creating poems like "Wiatrak" or "Fala" could have the same meaning later neither for the creator nor for the reader. Even so, the definition of Leśmian's symbol is of minimal importance in his mature poetry. The poet represents a phase in the development of Symbolism in which "symbols" had already diminished in importance. Even in its beginning stages, as coined by Verlaine, the symbol was conceived of as a kinetic phenomenon. Though in the early years the Symbolists were preoccupied with the definition of the symbol, their zeal diminished, as can be seen in works of such Symbolists as Tancrède de Visan, Jean Royère, and later Edouard Dujardin and others. Rhythm was the primary attraction for the Symbolists, who saw the Symbolist movement as an attitude. Symbol, originally envisioned as a stylistic phenomenon, became a poetic property. All these tendencies are reflected in Leśmian's poetics.

One other phenomenon of great significance in the imagery of Leśmian's poetry is the *grotesque*. Almost from the start, we detect opposing elements in Leśmian, where a lust for life is linked with an obsession with death, and the real is linked to the supernatural. Later, when nature appears enigmatic to him, he is equally skeptical and ironic toward life and death. He feels lost, and everything in life becomes absurd. At this point the grotesque appears intensified in Leśmian's work. Contradictions accumulate, creating a dynamic tension. Due to the morbidity of some motifs, critics like Marian Pankowski consider Leśmian's entire work to be permeated with baroque aesthetics. Pankowski maintains that the absurd,

> . . . a most outstanding . . . baroque motif, where exaggeration is the most important feature, persists throughout Leśmian's entire creative work.
>
> Leśmian's humor has a baroque quality. . . . It is grotesque, biting, shocking, sensual, daring, and bordering on bad taste.[48]

Although this interpretation of Leśmian's work is exaggerated and somewhat inaccurate, it is true that the grotesque plays a great role in Leśmian's poetry. It is formulated on different levels, starting with word formation and combinations of words. A good example of the latter is the poem "W pałacu królewny śpiącej" ("In the Palace of the Sleeping Princess"):

Królewna dłoń o martwe zraniła wrzeciono.
Szerzy się snu zaraza! . . . Śmierć drzemie u płotu . . .
Drzewa, jawą parując, posnęły zielono.
Motyl zawisł nad studnią skrzydłami bez lotu.
Mrużąc przygasłych ślepi pilne ametysty,
Kot do snu łeb przypłaszczył na perłach w szkatule.
Pies się zwinął oszczędnie w kłębek wiekuisty,
Ogonem myśl o ludziach zaznaczając czule. / . . . /[49]

The princess pricked her palm on a dead spindle. / The plague of dreams is spreading! . . . Death dozes at the fence. . . . / Steaming with wakefulness, the trees fell into a green sleep. / A butterfly hung suspended on flightless wings above the well. / Squinting the watchful amethysts of its dull-lidded eyes, / To sleep the cat flattened his head against the pearls in the casket. / The dog rolled himself sparingly into an eternal ball, / Tenderly marking with his tail a thought about people. / . . . /

This part of the poem demonstrates that the plot development is based on the grotesque, which also appears in separate formulations within the plot, e.g., ". . . do dna nicość z sadłem za pan brat przywarły;" (". . . hobnobbing with lard, nothingness got stuck to the bottom"). Sometimes the juxtapositions of the abstract with the concrete, so basic to Leśmian's poetry, take on a grotesque tinge: for instance, "ruchem snu i kota" ("as with the movement of a dream and of a cat"). Thus, in Leśmian's poetry the grotesque is one of the constant possibilities, and is expressed both in individual words (some "strange" words present in his poetry are of a grotesque nature), and in the juxtaposition of images.

A good example for juxtaposing images for the purpose of achieving the grotesque is the stylized ballad "Dusiołek" ("A Choking Nightmare"). It is chosen as representative of similar poems, e.g., "Śnigrobek," "Zmierzchun," "Kocmołuch," and others. An excellent analysis of this ballad has been rendered by Kazimierz Wyka.[50] However, I shall try to show how well "Dusiołek" realizes Bergson's ideas on the comic, the absurd, and the grotesque. Leśmian uses intentional "mechanization," which Bergson considers essential to create an absurd, grotesque situation.[51] According to the philosopher, the latter arises when

> it belongs to two altogether independent series of events, and is capable of being interpreted in two entirely different meanings at the same time.[52]

In this poem we have an evolution of events that are unexpected and therefore essential in creating the grotesque. "Dusiołek" represents a combination of two contrasting backgrounds. It is a semistylized Romantic ballad combined with loose folk stylization. The poet treats the folk elements with intentional exaggeration, thus creating doubt in the reader's mind. The hidden narrator relating the story is equally presented in an exaggerated manner. His observations hint at the presence of onlookers. The story is that of a traveling peasant, Bajdała, who, while taking a nap, is choked by a nightmare (Dusiołek). His restless dream is witnessed by the narrator and onlookers. The narrator's unexpected observations are comic because "an absurd idea has been fitted into a well established form."[53]

/ . . . / Nie wiadomo dziś wcale,
Co się śniło Bajdale?
Lecz wiadomo, że szpecąc przystojność przestworza,
Wylazł z rowu Dusiołek jak półbabek z łoża.

Pysk miał z żabia ślimaczy—
(Że też taki żyć raczy!)—
A zad tyli co kwoka, kiedy znosi jajo.
Milcz, gębo nieposłuszna, bo dziewki wyłają! / . . . /[54]

No one knows at all today, / What Bajdala dreamed about? / But it's a fact that a Choking Nightmare, / Blemishing the handsomeness of infinity, / Crawled from a ditch like some half-hag from her bed. /

It had a snaily frog-snout— / (That such a creature dare to live!)— / And a rear as big as a cackling hen laying an egg. / Quiet, disobedient mug, or the wenches'll give you hell! / . . . /

The narrator's contradictory observations create, at the outset, an effect of parody. No one knows what the peasant dreamt about, yet he describes the dream and the apparition in realistic terms, even using a digression. He is even reprimanded for using vulgar language by one of the onlookers, who threatens him with the reaction of the wenches.

The series of events becomes grotesque by mutual interference of all present, as the narrator engages even the natural phenomena to witness the unusual event.

/ . . . / Dmucha w wąsy ze zgrozy, jękiem złemu przeczy—
Słuchajta, wszystkie wierzby, jak chłop przez sen beczy! / . . . /[55]

/ . . . / He puffs through his moustache in horror, spurning the evil one with a moan— / Hey, listen, all you willows, how the peasant bleats in his sleep! / . . . /

The humor of the story is further heightened when the awakened peasant, Bajdała, reproaches the horse and the ox for failing to annihilate the nightmare choking him in his dream:

/ . . . / Rzekł Bajdała do szkapy:
"Czemu zwieszasz swe chrapy?
Trzebać było kopytem Dusiołka przetrącić,
Zanim zdążył mój spokój w całym polu zmącić!"

Rzekł Bajdała do wołu:
"Czemuś skąpił mozołu?
Trzebać było rogami Dusiołka postronić,
Gdy chciał na mnie swej duszy paskudę wyłonić!" / . . . /[56]

Said Bajdala to the nag: / "Why do you let your nostrils droop? / You should have toppled and trampled the choking nightmare with your hoof / Before it could trouble my rest all over the field!" /

Said Bajdala to the ox: / "Why did you begrudge your labor? / You should have chased away the Choking Nightmare with your horns, / When it wanted to smother me with the foulness of its soul! / . . . /

As is customary for primitive man, reality and the supernatural or the dream are treated in the same manner. Therefore, Bajdała ("The Prattler") reproaches his animal friends for not coming to his rescue when his rest was disturbed in the "entire" field. There we have a double connotation: This form can be simply dialectal or assume a philosophical universal meaning. This episode fits Bergson's idea perfectly that *"a comic absurdity is of the same nature as that of a dream."*[57] Yet the climax of the grotesque is achieved when there occurs a transposition of "the natural expression into another key."[58] Bergson's idea here again finds a perfect realization:

/ . . . / Rzekł Bajdała do Boga:
"O rety—olaboga! / . . . /
Nie dość Ci, żeś potworzył mnie, szkapę i wołka,
Jeszcześ musiał takiego zmajstrować Dusiołka?"[59]

Said Bajdala to God: / "Help—for God's sake! . . . / Isn't it enough that Thou hast monstrously created the nag, the little ox and me, / Didst Thou have to contrive such a Choking Nightmare?

The poet uses the natural expression of a simple half-witted peasant to pose a highly philosophical and ethical question. This question is symbolic in nature: the confrontation between innocence and the evil that dominates the world. Thus, two contrasting levels of consciousness; the simple, folkloric and the complex, philosophical, have been merged by the poet to attain the heights of humor and grotesque. The believing peasant's question was transposed into an indictment of God, bringing to absurdity the issue of God's creation. This is aided, as has been pointed out earlier, by appropriate lexical means (cf. chapter 3); the idea and form are indivisible. The grotesqueness of the idea is expressed by the grotesque in the form, by juxtaposing various levels of language: dialect, archaisms, colloquialisms, literary language, and "Leśmianisms" (neologisms) even within one verse. We have a syntactical mixture of statement, narration, digression, apostrophe and dialogue.

In the last phase of Leśmian's works, the comic is often fused with eschatology. He finds the world illusory, senseless. The chaos reigning in this world is best illustrated in the poem "Wiosna" ("Spring"):

Takiej wiosny rzetelnej, jaką w swym powiecie
Widział Jędrek Wysmółek—nikt nie widział w świecie!

Poprzez okno karczemne łeb w bezmiar wyraził
I mało się w durną mgłę nie przeobraził!

Lecz umocnił się w karku i nieco przybladłszy,
Łbem pochwiał dla otuchy, i splunął i patrzy . . .

Jego własna chałupa wraz z babą i sadem
Odwróciła się nagle nieproszonym zadem.

Wieprz—znajomek, nie większy na pozór od snopa,
Biegnie w skradzionych portkach Magdzinego chłopa. / . . . /[60]

Such an honest spring, as in his district / Andrew the Tarred saw—nobody'd ever seen in this world! /

He poked his huge head out the pub window into the boundlessness / And was almost turned into a foolish mist! /

But he stiffened his neck and, paling a bit, / He shook his huge head to pluck up his courage, and spat and keeps looking . . . /

His very own hut with his woman and orchard / Turned about suddenly its unbidden backside. /

The pig—an old friend, no bigger at first glance than a sheaf of wheat, / Runs in breeches stolen form Magda's swain. / . . . /

Here we have again a drunken simpleton's view of the world. The narrator describes the incongruous events in all seriousness mixing language levels and stylistic devices to heighten the comic effects.

This poem represents the world turned upside down, recalling in its theme and plasticity Chagall's paintings. The chaos and the grotesqueness of the imagery present the world in upheaval and echo as well Gogol's incongruities in *The Tale of How Ivan Ivanovich Quarreled with Ivan Nikiforovich* (cf., the event with the pig). It should also be added that the grotesque is manifested in the sensuality and brutality of the physically maimed (cf., the cycle *The Maimed Songs*, "Pieśni kalekujące," and especially the poem "Zaloty" "Courtship"). The element of Russian folklore (cf., *byliny*) is also evident in Leśmian's poetry, where the juxtaposition of extreme cruelty with childlike innocence (cf., Vasilii Buslaev of the Novgorod *byliny*) creates the most refined kind of the grotesque which is expressed in a language at once affectionate (using diminutives) and macabre. Jacek Trznadel's opinion of Leśmian's grotesque as "the last stage of overcoming aesthetics"[61] is fully shared by this writer.

Every literary work demands an analysis of its verbal texture, regardless of the importance the writer himself ascribes to it. However, in the case of Leśmian for whom the word was *myth* and myth-creating, the analysis of language is imperative. Wyka remarks the following on the subject

A literary work represents an indivisible whole. Only our scrutinizing schemes cut it into pieces. However, the road to the mystery of a work of art can vary. There are writers in whose work we enter the mysteries by means of verbal expressions, and where the analysis progressing from the lexical vestment to the reflective essence (basis of thought) is the right one.[62]

There is no doubt that this ideal approach in analyzing artistic work applies especially to Leśmian, whose ideas on the subject of language have been discussed in chapter 2.

However, Leśmian's language requires a separate and exhaustive study, far exceeding the scope of this work. Of necessity, I shall treat the subject superficially, giving the reader some idea of the function of this "peculiar" language, representing virtually an inexhaustible treasure. Leśmian's so-called "strange" words are not mere concoctions created to fill a void (as has been assumed by some critics);[63] They are a uniquely "motivated,"[64] an indispensable means of expressing an equally unusual philosophy in poetic images. I shall attempt to show briefly how the structure and the semantics of the poet's neologisms serve as a key to the understanding of his metaphysics.

As discussed in previous chapters, time, as an element, exists in Leśmian's poetics only insofar as it can be represented by a *word* or accumulated in a work of art. Therefore, Leśmian aimed at creating a poetic language which would incarnate the time element. This concern in creating words is limited exclusively to fit his own poetic context, and only within its realm do they have a poetic meaning.

/ . . . / I zachłanną radością mąci mu się głowa,
Gdy ujmie niepochwytność w dwa przyległe słowa! / . . . /
("Poeta" ["The Poet"])[65]

/ . . . / And his head is a-spin with joyous delirium. / When he pins down elusiveness with two adjacent words! / . . . /

In this programmatic and somewhat autobiographical poem, the primary function of the word is to capture the elusive moment in an ever-changing reality. Yet, this is a rare feat for a poet serving contemporaneity, for whom "Słowo się nie spokrewnia z pozasłownym trwaniem— / Porównanie się stało tylko porównaniem." ("The word is not related to extralingual duration— / A simile became only a simile.")[66]

In contrast to this, Leśmian's words have a "direct contiguity to a situation in constant flux. . . . They do not describe it, they only signalize it"[67] by way of a synthetic image. A poetic statement expressing a fleeting moment can only be understood in a given situation and in a given time, for it fits only a single occurrence.

Another function of the word is to express phases in the process of the ceaseless metamorphosis of every phenomenon. This partially explains the "haphazardness" (*bylejakość*) of many words which, like the phenomena they connote, barely have time to become incarnated. A good example is the following:

/ . . . / Pocałunki dla cię, chłopcze, w ostrą stal uzbroję,
Błysk—*niedobłysk* na *wybłysku*—oto zęby moje! / . . . /
("Piła" ["The Saw"])[68]

/ . . . / Kisses for you, my lad, will I arm with sharp steel, / A glint—an unglint now a-glint—*these are my teeth! / . . . /*

Here we have affirmation, negation, and emanation of a phenomenon expressed (by the lover—the saw) in a parallel juxtaposition, used often in Russian folklore, especially in riddles. In fact the distich resembles a riddle. The effect of such use of language is very much like that of a movie, where now you see the image, and now you don't.

The use of prefixes like un-, non-, connotes, as a rule, a certain lack in the context of a word. In Leśmian's poetics, the lack and excess coexist side by side, as do other antonyms. This careless juxtaposition is but one example of Leśmian's *bylejakość*, originally analyzed by Sandauer.[69]

The state of metamorphosis is closely connected with the state of becoming, a very vital state in Leśmian's aesthetics. He is a poet who, in his creative evolution, is constantly trying to capture the stage just between *res nullius* and before a person or a thing becomes incarnated (cf., *niedobłysk* ["an unglint"] in "Piła"). That is why his images protrude halfway out of the substance from which they try to free themselves. This is the case in "Ballada bezludna" ("The Desolate Ballad"):

/ . . . / A to jakaś mgła dziewczęca chciała dostać warg i oczu,
I czuć było, jak boleśnie chce się stworzyć, chce się wcielić,
Raz warkoczem się zazłocić, raz piersiami się zabielić— / . . . /[70]

/ . . . / And then a kind of girl-like haze wanted to have lips and eyes, / And one felt how painfully it wanted to be created, wanted to become flesh, / Now with golden braid to shimmer, now with snow-white breast to sparkle— / . . . /

The poem reminds one of the unfinished sculptures of Michelangelo Buonarroti in the Academy Gallery in Florence, where only a part of the body has been formed, the rest being still rooted in the marble rock. To recreate such fleeting unrepeatable images requires a special language. In Leśmian's aesthetics the word is an autonomous entity. It must be self-sufficient. One can say that due to the structure of the neologisms, consisting often of single or compound prefixes (often antithetic), they represent in a sense a contracted syntactical unit. They can constitute a poetic image by themselves. Thus, the verb *zanieistniał* expresses, in effect, a whole sentence—i.e., the state of becoming, of existing, and of a subject's ceasing to exist. Such words, not only express different levels of meaning, but also are capable of fulfilling various functions and concepts basic to Leśmian's poetics.

To express things in action and deed (synonymous with life in Leśmian's aesthetics) he used a language replete with nouns pertaining to deeds, and a verbal texture with prefixes connoting the state of emanation. Each morpheme of the word is charged with a metaphysical connotation.

I ona, nim *wylgnęła* z rąk uboczem ciała. ("Niedziela," *N.* ["Sunday"])
("And she, before she *slipped* [out] with her body sideways from his grasp.")

(*Ubocze* is a neologism based on an archaic noun: *ubocz*—see Linde—which means "a place to the side." Leśmian's neologism is a noun of neuter gender, implying "with the side," "sideways.")

Gdy chciał na mnie *paskudę* swej duszy *wyłonić*. ("Dusiołek," *Ł*. ["The Choking Nightmare"])
("When he wanted to *smother me with* the *foulness* of his soul.")

(In English, the act of *emanation* does not come through. The neologism *paskuda* is, according to Bogumił Linde, of Russian origin. It is derived of two words *pakost'* ("dirt") and *skuda* ("poverty").

A kiedy księżyc *wyotchłanił przerażone niebiosy* ("Baśń o ryc. . . ." *Legendy tęskn.* ["The Tale about . . ." *Legends of Longing*])
("And when the moon *called into being* the abyss of horror-stricken heavens.)

Aż zamęt ich podziemnych szmerów i hałasów *wyprzejrzyści* się nagle w okrzyk lazurowy. ("Zamyślenie," *Ł*. ["Meditation"])
("Until the welter of subterranean noises and tumult / Shall suddenly *grow into* a *pellucid* azure outcry.")[71]

To express the state of becoming and fading away, he also fuses verbs with prefixes: *za-*, *od-*, *do-:*

Zabłękitnij—odbłękitnij . . . ("Pan Błyszczyński," *N*.)
("*Become azure—cease being azure* . . ."), or ("Be azure—be not azure.")

With this incantation the protagonist urges his creation, the maiden, to continue acting, thereby prolonging her existence.

I księżyc co na dachach *dolśnił się* do czczości ("Pejzaż współcz." *N*. ["Contemporary Landscape"])
("And the moon that on the roofs *gleamed to* futility, . . .")

. . .pył biały w słońcu *zaprzejrzyściał* ("Majka," *Kl. p.*)
(". . . the white dust *became suddenly transparent* in the sun.")

I duch zrozumiał, że i strzechy słoma
Powinna pierwej *zazłocić się* słowie ("Spowiedź," *N*. ["A Confession"])
("And the spirit knew that even the straw of a thatched roof / Should first *assume a golden hue* in the word.")

Coś się chciało *zazłocić,* lecz zabrakło czasu ("Strumień," *N.* ["A Stream"])
("Something *would have glimmered gold,* but time ran out.")

(This verse explains why a complete state cannot be fully achieved.)

Nominal verbs prevail in this phase. The phenomenon of tautology proves the autonomy, the totality of "a thing within itself." We find the following examples:

Stodoła się stodoli ("The barn barns itself")
Topola się topoli ("The poplar tree poplars itself")
("Stodoła," *Ł.* ["The Barn"])

This action originating in tautology was first discussed by Adam Szczerbowski.[72] Sandauer called it the "dynamization of a vicious cycle, the circumference of which is closed by a motion of the predicate wound around its own subject."[73] Roman Jakobson calls words based on the same root "etymological figures" (cf., footnote 133, chapter 3). The static quality of the noun has been changed, put into motion by the verb derived from it, thereby shedding a different light on the process of becoming. Other tautological expressions taken from Russian folklore, e.g., *wolna wola,* cf., *Elijah,* "The Hut," serve as incantations.

The stage of a slowed-down process of becoming or eternal becoming and of prolonged action is characterized by verbs with compound prefixes, a phenomenon more prevalent in Russian than in Polish.

Świat się już dla mnie dosyć *nanicestwił i naustronił*
I jam dość się dla świata *naczłowieczył* i *naśnił!*
("Słowa do pieśni bez słów," *N.* ["Words to the Song Without Words"])

("I have already *had my fill* of a world *made nothing* and *remote* [*to excess*]. / And the world has *had its fill* of me *made human* and *dreamy* [*to excess*].")

Here the prefix na-, + się—means to do something to one's fill, to excess. These verbs: *na-u-*stronił się, *na-*nicestwił się, are of Russian derivation according to Linde. A Russian rendering of the first verse will show that the neologisms grow naturally out of that language: "Svet dla menia uzhe dostatochno *nau*-nichtozhylsia i *nau*-stranilsia." The same is true for the compound prefix poroz-,:

Porozbujał pieśń górą w dwa ruczaje niestałe ("Dąb," *Ł.* ["The Oak"])
("The song at the top he set swinging in two wavering streams.")

This concrete image is created by the crown of the oak, which divides the blue sky into wavering streams as it sways.

Especially verbs formed by adjectives, ending in -eć, as in the following examples, that connote the process of attainment of an attribute, are used more often in Russian (cf., *belet'*):

Kto tam z nocy na północ na burzę i zawieję
Tak bardzo *człowieczeje* i tak *bożyścieje?* ("Żołnierz," *Ł.* ["A Soldier"])
("Who there northwards out of the night into the storm and blizzard / *Appears* so *manlike* and so *godlike?*")

W mgłach *daleczeje* sierp księżyca . . . ("Szewczyk," *Ł.* ["The Little Shoemaker"])
("The moon's crescent *glows distant* in the mist . . .")

Czmurowi . . . *sobacząc.* ("Dwaj Macieje" ["The Two Matthews"])
("Cursing at Chmur.")

The same connotation is found in verbs with compound prefixes przypod-: (cf., "pripodnimat'sia"):

Nadaremnie się obłok słońcu *przypodzłaca* ("Sen," *N.* ["A Dream"])
("The cloud *endears itself gold-like to* the sun in vain.")

The prefixes: *powy-, poroz-, poza-;* are used in Polish only occasionally: "*powy*pełznąć," "*poza*wrzeć," "*powy*rzucać," "*poza*rastać," connote repetition of action or of a gradual process. They are, however, used frequently in Russian ("*povy*brasyvat'," "*poza*byt'," "*poza*rastat' "). (Linde gives many Russian examples which indicates their influence on Polish).

Existence and nonexistence were the two poles of Leśmian's constant oscillations. To express this phenomenon, the poet uses compound prefixes: *zanie—, zbez—,* of which only four verbs appear in colloquial Polish; these verbs are, therefore, Leśmian's original creation. Acting as a syntactical shortcut, they insinuate paradox and, as a sort of synecdoche, they express in a "molecule," the microcosm of Leśmian's metaphysics:

Spróbujmy we troje *zanieistnieć* w słońcu ("Pururawa i Urwasi," *Ł.*)
("Let us try, we three, *to cease existing* in the sun")

Zielona zjawa swe dłonie *zbezcieleśnia* ("Pan Błyszczyński," *N.*)
("The verdurous spectre *disembodies* its hands.")

Indicating growth and development with a broader sweep, Leśmian uses many verbs with the prefix *roz-*, which is used even more in Russian than in Polish.

I jak drzewo pod ziemię w nagły żal się *rozklęka!* ("Dąb," *Ł.* ["The Oak"])
("And how beneath the earth the tree *sinks to its outstretched knees* in sudden grief!")

Jak trudno czasem żal *rozbiałośnieżyć* ("Aniołowie," *S.* ["The Angels"])
("How difficult it is at times to dispel grief by *making it snow-white.*")

Even in some participial forms the same prefixes are used:

. . . wygląda raczej jak *rozemknięty* miraż . . . ("Baśń o rycerzu," *R.*)
(". . . it looks rather like a mirage flung open . . .")

Existence, nothingness, as well as negation of existence have their philosophical origin in Bergson's *Creative Evolution* (in which a whole chapter is devoted to "Nothingness"). Nonexistence, negation, nothingness, expressed by using nouns and adjectives with the prefixes *bez-*, *nie-*, do not have the connotation, as interpreted by Sandauer, of "destructive prefixes of negation." Instead, Leśmian understands nothingness as a kind of partial nothingness which remains after a thing is no longer present. In this concept he echoes Bergson:

The void of which I speak . . . is, at bottom, only the absence of some definite object, which was here at first, is now elsewhere, and insofar as it is no longer in its former place, leaves behind it . . . the void of itself.[74]

The idea of absolute nothingness ("naught"), in the sense of total annihilation, does not exist in Leśmian's aesthetics, as his poetry makes obvious. That is why the use of negative prefixes is rather an expression of a passing phase in existence; from the total presence to a concretization of the nonexistence. The negative prefix endows the word with a dual meaning. A careful study of the texts shows clearly that the negation is superimposed over the negated world, and therefore does not exclude its existence.

Puść mnie tam—w *bezbożyznę!* (*Eliasz, N.* ["Elijah"])
("Let me in there—into *godless space.*")

Aż zabrnął . . . /
W taki *bezświat* zarosli, w taki *bezbrzask* głuchy ("Topielec," *Ł.* ["The Drowned One"])
("Until he waded / . . . / Into such an *unworld* of thickets, into such a still *undawn,*")

Wróć mi wolę ruczajną, wróć sławne *bezczasy!* ("Pururawa i Urwasi," *Ł.*)
("Give me back the will of the stream, give me back the *neverness* of renown!")

I nęcił ust zdyszanych tajemnym *bezśmiechem* ("Topielec," *Ł.*)
("And tempted him with panting lips mysteriously *laughless*")

I z wozu gasnącego w *bezświat* się wychylił (*Eliasz, N.* ["Elijah"])
("And from the waning flames of [his] chariot he leaned out into the *unworld.*")

Kocham cię za twojego obłędu *bezwinę* . . . ("Do śpiewaka," *Ł.* ["To The Singer"])
("I love you for the *unguilt* of your madness . . .")

Negation runs through the entire work of Leśmian. It has its roots primarily in Russian folklore and parallels Russian Symbolist aesthetics. It is the ever present theme, although the stimuli differ depending on the period in his creation. The poet also uses verbal forms with the prefixes *nie-* and *bez-:*

I coraz bardziej sobie *niedostrzeżny.* ("Niezn, podr. S. Ż.," *S.*)
("And more and more *undiscernible* to myself.")

Śmierć jest dla nich pędem w *niepochwytne* cienie ("Skrzeble," *Dz.* ["The Rodents"])
(Death for them is an onward rush into *uncaught shadows.*]

Like the Russian Symbolists, Leśmian creates abstract nouns—a special forté of Balmont (cf., his "Bezglagol'nost' ").

W głuchą *bezleśność* i nudną *bezpolność* ("Niezn. podr. S. Ż.," *S.*)
("Into a deaf *forestlessness* and a dull *fieldlessness*")

This category of nouns attains an adjectival connotation and a concreteness in Leśmian's poetry. There are some Leśmianisms that seem to have obvious Russian origins. These are nouns with suffixes which are not very productive in Russian word formation, e.g., *-ba, -da, -ak, -anka, -uszka,* and *-ost'*. In Leśmian's works we find nouns such as *dziejba, paskuda,* (see Linde), *niepodoba, sitak, cichanka, śmiertuszka, spojrzystość,* etc. Except for the last, all of these neologisms have one thing in common: they connote concreteness. Leśmian also uses truncated nouns, the stems of which are of Slavic origin.[75]

Another possible folkloric Russian influence seems to me to be Leśmian's usage of some compound adjectives, although some of these are also Polish archaisms:

Płaszcz szkarłatny, *złotobrzeżny* . . . ("Baśń o rycerzu," *R.*)
("A scarlet cloak, *gold-trimmed* . . .")

Anioł błękitnooki i *złocistobrewy* ("Noc," *S.*)
("An angel azure-eyed and golden browed.")

The influence of folklore was of great importance in Leśmian's language, as can be seen in his letter written to the newspaper *Ponowa:*

. . . It seems to me that a kinship based upon the freedom of spirit and cognition of the real folkloric world with that of the "beyond" will release new sources. These sources will revive a language which conceals incalculable creative possibilities. . . . It will serve as an everlasting dissemination of pre-dawn recollection, of primeval impressions, eternal manifestations, and even of elements which never yet materialized ["widów-niewidów"]. [Cf., the juxtaposition of antinomies of Russian origin.]

The ritualistically inspired conception of art on the part of the folk, will inhibit [the artists'] flights of imagination above the gray "commonplace." It will force them to gather on the colorful, concrete lowlands. . . .

Language becoming primeval will impose upon the poet its remote "dream world" ["śni mi się"].[76]

From Russian folklore comes the parallel juxtaposition of attributive nouns and antonyms:

Księżyc—Królewicz z błękitów baśni ("Wierzba," *R.* ["The Moon Prince" from the fairy tale "The Willow Azure"])
widy—niewidy ("List do red.," *Ponowy* ["Sight(s)—unsight(s)"])
koszula—ciasnocha ("Alcabon," *N.* ["Shirt—snugger."])
czapka—niewidymka ("Z rozm. o B." ["Invisible—cap."])
Za ugorami podźwignął swe brzemię
Sam pług—włodyka ("Spowiedź," *R.* ["Confession"])
("Beyond the fallows his burden raised / The plow himself—the master.")

Here we have a folkloric reference to the prehistoric Russian *bylina* and to Mikula Selaninovich—the peasant—*bogatyr'* (vladyka).

I poburzył organy rąk swych zmorą—niezmorą ("Dąb," *L.*)
("And smashed the organ with its ghostly-unghostly hands.")

Wyrzuca szepty—perły i jęki—korale ("Wobec morza," *S.* ["Towards the Sea"])[77]
("Casts out whispers—pearls and moans—corals")

In each of the language categories discussed above, superficially we find definite traces of Russian.

Such is the case in the dialecticism of verbs in the first person plural of the present tense—*Będziem, możem, kładziem się, odbierzem, stoim, pójdziem*—which is the normal first person plural form of Russian verbs. Cf., *budem, mozhem, klademsia, otberem, stoim, poidem,* etc.

Verbs like *kołychać,* ("to swing," "to rock") is a borrowing from the Russian—*kolykhat'.*

Also some generic nouns (consisting of roots or stems only) are of Russian origin: *wid, twardź;* cf., with *vid, tverd'*—the latter is a Russian archaism in *Pesni Vasilisy Premudroi; rzadź*—as an assimilation to such Russian nouns as *priad'*. Here also belong the truncated neologisms, such as *sprzęg;*—cf., with *upriazh; (spriagat')* in Russian.

Compound nouns such as: *białydnia—dobrawoli,* are derived from Russian folklore especially from *byliny.*

Some nouns ending in an unproductive suffix: *-ba, -da; -okha; -ikha; -izna; -ok* (mentioned above), have been pointed out by Linde as being more prevalent in Russian: *dziejba, paskuda*—cf., *"svad'ba"* etc., *"tańczyć przysiudy"* ("to dance *prisiudy*"—part of the gopak); Rozwalicha—cf., Russian *portnikha,* etc., *ciszyzna, bezbożyzna*—cf., Russian *dorogovizna, dziadok*—cf., *dedok* ("an old man; beggar" in "A Beggar's Ballad").

Nouns used adverbially: *na przychlipkę*—cf., *prikhlebnut', v prikhlebku, v prikusku; z niedaleczka*—dialectal Russian and Polish (see "The Two Matthews").

It seems to me that "Czmur" is not used in the above poem for its onomatopoeic effect (as pointed out by Papierkowski), but is rather an adaptation of "Chernomor"—also a name of the sorcerer in Pushkin's *Ruslan and Liudmila.*

According to Przyboś, many of Leśmian's neologisms find no equivalents in Linde or Karłowicz.[78] Zawodziński does not find sources either for many "Leśmianisms" in the Polish language. Yet, many of them are based on Russian, which is especially evident in his dialectical words based on Russian folklore. However, substantial proof of this could only be given in a separate study.

All of these "strange" Leśmianisms have yet another aim. They are not used to express philosophy, ridicule, and the grotesque exclusively. It is perhaps the only Symbolist language endowed with a strong element of parody. The strange word combinations evoke humor in Leśmian's poetry. This was his intention as he stated in his esssays on rhythm. He wanted to create laughing words. At times this is their only function. Such is the case in the description of Indra in the guise of a peacock:

Porzucił praistnienia zjesieniałość górną,
By się nasnuć w jej oczy tak barwno i piórno! ("Dżananda," *N.* ["Djananda"])
("He abandoned the lofty autumnedness of primeval existence, / To spin and spin before her eyes, so colorful and feathery! / ")

This analogy evokes laughter. The poet Zbigniew Bieńkowski says that his "word oozes with humor. . . . The poet had no intention of enriching the scope of the Polish language . . . the humor of a word has only this in common with the humor of a joke: it dies when repeated."[79] Leśmian was interested mainly in expressing and evoking the singular, specific moment, in this case the funny side of life.

A słowa się po niebie włóczą i łajdaczą—
I udają, że znaczą coś więcej niż znaczą! . . .
"Poeta," *N.* ["The Poet"]

But words roam the heavens and carouse— / And pretend they mean something more than they do! /

Leśmian's words are the primary level of expressing his aesthetics. In achieving this, he lives up to his "myth of genesis," creating as did the "natural" poet. A. Sandauer arrived at an excellent analysis of Leśmian's philosophy through a partial decoding of Leśmian's "strange" words. Having discussed, somewhat superficially, the words used for expressing his poetic ontology, I shall in conclusion present briefly the structure of Leśmian's poetic image as his poems smallest syntactical, contextual unit.

Images in Leśmian, as in all poetry, are a matter of language. Here we shall discuss certain specific characteristics of that language, namely those to which critics and analysts of poetry have given the most attention. As was demonstrated above, Leśmian's language is very distinctive, individual, and inimitable, distinguished by the presence of words and phrases unknown to the contemporary Polish literary language. Such an attitude toward language was part of the literary program of Młoda Polska. The poetry of that epoch created certain conventions for shaping a new language, but the main purpose of such a formulation was to subjugate it in evoking an emotional atmosphere. Leśmian, on the other hand, directs his linguistic quests towards cognition: the word is to convey the uniqueness and singularity of phenomena. It was believed that the basic linguistic achievement in Leśmian's poetry was the creation of neologisms, but more careful investigations have revealed that archaisms, dialectisms and colloquialisms play an equally important role in his language.

The individuality of the poet's language appears not only in his choice of particular words; his innovations consist, most of all, in bringing out nuances of meaning through context. For example, in the combination "przywidzenia kalinowe"—"Łąka" ("cranberry apparitions" ["The Meadow"])[80] the epithet *kalinowe* takes on new meanings; it is not merely a word derived from *kalina*, but is much more general in content and, significantly, somewhat enigmatic at the same time; for it can serve as an epithet indicating anything that is part of nature.

In general, it is characteristic of Leśmian that the combined words may be only loosely related semantically, even in a given context; this is particularly true of the modifiers, e.g., "umówny kwiat" ("Niewiara") ("conventional flower" ["Disbelief"]) "nudny wóz ("Do siostry") ("tedious wagon" ["To My Sister"]).[81] But no matter how loose, such juxtapositions are never accidental; they are of value functionally and are defined through the context. This context permits the use of nonce words which have a specific meaning only in a given group of words or word formations. (Cf., the verb *napurpurzać* ("To grow more and more purple") in the poem "Zwiewność" ["Etherealness"]).[82] Leśmian intensifies the capacity of language to attain such momentary, occasional meanings, thereby obtaining unusual effects.

His innovations are most evident in his phraseology in that he creates new syntactic relationships between words. For example, in "Schadzka"[83] ("A Rendezvous"), we have such formulations as "purpurowieje w niebiosy" ("to glow purple into the heavens"), and "drzwi w słońce otworzę" ("I shall open a door into the sun"). In "Cień," *S.* ("The Shadow") "Jeno pragnę powrócić w ten kraj, ("Only I wish to return to this country"). These are the poet's own stylistic devices, since, in the Polish language, verbs and the preposition *w* ("into") are combined differently. In this, the poet betrays Russian influences. The normal usage for the preposition *w* ("into") and *na* ("on") with verbs of motion take the Accusative case equal to the Nominative case for inanimate nouns. Cf., also such a syntactical structure as:

Wszyscy na koń już *siedli,* by jechać po sławę ("Mimochodem," *N.* ["By the Way"])
("All had already got on their steeds to ride for glory.")

The use of the preposition *na* ("on"), with the Acc.—Nom. of an animate noun with a verb of motion, is rather a Russian syntactical feature. This Polish archaism is used normally in modern Russian, as is the usual "na loshad' " ("onto the horse"). Thus Leśmian seems to have attained, through a new combination of words, highly unusual and original phrases. The use of the Dative is shown in "Strumień na oślep ku słońcu się pali" ("The stream burns blindly toward the sun") in "W polu" ("In the Field").[84]

Gdzie się las upodobnia łące ("Topielec" ["The Drowned One"])
("Where the forest resembles the meadow")

I czarnej barwie odtąd przynależą. ("Niezn. p. S. Ż." ["The Unknown . . ."])
("And from now on they belong to the black hue")

Here again the poet uses the verb with the Dative case without a preposition which is proper for Russian rather than for Polish. Sometimes, word combinations of this kind make possible a poetic abbreviation as well as the elimination of description. This purpose is served also by employing unusual adverbial expressions, as well as abverbs or entire phrases, e.g., "pieśń moja czerwcami gorąca" ("My bosom hot as June's")—note the Russian influence in the simile expressed by the Instrumental case—in "Ballada bezludna" ("The Desolate Ballad").[85] When the author introduces a phrase that might seem banal, he makes it more concrete and develops it in an unusual manner (see, "U wód Hiranjawati" ["At the Waters of Hiranjavati"]).

Szło za mną w krok życie,
Szło, skomląc o kęs ciała i tucząc się troską,
Szło z tej nędzy człowieczej w tamtą nędzę boską.[86]

/ . . . / life followed in my footsteps / It followed me, whining for a bit of flesh and gorging itself on worry, / It followed me from this human poverty into that godly one. / . . . /

Here anthropomorphism has transformed an abstract image of life into an autonomous entity invested with desires of its own. There is an inversion—a frequent occurrence in Leśmian's imagery; here life actually follows the protagonist. Such commonplaces as "a piece of bread" and "gorging oneself on food" are altered in a novel way to best express the author's philosophy. The emphasis placed on phraseology indicates the function of the word in the composition of this poetry. Composition itself plays an equally important role in Leśmian's poetics. Before I move on to a discussion of this, I would like to consider Leśmian's images and their sources.

MOTIFS, MYTHS, FOLKLORE

Leśmian's poetry is highly original in the area of images and themes, which does not mean that the author merely took his themes and motifs "out of thin air." On the contrary, Leśmian turned to many traditions and made use of them in a variety of ways. His originality often consists in applying a new and creative treatment to traditional motifs. The conception of these motifs is among the most archaic and determines the particular character of the fantastic and the irrational in his poetry. The author's attitude toward these traditional themes and motifs is as though he invented them himself; he somehow identifies with their mythical creators.

The most important source of Leśmian's motifs is Slavic mythology, Polish and Russian in particular, conceived rather broadly. Its use was not only due to a fascination with "primordiality," but also found justification in literary history, since Symbolism included an interest in past eras—antiquity and folk imagery (cf., Maeterlinck and Ivanov). In Poland, the most prominent expression of this interest is to be found in certain dramas by Stanisław Wyspiański and was also present in lyric poetry, in the ballads by Bronisława Ostrowska, however, that interest did not produce major literary results in lyric poetry until Leśmian. He did not use the existing motifs or themes in a slavish manner. In the poem "Pszczoły" ("The Bees"), for example, Leśmian made use of an old Slavic belief in an original way that bees travel to the other world to maintain contact with the dead. In this typical work, myth is a point of departure; the poem becomes understandable, not as an allusion, but as an entity in its own right; even a reader who has never heard of the myth can understand the poem.

Hindu mythology is the second major source (cf., the long poems *Asoka, Pururawa i Urwasi, U wód Hiranjawati* ("At the Waters of Hiranjavati"). An interest in Hindu culture and mythology was characteristic of Young Poland (Młoda Polska). Many translations were published in *Chimera,* usually from secondary sources. As mentioned previously, the greatest popularizer of old Hindu poetry was Antoni Lange, who translated many epic texts, the long poem *Nal and Damajanti,* and who edited an anthology of Hindu epic poetry. Leśmian also wrote a review of *Ramayana.*

From the Polish literary Renaissance, Leśmian borrowed the most important theme of Jan Kochanowski, the bard from Czarnolas ("Black Forest"—Poland's Parnassus), the death of the heroine Urszula Kochanowska. Leśmian uses only a few West European literary themes combining them occasionally with others. Such is the case with the poem *Pururawa i Urwasi,* where he introduced a motif into one of the songs from *Rigveda,* from the myth of "Eros and Psyche." In the poem "Dziewczyna przed zwierciadłem" ("The Maiden Before the Mirror"), the poet actually developed the theme used by Giambattista Marino in his sonnet, "La donna allo specchio," which, in turn, echoes some sonnets of Petrarch. The Polish poet's transformation of the theme itself, and the stream used as a metaphor for the mirror, can be found in "Hérodiade" by Stéphane Mallarmé. Leśmian also paid homage to the themes of Don Quixote and to Ossian. All of these themes are transformed, however, and serve mainly as a point of departure for a new creation.

Archaic themes from other sources appear only incidentally. In his early period, Leśmian referred to current ballad and fairy-tale motifs. The secondary source with respect to West European folklore, was an anthology by Edward Porębowicz, *Pieśni ludowe celtyckie, romańskie, germańskie,* published in 1909, which Leśmian reviewed and whose influence upon him was mentioned by Szczerbowski as pointed out above. It is characteristic of Leśmian that he makes very little use of sources and themes which played a dominant role in European (including Polish) poetry: Greek mythology, the Bible, and Christianity. Only one work, "Akteon," is based entirely on a Greek myth; the Bible is used in the long poem, *Eljasz* ("Elijah"), in addition, there are sporadic references to certain motifs and themes, such as the Last Judgement. It is interesting to note that although not drawing on these themes, Leśmian nevertheless often introduces the atmosphere of those worlds in their primitive, pristine epochs. He makes use of the Dionysian spirit of ancient Greece, of gnosis in early Christianity, and of the Hebrew spirit as expressed through the prophet Elijah. Themes of Christianity are either greatly transformed (see, "Betleem" ["Bethlehem"]) or treated merely as a point of departure for creating images of his own (see, "Strumień, ["The Stream"], "W czas zmartwychwstania" ["At the Hour of Resurrection"], "Żołnierz" ["A Soldier"]).

In the poem "Betleem," we can see how the evangelic theme is treated in this way, only as a point of departure:

Sen mię ze snu obudził. Przespałem byt drobny
Gwiezdnej smugi na rzęsach. Śniła się—dlaczego?
Chciałem razem z Magami iść w świat, niepodobny
Do żadnego z tych światów. Wiem, że do żadnego!

Biegnę w mrok, byle biegnąć! Może ich dogonię,
Choć mi trudno przeczuciu opierać się złemu.
Już widzę pierwsze stada, śpiące na wygonie,
I światła w Bogu ślepych oknach Betleemu. / . . . /

Gdzie Magowie? "Odeszli. Badacze ich cienia
Głoszą, że wraz z kadzidłem i mirrą i złotem
W kurz się marny rozwiali pod tej karczmy płotem,
Gdzie droga w nicość skręca. Tyle—ich istnienia."

Gdzie Maryja? "Mów o Niej z niebem lub mogiłą.
Nikt nie wie—i nikt dzisiaj nie odpowie tobie."
A gdzie Bóg? "Już od dawna pochowany w grobie,
Już szepcą, że go nigdy na świecie nie było!"—[87]

A dream woke me from my sleep. I'd slept through the minute existence / Of a starry trail upon my lashes. It came in a dream—what for? / I longed to go with the Magi to a world unlike / Any of these worlds. I know it's unlike any! /

I run into the gloom, just to be running! Perhaps I shall catch them, / Although it's difficult for me to defy an evil foreboding. / Already I see the first herds sleeping in the pasture, / And lights in Bethlehem's God-blind windows. / . . . /

Where are the Magi? "They've gone. Explorers of the shadows / Assert that with their incense and their myrrh and their gold / In wretched dust they blew away under this pothouse fence, / There, where the road bends to nothingness. So much—for their existence."

Where is Mary? "Talk of her with Heaven or the grave. / No one knows—and today no one shall answer you." / And where is God? "He lies long since buried in the grave. / Already there are whispers that he never existed in this world!"—

The Magi (the poet among them) are not worshippers—they are seekers after new, unknown values. Thus, the poet introduces philosophical problems into the history of the New Testament foreign to the original. The emphasis is placed upon the process of seeking and not finding. Here the poet arbitrarily combines various evangelic motifs and themes (e.g., Mary Magdalene in the last stanza). The vision of Bethlehem becomes a cosmogonic vision. This poem is a good example of Leśmian's treatment of traditional motifs: he is interested, not in repeating the themes, but in transforming them in order to extract a new content and a new essence from the ancient material. This is why he takes such great liberties in developing this type of theme. The poet brings them close to his own poetic system, but he does not subjugate himself to their influence.

In his use of folkloric motifs, Leśmian takes advantage of a large repertoire,[88] but again, he treats these themes quite differently than did the Romantics Brodziński or Mickiewicz, or later poets who stylized folk poetry and who wrote in a manner resembling folk songs (the most typical being Teofil Lenartowicz and Maria Konopnicka). Leśmian does the opposite: he incorporates folkloric themes, motifs and concepts into his own poetic system. Here, "Piła" ("The Saw") may serve as an example. In this work Leśmian draws upon a folk motif, but does not imitate the external characteristics of folk poetry. He takes a certain plot outline from folklore, but uses it as a means of realizing his philosophical aims (here the perspective of death precludes the attainment of man's striving). Imitation, in itself, is of no aesthetic value for Leśmian which is why it is extremely difficult to speak of his "folk stylization" in the usual sense of the word. Despite the fact that he introduces, not only folk motifs and themes, but even particular forms (such as a nonsense refrain, "dyny moje, dyny," in "Piła"),[89] his ballads based on folklore are, as a rule, far more thought-provoking than the original folkloric example. Sometimes, he even treats a philosophically charged type of ballad with humor, as in "Dusiołek" (discussed above). Generally, he may develop a motif in a humorous manner even when the prototype has not assumed that form.

One can safely state that the more conventional and contemporary the motif, the more humorous is Leśmian's formulation. The clearest example of this tendency is the grotesque "Kopciuszek" ("Cinderella"). The grotesque in this poem is expressed by an intentional equalization of heterogeneous objects of both the symbolic and realistic levels. A good example is the symbolic inequality of the rat-steed as well as the collision of words with different emotional connotations (catachresis) as, "łachmanów rozmarzonym zgrzebiem" ("In dreamy hempen rags"). The accumulation of these phenomena is especially apparent in the last stanza:

/ . . . / Bicz zaświstał! Ruszyły rumaki z kopyta!
Złe jary—wyrwy w złudach, zmór pełne kałuże!
Przepaść śni się łbom końskim! Śmierć za koła chwyta!
Baczność, durny woźnico! Oszalały szczurze!

Już zmyliłeś otchłanie! . . . Brniesz w nicość po grudzie!
Mrok się zaśmiał! . . . Strach—spojrzeć! Duch blednie człowieczy!

Pędzą konie! O, Boże! Szczęść myszom w ich cudzie! . . .
Grzmi kolasa! O, Boże! Miej dynię w swej pieczy! . . .[90]

/ . . . / The whip gave a whistle! The steeds were off like a shot! / Evil ravines—furrows in delusions, puddles full of ghosts! / The brink is the dream of the horses' heads! Death catches at the wheels! / Hold on, you foolish coachman! You crazed rat! /

You've confused the abysses! . . . You're blundering across this clod of earth into nothingness! / Darkness burst out laughing! . . . It's a fright to see! The human spirit pales! /

The steeds gallop on! O God! Speed the mice in their miracle! . . . / The carriage rumbles! O God! Keep the pumpkin in thy care! . . .

The poet transforms a conventional theme, not only by presenting it in a macabre way, but also by equating the original plot (the story of Kopciuszek) with the process of writing about it. In addition, the poet here has exploited the traditional motif of transformation for nontraditional purposes (the rat-steed, the pumpkin-carriage).

Leśmian uses folk motifs in various ways. His adaptation of the folk song is not limited to their motifs, but can be discerned also in his choice of words (mainly of dialectal origin) and in the introduction of devices common to folk songs. The use of common folk expressions such as "oj-da, oj-da-dana" in "Ballada dziadowska" ("The Beggar's Ballad") is incidental. The introduction of refrains is also important, as in the poems "Dąb" and "Matysek":

Grajże, graju, graj
Dopomóż ci Mag,
Dopomóż ci, miech, duda
I wszelaka ułuda!
("Dąb" ["The Oak"])

Play then, o player, play, / Let May help you, / Let the bellows help you, and the pipe, / And every delusion!

Takie było Matyskowe granie,
Zanim pieśni nastało konanie.
("Matysek" ["Little Matthew"])[91]

Such was Little Matthew's playing, / Before the throes of death began. /

The invocational refrain used in "Dąb" is very characteristic of the Polish folk song. The refrain used in "Matysek" has an important compositional role, for it follows and links the three stanzas, each of which constitutes a compositional unit of this poem. Most important in Leśmian's poetry is the adaptation of parallelisms, which became one of the main compositional devices in his poetry. This aspect is evident in the poem "Matysek," in which each stanza begins with the same two verses:

Grał w lesie Matysek na skrzypkach z jedliny—
I wygrał i wygrał—płacz zmarłej dziewczyny.[92]

Little Matthew played in the forest on a fir-wood fiddle— / And he won, he won—the tears of a dead maiden. /

It is most characteristic that Leśmian selects from folklore, not the established patterns of folk songs characterized by "direct" lyricism, but works that are narrative in structure. That is why he often stylizes the subject of his poems as a folk narrator (e.g., "Mak," "Zielony dzban," ["The Green Jug"] *Dwaj Macieje* ["The Two Matthews"]). This approach is related to his aim of limiting the Impressionist lyrical "I" and its direct emotional confession. The stylization of the folk narrator in such poems, as in the three just mentioned, is expressed as well by the literal or allusive usage of folkloric language and also by syntactical features. The most important element is the stylization of a simple, completely unrestrained narrative. When we read the poem, we find ourselves as though in the direct presence of the narrator. He speaks in such a way that he preserves the vivid flow of the narrative. He achieves this by deliberately repeating himself. In the poem "Mak" this folk narration is manifested in the use of dialect and in the repetition of the refrain:

Za chruścianym stanęła witakiem,
A boginiak już czyhał za krzakiem—
Pogiął kibic, zagarnął twarz białą
I mięśniami pościskał jej ciało!
 A ty śpiewaj, śpiewulo—
 A ty zgaduj, zgadulo!
I mięśniami pościskał jej ciało. / . . . /
("Mak" ["Poppy"])[93]

She stopped beyond the wattle fence, / And the ghost-rapist already lay in wait behind the bush— / He bent her waist, he grabbed her white face / And with his muscles he squeezed her body! / But you, you singer, sing— / But you, you guesser, guess! / And with his muscles he squeezed her body. / . . . /

In the poem "Zielony dzban" the folk narration is expressed by means of negative parallelisms:

To nie stu rycerzy, lecz sto trupów leży!
Nie sto trupów leży, jeno stu rycerzy!
 A nie dla nich ruczaj dzwoni,
 A bór szumny od nich stroni,

Jeno wicher we sto koni
Znikąd ku nim bieży. / . . . /

Stopy moje—bose, skronie—złotowłose,
Kochałam, płakałam, zmarłym wodę niosę,
Oczerstwijcie ból wasz słony,
Smakiem śmierci podrażniony,
Cały ranek w dzban zielony
Ciułałam tę rosę. / . . . /
("Zielony dzban" ["The Green Jug"])[94]

It's not a hundred knights, but a hundred corpses lying! / Not a hundred corpses lying, but only a hundred knights! / And it's not for them the brook rings, / While the rustling forest shuns them, / Only a gale, like a hundred horses / From nowhere rushes toward them. / . . . /

My feet—are bare, my temples—golden-haired, / I loved, I wept, I carry water for the dead, / Refresh your salty pain, / Inflamed by the taste of death, / All morning in the green jug / I gathered this dew. / . . . /

The intricate composition of the poem as well as the imagery serve to emphasize the grotesque. This type of negative-parallelism structure, frequently fortified by inner rhyme, appears in Russian folklore. (Cf., chapter 3). The negative parallelism is implied in the second stanza: "Stopy moje—bose, skronie—złotowłose," or in

/ . . . / Wypić—wypijemy, lecz nie ożyjemy, Na polu w kąkolu żal się chwieje niemy, / . . . /[95]

/ . . . / Drink—we will, but we shall not come back to life, / In the field, in the corn cockle mute sorrow sways, / . . . /

In the long poem *Dwaj Macieje* ("The Two Matthews") Leśmian achieves a "chatty" quality through the use of words characteristic of folk tales ("i basta," "and that's that") and the often repeated narrative formula of the type: "Rzekł Maciej do Macieja" ("said Matthew to Matthew"). The concreteness, minutiae of detail, and stylized simplicity are closely connected with the metaphysical issue. It is precisely in Leśmian's use of the narrative in this work that we discern his close ties with Russian folklore and especially with the genres of *byliny* and *skazki. Dwaj Macieje* best represents this tendency. It also illustrates the fact that Leśmian never imitates a genre, but uses those aspects which most aptly suit his purpose. The poem is an amalgam of *bylina* and *skazka,* with an apostrophic beginning "Pleć pleciugo!" ("Prattle prattler!") reminiscent of the apostrophe in *Slovo o polku Igoreve,* "O Bojan, solovei starogo vremeni!" (O Boyan, you nightingale of olden time!") The marked similarity of this poem to the Russian folklore genres deserves a special study. Here I shall only give a brief analysis of its structure, style, and language.

Dwaj Macieje has some characteristics of an epic, but it can be classified as a so-called "contaminated" genre, a merging of a Russian *bylina* and *volshebnaia skazka* (a magic fairy tale), philosophical in scope. The structure is that of a *skazka* and consists of four parts: The first part, *priskazka,* an antecedent and an unrelated part, is here the apostrophe: "Prattle prattler!" It is followed by the second part, *zachin,* a beginning, which is a topos: "Once upon a time there sat Matthew with Matthew on a hill." The third and most important part is *povestvovanie,* the narration. It starts with "the second Matthew said to the first." The plot is then developed in a dialogue between the two protagonists. It is a serious dialogue, replete with verbal clichés and proverbs. It deals in a humorous way with a serious, philosophical issue—life and death. The heroes, two peasants, reject death which precludes all pleasures of earthly existence. In order to "endure—and that's that!" ("trwać i basta!"), they determine to find the herb of immortality which is guarded by Czmur, the sorcerer. Here follows the usual bragging about their respective strength, characteristic of the genre of *bylina.*

The narration of a magic fairy tale resembles also that of the *byliny.* The exploits of the two protagonists—*bogatyri* ("giants") —starts out with the usual retardations: "They went and walked forward, across, and diagonally." Here we have a compositional device of a "stepwide narrowing." The actions of the protagonists are often accompanied by *troichnost'* ("the triad") a characteristic type of repetition and retardation, as is the case above. In their dialogue they use repetitions, diminutives (z *niedaleczka, jestku, pitku*—"from none to far" "eating, drinking"), hyperboles, apostrophes, fixed epithets (e.g., "bestia nieczysta," the Russian connotation of the devil). Metaphors are usually reduced to similes only. The internal rhyme and rhythm is used frequently for emphasis. Totemism is employed here as in the *byliny*, a bird "gil" comes to the aid of the protagonists, forewarning them (cf., "solovei razboinik" in the *Il'ia Muromec* cycle of *byliny*). The Matthews emerge victorious over Czmur, as the possessors of the herb of immortality which they cannot digest. They decide to give it to the weeping, suffering god, "Płaczybóg" and to die as men. The ending—*iskhod*—is brief. "One said that night approaches and the other that it dawns, and so they died."

The mythical character of Leśmian's poetry has long been of interest to critics. One can speak first, of the way he treats existing myths: In "Akteon" ("Acteon") the myth is related in the first part, introduced by a quotation of sorts ("Powieść o Akteonie: . . .") ("The Tale of Acteon: . . .") as a point of departure. Akteon, transformed into a deer, is dehumanized and suffers the torture of not being able to express himself before dying as an animal:

/ . . . / Nikt nie poznał po głosie i po znoju rany,
Że to człowiek—nie jeleń! Duch—upolowany!
Nikt nie zgadł tajemnicy narzuconych wcieleń!
Musiał być tym, czym nie był! I zginął, jak jeleń!

/ . . . / No one could tell by his voice and the hurt of his wound, / That he was a man—not a deer! A soul—hunted down! / No one could solve the mystery of imposed incarnations! / He had to be the one he wasn't! And he perished as a deer! / . . . /

The myth of the first part allows the poet to develop his poetic expression as though through analogy to this myth.

I jam niegdyś był inny. Dziś jeszcze się złocę,
A złociłem się bardziej . . . Świadkami—złe noce! / . . . /
Przemieniony w człowieka za nędzę mej zbrodni,

Dźwigam obce mi ciało w blask Bożej pochodni! / . . . /
Kto mni pozna po głosie, że to ja tak śpiewam?
Milcz, głosie! Nie mój jesteś! Swego już nie miewam . . .
Majacząc cudzych kształtów zgubną niepodobą,
Nawet w śmierci godzinie nie mogę być sobą!
Krwawą zmorę jelenia unosząc śród powiek,
Próżno wołam o pomoc!—I ginę, jak człowiek![96]

And I was once someone else. Today I am still golden, / But I was once a brighter gold . . . My witnesses—the evil nights! / . . . / Changed into a man for the baseness of my crime, / I bear an alien body into the radiance of God's torch! / . . . /Who shall know by my voice that it is I who sing / Be silent, voice! You are not mine! My own I no longer possess . . . / Looming like the fatal unlikeness of alien forms, / Even at the hour of my death I can't be myself! / Carrying away the bloody nightmare of the deer between my eyelids, / In vain I call for help!—And I perish as a man!

The second part speaks about the drama of man, no longer united with nature and independent of it. The tragedy consists in being *degraded* to the status of man from a state of fuller awareness. The protagonist must die as man. The poet here does not identify with the myth and makes a point of keeping his distance from it. He presents the drama stemming from a reverse situation.

An example of a different attitude towards a myth is provided by the poem "Strumień" ("The Stream"):

Mrok się z mrokiem porównał, żałoba—z żałobą.
Coś się chciało zazłocić, lecz zabrakło czasu.
Zbył się strumień swych brzegów, powstał całym sobą,
Wyprostował się w wieczność i szedł środkiem lasu.

Szedł do krzyża w pustkowiu, gdzie gwiazd swych niepewna
Nieskończoność się krzepi westchnieniami mięty—
I pierś swą strumienistą przymartwił do drewna
I zawisł, z dobrawoli na krzyżu rozklęty.

Po co ci, Senna Falo, na krzyżu noclegi?
Za kogo, Dumna Wodo, chcesz marnieć i ginąć?
Za tych, co już przeżyli dno swoje i brzegi—
Za tych, co właśnie odtąd nie mają gdzie płynąć.[97]

Dusk became like dusk, mourning—like mourning. / Something would have glimmered gold, but time ran out. / The stream cast off its shores, arose with its whole self, / Stood up into eternity and went through the middle of the forest. /

It went to a cross in the wilderness, where, uncertain of its stars, / Eternity gathers strength from the sighs of the mint— / And mortified its stream's breast against the rough wood, / And hung willingly on the cross, accursed. /

Of what use to you, Sleepy Wave, are a night's lodgings on the cross? / For whom, Proud Water, would you perish and be squandered? / For those who already have outlived their bed and their shores— / For those who from this point have nowhere to swim. /

The poem uses the Crucifixion as its motif. Rather than speak directly about it, the poet insinuates. He introduces this motif into a group of poetic images in which nature is the basic elemental force, and thus he somehow equates Christ with the stream. This is an example of a far-reaching assimilation of myths. Such adaptation plays a very important part in Leśmian's poetry, and typifies his attitude toward existing motifs.

Secondly, one can speak, as it were, about *poetry understood as myth,* that is, of poetry taking on the function of myth. This kind of definition may be applied to Leśmian's poetry if only because his poetry contains those elements which are usually important in all myths. It is noteworthy that almost all of Leśmian's poems evoke a primeval and prehistoric past in which man is primarily still an element of nature. In this primeval past, nature is treated anthropomorphically, as it is in actual myths; the distance is not concrete, hence the role of such phenomena as nothingness and infinity. Man not only believes in the existence of animated nonmaterial beings, but can even come into direct contact with them. Just as in myths, God finds himself in direct contact with man and personally intervenes in his affairs. In Leśmian, the fantastic is therefore not conventional; rather, it represents an attempt to construct myths by means of poetry. The mythical aspect of this poetry, so understood, finds its expression in the frequent use of the "theme of genesis," of the coming into being of the world and of man. This occurs, for example, in "Ballada bezludna" ("The Desolate Ballad") and especially in *Pan*

Błyszczyński. The poet's formulation of this theme differs from that used in myths about genesis: rather than show a creative process resulting in success, he shows the same process ending in failure. This difference does not obliterate the importance of the association with myth. It is in formulating poetry as a myth that Leśmian's ties with Symbolism are evident, since Symbolism aspired to this kind of interpretation of poetry as magic. Pan Błyszczyński's creation results from the "genesis of spirit,"[98] and from the mere blink of an eye:

Ogród pana Błyszczyńskiego zielenieje na wymroczu,
  Gdzie się cud rozrasta w zgrozę i bezprawie.
Sam go wywiódł z nicości błyszczydłami swych oczu
  I utrwalił na podśnionej drzewom trawie. / . . . /[99]

The garden of Pan Blyszczynski is a patch of green against the ending darkness, / There, where miracle proliferates into horror and lawlessness. / From nothing he created it himself with the glitterings of his eyes / And fixed it on grass dreamed up to the trees. / . . . /

The poem's dedication to Kazimierz Wierzyński: "to his vital struggle with the ghosts of contemporaneity and to his conquest of creative transformation," clearly shows *Pan Błyszczyński* as Leśmian's attempt at a similar conquest. This programmatic, philosophical poem was of great import to its creator.[100] It is interesting to note that Pan Błyszczyński—the protagonist—is, in some Polish dialects, the name given to God. Thus, again, Leśmian uses a folkloric element to express his poetic creed. As in other works before, this one again challenges God's creative powers. Pan Błyszczyński, the poet-demiurge supersedes God by conjuring in his presence a new gardenlike existence, the miracles of which defy the terror and lawlessness of the two existences created by the latter. Pan Błyszczyński invites God to his garden, conceding that he created it because of his doubts about the hereafter. Although he realizes that this third existence is short-lived, it is a magical creation that offers many paths to man and defies causality:

Wyłoniłem z mroku orgód, oderwany od przyczyny,
Rozkwieciłem próżnię, namnożyłem ścieżek— / . . . /[101]

/ . . . / From darkness I called into being a garden, detached from cause, / I flower-bedecked a void, I multiplied the paths— / . . . /

The created garden exists on the borderline between existence and nonexistence, forced to existence under the careful watch of Pan Błyszczyński:

/ . . . / Pan Błyszczyński sprawdzał ogród, czy dość czarom jego uległ—
I czy szum i poszum dość jest rzeczywisty—
I czy liszaj na dębie—jadowity brzydulek—
Dość się wgryza w złudną korę i w pień śnisty? . . .

Badał jeszcze, czy ptak-lilia dość skowrończo w przyszłość śpiewa,
I czy wąż-tulipan wiosny jest oznaką . . .
I spojrzeniem przymuszał przeciwiące się drzewa,
By do zwykłych podobniały jako-tako . . . / . . . /[102]

/ . . . / Pan Błyszczyński inspected his garden, did it conform to his magic— / And were the rustlings and hissings real enough— / And was the tetter on the oak—a venomous little ugly thing— / Gnawing enough into the illusory bark and the dream-saturated trunk? . . .

He also observed, whether the bird-lily sang enough like a nightingale into the future, / And whether the snake-tulip was the sign of spring . . . / And with a look he forced resisting trees, / To resemble ordinary ones somewhat . . . / . . .

Noticing a beautiful maiden emerging from the thicket of dreams, God asked who had created her. Pan Błyszczyński answered: "Nikt, bo przyszła bez życia / I bez śmierci, więc nie żyła i nie zmarła . . . / . . . / Wszystko rozumiem, prócz tej jednej dziewczyny, / Prócz tej jednej, którą kocham!" / . . . /[103]

No one, for she came without life / And without death, therefore she did not live and did not die . . . / . . . / All I understand, but this one maiden, / But this one that I love! / . . . /

The maiden, as in the ballad by that title and in the *Pesni Vasilisy Premudroi,* symbolizes myth-poetry which remains a mystery to the poet. He implores the magic apparition to share her secrets. Clutching her he sprinkles starry glitter in her eyes to prolong her existence. But the maiden disintegrates into nothingness. As "the Greeks maintained that out of nothing, nothing can be created, *ex nihilo nihil*,"[104] so, too, the garden disappeared.

/ . . . / Ustał cud dziewczyński . . .
O, wieczności, wieczności, i ty byłaś w ogrodzie!
I był blady, bardzo blady pan Błyszczyński.[105]

The miracle of the maiden came to an end . . . / O, eternity, eternity, you too were in the garden! / And pale, very pale was Pan Błyszczyński. /

Thus, the protagonist of the title is a metaphor of the poet-magus who has lost the power of magic; with it, the beyond—the realm of the third existence—was terminated.

It is easy to understand why Leśmian attached great importance to this work, and why it was so dear to him. This poem and *The Two Matthews* were his last works, written and published about a year before his death. The foreboding of his end apparently intensified the poet's tragic realization of the transitory nature of the garden-existence he had created despite the fact that "eternity" was present in his creative realm. He probably did not believe that he would achieve fame, as indicated by a poem in the cycle *Mimochodem* ("By the Way"). Like the two Matthews he was resigned to die as a man (cf., "Akteon"), but he did not believe in a life hereafter.

Leśmian is not limited in his poetry to motifs and themes which are derived from mythology and folklore. The theme of existence and nothingness, of nature, of God, of the Apocalypse, were discussed previously. The motifs and themes of his early poetry demonstrate his kinship with the aesthetics of Decadence and with the aesthetics of the Russian Symbolists of the second generation. The resonance of "void," which we find in Viacheslav Ivanov, Andrei Bely, and Aleksandr Blok persists in Leśmian's lyrics to the very end (note the influence of Schopenhauer):

/ . . . / Dziś, gdy ogród zaszumi lub zaskrzypią drzwi,
Zrywam się aby stwierdzić pustkę beznadziejną.
("Wyznanie spóźnione" ["Belated Confession"])[106]

/ . . . / Today, when the garden starts to rustle or the doors begin to creak, / I start up to ascertain the empty hopelessness. /

or:

Za miastem na odludziu—rozpacz i Niedziela!
Puste niebo zaledwo ziemi się udziela.
("Niedziela" ["Sunday"])[107]

On the outskirts of the city, in a secluded spot, are—despair and Sunday! / An empty sky barely pays attention to the earth. /

The grotesque of such a "void" has been pointed out by Jan Tuczyński[108] in Leśmian's poem "Zwiewność," especially since the realia are presented with utmost plasticity and naturalism:

Brzęk muchy w pustym dzbanie, co stoi na półce,
Smuga w oczach po znikłej za oknem jaskółce.
("Zwiewność" [Etherealness"])[109]

The buzzing of a fly in an empty jug that stands on the shelf, / The streak left in the eyes by a swallow vanished outside the window. /

It is natural that the theme of the void grows in Leśmian's later poetry proportionately to the pessimism of his last period, hence the intensification of activity to fill this void.

The theme of love is recurrent in Leśmian's poetry. His erotics are among the finest ever written. The cycle *W malinowym chruśniaku* ("In the Raspberry Thicket") reveals a tender, sensual intimate feeling, often expressed through insinuation. As Mieczysław Jastrun has observed, these poems are unique in Polish literature. With the exception of Mickiewicz, no one has expressed love so powerfully and yet so simply.[110] The intimacy is expressed by means of allusion, clarity, brevity, and conciseness. This cycle represents the optimistic and happy period in the poet's life. The cycle *Trzy Róże* ("Three Roses") is a combination of the erotic theme and philosophy. The erotic "Wyznanie" ("Confession") has autobiographical connotations, alluding to two simultaneous loves. (Some love lyrics in this cycle are similar to those of Akhmatova. The brevity and simplicity of language reminds one of her *govorok*):

Ja tu stoję za drzwiami—za klonowymi,
I wciąż milczę ustami—rozkochanymi.
Noc nadchodzi w me ślady—tą samą drogą,
Pociemniało naokół—nie ma nikogo!

Od miłości zamieram—chętnie zamieram,
I drzwi twoje rozwieram—nagle rozwieram,
I do twojej alkowy wbiegam uparcie,
I przy łożu twym staję, niby na warcie!

Żaden lęk mię nie zlęknie i nie wyżenie,
Nawet rąk twych po murach spłoszone cienie,
Choćbyś mnie zaklinała wszystkimi słowy,
Już ja nigdy nie wyjdę z twojej alkowy![111]

Here I stand behind the doors—behind the maple doors, / And keep a constant silence with my lips—my lips in love. / Night approaches in my footsteps—by the same path, / All around it has grown dark—there's nobody about! /

From love I waste away—gladly I waste away, / And your door I open—suddenly I open, / And into your alcove I run stubbornly, / And by your bed I stop, as though on guard! /

No fright shall frighten me or drive me away, / Not even the startled shadows of your hands upon the walls, / Not even if you should beseech me with all manner of words, / Never again shall I leave your chamber!

In this erotic the intimate tone of a personal experience merges with a folksy tone, approximating a song, created by the repetition of phrases in the first two verses, stanzas one and two. The theme of love differs markedly in character and treatment from that of the Decadent and later Russian Symbolists. It lacks the quality of excess and morbidity. In the erotics scattered in *Napój cienisty* the tone is subdued, the love is more humane, and pessimism prevails.

Perhaps the most important motifs are those common to the poetry of all ages, such as "shadow" and, above all, "dream" ("dream," which in Polish means also revery, is a most frequently used word throughout Leśmian's entire work). He admits that he can come closest to eternal life through revery and calls himself "a mad recollector of nonexistent events."[112] It fits the aesthetics of Romanticism and Symbolism. The duality of every phenomenon is constantly expressed in Leśmian's poetic world which oscillates between dream and reality and which is based on the "duality" of every manifestation.

Wacław Kubacki, paraphrasing a Polish critic of the Romantic era, finds his observations most fitting for Leśmian's poetics:

> A reflection in water or a mirror, a shadow of an object, an echo of a sound—these are the secondary, illusory forms of existence; another somewhat dematerialized form of phenomena, the reminder of nonexistence. To the physical chain "thing, shadow, destruction corresponds a humanistic chain: reality, dream, extinguished consciousness (death)."[113]

In Leśmian's pantheistic world there is no separation between these phenomena, all are part of the same existence. These motifs and images enumerated above appear consistently in Leśmian's poetic world as props for the strife between existence and nonexistence, for the ceaseless incarnations and metamorphoses, for the eternal struggle between life and death. Leśmian's poetic world is built on these antinomies. His life is a dream (cf., the Calderónean "La vida es sueño"). His art is a dream within a dream—"Ja tol'ko son vo sne!" ("I am only a dream within a dream")[114] says his Vasilisa Premudraia—the incarnation of myth (that is, of poetry). Dreams, shadows, reflections are the only means by which Leśmian can introduce the reader to his conjured, ephemeral, third existence. And, although they are but traces of the material world, we can identify with them, especially since they are presented as a tangible part of Leśmian's reality.

The motifs of "shadow" and "dream" appear in his early poetry and in *Sad rozstajny* mainly as metaphysical embellishments.

There is hardly a poem without them.
In the shadow:

Cień mój co we dnie się kładł na złocisty łan.
("Wieczorem"["In the Evening"], p. 7)

My shadow that in the daytime lay down on a golden cornfield. /

Słońcem pocięty wzdłuż upada cień pasiasty . . .
("W słońcu" ["In the Sun"], p. 12)

Cut lengthwise by the sun, a striped shadow falls . . . /

Cf., also the poems "Cień" and "Pieśń o ptaku i cieniu" ("The Shadow" and "The Song of the Bird and the Shadow") and this third collection of his work: *Napój cienisty* (*Shadowy Potion*).
In the dream:

Sen miałem—ale jaki?
Przypomnieć już nie mogę.
("Róża" ["A Rose"], p. 8)

I had a dream—but what kind? / Already I can't remember. /

Śnił mi się jej śpiew, pląsy
Sen zbiegła wzdłuż i wszerz. / . . . /

Sen zbiegłem, goniąc ciebie.
("Zmory wiosenne" ["Spring Nightmares"], p. 18)

I dreamt of her singing, dancing / She ran the length and breadth of my dream. / . . . /

I ran through my dream, chasing after you.

The dream multiplies into a double dream:

. . . zaledwie snem we śnie
("Aniołowie" ["The Angels"])

. . . barely with a dream in a dream /

In "Szmer wioseł" ("The Plashing of Oars"), the motifs of reflection, reality and dream are all combined. Such is also the case in this early programmatic poem, where the echo and reflection attain autonomy and convey a profound idea:

Dwa zwierciadła, czujące swych głębin powietrzność,
Jedno przeciw drugiemu ustawiam z pośpiechem,
I widzę szereg odbić, zasuniętych w wieczność,
Każde dalsze zakrzepłym bliższego jest echem.
("Prolog" ["Prologue"])[115]

Two mirrors that feel the airiness of their depths, / I place one against the other in haste, / And I see a series of reflections thrust into eternity, / Each farther one a congealed echo of the nearer. /

Art is a tunnel of mirrors—representing, by means of reflection and echo, a durable link between the present and the mythical past. The "two mirrors" and, later, "two candles" symbolize art's relationship to reality. The candles continue illuminating the tunnel. Art is eternal and emerges victorious over the transitoriness of life.

In Leśmian's mature poetry "dream" becomes a structural device of his poetic work. In *Łąka,* the structure of the cycle *Trzy Róże* ("Three Roses") as well as of the title poem itself is based on a "dream." In *Napój cienisty* dream becomes the theme of an entire poem (cf., "Sen"). In this volume the poet intensifies the illusory nature of the world by combining dream with the reflection in the water:

Tylko brzoza, kwitnąc w światów mnóstwo,
Całe swoje w snach odmilkłe brzóstwo
Z nagłym szeptem wcudnia do strumienia,
Gdzie raz jeszcze w brzozę się zamienia.
("Wieczór" ["The Evening"])[116]

Only the birch, blossoming into many a world, / Losing in dreams its whole silenced birchness / Enters it miraculously with a sudden murmur into the stream, / Where it once again changes itself into a birch.

The intensification of "shadow" in *Łąka* corresponds to the intensification of "dream" in *Napój cienisty.* (Cf., the cycle *W nicość śniąca się droga* ("A Road Dreaming into Nothingness"):

"Pająk w nicość sieć nastawił, by pochwycić cień jej cienia." ("Ballada bezludna" ["The Desolate Ballad"]). ("The spider set up a web into nothingness, to catch the shadow of its shadow.") "Znikomek" ("The Evanescent One") is lost in "w cienistym istnienia bezładzie." ("in the shadowy chaos of existence").

Another theme running through Leśmian's poetry is the play between life and death, and love and death, a Romantic theme that assumes attributes of Hindu philosophy. Death, like everything in Leśmian's ontology, is not a finite state. Except for life, the same uncertainties, the same fears persist in the grave (Cf., "Cmentarz"—["The Cemetary"]). At times, the theme of death is treated humorously. In "Za grobem" ("Beyond the Grave"), death frivolously blows golden bubbles with the remains of life. With the separation of realms absent, not only does death intrude upon life, but the reverse is also true. (Cf., "Pszczoły ["The Bees"] which swerve toward the realm of death.) In the autobiographical poem "Ubóstwo" ("Poverty"), there is defiance against death's emptiness because of which the forgotten loved ones die a second death. (Cf. also "Śmierć wtóra" ["Repeated Death"]).

The theme of love and death is treated at times with tenderness and humaneness, as in the poem "Do siostry" ("To My Sister"). However, in "Śnigrobek" it is presented in a morbid way. Here, along with the desire for death we have a lust for the maiden's corpse.

The ghost of existence becomes an obsession in *Napój cienisty*, as in the following examples:

Nic nowego za grobem! Nic poza tą bramą,
Gdzie się duchy zlatują ku istnienia plewom!
("Noc" ["The Night"])

Nothing new beyond the grave! Nothing beyond this gate, / Where spirits come flying toward the chaff of existence!

A wszechświat, co już stał się czymś w rodzaju mitu—
Ożywiony pogrzebem—pomyślał, że trzeba
Zmienić cel nieistnienia i miejsce—niebytu.
("Snigrobek" ["Gravedreamer"])

And the universe, which had already become something of a myth— / Cheered by the funeral—thought it should / Change the goal of nonexistence and the place—of nonbeing.

Czy to—byt, czy to—niebyt tak wrzawnie się tłoczy?
("Dookoła klombu" ["Round the Flowerbed"])[117]

Is it—being, or is it—nonbeing crowding so noisily?

The illusion of existence is incarnated in "Lalka" ("The Doll"). All the metaphysical devices are put to use: reality, dream, existence, nonexistence. Kubacki calls this occurrence a "phenomenalistic reduction."[118]

For Leśmian, for whom there are no limits and for whom there is no differentiation between various realms, such a reduction is possible. "The Doll" exists and so do "The Bees" which can change their existence at will in either realm. The paradoxical treatment of the contrasting poles of existence become at the end unsettling even to "The Evanescent One"—the poet himself.

COMPOSITION, GENRE, VERSE

The composition of Leśmian's poems is characterized by what is true of almost all poets, that the poetic "I" ("the lyrical subject") occupies a distinct place and fulfills diverse functions. Leśmian's earliest works, mainly those collected in *UR*, in this respect resemble the typical conventions of the poetry of Młoda Polska. The main factor in the composition is the lyrical subject who relates his experience directly—this is known as *lyric poetry of confession.* Images are subordinated to the subject. One does not speak in these poems about how things are, but rather about how the poetic "I" is reacting to them emotionally. From his later works, a characteristic example would be the poem "Sen wiejski" ("A Village Dream"), written in 1916, although it is a rare specimen for Leśmian's mature poetics:

Śni mi się czasem wieś, którą wbrew losom
Wysiłkiem marzeń przymuszam do trwania,
Czując, jak przymus co chwila jej wzbrania
Zniknąć, gdy właśnie zmyślonym niebiosom
Oczyma ledwo naznaczyłem w próżni
Miejsce spotkania snu mego z błękitem. / . . . /[119]

At times I dream of a village that, despite the fates / I force to endure by the strength of my dreams, / Feeling how that force from moment to moment forbids it / To vanish, while at that moment for the heavens I imagined / With my eyes I barely had marked in the void / The meeting place of my revery with the azure. / . . . /

Here the images, subordinated to the poetic "I," are, as is often the case in Leśmian's mature works, figments of its imagination, bordering on the supernatural.

By the time Leśmian wrote *Sad rozstajny* he had already overcome this conventionality which was quite hackneyed by the turn of the century. In these conventional poems, opposing the "I" against the world was mandatory. The latter was only an object of experience and emotional evaluation. In poems of his mature period, this structure was replaced by another; the lyrical "I" is presented in direct contact with the world, in a sort of dramatic collision. This results in a change of structure in the lyric monologue. The "I" does not state its experience; instead, it is depicted in the course of the manifestation of the experience.

Let us compare two works typical in this respect, "Modlitwa" and "Do siostry." Their content develops as though before the reader's eyes, rather than being transmitted as something ready and done. Therefore, the present tense usually prevails even though the past tense may be used grammatically (typically, the two tenses alternate in these poems). Sometimes the lyric "I" only enumerates specific elements. This is well illustrated in "Modlitwa" ("A Prayer"):

Za młodych lat szeptałem żarliwie i skrycie
Modlitwę o wydarzeń tragicznych przeżycie—
O łzę, która się w oczach rosiście przechowa
Na pokarm dla mgieł nocnych i na treść—dla słowa.

I nastał dzień, co zgrozą poraził mi duszę—
I musiałem go przeżyć . . . On wiedział, że muszę . . .
A już stało za drzwiami to Złe, co niweczy
Szumy mego ogrodu nad gęstwą wszechrzeczy.

Zasłuchany boleśnie w lada szmer na dworze—
Nie wiem, kto w drzwi zapuka? Kto jeszcze przyjść może?
I ze trwogą wspominam, sny tłumiąc bezsterne,
Nieoględnej modlitwy słowa łatwowierne.[120]

In my youth I whispered fervently and secretly / A prayer for the survival of tragic events— / For a tear to be preserved like dew in the eyes / As nurture for night mists and essense—for the word. /

And there came a day that paralyzed my soul with horror— / And I had to live it through . . . It knew I must . . . / And behind the doors already stood that Evil which annihilates / The sounds from my garden over the thicket of the universe. /

Listening painfully enrapt for any sound outside— / Do I not know who shall knock at my door? Who yet may come? / And quelling my rudderless dreams, with fear I recall / The naive words of my rash prayer. /

Here the lyrical hero does not present his emotional experiences as a finite event. His emotional world unfolds as the poem develops. The past tense used in the first two stanzas is a means of reconstructing his past and a means of speaking his mind. Therefore there is no contradiction between the past and present tense of the last stanza. This is how Leśmian almost always contemporizes the past.

The poem, "Do siostry" ("To My Sister"), is characteristic for other reasons:

Spałaś w trumnie snem własnym tak cicho, po bosku,
Nie wiem, czy wszystkich naraz pozbawiona trosk?
W śmierci taka zdrobniała, niby lalka z wosku . . .
Kocham ten ubożuchny, ten zbolały wosk!

Trup jest zawsze samotny! Sam na sam z otchłanią! . . .
  A właśnie ja—twój brat—
Suknię Tobie sprawiłem za dużą i tanią,
  Suknię—na tamten świat!

W każdym zgonie tkwi zbrodnia, co snem się powleka,
Chociaż zbrodniarza brak . . .
Wszyscy winni są śmierci każdego człowieka!
O, tak! Na pewno—tak! / . . . /[121]

You slept in your coffin with a sleep of your own, so quietly, so godlike, / At once freed of all dreams? I do not know. / So shrunken in death, like a waxen doll . . . / I love this poor, this woeful wax! /

A corpse is always lonely! Face to face with the abyss! . . . / And it was I—your brother— / Who bought a dress for you, too large and too cheap, / A dress—for the other world! /

In each death there lies a crime, coated with a dream, / Though the criminal is missing . . . / All are guilty of the death of each man! / O yes! Yes indeed! / . . . /

Although the form is that of addressing a second person, it is neither a conventional "Du-Lyrik" nor a rhetorical creation. In the course of "speaking" to the other person generalizing reflections appear. This composition is somewhat similar to the *Crimean Love Sonnets* by Adam Mickiewicz. The poem, as a whole, creates a specific portrait of the heroine mentioned in the title. At times, in the third collection of Leśmian's poems, the lyrical "I" appears in a condensed form, and in a way it introduces separate events by means of narration, as in the following example:

Dawniej mi się zdawało, żem z *mroków chaosu*
Wybiegł w świat—niepochwytny i wolny od losu.

Że najtrwalszy ze wszystkich przywidzeń i dziwot—
Sam o sobie śnię powieść—sam klecę mój żywot. / . . . /

Dziś wiem, że w zło się trzeba, jak w szelest, zasłuchać—
Że je łatwiej wykrwawić, niżli udobruchać.

Mgła mi z ręki wróżyła . . . Pamiętam szept cienia . . .
Nim cios we mnie uderzył—wprzód zbrakło zbawienia.

A gdym wołał o pomoc—tak nagle się stało,
Jakbym najpierw miał ranę, a później—to ciało . . . / . . . / [Italics mine.]

("Klęska" ["Defeat"])[122]

Once it seemed to me that from the darkness of chaos / I had run into the world—elusive and free of destiny. /

That, as the most lasting of all delusions and wonders— / Alone I dreamt a tale about myself—alone I shaped my life. / . . . /

Today I know that, just as for the faintest sound, one must listen with all ears for evil— / That it is easier to drain it of its blood than to appease it.

A mist predicted from my palm . . . I recall the whisper of a shadow . . . / Before something hit me—my salvation expired. /

And when I cried out for help—it suddenly was / As if I'd first had the wound, and later this body . . . / . . . /

Even in this poem, which could be considered one of his few autobiographical works, Leśmian clearly avoids the direct lyrical "I." This is characteristic of his attempt to objectify statements about himself, allowing the reader to form his own opinion. An account is given of observations and life experiences perceived from the vantage point of time. The observations are direct, the images concrete, vivid, as though the experiences were unfolding right before our eyes.

Leśmian uses the poetic "I" in two ways: as the poet's *porte-parole* (as illustrated above) or as representing a person whom it is impossible to identify with the poet. Such an example is the poem "Lalka" ["Doll"]: "Jam—lalka. W mych kolczykach szkli się zaświat dżdżysty" ("I am a doll. In my earrings sparkles the rain-wet beyond").[123] A similar phenomenon can be seen in his cycle of Russian poems, *Pesni Vasilisy Premudroi* ("Songs of Vasilisa the Wisest"):

Ia—solnechnaia byl', ia—mudraia carevna,
Liubimica nebes i lesa i ruch'ia,—
Ia—golos bytiia tainstvenno zapevnyi,—
Vsem obruchennaia, i vse zhe ia—nich'ia! / . . . /[124]

I—am the sunlit song of the past, I—am the wise daughter of the tsar, / The darling of the heavens, the forest and the stream,— / I —am the voice of existence that mysteriously sets the tune,— / Betrothed to all, yet I belong—to none! / . . . /

In the case of both poems there is a high degree of stylization, but both examples of the poetic "I" share the feature that the "I" is always shown in some situation which has an impact on the dynamic form of the statement. An example is the cycle *W malinowym chruśniaku,* in which the situation between the lyrical "I" and the other person is of dominant significance (which is what happens in the majority of Leśmian's erotic verse). This kind of situation permits the author to depict the "I" as an element of the image, and not as the originator of a statement only. The last stanza is, as a rule, climactic and elucidating. Sometimes this element appears episodically, as though under the domination of the image. Such is the case in the poem "Zwierzyniec," discussed earlier.

The narrative works (some of them also written in the first person), are as important to Leśmian's poetry as the direct lyrics discussed above. Leśmian considered narration to be a language arrangement that could serve epic poetry and also be a form of lyrical expression; it serves both functions in his work. This lyric quality in his narration does not appear (as was the case in the majority of narrative poetry of Młoda Polska), in such standard lyric devices as epithets with an emotional value. In Leśmian, things are much more complicated. The lyric quality of narration manifests itself in the fact that the story is not treated as an objective account of that which happens.

Leśmian's lyrical images are often built on a synthesis of two poetic worlds, the imaginary and the material, invested with a sensual and plastic quality. A concrete, mundane narration or event becomes transformed into a bridge between the real and the world beyond:

Puściła po stole swawolący wianek.
"Kto go chwyci pierwszy—ten mój ukochanek."

Pochwycił tak ściśle, aż się kwiaty zwarły.
"Skąd ty jesteś rodem?"—"Ja rodem—umarły!"

"Co się stało wokół, że świat mi się mroczy?"—
"To ja własnoręcznie zamykam ci oczy . . ."

"Już mnie nigdzie nie ma i nigdy nie będzie!"—
"Nie ma ciebie nigdzie, bo już jesteś wszędzie."
("Puściła po stole swawolący wianek"
["She flung her playful chaplet on the table"])[125]

She flung her playful chaplet on the table. / "He who catches it first —shall be my lover." /

He grasped it so tightly, the flowers closed. / "Where are you from by birth?"—"By birth—I am dead!"

"What has happened all about, that the world grows dark for me?"— / "It is I closing your eyes with my own hands . . ." /

"I am already nowhere and shall never be!"— / "You are nowhere because you are already everywhere." /

(*Ukochanek*—is a good example of Leśmian's rejuvenation of existing words. From the passive participle *ukochany*—"beloved," Leśmian takes the prefix *u* and attaches it to the existing noun *kochanek*—"lover," creating a neologism.)

The poem represents a situation which starts out as a point of departure for further events. The discerned characters, one of whom appears to be a phantom, carry on a conversation. Thus, in the course of events the reader focuses his attention on the characters. The initial situation introduces further events. At the end, the concreteness gives way to a paradox in the two last verses. This is the kind of lyric that could be considered a "lyric of situation," a term coined by Henryk Markiewicz.

The characteristic feature of this type of lyric is the fact that the hero is not the author but an outsider. The feature of a "situation" is usually determined by the use of a specific kind of expressive device, somewhat approximating drama and epic poetry. The difference is that in this "lyric of situation" the dramatic and narrative elements are subordinated to the lyrical aspects.

Here, in contrast to drama and the epic, narration and situations are not the basic means of expression. They are absorbed by the reader together with the emotion expressed in the lyric. This "lyric of situation" plays a prominent role in Leśmian's poetics. In this, he is a forerunner of Expressionism. The most remarkable feature in the composition of these lyrics is its ties with philosophy. A juxtaposition of loosely connected concrete images expresses a highly abstract thought. The maiden, a symbol of myth-creating powers, is the one who entices poets. The poet closes her eyes, that is—of inspiration. However, doubts of her lasting powers are dispersed by the poet's statement that myth is eternal and therefore exists everywhere. As observed by M. Głowiński, it constitutes

> a paradox; in the "lyric of situation," at times very elemental, saturated with sensuality, philosophical elements predominate. They are rooted in the image, and in the behaviour of the grotesque protagonists.[126]

Thus the relating of an event is used to create a new poetic world.

Sometimes a story is used to create a specific poetic world. Its mimetic functions are often replaced by depictive ones. This does not interfere with the character of the narration, which is very exact, at times even minutely detailed, sometimes existing side by side with a description of similar characteristics. Such are the poems of "Don Kichot" and "W locie." The first poem starts as follows:

W jednym z pozagrobowych parków, uroczyście
Zamiecionym skrzydłami bezsennych aniołów,
W cieniu drzew, co po ziemskich dziedziczą swe liście
Pożółkłe i zbyteczne—z duszą, niby ołów,
Ciężką, chociaż pozbytą życia nędz i lichot,
Na ławie marmurowej wysmukły Don Kichot
Siedzi, dumając nad tym, że dumać nie warto.
I pośmiertnym spojrzeniem, co nie sięga dalej,
Niźli dłoń rozmodlona, obrzuca głąb alej,
Gdzie ślad życia na piasku starannie zatarto. / . . . /
("Don Kichot" ["Don Quixote"])[127]

In one of the parks beyond the grave, solemnly / Swept by the wings of sleepless angels, / In the shadow of trees that inherit from earthly ones their leaves / Yellowed and superfluous—with a heart heavy as lead, / Though freed of life's wants and shoddiness, / On a marble bench slender Don Quixote / Sits thinking that thinking has no purpose, / And with a posthumous glance that reaches no farther / Than his prayerful palm, he casts down deep avenues, / Where on the sand every trace of life has been carefully erased. / . . . /

In this poem the description has a very detailed and specific character. However, it is not something external to the story of Don Quixote, treated in a narrative way. At first, the description gives the impression of an etched background, but, in actuality, it has a much more important role. Here, as in Leśmian's other poetry, there is, as a rule, no division into a static background and dynamic action. Dynamic elements appear already in the description. They are infused with dramatic elements even into the realia and the portrait of the hero. (This is exemplified in verses: 3, 4, 5, 8, 9, 10.) Characteristic of this kind of description is an extremely complex syntax. Also of note is the frequent use of enjambements—an unusual feature of Leśmian's mature poetry—to convey an ongoing process. We find another example in the poem "Wieczór":

Słońce, zachodząc, wlecze wzdłuż po łące
Wielki cień chmury, ciągnąc go na wzgórza,
Zetknięte z niebem, co życie, gasnące
Pod barw przymusem—w głąb marzeń przedłuża. / . . . /
Chłonąc czar drętwy samego patrzenia
We wszystko naraz, w nic zasię z osobna . . .
Wpobok, zaledwo do siebie podobna,
Wyolbrzymiona wobec próżni świata,
Krowa się w świetle różowi łaciata,
Co jednym rogiem pół słońca odkrawa,
A drugim wadzi o daleką gruszę . . . / . . . /
("Wieczór" ["Evening"])[128]

The setting sun draws across the meadow / The huge shadow of a cloud, pulling it up hills, / Joined to a sky that extends a life fading / Beneath the force of colors—into the depth of dreams, / . . . / Drawing the lifeless magic of the look itself / Into everything at once, while into nothing by itself . . . / Sideways, barely looking like itself, / Immense against the emptiness of the world, / In the light glows pink a speckled cow, / That with the one horn carves half the sun away, / And with the other obscures a distant pear-tree . . . / . . . /

This syntactical tendency appears exclusively in stichic poems, and is not known in stanzaic works. The animated description is extraordinary in its plasticity. (It is reminiscent of one of David Burliuk's primitive paintings, with a pink cow in the foreground.)

In the poem "W locie" the description does not fulfill the role of a prelude, but becomes incorporated in the narration itself:

Na potworze, z majaczeń wyległym rozbłysku,
Mknę, *kresów nienawidząc,* w wieczystą swobodę,
W nieskończoność, *co szumiąc,* pieni mu się w pysku,
Aż nagle zwierz mój trafia *na lęk,* na przeszkodę
I w miejscu, gdzie dla oczu kończą się błękity,
Staje dęba! Wiem dobrze: tu—Bóg jest ukryty!
Zastygły w zlękłym skoku nad otchłanią wiszę,
Pełno w niej jego spojrzeń i głos jego słyszę:
"Jam—twój kres! Czekam na cię—na swego przybłędę,
A gdziekolwiek podążysz—tam ja z tobą będę!"
W grzbiecie mego zwierzęcia zmacałem kark Boga!
Onże tak mię unosi w szału bezzacisze,
Jakby wspólna nam była w bezpowrotność droga?
Tak, to—on! Wiem na pewno i głos jego słyszę;
"Jam—twój kres! Czekam na cię—na swego przybłędę,
A gdziekolwiek podążysz—tam ja z tobą bedę!"
Do głosu tego w niebie dusza ma nawyka,
A pęd mój nie ustaje, a zwierz mój nie znika!
("W locie" ["In Flight"] [Italics mine])[129]

Atop a monster sprung from the flaring of hallucinations, / I speed, hating limits, *into eternal freedom, / Into the endlessness* that, hissing, *foams in his snout, / Until suddenly my beast encounters* fear, *an obstacle, / And, at the place where for the eyes the azures end, / He rears up! Well I know: here—God is hidden! / Petrified in a frightened leap, I hang above the abyss, / It is filled with his gazes and his voice I hear: / "I am—your limit! I await you—my straggler, / And wherever you will hasten—there shall I be with you!" / . . . / In the spine of my beast I felt God's nape! / It is he who bears me off to insanity's disquiet, / As if the path of no return were common to us? / Yes, it is—he! I know for certain and his voice I hear: / "I am—your limit! I await you—my straggler, / And wherever you will hasten—there shall I be with you!" / My soul grows accustomed to this voice in the sky, / And my speed does not diminish, and my beast does not disappear!*

Here description merges with narration, including even a kind of dialogue between the narrator and God. The unique minuteness of detail in the narrative is strengthened by introducing supplements, defining the character of action or the way of its realization (i.e., "Kresów nienawidząc, ["hating limits"], "szumiąc" ["hissing"]). Juxtaposed parallels, such as "na lęk, na przeszkodę" ("toward fear, toward an obstacle"), or the repetition of God's statement to the narrator are also used to achieve this purpose. This intricate composition successfully conveys the merging of satanism with the divine, due to "the flight," the onward rush, of Leśmian's creative evolution. This symbolic flight liberates the poet's creative powers from the influence of God, which they supersede.

The impersonal character of the narration can sometimes be explained by its purpose, which is to create a myth. Minuteness of detail coexists with the fantastic of the theme and can be varied in character. It can consist in relating one fact to which the whole poem is devoted (e.g., "Wół wiosnowaty" ["A Springtime Ox"]), in which case the narration is continuous. Or it may even consist of individual episodes arranged in a parallel manner which, together, form a tightly delineated whole (cf., "Wiosna" ["Spring"], "Marcin Swoboda" ["Martin Swoboda"]). Exactness in the treatment of episodes is always explained by their place in the composition. Frequently, the narrator is stylized into a naive storyteller who speaks about events chattily, using simple words (we find this in many of the ballads, cf., *Dwaj Macieje*. The use of narration in Leśmian's poetry has an enormous range, for it is used to relate that which is usually the object of description, namely, natural phenomena. This is connected with their dynamic treatment. Nature here is not a passive object but is always in the process of becoming. For these reasons, it is difficult to draw a strict line between description and narration in Leśmian's poetry, as is the case particularly in the ballads (see below).

In many poems, particularly in the narrative works, a very important phenomenon occurs, vital for the composition of Leśmian's poetry, i.e., *parallelisms.* Their usage is connected with, but not limited to, folk stylization. The parallelism consists in juxtaposing, as equivalent, different kinds of phenomena, objects, and situations. This leads to a certain uniformity of style (especially of syntax). Parallelism appears in different forms. Sometimes it includes even the smallest units of composition, appearing in individual verses. A good example is the poem "Dąb" "The Oak":

Bił prawicą na lewo, a lewicą na prawo,
Pokrzyżował ryk z jękiem, a lamenty ze wrzawą,
Aż z tej dudy—marudy dobył dłonią sękatą
Pieśń od wnętrza zieloną, a po brzegach kwiaciatą.
Wyszli święci z obrazów, bo już mają we zwyku,
Że się garną śmierciami do śpiewnego okrzyku.
I Bóg przybył skądinąd, niebywały w tej porze,
Niebywały, lecz cały zasłuchany! O, Boże!

Grajże, graju, graj
Dopomóż ci Maj,
Dopomóż ci miech, duda
I wszelaka uluda! / . . . / [Italics mine.][130]

He thrashed his right hand to the left, *and his* left hand to the right, */ He crossed a roar with a moan and laments with a din, / Until from the bagpipe—moper he drew with his gnarled hand / A song green on the inside and flowery at the edges. / The saints left their pictures, for it is already their wont / To cling with their deaths to melodious outcry. / And from somewhere else God arrived, unusual at this season, /* Unusual, but listening *enrapt! O God! /*

Play, *then, o* player, play, / Let *May* help you, / Let *the bellows* help you, *and the pipe / And every delusion! / . . . /*

The first verse especially exemplifies the internal parallelism of syntax and rhyme. Note also the internal rhyme in the third verse before the caesura: *dudy—marudy,* and in the ninth: *niebywały—lecz cały.* (Here we have also a truncated nominal neologism:

zwyk from *zwyczaj*.) Anaphora, representing the smallest feature of internal parallelism (see refrain), was frequently used by Symbolists, but its use is limited in Leśmian's poetry. However, the use of refrains, the most popular form of epiphoric structure (a repetition which is a truly prosodic phenomenon), is characteristic of many of Leśmian's poems. Note also the repetition in the first verse of the refrain built on tautology. The epiphora appears also within the structure of a stanza. Numerous examples may be found in the cycle *Trzy Róże* ("Three Roses"):

/ . . . / Od miłości zamieram—chętnie zamieram,
I drzwi twoje rozwieram—nagle rozwieram . . . / . . . /[131]

/ . . . / From love I waste away—gladly I waste away, / And your door I open—suddenly I open, / . . . /

(The epiphora was not developed by the Russian Symbolists, except for such known examples as Zinaida Gippius's "Pesnia," and Balmont's "Gornyi korol'.")

Often the parallelism occurs jointly with enumeration, as the following example demonstrates:

/ . . . / Przyszły do mnie motyle, utrudzone lotem,
Przyszły pszczoły z kadzidłem i mirrą i złotem,
Przyszła sama Nieskończoność,
By popatrzeć w mą zieloność—
Popatrzyła i odejść nie chciała z powrotem . . . / . . . /
("Łąka" ["The Meadow"])[132]

/ . . . / There came to me butterflies, weary from flight, / There came bees with incense and myrrh and gold, / There came Boundlessness itself, / To take a look at my verdure— / It looked and would not go back . . . / . . . /

Here we have another example of the usage of anaphoras. The writer also uses parallelism to combine heterogeneous elements and situations into a whole. The poem, "Migoń i Jawrzon" ("Wink and Jawrzon"), illustrates this best:

Niewidomską czapulę wdział Migoń na głowę
I poszedł do Jawrzona w sady czereśniowe. / . . . /

"Po głosie zgadnij wroga, co cię dziś nawiedził,
I wyznaj, żeś czarami mą zbrodnię wyśledził!

W jednym ulu ukryłeś—westchnienie mej winy—
W drugim—duszę zabitej przeze mnie dziewczyny. / . . . /"[133]

Migon put the invisible cap on his head / And went to Jawrzon in the cherry orchards. / . . . /

"By his voice guess the enemy that has visited you today, / And admit you have detected my crime with magic! /

In one beehive you have hidden—the sigh of my guilt— / In the other—the soul of the maiden I killed. / . . ."

In this ballad the narrative is fused skillfully with the dialogue between the rival suitors. The absurdity of their existence is accented by Migon's (Wink's) invisibility and emphasized structurally through the use of anaphora.

The last distich is one of the best examples of the element pointed out above.

Sometimes, parallelism, rather than being confined only to episodes, is the organizing force for the whole composition of the poem. As a rule, parallelism is not a mechanical repetition of one structure; Leśmian uses the distich of the ballad because of its flexibility as a vehicle for introducing changes. His awareness of the genesis of the ballad and its function has been expressed in his interview with Boyé:

I think that folk songs were created without any consideration for print. This is why the poet had to resort to a mnemonic technique in art. This is the reason for their influence upon my work. In my ballads there often occur distichs which are easily memorized. Besides, there is another thing: I never transfer a sentence to the next verse.[134]

Preserving all the strictness of the stanza, Leśmian manages to make it more flexible by introducing an element of freedom. The role of the distich has a dual meaning; it preserves the structural frame, but poetically it yields effective results when certain liberties are taken within its structure.

This effectiveness is realized by means of parallelisms. The fact that it constitutes a small unit within the distich gives it a wide range of possibilities. Preserving the basic contour of the parallelisms, Leśmian resorts to changes within their limits. This is achieved by introducing a certain parallelism of "a lower order . . . whereby in one poem there can exist a few 'subparallelisms'."[135] These are often contrasting in nature, but are eventually summarized in the parallelisms of the composition as a unit. Thus repetition is the element of change in Leśmian's ballads which Głowiński calls "varied parallelisms."[136]

This phenomenon can be observed even within one stanza, as is the case in the following poems:

Pod jaworem—dwa łóżka, pod jaworem—dwa cienie,
Pod jaworem—ostatnie, beznadziejne spojrzenie.
("Dwoje ludzieńków" ["Two Wretches"])

/ . . . / Under the sycamore—two beds, under the sycamore—two shadows, / Under the sycamore—a last, hopeless look. / . . . /

Grzmią wozy, chrapią konie i dzwonią kopyta—
Lśni kurzawa ku słońcu bezrozumnie wzbita!
("Dookoła klombu" ["Round the Flowerbed"])[137]

/ . . . / Carts rumble, horses snort and hooves ring— / A cloud of dust, stirred senselessly up to the sun, sparkles! / . . . /

/ . . . / A nie kochała tak tkliwie, a nie kochała tak czule,
Że nikt w jasnym uśmiechu nie trafił myślą na bóle. / . . . /
("Dusza w niebiosach" ["A Soul in Heaven"])

/ . . . / But she did not love so tenderly, and she did not love so warmly, / So that no one in his thoughts happened on the pains in her bright smile. / . . . /

We find in the initial hemistichs of verses, in the first two examples, a full parallelism where the caesura acts also as a syntactical division. In the third example there are three parallel syntactical units in the first verse. In all three examples the beginning of the succeeding verse intensifies the suggestiveness of the preceding verse. In the first distich the repeated unit (a lexical anaphora) returns and is developed in a different manner, thus introducing an essential change within the range of a parallel unit.

The possibility of formulating this "varied parallelism" is derived from the expansive capacity of the distich. The change can be expressed in either one or in the cluster of sentences. These limits coincide with the key points of the verse. This explains why parallelism within the distich became the basic compositional factor for Leśmian's poetry, especially for his ballads. This factor performs a dual function, for while it preserves similarity (i.e., structure), it introduces dissimilarity at the same time. It should be pointed out that Leśmian resorts to external parallelism, such as the anaphora, relatively rarely.

The role of parallelism in the composition of poems (particularly of narratives), lies in the fact that Leśmian does not combine phenomena in a chain of cause and effect; parallelism permits their juxtaposition. It is a specific means of introducing order.

Leśmian's poems are always outstanding in their evocative, precise, and closed compositions; in this they differ from the atmosphere prevalent in Impressionism of the turn of the century. Their expressiveness is determined as much by the specific structural feature of the image as by the stylistic devices. Each poem represents a closed unit of meaning. This is true even when the work consists of a grouping of seemingly loose elements, such as images, situations, etc. None of these elements are singled out, each, rather, playing a definite role in the whole. Leśmian has a fairly large number of poems of this type: the looser the factors, the more evocative is the composition of the whole. Usually, the meaning of a work is elucidated by the ending. Noteworthy examples are "Wieczór" and "Noc," in both of which "momentary mythology" appears next to sentences rather general in character.

Here we have an example of how a single verse represents, in a sense, an autonomous connotational unit. Each of the verses is like a separate atom:

/ . . . / Kto w nie spojrzy—zrachuje dwie cisze.
Dal się w oczach umyślnie kołysze.
Wieczór różnie niszczeje po krzakach,
Cień do rowu włazi na czworakach. / . . . /
("Wieczór" ["Evening"])[138]

/ . . . / Who will look into them—shall count two silences. / In the eyes the distance sways deliberately. / Evening wanes in various ways on the bushes, / Shadow crawls on all fours into the ditch. / . . . /

Such regularity (verse equaling a sentence) appears only in certain fragments of the text, since otherwise the cumulative effect would be monotony. Nevertheless, this device reveals a tendency characteristic of Leśmian, who uses it to assure, among other things, the rhythmical expressiveness of a poem. These autonomous sentences (see quotation above) do not by any means lead to a looseness of composition, but are subjugated by the overall compositional design. The poet strives to arrange facts to parallel each other on one plane, considering them of equal importance.

When speaking about the relationship of a sentence to a verse, it should be stressed that Leśmian uses the caesura, as mentioned previously, as an important component in the development of syntax in a given poem. The correspondence of the two is an aspect of symmetry. (Cf., "The Oak" discussed above). This is also evident in the following:

/ . . . / Nic nowego za grobem! Nic—poza tą bramą,
Gdzie się duchy zlatują ku istnienia plewom!
A cokolwiek się stanie—stanie się to samo—
Tych zdarzeń powtarzalność ciąży nawet drzewom! / . . . /
("Noc" ["Night"])[139]

/ . . . / Nothing new beyond the grave! Nothing—behind this gate, / Where spirits gather, flying toward the chaff of existence! / And whatever happens—happens in the same way— / The repetition of evil events weighs heavily upon the trees! / . . . /

The first and third verses are of importance. The caesura strengthens the statement.

Due to all the elements presented above, there appears a homogeneous whole with clear contours. Such striving toward expressive structure finds its strongest manifestation in symmetrical composition. In poems of this type a strict balance is maintained among the individual elements. This is apparent when parts are pitted against one another as in the poem "Jam—nie Osjan! . . ." ("I Am—not Ossian! . . .").

Jam—nie Osjan! W zmyślonej postaci ukryciu
Bezpiecznie śpiewam moją ze światem niezgodę!
Tarczą złudy obronny—zyskałem swobodę,
Której on by zapragnął, gdyby tkwił w tym życiu. / . . . /

Nikt się nigdy nie dowie, czym byłem dla siebie—
Dla innych chciałbym zawsze być tylko Osjanem.

Tak rzekł śpiewak, lecz własnym smutkom nie podołał,
I nagle: Boże, Boże!—do Boga zawołał.

Jam—nie Bóg! Twarzy mojej spragniony zatraty,
Maskę Boga przywdziałem—zdradziecko pokrewną,
I za Niego stworzyłem bezrozumne światy,
Tak, jak On by je stworzył . . . Na pewno! Na pewno! / . . . /[140]

I am—not Ossian! Secure in the refuge of my imagined form / I sing my discord with the world! / Armed with a shield of delusion—I attained a freedom, / That he would have wanted, had he been stranded in this life. / . . . /

No one shall ever know what I was to myself— / For others I would always like to be just Ossian. /

Thus spoke the singer, but with his own sorrow he could not cope, / And suddenly: God, God!—he cried out to God. /

I am—not God! Eager for the ruin of my face, / I put on the mask of God—a perfidiously similar one, / And in His place I created demented worlds, / Just as He would have created them . . . Yes indeed! Yes indeed! / . . . /

In this poem, the contrast manifests itself in that each part may represent a monologue of a different person; one part is supposed to be an answer to the other. Where different versions of one situation are presented, the balance is most apparent, e.g., "Matysek" ("Little Matthew") and "Dziewczyna" ("The Maiden"). Sometimes there is a repetition of the same type of composition representing a specific stanzaic structure, as in "Alcabon."

Był na świecie Alcabon. *Był, na pewno był!*
O brzóz przyszłość wiódł z mgłami walki nieustanne.
Próżnię życia na karku dźwigał z całych sił!
    "Tere-fere!"—tak śpiewał,
    Gdy się śmierci spodziewał.
Aż pokochał osiadłą na strychu Kuriannę.

Dur go pchał wzwyż po shodach. *Dur, na pewno dur!*
We łbie miał złote mroczki i srebrne zamiecie,
Gdy wspinając się ku niej, dawał baczny zór
    Na czar, co się po cichu
    Tak utrwalał na strychu,
Jakby miejsca zabrakło gdzie indziej na świecie. [Italics mine.][141]

Once in the world there lived *Alcabon.* He lived, indeed he lived! / *He fought incessant wars with the mists for the birches' future. / With all his strength he bore the emptiness of life on his shoulders! / "Tere-fere!"—so he sang, / While awaiting death. / Till he fell in love with Kurianna, who had settled in the attic. /*

Folly *pushed him up the stairs.* Folly, indeed folly! / *He had little golden glooms and silvery snowstorms in his head, / While climbing toward her, he gave a close look / At the magic that quietly / Had fixed itself in the attic, / As if there were a lack of space elsewhere in the world. / . . . /*

This poem is a humorous ballad and, to a certain extent, an expression of self-irony on the part of the poet. The narrator attempts to convince himself of Alcabon's existence and of his exploits using an intricate composition and a colloquial language. The first verse of each stanza contains a repetition—an inner, syntactical parallelism. The structure and meaning of the stanza, which has a refrainlike part in the fourth and fifth verse, help to accentuate the parody. The intensity of these formal assurances creates a totally opposite effect, revealing the uncertainty of existence and the absurdity of all human deeds.

The strict adherence to composition in Leśmian's poems was unusual against the background of the Impressionist poetry of Młoda Polska. Aspirations to such rigor did not characterize poetry until the period between the wars. In this regard, Leśmian seems to parallel the later development of Polish lyric poetry. However, he shows his virtuosity and extreme variety in the stanzaic structure.

Poetic genres are, traditionally, fixed means of composition. Leśmian's poetry—like all poetry since the times of Romanticism—cannot be categorized by genre, since it develops outside genres, except for the one genre that can be clearly discerned—the *ballad*—which occupies a dominant position in his work.[142] The ballad was one of the favorite literary genres of Młoda Polska. Its ballads gravitated toward an epic variant, following a symbolic fairy-tale line, as written by B. Ostrowska and L. Staff, or the lyrical-psychological variant, lacking in objective narration, whose foremost exponents were Tetmajer and Kasprowicz (cf., his "Ballada o słoneczniku" ["A Ballad about the Sunflower"]). Leśmian outgrew this tradition as well as that of the Romantic ballad, although his "Ballada Dziadowska" ("The Beggar's Ballad") draws on Mickiewicz's "Świtezianka" ("The Water Nymph of Switeź") for motifs. His ballad is a grotesquery of the Romantic plot. The ballad genre is found, not only in the cycle of that title, but also in the majority of Leśmian's narrative work (*Pieśni kalekujące* ["The Maimed Songs"], *Postacie* ["Characters"] and poems of other cycles).

If we leave out a few works of his earliest creative period (e.g., sonnets), we can say that Leśmian's ballads are unconventional in character. He ignores the traditional Young Poland treatment of contemporary motifs and rejects its trite, fairy tale, supernatural aspect. His themes are drawn from areas of folk imagination heretofore unexploited. Sometimes the themes do not originate in tradition at all—the most typical example being "Ballada bezludna" ("The Desolate Ballad"). The ballad, for Leśmian, is not a means for achieving effects of atmosphere, but rather a form in which philosophical problems and tenets are expressed. In one of these philosophical ballads, "Dziewczyna," this is achieved, not through direct statements, but through the structure of the plot and the presentation of the protagonists. Here the poet uses the ballad as a vehicle to express his perseverance in trying to break down the barrier of the mystery of life. The superhuman efforts expended in finding out what life is all about is invested in real and supernatural heroes. Their failure is his failure. Yet, even in this ballad, the lyric quality is absent; instead, he objectifies and dynamizes his poetic expression. Dynamization in his ballads "becomes intensified to the point of fierceness, which nothing can resist."[143]

Leśmian's ballad represents the extreme of the device "lyric of a situation." Unlike in the Romantic prototype, Wyka finds that

> the element of the fantastic in the traditional ballad was transferred into . . . form [i.e., plot] and language. This difference is of equal importance to the work of art as a whole and also serves as a link in the evolution of Leśmian's ballad. The ballad quality is contained in the fantastic element of the poet's word formation, yet the magic of the word is still [partly] accompanied by some elements of the fantastic ballad, i.e., that of the content.[144]

The new content and the new hero are introduced by means of ironic tragedy. Everything in the plot turns out to be catastrophic (cf., "Ballada dziadowska" and others).

The vast majority of ballads are based structurally on a plot presenting a defined sequence of events; thus, its fabular character is not treated in an epic manner. In accordance with the traditions of the ballad, there is an obligatory abbreviation in the presentation of events. We can even speak of fabular ellipses, which means that individual events are not mentioned and yet have an impact on the general sequence of events, leaving the reader to figure them out. Thus selected, the events are outstanding in their concreteness, always clearly defined, and occupy an important place in the dramatic development. As a rule, the plot is clear-cut in structure and ends with the event to which all the preceding ones have been leading. If one may speak of degrees of plot structure, then they exist in Leśmian's work. The works presenting a single conflict ("Piła," ["The Saw"], "Migoń i Jawrzon") are strictly fabular in character, as are those in which a single event is presented in various stages of development ("Dziewczyna"). The plot is less fully developed in works structured around a single element, figure, place, etc. ("Bałwan ze śniegu" ["The Snow Man"], "Karczma" ["The Inn"]). In general, direct lyricism is absent in those ballads in which the narrator appears as a definite person, where he is usually stylized into a folk storyteller (a prattler, "bajarz"; cf., to the Russian "bakhar' ").

The basic stanzaic structure for the ballad is the distich. The distinction of Leśmian's distich lies in the fact that it differs decidedly from old examples of the form as well as from the traditional distich of the nineteenth century. It has a different function from that of other stanzaic forms. Leśmian employed it as a compositional feature of distinctive expressiveness. Outwardly, the distichs look alike. They are descriptive and narrative in nature and they use a thirteen-syllable verse, the so-called Polish Alexandrine. They are distinguished from the stichic poem by the laconic style and flexibility within the frame of the distich. As mentioned before, in the discussion on parallelisms, the syntax can vary, and consists of small units, which accounts for its distinctness. In spite of presenting a closed unit of both syntax and rhyme, with a pronounced caesura and clausula, Leśmian manages to make it flexible. This is due largely to his use of parallelism. Parallels, as a rule, are more pronounced in a distich. In some poems Leśmian is very strict in the use of parallelism, so that all the stanzas create one unified whole:

/ . . . / Wychynęła z głębiny rusałczana dziewczyca,
Obryzgała mu ślepie, aż przymarszczył pół lica.

Nie wiedziała, jak pieścić—nie wiedziała, jak nęcić?
Jakim śmiechem pośmieszyć, jakim smutkiem posmęcić?

Wytrzeszczyła nań oczy—szmaragdowe płoszydła—
I objęła za nogi—pokuśnica obrzydła.

Całowała uczenie, i łechtliwie i czule,
Oj da-dana, da-dana!—tę drewnianą, tę kulę!

Parskał śmiechem dziadyga w kark poklękłej ułudy,
Aż przysiadał na trawie, jakby tańczył przysiudy. / . . . /
("Ballada dziadowska" ["A Beggar's Ballad"])[145]

/ . . . / A mermaidlike maiden peered out from the depths, / She splashed him in the eye till he crinkled half his face. /

Didn't she know how to caress—didn't she know how to entice? / With what kind of laughter to make someone laugh, with what kind of sadness to make someone sad? /

She rolled her eyes at him—emerald-green startlings— / And embraced his feet—the devilish temptress. /

She kissed him expertly and ticklingly and tenderly. / Of—dana, da—dana!—this wooden, this crutch!

The old geezer burst out laughing into the kneeling phantom's nape, / Till he squatted on the grass as if dancing the gopack. / . . . /

The events appear in a natural, orderly sequence of plot development. This very expressive parallelism of the first, second, and third distichs is emphasized by the corresponding metric structure of the precaesura and the postcaesura elements (in this fourteen-syllable verse). It expresses the dynamism of the moving water nymph. The fifth stanza, expressing the old man's reaction, is entirely different; it is less distinct. Therefore, the preceding stanzas are more pronounced, focusing our attention on the action of the water nymph. As a rule, Leśmian exposes his heroes to extreme danger, which usually comes from extraneous forces. In this case it is the water nymph who drowns the old beggar. Here, under the guise of parody, we find Leśmian's poetic creed. Though the old man dies the wooden leg, liberated, surfaces triumphantly. As a part of nature it is autonomous and indestructible, while human life, despite its spiritual baggage, is transitory.

Sometimes the poet combines the structure of the distich with that of a riddle:[146]

Tyś całował dziewczynę, lecz kto biel jej ciała
Poróżowił na wargach, by cię całowała?

Tyś topolom na drogę cień rzucać pozwolił,
Ale kto je tak bardzo w niebo roztopolił?

Tyś pociosał stodołę w cztery dni bez mała,
Ale kto ją stodolił, by—czym jest—wiedziała?

Stodoliła ją pewno ta Majka stodolna,
Do połowy—przydrożna, od połowy—polna.

Ze stu światów na przedświat wyszła sama jedna
I patrzyła w to zboże, co szumi ode dna.
("Stodoła" ["The Barn"])[147]

You have kissed a girl, but the whiteness of her body / Who made rosy on her lips, so that she would kiss you? /

You have let poplars cast their shadows on the road, / But who poplared them so high into the sky? /

You have hewn a barn in almost four days, / But who barned it, so—it would know—what it is? /

It was barned for sure by this barny Majka, / From the waist down—like the roadside, from the waist up—like the field. /

From a hundred worlds into the dawn of this world she went out along / And looked into this rye that rustles from the bottom.

Here the device of the puzzle is a decisive structural feature, further intensifying the ties of the ballad to folk poetry. The first three stanzas are a unit due to the syntactical similarity (that is, questions). They represent an introduction. The fourth stanza is an answer. Thus the whole poem has the appearance of a puzzle.

The same is true of the language, representing, as mentioned earlier, an autonomy, a "vicious cycle" expressed by "etymological figures."

In other cases, the parallelism becomes complex, consisting of several elements, introductory narratives and direct statements of the protagonists, as is the case in the philosophical ballad "Dziewczyna." A parallelism even occurs in the structure of the plot of this ballad. The attempt to free the girl from behind the wall is repeated by twelve men, then by their shadows, and, finally, by the hammers themselves. Thus, the narrative of these attempts is modified only by the change of protagonists. Into the long narratives are interpolated a direct, one-verse address by each of the twelve protagonists to the other eleven: "O, prędzej skruszmy zimny głaz, nim śmierć Dziewczynę rdzą powlecze!" ("O, let us swiftly crush the cold stone before death covers the Maiden with rust!"). Repetition of this apostrophe is a very effective means of dramatization. Sometimes the structure is based on juxtaposed syntactical combinations without conjunctions, in asyndeton (cf., "Wiosna," quoted earlier). This structure contributes to the evocation of a comic effect.

In those ballads with a more developed plot, an important part is played by the various commentaries. The lyrical "I" is subjugated to the narrator. The use of dialogues and monologues, characteristic of Leśmian's ballads, further heightens their dynamism. A good example is the following poem:

/ . . . / Jego kochanka z różańcem w ręku
Zawodzi pełna skargi i jęku: / . . . /

Rozważył rycerz, że w słowach—zdrada.
I po dawnemu leżąc powiada: / . . . /

I zamilkł rycerz—dumnie i godnie—
I po dawnemu leżał wygodnie. / . . . /
("Ballada o dumnym rycerzu" ["Ballad of a Proud Knight"])[148]

/ . . . / With a rosary in her hand his lover / Laments, filled with plaints and wailing: / . . . /

The knight pondered that in the words—there is treachery. / And lying down as of old, he says: / . . . /

And the knight fell silent—proudly and worthily— / And as of old he lay comfortably. / . . . /

This ballad is based on two statements of the protagonists. There are three narrative interpolations that have a definite compositional function. The first, serves as an introduction, the second, as an interlude between the two statements.

In other cases, a text of secondary importance appears within one distich with a direct statement or question:

/ . . . / A Bóg z nieba zawołal: "Wstyd dziewczyno młoda!
Nie poznałaś? Jam poznał! To—Marcin Swoboda!"

I pobladła dziewczyna, i odrzekła: "Boże!
Już to ciało Marcinem dla mnie być nie może! . . ." / . . . /
("Marcin Swoboda")[149]

/ . . . / And God shouted from heaven: "Shame, young maiden! / Do you not recognize him? I recognize him! This is Martin Swoboda!"

And the maiden paled and answered: "O Lord, / For me this body no longer can be Martin! / . . . /

In some cases parallelism is achieved by means of distichs which represent an identical compositional unit. We find in the ballad "Strój" ("Attire") a descriptive narrative stanza and a purely narrative introductory distich followed by four distichs, in which the first verse is narrative, while the second is a direct pronouncement:

/ . . . / Podawali ją sobie z rąk do rąk, jak czarę:
"Pojmy duszę tym miodem, co ma oczy kare!" / . . . /[150]

They passed her round from hand to hand, like a goblet: / "Let us ply the soul with this mead, that has black eyes!" / . . . /

This kind of dialogue used in certain distichs is an important factor for their parallel organization. Whereas a monologue is a singular statement, the parts of a dialogue when repeated provide variety. Leśmian adheres to uniformity in his use of dialogue. Stichomythia is a phenomenon he often uses in various ways. It manifests itself in such poems as "Urszula Kochanowska":

/ . . . / "Zbliż się do mnie, Urszulo! Poglądasz, jak żywa . . .
Zrobię dla cię, co zechcesz, byś była szczęśliwa."

"Zrób tak, Boże—szepnęłam—by w nieb Twoich krasie
Wszystko było tak samo, jak tam—w Czarnolasie!"— / . . . /[151]

/ . . . / "Come closer to me, Ursula! You look as if you're alive . . .
/ I shall do for you what you desire, so that you shall be happy. /

"Do so, o Lord—I whispered—so that in the beauty of Thy heavens
/ Everything shall be the same, as there—in Czarnolas!— / . . . /

Before commenting on the structure of the poem, it should be pointed out that its heroine is also a child as was her prototype in Jan Kochanowski's "Threnodies." The naïveté of the dialogue is kept within the stylization appropriate to a child's language. To the child, Czarnolas (the estate of her parents) is the "true heaven" to which she longs to return. This is an example of the statement of a protagonist utilized in a distich. As rightly observed by M. Głowiński, in most cases "the distich is the smallest unit of dialogue realizing the principles of stichomythia."[152] By using it, Leśmian demonstrates his aspirations for uniformity and symmetry. A distich lends itself to their realization. However, there are many examples where stichomythia is used within one verse only. We find this phenomenon in three distichs of the second ballad mentioned below:

/ . . . / "Kiedyż ty mnie podpatrzysz, jako w ciebie dyszę?"
"Nigdy cię nie podpatrzę! Dość, że dech twój słyszę!"

"Czemuż nie chcesz oczyma wyjść szczęściu na drogę?"
"Po cóż jeszcze mam widzieć to, co kochać mogę?"

"Chciałbym w oczach twych odbić radość, co mózg mroczy!"
"Bądźże mi niewidzialny, póki mam te oczy." / . . . /
("Pururawa i Urwasi" ["Pururava and Urvasi"])[153]

/ . . . / "When will you peek at me, the way I puff and blow at you?" / "Never shall I peek at you! It's enough that I hear your breath!" /

"Then why won't you meet happiness halfway with your eyes?" / "Why must I see that also, which I can love?" /

"I would like to mirror in your eyes the joy that darkens my brain!" / "Be then for me invisible for as long as I have these eyes." / . .

This kind of composition quickens the pace of events and the conversation between the two lovers, Pururava and the Indian water nymph. The vivid, spontaneous exchange gives the impression that the reader is eavesdropping on the lovers' intimacies. We find distichs used in diverse ways in this ballad. The narrative, or introductory distichs, are followed by those distichs that combine narration with direct speech, as well as by those that represent distichomythia, and, finally, those shown above. This variety of position accounts for the rapid and dramatic pace in the development of the plot. Especially in the combination of narrative forms with dialogue, within the limits of its stanzaic structure, the poet was able to reach his goal without resorting to a stagnant scheme.

As a rule, Leśmian employs the distich in poems of a narrative nature. Most of the poems, especially in *Napój cienisty*, are closely related to ballads; Głowiński calls them "balladic distichs." The term specifies the type of distich developed by Leśmian, the nature of which is close to folk poetry. The narration and the neatly framed dialogue represent a factor of folk stylization. The distich, which in the nineteenth century was limited in scope and used only occasionally as a means of stylization, assumed an entirely new role in Leśmian's transformation of this verse form: It became a folk stylization employed by the poet as a means to an end, not as an end in itself. "Leśmian's poetic creation seems to be a landmark, a culminating point in the development of the distich."[154] It contributed to the wide usage of the distich in the poetry written in Poland in the twenties.

Because of the plot structure, protagonists play an important role in ballads. They may be people, or fantastic creatures ("Urwasi' "), or animated objects ("Lalka" ["A Doll"]). Most frequently, an "ordinary" man in the ballads is in contact with ghosts and other representatives of "the other world," resulting in a dramatic conflict between the two. This is evident in "Ballada dziadowska," "Świdryga i Midryga," "Pururawa i Urwasi," and others. The poet treats both kinds of figures in the same way; since he does not differentiate between them, ghosts and other fantastic creatures are thought of as materialized, real beings.

Leśmian presents his protagonists, not by describing them or by relating their past, but through their participation in actual events. They appear in explicit situations, and only those situations permit the display of their characteristics. Character presentation of this type is related to the ballad tradition, but Leśmian intensifies this aspect. Presenting the protagonist in a definite situation gives the poet leeway to quote the heroes' statements; such direct quotation plays an important part in the ballads. Sometimes, the quotations are soliloquies, but often they are in the form of a dialogue which is dramatic in character, not merely relating events, but advancing them (as has been shown above). From the point of view of style, these quotations are basically not different from narration. Leśmian's poetic language is similarly formed in both cases (e.g., dialect, folkloric stylization, or *gawęda* ["prattling"] can occur in both quotations and narration).

Leśmian's ballads have great versatility. Some poems present a clear philosophical problem, e.g., "Bałwan ze śniegu":

Tam—u samego lasów brzegu,
Gdzie kruk—jedyny pustki widz,
Ktoś go ulepił z tego śniegu,
Co mu na imię: biel i nic . . .

Na głowę śmieszną wdział czapulę,
A w bok żebraczy wraził kij—

I w oczy spojrzał mu nieczule
I rzekł na drwiny: "Chcesz—to żyj!"

I żył niezgrabny, byle jaki,
A gdym doń przyszedł śladem trwóg—
Już weń wierzyły wszystkie ptaki,
Więc zrozumiałem, że to—bóg . . . / . . . /
("Bałwan ze śniegu" ["The Snowman"])[155]

There—at the very edge of the forest, / Where a raven is the emptiness's sole witness, / Someone molded him from this snow, / Which is called: whiteness and nothing . . . /

He put a cap on the silly head, / While into the beggar's side he stuck a stick— / And looked him heartlessly in the eyes / And said with a sneer: "Live—if you want!" /

And he lived, a clumsy, slapdash thing, / But when I came to him in the path of fear— / All the birds already believed in him, / And that is how I knew that this was—god . . . / . . . /

Here the animated snowman symbolizes divinity identifiable with creative power and the poet himself. This work deals with Leśmian's philosophical theme of theodicy, as he understood it.

Other ballads are grotesque, humorous, and macabre. The cycle *Pieśni kalekujące* ("Maimed Songs"), demonstrates an almost brutal compassion for the condition of the physically deprived. The following poem from this cycle is an illustration of this:

Nędzarz bez nóg, do wózka na żmudne rozpędy
Przytwierdzony, jak zielsko do ruchomej grzędy,
Zgroza bladych przechodniów i ulic zakała, / . . . /
Toczy się bałamutnie do dziewki z podwórza,
Do przystani stóp bosych—i ducha wynurza
Z łachmanów i wyciąga paździory swych dłoni
Ku jej zębom śnieżystym i tak mówi do niej:
"Kocham strzęp twojej błotem zbryzganej spódnicy,
Kocham głośny twój oddech! Na całej ulicy
Ty jedynie mym ustom bywasz tak potrzebna! / . . . /
Ona mu się broni,
A on mówi do niej:
"Wszak musi ktoś pokochać to, co już się stało—
I ten wózek męczeński i korbę zbolałą,

I żadzę w resztkach cielska, jak w zgliszczach, poczętą,
I ten ochłap człowieka, co chce być przynętą!
Odsłoń czar w mej brzydocie! Znijdź z wyżyn do karła! / . . . /
("Zaloty" ["Courtship"])[156]

To a little wagon, for a strenuous run a legless beggar / Fastened himself, like a weed to a moving garden patch, / Terror of pale passersby and disgrace of the streets, / . . . / He rolls along bafflingly flirtatious to the harlot from the courtyard, / To the haven of her bare feet—and brings his soul to the surface / From his tatters and reaches his palms' claws / Toward her snowy teeth and speaks to her: "I love the shred of your skirt bespattered with mud, / I love your loud breath! On the whole street / Only you are so needed by my lips!" / . . . /

She resists him, / And he speaks to her: /

Why, somebody must fall in love with what has already happened— / And this martyr's little wagon and its aching crank, / And the lust in remnants of flesh, as if conceived in smouldering ashes, / And this scrap of a man that wants to be a lure! / Reveal the magic in my hideousness! Descend from the heights to a dwarf! / . . . /

The courtship of the girl by the sensual cripple, whose torso is tied to a wagon, is represented in a tragic and grotesque way, intensified by the naturalistic description of every detail. The cry of anguish for sexual love from this remnant of a human body is pathetic, tragic, and revolting (cf., Baudelaire's unhealthy eroticism). This work is structurally interesting. As is customary for a ballad, it begins with a long stanza, combining a narrative and monologue. Two subsequent stanzas are monologues. The narration and the cripple's monologue are interrupted by a refrain after each part. The drama is heightened by various rhetorical devices. The language is a combination of archaisms, colloquialisms, and neologisms that intensify the grotesque situation. When denied love, the cripple runs away into the unknown in search of a possible love adventure, even if it is to come from a beast or a worm.

Some ballads, such as "Alcabon," are humorous, other genres play no great part in Leśmian's poetry and occur only sporadically. Erotics comprise a large group of works, yet these cannot be treated as a separate genre, since they vary in composition and are related to different traditions. (Even those which are decidedly "personal lyrics" deserve a separate study.) We can call a certain group of poems elegies, although Leśmian himself never so described any of his poems. Several autobiographical works are elegiac in character, particularly those concerned with memories of childhood ("Ze wspomnień dzieciństwa" ["From Recollections of Childhood"], *UR*; "Wspomnienie," "Ubóstwo," "Z lat dziecięcych"). Here are excerpts from some of them:

Przypominam—wszystkiego przypomnieć nie zdołam:
Trawa . . . Za trawą—wszechświat . . . A ja—kogoś wołam.
Podoba mi się własne w powietrzu wołanie—
I pachnie macierzanka—i słońce śpi—w sianie. / . . . /

A jeszcze? Co mi jeszcze z lat dawnych się marzy?
Ogród, gdzie dużo liści znajomych i twarzy—
Same liście i twarze! . . . Liściasto i ludno! / . . . /

I pokój, przepełniony wiosną i upałem,
I tym moim po kątach rozwłóczonym ciałem—
Dotyk szyby—ustami . . . Podróż—w nic, w oszklenie—
I to czujne, bezbrzeżne z całych sił—istnienie! / . . . / [Italics mine.]
("Z lat dziecięcych" ["From Childhood Years"])[157]

I recall—everything I won't be able to recall: / The grass . . . Beyond the grass—the universe . . . And I—call to someone. / My own call in the air pleases me— / And there is a scent of thyme—and the sun sleeps—in the hay. / . . . /

And what else? What else from years past occupies my thoughts? / The garden, where there is a multitude of familiar leaves and faces— / Nothing but leaves and faces! . . . Leafy and crowdy! / . . . /

And the room, filled to the brim with spring and sweltering heat, / And with this body of mine stretched out in the corners— / The feel of the window-pane—against my lips . . . A journey into nothing, into window-glazing— / And this keen, boundless, with all one's strength,—existence! / . . . /

The concreteness of the recollections makes the poem extremely vivid, heightening the longing for the minutiae associated with childhood. The nostalgic feeling for the intensity of a child's existence, as expressed in the last verse is particularly wistful. The images and actions of the past, be they real or phantasmal, are juxtaposed haphazardly—as though related by a child.

The following elegiac poem is especially autobiographical:

Każde zmarło inaczej śmiercią strasznie własną! . . .
Ciało matki i ojca i siostry i brata . . .
Dziś rysy waszych twarzy w pamięci mi gasną,
Umieracie raz jeszcze śmiercią spoza świata.

Już nie umiem zobaczyć siostry mej uśmiechu—
I tego, jak konając, padła na podłogę . . .
Brat mglisty i niecały śni mi się w pośpiechu—
I głosu, którym mówił, przypomnieć nie mogę. / . . . /
("Ubóstwo" ["Poverty"])[158]

Each one died a death horribly its own! . . . / The body of my mother and father and sister and brother . . . / Today the features of your faces fade in my memory, / And once more you die a death from beyond the world. /

No I can no longer see my sister's smile— / And how she fell to the floor when she died . . . / Hazy and unwhole, my brother appears to me fleetingly in a dream— / And the voice with which he spoke I can't recall. / . . . /

Remembering the loss of his beloved family, they die a second time in the process of recollection, intensifying the tragedy.

The following elegy is outstanding for its concreteness of description. The poet seems to be looking at things as through a magnifying glass:

Lubię wspominać te dziecięce lata,
Gdym zaniedbując całą resztę świata,
W znajome pole szedł razem z pastuchem / . . . /

Naówczas wpodłuż kładłem się na trawie,
Ażeby badać skrycie i ciekawie
Znajomą łąkę, oglądaną spodem,
Co rozumiejąc, czym jest taka chwila,
Sama przede mną swą gęstwę rozluźnia,
By mi ukazać, jak się cień motyla

Tuż za skrzydłami po kwiatach opóźnia,
I jak bąk w futro odziany tygrysie
Na złotym jaskrze, olbrzymiejąc, skrzy się, / . . . /
("Wspomnienie" ["Reminiscences"])[159]

I like to recall those childhood years / When, ignoring the rest of the whole world, / I would go with the shepherd into the familiar field / . . . /

In those days I stretched lengthwise on the grass, / Secretly and curiously to explore / The familiar meadow, as seen from underneath, / Which, understanding what such a moment means, / Would of its own loosen its thicket before me, / To show me how the shadow of a butterfly / Nearby trailed behind the wings upon the flowers, / . . . / And how a beetle dressed in tiger's fur, / Growing immense, sparkled on a golden buttercup, / . . . /

In the concreteness with which Leśmian presents his images, he can be compared only to Adam Mickiewicz. The plasticity is Cézannesque.

Elements of the idyl are present in "Sen wiejski" ("Village Dream"). It is typical of Leśmian that except for his earliest period he wrote no sonnets, despite the mania for sonnets in the period of Młoda Polska (the sonnet plays a large role in the creative output of Tetmajer, Kasprowicz, and Staff). Leśmian's longer works are very varied, and cannot be defined easily as belonging to any one genre. They often represent an amalgam of folk song, fairy tale, and epic (cf., *Dwaj Macieje, Pesni Vasilisy Premudroi,* and others).

Leśmian remains faithful to the most classic usage of the metric systems in Polish poetry, namely, to syllabic and syllabo-tonic verse, although during the period of his greatest creative activity tonic verse and free verse become more and more important. His choice is motivated by the fact that he considers *rhythm to be the most essential and expressive factor of poetry.* In this area of traditional versification, Leśmian introduces variety and differentiation. He does not limit himself to the use of the most classic meters (the eleven-foot syllabic and the thirteen-foot syllabic verse), but introduces also longer meters which appear rather seldom in Polish poetry, such as the fourteen-foot syllabic verse (in "Dwoje ludzieńków ["Two Wretches"]), the sixteen-foot syllabic verse (in "Dusza w niebiosach" ["A Soul in Heaven"]), and even the seventeen-foot syllabic verse (in "Dziewczyna"). He also incorporates relatively rare types of traditional meters, such as the (8 + 5) thirteen-foot syllabic verse (normally used as 7 + 6), as in the poem "Wyruszyła dusza w drogę. . . .":

Wyruszyła dusza w drogę . . . Dzwonią we dzwony.
"Gdzie są teraz moje sady? Gdzie moje schrony?"

Zawołały wszystkie lasy, pełne motyli:
"Spocznij, duszo, w naszym cieniu—nie zwlekaj chwili!"

"Jakże mogę w waszym cieniu spocząć niezwłocznie,
Kiedy sama jestem cieniem, gdzie nikt nie spocznie!"

Zawołała wonna łąka, zalśniona rosą:
"Koś mnie sobie na użytek złocistą kosą!"

"Jakże mogę ciebie kosić, łąko zielona—
Kiedy sama kosą śmierci jestem skoszona!" / . . . /
("Wyruszyła dusza w drogę . . . Dzwonią dzwony" ["The soul set out on a journey . . . The bells are ringing"])[160]

The soul set out on a journey . . . The bells are ringing. / "Where are my orchards? Where are my shelters?" /

Cried all the forests, filled with butterflies: / "Rest, o soul, in our shadow—don't delay an instant!" /

"How then can I rest in your shadow without delay, / While I myself am a shadow, where nobody shall rest!" /

Cried the fragrant meadow, sparkling with dew: / "Scythe me to your own avail with a golden scythe!" /

"How then can I scythe you, o green meadow— / When I myself am scythed by the scythe of death!" / . . . /

This unusual placing of the caesura after the eighth syllable, coinciding with the syntactical units in the two first distichs in this poem, produces an emphatic rhythmical effect. The role of metrical structure in a poetic work is illustrated exceptionally well. The protagonist here is the soul. Leśmian borrows such medieval folkloric motifs as the soul, on the way to heaven, meeting the meadow; the scythe (associated with death); and, finally, God in heaven. However, as is almost always the case with Leśmian, the adopted motifs are stylized and transformed. The soul is autonomous, has a life and mind of its own; it does not delight in reaching heaven, on the contrary, it blasphemes before God, desiring His death. (Cf., the irreverence shown to God and heaven by Ursula Kochanowska.)

In this ballad the dialogue propels the action. As is customary in folklore, it is a dialogue whose pronouncements are both simple and lapidary, and form parallelisms. Some distichs equal a single pronouncement of either God or of the soul. The meter used is trochaic, especially in the eight syllables preceding the caesura, after which there is, at times, a mixture of trochees and amphibrachs. The trochees of the first part accentuate the pace of the soul's wandering and the urgency of the pronouncements and events which accompany it on its way. The caesura, coinciding with the end of a syntactical unit, stresses the autonomy of the soul and the folk stylization of the dialogue. It also gives the verse a scanning quality, where retardation of the pace in the postcaesura part acts like an echo. This thirteen-syllable verse (8 + 5) ties Leśmian's work to folklore, but in a highly original, stylized way. Though unusual, this verse form had been used originally by Jan Kochanowski[161] for folk stylization. Its use, therefore, is not accidental in Leśmian's poetry.

This poem illustrates a tendency typical of the way in which Leśmian treats poetic construction as a means of folk stylization. Usually, for reasons of stylization, Leśmian uses *syllabo-tonic versification* which had earlier been used for the same purpose by Lenartowicz and Konopnicka. Leśmian, however, frees it from excessive melodiousness and automatic repetitiveness. This exemplifies his creative attitude toward existing forms. However, aside from its folkloric value, this poem is also important as an illustration of Leśmian's eschatology.

An interesting example of Leśmian's versification is the philosophical ballad "Dziewczyna," consisting of seventeen syllables with a caesura after the eighth syllable (8 + 9):

Dwunastu braci, wierząc w sny, zbadało mur od marzeń strony,
A poza murem płakał głos, dziewczęcy głos zaprzepaszczony. / . . . /

Porwali młoty w twardą dłoń i jęli w mury tłuc z łoskotem!
I nie wiedziała ślepa noc, kto jest człowiekiem, a kto młotem? / . . . /

Ale daremny był ich trud, daremny ramion sprzęg i usił!
Oddali ciała swe na strwon owemu snowi, co ich kusił!

Łamią się piersi, trzeszczy kość, próchnieją dłonie, twarze bledną . . .
I wszyscy w jednym zmarli dniu i noc wieczystą mieli jedną! / . . . /
("Dziewczyna" ["The Maiden"])[162]

Twelve brothers who believed in dreams explored the dream side of a wall, / And beyond the wall there cried a voice, a maiden's voice spent in vain, / . . . /

They took up their hammers in their hard palms and fell to striking the wall with a din! / And the blind night could not see which was a man, and which a hammer? / . . . /

But in vain was their labor, in vain their shoulders' link and strain! / They squandered their bodies for the dream that lured them! /

Chests break, bones crack, palms molder, faces pale . . . / And all died the same day and had the same eternal night! / . . . /

In Polish versification, the caesura is usually feminine, but in "Dziewczyna" we have a masculine caesura throughout. In this case it is, of course, a stressed monosyllabic word. It catches the ear much more easily because it stands out acoustically. That is, one can easily divide a distich and arrive at a quatrain (8, 9, 8, 9), but this would only represent a graphic change (rhyming: a, a, b, a), not a change in versification. Leśmian wrote the seventeen-syllable verse intentionally—the whole metric composition of the poem is iambic. It is an eight-foot iambic verse, thus very rare in Polish poetry. The folkloric influence is not discernible in this ballad. The metrics suited the philosophical ideas of the poem which consists of three parts: the skeptical, the stoic, and the tragic. The changing moods are accompanied by the feverish action of demolishing the wall; emphasized by the iambic meter. The expanded verse allows for a more detailed description of events and thoughts, while retaining the rhythmic beat.

In the realm of strophics (stichic poems are used with relative rarity by Leśmian), the poet usually makes use of classic stanzas, mostly of quatrains. However, in narrative works he assigns an important role to the couplet. There are also stanzas that are not so firmly fixed in tradition, e.g., a stanza in the poem "Łąka."

Czy pamiętasz, jak głowę wynurzyłeś z boru,
Aby nazwać mnie Łąką pewnego wieczoru?
    Zawołana po imieniu
    Raz przejrzałam się w strumieniu—
I odtąd poznam siebie wśród reszty przestworu. / . . . /[163]

Do you remember how you stuck your head out of the forest, / To call me Meadow one certain evening? / Called by name / I looked but once at myself in the stream— / And since then I shall know myself in the rest of space. / . . . /

This stanza has an unusual structure of 14, 13, 8, 8, 13-syllable verse, following one another. The feminine rhyme persists throughout, mostly of nominal genitive endings. Equally unusual is the poem *Pan Błyszczyński,* the standard form of which (17, 11, 17, 11 syllables) was of particular importance for the poet —as related by his daughter—according to whom the metrical form of this work is an amalgam of the epic of Roman antiquity and of Slavic folk poetry.[164] Another deviation from tradition is a tercet (a triply rhymed stanza), as in the poem "Asoka" differing from the classic tercet, or the *terza-rima*:

Król Asoka, na wzgórza smuklejąc odsłoniu,
Patrzał zowąd na wroga, co poległ na błoniu,
I rozżalił się duchem na wronistym koniu. / . . . /
("Asoka")[165]

King Asoka, gaunt on the hill's prominence, / Gazed at the enemy who had fallen on the pasture ground, / And, astride his raven steed, grew bitter in spirit. / . . . /

In the realm of rhyme, Leśmian consistently conformed to the classical full rhyme, in spite of the fact that in Poland during the between-war period the traditional rhyme yields to a use of inexact rhyme and assonance.

An attempt has been made to demonstrate Leśmian's way of presenting the great differentiation of motifs, themes, plots, and images in his poetry, and his method of creating poetic language. The poetic word is one of the most significant elements of Leśmian's originality. His is an active myth-creating attitude toward the word. That is why the poetic word can be considered as a microcosm of his aesthetics.

Leśmian does not directly continue any of the traditional styles of the historical periods of Polish poetry nor of any of the great poets. Yet, despite his great innovations, his attitude toward Polish literary traditions (outside of the Russian) plays a great part in his poetry. Sometimes, though rarely, it is manifested in stylization of traditional literary and folkloric motifs. In his earliest period, Leśmian adopted some of Juliusz Słowacki's mannerisms: his ornamentation, his overabundance of images, and his direct lyricism. Connections with Mickiewicz are important to Leśmian's mature literary output. For example, the descriptions in "Wół wiosnowaty" ("A Springtime Ox") are reminiscent of descriptions in *Pan Tadeusz.* However, Leśmian does not simply imitate external devices, but rather creates them anew. His originality is expressed in the fact that Leśmian introduced folkloric elements into poetry that was philosophical in character. His relationship to tradition does not consist of imitation, but of taking advantage of the elements of tradition for his own poetic purposes.

In the inter-war period Leśmian remained in the background of literary life. Still, "There is hardly a twentieth-century poet, who, having met Leśmian, did not succumb to . . . his enchantment."[166] His hidden influence was felt equally by the "Skamander" poets, particularly Tuwim in his neologistic searches, and by the poets of the Cracow Vanguard, who were particularly fascinated by Leśmian's imagery, without admitting it at the time. Interest in Leśmian grew somewhat in the late thirties because of the metaphysical inclination of contemporary poetry. Leśmian also has had his followers (the lesser known Bronisław Przyłuski and Stanisław Rogowski).

"Banished" in the years between 1949 and 1955, Leśmian has, since then, achieved recognition as one of the classics of Polish poetry and its most outstanding poet since Norwid. Literary historians, poets, and essayists all write about him. Leśmian also has had an impact on the exuberantly developing poetry of the post-thaw years. Young poets are fascinated by the magic of his language, its primordial vigor and philosophical depth, and his constant search for new values and methods of poetic expression. Leśmian is among those classic writers who will continue to exert an influence on the development of Polish poetry.

Notes

1: The Perspective of Time

1. Unless otherwise noted, I have translated all foreign quoted materials and am solely responsible for their accuracy.

2. Czesław Miłosz, *The History of Polish Literature*, London, 1969, p. 347.

3. Julian Przyboś, "Słowo o Leśmianie," *Poezja*, 1967, no. 12, p. 13.

4. Manfred Kridl, *A Survey of Polish Literature and Culture*, The Hague, 1956, p. 417. The author devotes only nine lines to Leśmian, without any mention of his last two books of poetry. This meager evaluation is, moreover, totally inaccurate. Kridl claims that Leśmian's work is concerned mainly with nature and countryside ". . . the conception of nature has nothing in common with either pantheism or anthropomorphism." Yet, these are elements which are most essential to Leśmian's poetics. Kridl's *Anthology of Polish Literature*, New York, 1957, does not include a single poem by Leśmian. He also chose not to mention the poet in his article on Polish poetry in the *Princeton Encyclopedia of Poetry and Poetics*, Princeton, 1965.

Julian Krzyżanowski, *Neoromantyzm Polski, 1890-1918*, Wroclaw-Warsaw—Krakow, 1963, p. 142. The eminent literary historian found that Leśmian's curse was his rhyme and rhythm, giving as an example of clumsiness: "we kwiaty," "we ślubne" ("into the flowers," "into the wedded ones"). Yet, Leśmian excelled in these two aspects of prosody. It would seem unlikely that the author should fail to associate these examples with Leśmian's predilection for the folkloric inner parallelisms, especially characteristic of Russian folklore.

5. Edward Boyé, "Dialogi akademickie," *Szkice literackie*, Warsaw, 1959, p. 501. The poet mentions his debut in an interview with the author. (Hereafter, this work shall be referred to in all chapters as *SL*.)

6. Michał Daszkiewicz-Czajkowski, "Leśmian w młodości," *Wspomnienia o Bolesławie Leśmianie*, ed. by Zdzisław Jastrzębski, Lublin, 1966, p. 115. (Hereafter, this collection of essays shall be referred to as *Wspomnienia o BL*.)

7. The favorable critics—Adam Szczerbowski, Ostap Ortwin, and Stefan Napierski—were his friends, and their literary influence was limited.

8. It is well known that Socialist Realism, prevalent in Poland during the period from 1949 to 1955, branded all avant-garde poetry as decadent. After the political thaw of 1956, Polish poetry underwent a change, and is at the present time considered to be among the most philosophically oriented poetry in Europe. The discovery of Leśmian after 1956 is due, in part to the interest of young people, who see in him the most persistent seeker after "pure art"—art as religion and philosophy. Cf., Czesław Miłosz, *Człowiek wśród skorpionów*, Paris, 1962, p. 25.

9. Jacek Trznadel, *Twórczość Leśmiana*, Warsaw, 1964.

10. Cf., the reminiscences of Anatol Stern, in, "Powroty Bolesława Leśmiana," *Wspomnienia o BL*, p. 337.

11. Bolesław Leśmian, *Utwory Rozproszone, Listy*, Warsaw, 1962, no. 106, p. 347. In a letter to the Czech poet František Kvapil, Leśmian gives the year of his birth as 1878. Yet, on his tombstone in the Powązki cemetary the date is given as 1879. (Hereafter this work shall be referred to in all chapters as *UR, Listy*.)

12. This information comes from Jan Brzechwa (Jan Lesman), "Niebieski wycieruch," *Wspomnienia o BL*, p. 81. The author was Leśmian's first cousin.

13. Maria L. Mazurowa, "Podróże i praca twórcza Bolesława Leśmiana," *Wspomnienia o BL*, p. 46. The poet's eldest daughter draws a picture of her father's childhood which is reminiscent of incidents taken from Gogol''s *Vii*. Another incident involving a cat reminds one of the story *Old World Landowners*.

14. Mazurowa, op. cit., p. 48. The daughter's account of this episode differs quite a bit (she had confused the dates) from the account given by Daszkiewicz-Czajkowski, op. cit., p. 115. Other sources give the date of Leśmian's imprisonment as 1895 to 1896. Cf., Kazimierz Wierzyński, *O Bolesławie Leśmianie*, Warsaw, 1939, p. 14.

15. Stern, op. cit., p. 344. This information was obtained from a letter received from Zieliński.

16. Henryk Hertz-Barwiński, "Nasze szkolne czasy," *Wspomnienia o BL*, Lublin, 1966, p. 112. This must have been Bal'mont, for no other Russian poet of the twentieth century translated Słowacki. Yet Leśmian writes in a letter to Przesmycki of meeting the Russian poet in Paris in 1905 as though for the first time.

17. There are several versions of the tale of the poet's pseudonym. According to Izabella Czajka-Stachowicz, Franc Fiszer thought it up. Maria Kuncewiczowa vividly described the scene to me. "Fiszer, a huge, Rabelaisian eccentric, the great wit of the period, looking down at his steady companion fretting at his feet, decided that Lesman was hardly a name fit for a poet. Doodling on a napkin, he came up with the pen name which fitted the poet like a glove, it smelled of the woods." (Leśny: adjective derived from *las,* forest, and *mian, miano* meaning name. The whole name sounds like one of Leśmian's neologisms.) This assumption, however, seems less probable, since the poet used this pseudonym prior to meeting Fiszer. Furthermore, Jan Brzechwa, op. cit., p. 84, also attributes its origin to Lange.

18. Leśmian, *UR, Listy,* no. 34 (to Przesmycki), p. 265.

19. With regard to Leśmian's cycles of Russian poems, there are two versions of what occurred. Brzechwa claims that Bal'mont inspired the poet. However, Włodzimierz Słobodnik, in "Pieśni mimowolne," *Wspomnienia o BL,* p. 245, recalls that Leśmian told him that he made a bet with the Polish-born Russian poet Vladyslav Khodasevich that he would write a cycle of poems in Russian if Khodasevich would write one in Polish.

20. *Edgar Allan Poe: Extraordinary Stories,* translated and with an introduction by Bolesław Leśmian, Warsaw, 1913-1914.

21. Bolesław Leśmian, *Klechdy polskie,* London, 1956. Originally Mortkowicz commissioned Leśmian to write a book of fairy tales for children. He found *Klechdy polskie* too sensual. Leśmian withdrew the ms. from print. It was later rescued by the poet's wife and daughter from the Warsaw-uprising fire. Somewhat damaged, the ms. reached England via the Mathausen concentration camp, Rome, and Argentina (the residence of Leśmian's widow until her death in 1964).

22. Leśmian, *UR, Listy,* no. 95, p. 332. Leśmian's complaints to Przesmycki convey his feelings very well; not only did he not consider himself a part of the Young Poland movement, he detested being considered as such:

> "I am considered here as an epigone of Young Poland!! I have earned quite an epithet!"

23. Mazurowa, op. cit., p. 67.

24. Krzysztof Miklaszewski, "Teoria i praktyka. Wokół Leśmianowskiej wizji teatru," *Ruch Literacki,* 1970, no. 1 (58), p. 20.

25. This fragment of a play was the subject of a study by Jacek Trznadel, "Piłka rzucona w zaświat," *Poezja,* 1967, no. 12, pp. 44-54.

26. Leśmian's love life presents a piquant side of his life and explains why erotics play an important part in his poetic output. He had a birdlike appearance—some compared him to a butterfly. According to Brzechwa, he carried on two love affairs simultaneously.

27. Hermina Naglerowa, "Przyjaciel z innego wymiaru," *Wspomnienia o pisarzach*, London, 1960, p. 58. In Franc Fiszer's presence, Leśmian showed an interest in current literary issues. His friend's giant stature had a reassuring effect and made the poet bolder. His shyness would give way to an innate sense of humor evidenced in anecdotes. One was about himself: "An empty carriage pulls up to the 'Café Ziemiańska,' stops, and out steps Leśmian."

28. Stern, op. cit., pp. 353-357. The author divulges the secret manipulations and his role in "the noble fraud" and "the historical correction" which resulted in Leśmian's nomination to the Academy.

29. Izabella Czajka-Stachowicz, *Wspomnienia o BL*, p. 300. According to this source, the young man courting Leśmian's daughter Wanda, when asked by the poet about his intentions, laughed sarcastically. He said he was a member of the ONR, a Polish fascist organization, and that it would be madness for him to marry a girl whose father was of Jewish descent. Enraged, the poet threw the suitor out. The emotional stress and humiliation were too much for his heart. Two hours later Leśmian was dead.

30. Brzechwa, op. cit., p. 103.

31. Jacek Trznadel, "Bolesław Leśmian," *Literatura okresu Młodej Polski*, Warsaw, 1968, p. 853.

32. Many works of Verlaine and other French and West European Symbolists were translated also by Zenon Przesmycki, but primarily by Antoni Lange. It should be added that Verlaine's works were also translated later by Leśmian, but his translations remained unpublished. His two-volume translation of Edgar Allan Poe, published in 1913-1914, was from the French of Baudelaire. Lange's articles, which played an important role in introducing the Polish reader to Symbolism, appeared in collections, the first volume of which, *Studies of French Literature*, came out in 1897, and the second, *Studies and Impressions*, in 1900.

It was Lange who introduced the term "Symbolism" into the current Polish literary language. Cf., Antoni Lange, *Literatura okresu Młodej Polski*, p. 15.

33. Reprinted in *Polska krytyka literacka* (1800-1918), Warsaw, 1959, IV, pp. 47-60.

34. Noteworthy are Henryk Markiewicz's observations in "Młoda Polska i 'izmy'," Kazimierz Wyka, *Modernizm polski*, Krakow, 1968, pp. 325, 326, about Ignacy Matuszewski's stand toward the term Modernism. Though he strongly advocated its adoption, he gave it only token attention in the title of his book: *Słowacki a nowa sztuka* (*modernizm*). In it, however, he equates Modernism with Romanticism and compares its artists to Słowacki.

35. Jeannine Łuczak-Wild, *Die Zeitschrift "Chimera" und die Literatur des polnischen Modernismus*, Lucerne and Frankfurt, 1969, p. 21.

36. Mieczysław Jastrun, "Od Baudelaire'a do Valery'ego," *Poezja i rzeczywistość*, Warsaw, 1965, p. 294.
37. Ibid.
38. It is obvious why Polish Symbolism, as envisioned and promulgated by Przesmycki, is called "Synthetic Symbolism." Cf., Wojciech Juszczak, *Wojtkiewicz i nowa sztuka*, Warsaw, 1965, p. 28.
39. However, in his explanation it is difficult to see any difference, as "the symbol must be a concrete image. . . . However, it must have its 'roots' in the darkness. Behind the concrete image endless . . . limitless horizons of the eternal . . . unchanging, incomprehensible essence of the thing must be exposed." Zenon Przesmycki, "An Introduction" to *A Selection of Dramatic Works by Maurice Maeterlinck*, p. lxvii.
40. Janusz Sławiński, "Recenzja 'Szkiców literackich' Bolesława Leśmiana," *Pamiętnik Literacki*, 1961, z. 1, p. 221.
41. Leśmian, *UR*, *Listy*, no. 2, p. 234.
42. Ibid., no. 4, p. 239.
43. Ibid., no. 59, p. 291. Leśmian contributed to the Paris edition of *Sztuka*. However, his remarks, as quoted, are directed at the Warsaw edition. The words *polskość* and *swojskość* have been rendered as accurately as English permits.
44. Ibid., no. 11, p. 249. Especially the last issues of *Chimera* can be considered almost anthologies. They consist of various genres and works expressing different literary trends. These anthologies are the best examples of the discrepancy between the poetry of Young Poland and a truly Symbolist poetry. The question of the extent to which Young Poland can and should carry the label of Symbolism was posed lately by such critics as Artur Sandauer, "Czas oswojony," *Poeci trzech pokoleń*, Warsaw, 1955, pp. 176-177; Jan Błoński in his essay "Poezja Kazimierza Tetmajera," *Życie Literackie*, 1959, no. 17. and by Michał Głowiński, *Poetyka Tuwima a polska tradycja literacka*, Warsaw, 1962, pp. 76-77.
45. Leśmian, *UR*, *Listy*, no. 84. p. 314.
46. Ibid.
47. Leśmian, "Z rozmyślań o poezji," *SL*, p. 89.
48. Miłosz, *Polish Literature*, p. 348.
49. Adam Czepiel (Stanisław Brzozowski), "Scherz, Ironie, und tiefere Bedeutung," *Głos*, 1904, no. 27.
50. Stanisław Brzozowski, "Miriam," *Głos*, 1905, no. 52. Brzozowski was not a cosmopolitan, therefore he did not find any merit in a work of art which did not reflect the geographic, historic or linguistic peculiarities of a nation. In short, he did not believe in abstract or universal art. Cf., Miłosz, *Człowiek wśród skorpionów*, p. 19.
51. Avanti (G. Glass), "In sacerdotes," *Głos*, 1904, no. 34. This author attacked Leśmian in a brutal, unprofessional manner.

52. Jan Lorentowicz, "Chimera," *Nowa Gazeta*, 1908, no. 196.

53. Hanna Mortkowicz-Olczakowa, "Wspomnienie o Leśmianie," *Bunt Wspomnień*, Warsaw, 1961, p. 124. The author writes of Leśmian's detachment from poetic groups. "He was at the beginning a powerful rival of the Skamander group."

54. Maria Mazurowa, letter of July 15, 1974. Immediately before this manuscript went to press, a letter arrived from Leśmian's daughter, Maria Ludwika Mazurowa, in which she states, "My father . . . was overwhelmed by the Skamandrites, who would not allow the publication of articles on Leśmian in *Wiadomości Literackie*, and at that time they were the oracle."

55. Ji (Jarosław Iwaszkiewicz), "Pierwszy zeszyt Czartaka," *Skamander*, 1922, no. 17, p. 126.

56. Wojciech Wyganowski, "O Bolesławie Leśmianie," *Wiadomości Literackie*, 1931, no. 8, p. 7.

57. T. Dworek, "Dziejba Lesmanów," *Prosto z mostu*, Warsaw, 1939, no. 1.

58. Feliks Zahora-Ibiański, "Noce umówione" *Myśl Polska*, 1936, no. 15.

59. The corroborating facts are too numerous to mention. Cf., Stern, op. cit., pp. 343-345.

60. Julian Przyboś, "Leśmian po latach," *Linia i gwar*, Krakow, 1959, vol. II, p. 91. It should be mentioned that Przyboś was a leader of the I Vanguard before World War II. Leśmian had polemicized with that group in his "Treatise on Poetry." However, it was Przyboś who severely reprimanded the poet Gajcy for his article in *Poezja*, in which he dismissed the works of Leśmian and Tuwim as alien to the Polish people.

61. Ibid., pp. 103-104 (italics mine).

62. Leśmian, "Wielki starzec," *SL*, pp. 433-434.

2: Leśmian as a Theoretician of Poetry

1. Adam Szczerbowski, *Bolesław Leśmian*, Warsaw-Zamość, 1938, Vol. VI.

2. Cf., e.g., ibid., p. 68.

3. Hieronim Michalski, "Wizerunek poety," *Pion*, 1938, no. 38, p. 3.

4. Julian Przyboś, "Leśmian jako eseista," *Sens Poetycki*, Krakow, 1963, p. 357.

5. Zenon Przesmycki, *Wstęp do: Wybór pism dramatycznych M. Maeterlincka*, Warsaw, 1894; reprinted in: *Polska krytyka literacka*, Warsaw, 1959, Vol. IV, p. 54.

6. Kazimierz Wyka, *Modernizm polski*, Krakow, 1968, p. 142.

7. Karol Irzykowski, *Czyn i słowo*, Lvov, 1913, p. 164.

"Miriam seems to be interested only for a single moment in a work of art, namely: in the one in which the work loses the original sensual, corporal character given to it by life and starts to sparkle philosophically, leaning towards something indefinable, corpselike. . . . Miram wants to look at works of art as a god, not as a man. This is the reason why he is indifferent to their usefulness, their practical role. The latter interests him only as an unfortunately necessary material, as a transition toward philosophical leanings in the direction of infinity. For in order that something should be able to lean in any direction, something must be written which has some kind of relationship to this wretched vale of tears. There must be mention of people, boats, sea lions, treasures, sadness, and so on."

8. Jeannine Łuczak-Wild, *Die Zeitschrift "Chimera" und die Literatur des polnischen Modernismus,* Lucern and Frankfurt, 1969, p. 29.

9. Stanisław Przybyszewski, "Confiteor," *Polska krytyka literacka,* (1800-1918), Warsaw, 1959, Vol. IV, pp. 154-155. Manfred Kridl, *A Survey of Polish Literature and Culture.* The Hague, 1956, p. 409. Cf., his views about the Manifesto of Przybyszewski and its discrepancy with his creative work. Kridl points out the opening words in one of his works: "In the beginning was lust. . . ."

A later example of a manifesto that failed to inspire worthwhile literary achievements is apparent in Polish Expressionism, the very extensive program of which was formulated within the journal *Zdrój* in the years 1917-1921. In spite of the profound manifesto, no valuable artistic works followed.

10. The vagueness of Symbolism as propagated in the manifestos failed to provide the cohesion necessary to prevent Young Poland from fractioning. Cf., Henryk Markiewicz, "Młoda Polska i 'izmy'," in Wyka, op. cit., pp. 338-339, where the author discusses its syncretic nature.

11. Artur Sandauer, "Poezja twórczych potęg natury," *Polityka,* Warsaw, 1968, 6, VII, no. 27, p. 6.

12. Jacek Trznadel, *Twórczość Leśmiana,* Warsaw, 1964, p. 52.

13. Bolesław Leśmian, *UR, Listy.* These poems were among the first written in 1896-1897, and were not included by the poet in his first volume of poetry *Sad rozstajny.*

14. This would apply especially to Leśmian who attached great importance to the very early stages of his development in childhood, because he considered it a period of the supremacy of feeling over consciousness and reason.

15. Zygfryd Krauze, "Ze wspomnień o Leśmianie," *Wspomnienia o BL,* Lublin, 1966, p. 186.

16. Jan Brzechwa (Jan Lesman), "Niebieski wycieruch," *Wspomnienia o BL,* p. 86; Maria L. Mazurowa, "Podróże i praca twórcza Bolesława Leśmiana," ibid., p. 62; and Włodzimierz Słobodnik, "Pieśni mimowolne," ibid., p. 244.

17. Edward Boyé, "W niepojętej zieloności," *Pion*, Warsaw, 1934, no. 23; also included in *SL*, pp. 497, 499. Cf., fn. 112.

18. Stefan Napierski, "Bolesław Leśmian," *Wiadomości Literackie*, 1931, no. 15, p. 8.

19. Michalski, op. cit., p. 3.

20. This letter refers to the modernistic journal edited and published by L. Szczepański in Krakow. The first issue appeared on the 24th of September 1897. In 1898 Stanisław Przybyszewski became its editor.

21. Leśmian, *UR, Listy*, Kiev, 1897, no. 2, p. 234. All dates are approximate. Cf., notes by Trznadel, p. 235. (The following letters referred to in this chapter were written to Przesmycki unless otherwise specified.)

22. Ibid., Kiev, 1898, no. 3, p. 236.

23. Ibid., Kiev, 1897, no. 2, p. 234.

24. Paul Verlaine, "Clair de lune," *Fêtes galantes*, Paris, 1869. In contrast to the poets who liked to depict hothouse gardens and the inner *paysage* of the soul, Leśmian's garden is at the crossroads (cf., the title of the first volume of his poetry, *Orchard at Crossroads*), which gives greater vision. Later the expanse widens to the open meadow (cf., the second volume—*Łąka*) then to the cosmos and stellar space. In the latter he shows some similarity especially to the Russian poet Derzhavin and such Russian Romantics as Tiutchev.

25. Leśmian, *UR, Listy*, Kiev, 1898, no. 3, p. 236.

26. The importance and stress which Leśmian places on achievement, action and heroism is pointed out by Kazimierz Wyka in his analysis of Leśmian's poem *Dziewczyna*, in an article entitled "O czytaniu i rozumieniu współczesnej poezji," *Polonistyka*, Warsaw, 1958, no. 6, pp. 10-11. In *Dziewczyna*, the author combines action and toil with the feeling of "necessary duty" and "the dictates of heroic aspiration." This poem was written in Leśmian's mature period, which indicates the consistency of his convictions.

27. Leśmian, *UR, Listy*, Kiev, 1898, no. 3, p. 236. The italicized line especially shows closeness to Bergson's idea of man perceived as a furrow.

28. Ibid.

29. Ibid., Leśmian, *UR, Listy*, Kiev, 1900, no. 5, p. 242.

30. Ibid., pp. 238-239.

31. Boyé, op. cit., p. 499.

32. Julian Przyboś, "Mój Leśmian," *Kamena*, Lublin, 30, XI, 1962, no. 22, p. 1.

33. In this concept of form Leśmian was a forerunner of the Russian Formalist school and of the English scholar Andrew Cecil Bradley, a propagator of the organic unity of form and content, expressed in his inaugural lecture of 1901: "Poetry for Poetry's Sake," *Oxford Lectures on Poetry*, Oxford, 1909, p. 19.

He called the unified whole, the "significant form." Leśmian understood poetic form exactly as did Bergson, whose works he could not yet have known at that time. Bergson's ideas about form are expounded especially in his *Creative Evolution* which was published in Paris in 1907. One should also mention Benedetto Croce's *Aesthetics,* translated by Douglas Ainslie in 1922.

Leśmian's concept of form makes him, in some respects, a possible follower of Friedrich Schiller, for whom (after Kant) form assumed an epistemological significance, and who later considered poetic form a force transforming blind intuition and impulse into the material of art.

34. Leśmian, *UR, Listy,* Kiev, 1900, no. 4, p. 238.

35. Ibid., Kiev, 1901, no. 10, p. 247. No such work under the mentioned title was printed. Evidently the poem was returned to Leśmian by Przesmycki in the summer for changes (cf., letters of the summer of 1901). It was dedicated to childhood (cf., *UR,* letter no. 11). All of which points to the conclusion that the fragment published in December 1901 in "Wędrowiec" was evidently a part of the poem *Pari-Banu.* This assumption leads to the acceptance of the poem *Wspomnienie,* which appeared in the second book of Leśmian's collected poems, *Łąka* ("Meadow" 1920), as a continuation of the long poem discussed above. As possible proof one can point out the similarity in style, imagery, general atmosphere, and also, the identical meter (i.e., the 11-syllable verse).

36. Ibid., pp. 46-48.

37. Ibid., Kiev, 1901, no. 11, p. 248.

38. Ibid.

39. Bolesław Leśmian, "Z rozmyślań o Bergsonie," *SL,* pp. 29-44. Cf., footnote 69.

40. Heraclitus (ca. 540-480 B.C.) believed that everything is in a state of flux and movement, like the stream of a river. He named this state *Panta rei,* which in Greek means, "everything flows." Any idea of permanency about anything was an illusion of the senses. Nothing exists but only *becomes,* and all becoming is the result of the conjunction of opposites. According to Heraclitus, strife is the father of all things. Cf., with Leśmian's "action" ("Leśmianowy czyn," as called by Maria Prodraza-Kwiatkowska in her article under this title in *Ruch Literacki,* Krakow, 1964, XII, z. 5-6). Cf., also with Bergson's philosophy of *élan vital* as a force opposing the entropy of matter and thus creating. "Becoming" is the principle of Heraclitus. It is indicative that Leśmian, who was yearning to express the process of becoming poetically, would mention this philosopher as early as 1901. Leśmian, *UR, Listy,* Kiev, 1901, no. 11, pp. 248-249.

41. Leśmian, *Niedopita czara, UR,* pp. 58-60, is a long poem published in Warsaw in *Wędrowiec* in 1902 and is one of his weakest works. It is stylistically bound to accepted canons of Young Poland. It also echoes Russian and Polish Romantic and post-Romantic poetry. However, even

in this poem there are truly original verses, worthy of the author of *Łąka* (Leśmian's second volume of poetry). It is hard to establish whether this poem was written before or after *Pari-Banu*.

42. Bolesław Leśmian, "Znaczenie pośrednictwa w metafizyce życia zbiorowego" [The Significance of Mediation in the Metaphysics of Collective Life], *SL*, pp. 45-65.

43. Leśmian, *UR*, *Listy*, Kiev, 1901, no. 11, p. 249.

44. Ibid. No such poem is known, unless its title was changed to *Niedopita czara*. No mention of the latter is to be found in Leśmian's correspondence, and it was written apparently, in the same year as *Pari-Banu*. Leśmian's opinion of the poem *Cień* and the sarcastic self-critical tone used to describe it, could very well apply to the poem *Niedopita czara*, for the reasons mentioned above (footnote no. 41).

45. Ibid., Paris, 1912, no. 86, p. 320. Here Leśmian expressed his concern about publishing his first volume of poetry. He was afraid that, after the high-flown style which the critics and readers were accustomed to, his poems might seem to them lacking in inspiration and content.

46. Ibid., Villeneuve-Saint-Georges (Seine-et-Oise), 1904, no. 44, p. 277. That he found narration most suitable for his poetry shows his deviation from the canons of Young Poland.

47. Ibid., p. 278. This work was inspired by his longing for the Ukraine, its setting. In a way, Leśmian can be considered one of the Polish poets of the "Ukrainian school," although, on the whole, his poetry is ungeographical.

48. Ibid., no. 88, p. 321.

49. Apparently the poet was referring to the long poem, *Łąka*, which opens the XI cycle of the second volume of poetry with the same title. Cf., Bolesław Leśmian, *Poezje*, ed. by Jacek Trznadel, Warsaw, 1965, pp. 250-257.

50. Leśmian, "Z rozmyślań o Bergsonie," p. 39.

51. Leśmian, *UR*, *Listy*, Paris, 1912, no. 85, p. 316.

52. Ibid., no. 86, p. 318.

53. Ibid., no. 88, pp. 321-322.

54. Except for the work cited below, Bolesław Leśmian, "Z rozmyślań o poezji" [A Treatise on Poetry], Rocznik, Warsaw, 1939.

55. Some articles were published in *Myśl Polska* under the pseudonyms Felicjan Kostrzycki and Jerzy Ziembołowski.

56. Bolesław Leśmian, *Sad rozstajny*, Warsaw, 1912. This first volume of poetry appeared concurrently with some essays of the *SL*, as the date of publication indicates, and were written at the same time.

57. Cf., Janusz Sławiński, "Recenzja 'Szkiców literackich' Bolesława Leśmiana," *Pamiętnik Literacki*, Warsaw, R.L. 11, 1961, z. 1, p. 222.

58. Ibid., p. 219.

59. This attempt was made by J. Trznadel in his book, *Twórczość Leśmiana*, cf., footnote 12. However, Trznadel, having drawn parallels between Leśmian's *SL* and his poetic work, chose to analyze Leśmian the

theoretician and Leśmian the poet mainly out of the literary context in which he belonged—namely as a proponent of Existentialism.

60. Sławiński, op. cit., p. 221.

61. Leśmian, "Mieczysław Smolarski: 'Pieśni i śpiewy rycerskie'," *SL*, pp. 287-288. In this review, Leśmian said that all these images and patterns which once required true artistry to create, had now lost their "prettiness" and put the reader to sleep. This observation shows once more the consistency of Leśmian's view on the obsolescence of reality. Even that which once was new, even sublime, loses its luster in another era. He adds that "these same words strung on a different cord could arouse, even now, our attention and curiosity." Cf., his essay "Przemiany rzeczywistości" [The Metamorphoses of Reality].

62. Jacek Trznadel, "Wstęp do Szkiców literackich," *SL*, p. 8.

63. Sławinski, op. cit., p. 221.

64. Leśmian, "To co się stało" [That Which Happened], *SL*, pp. 334-338. This is a review of the poetry of Aleksander Szczęsny, whose creative work showed how poetry can be inspired even by minutiae. Leśmian found this poetry full of magic. He found the poet capable of "catching with his golden fishing rod, from the surrounding reality, a living detail, full of . . . fresh meaning." Leśmian believed that "the poet ought always to be a bit too far out, and have a pitch higher than that of the 'gray everyman'. To spin a rainbowlike tale out of that which only a moment ago our eyes could only behold as a whirlwind of dust."

65. Ibid., "Kwiaty grzechu" ("The Flowers of Sin"), p. 229.

66. Sandauer, op. cit., p. 6.

67. Sławinski, op. cit., p. 219.

68. The myth system in Bergson's philosophy (for which he was attacked) was, apparently, one of the reasons why Leśmian was attracted to his philosophy. Myth, according to Leśmian, as the expression of evolutionary creative life, is the only means by which cognition of true reality can be achieved. According to Leśmian, only creative life is comprehensible to man. For him "to understand means to act, to create" (cf., article below, p. 37). In his philosophical essay: "Z rozmyślań o Bergsonie" Leśmian spins his cosmogenic myth as follows:

> "In the beginning there was a living whirlwind and dead matter at which the current struck suddenly. So began that which is beginning ever since . . . the living whirlwind (the *élan vital*, the onward vital impetus of the creative power), . . ." p. 35.

69. Leśmian, "Z rozmyślań o Bergsonie," *Nowa Gazeta*, Warsaw, 1910, no. 364, 366, 375-377; included in the *SL*, pp. 32-33. According to A. Sandauer, Leśmian's observation concerning the myth about ether preceded by two years Einstein's theory of relativity, which in fact, removed ether from the cosmos, thus depriving it of a uniform system. This, according to Sandauer, somewhat parallels the stratified cosmic

structure of Leśmian's poetry. Cf., footnote 4, p. 22, in Sandauer's article: "Romans z niebytem," *Samobójstwo Mitrydatesa*, Warsaw, 1968.

70. Giambattista Vico, *The Encyclopedia of Philosophy*, 1967, V. 5, p. 435. Cf., Leśmian's interpretation of myth with that of Giambattista Vico, an Italian philosopher of the eighteenth century, in his book *Scienza nuova:* "Myths (being neither false narratives, nor allegories), express the collective creative mentality of a given age. In the early stages, poetry and myths expressed the . . . wisdom of a people." *The New Science*, tr. by T. G. Bergin and M. A. Fish, Ithaca, N.Y., 1948, p. 104.

71. Leśmian, "Z rozmyślań o Bergsonie," *SL*, pp. 35-36.

72. Trznadel, *Twórczość Leśmiana*, p. 51.

73. Leśmian, "Z rozmyślań o Bergsonie," *SL*, p. 42. The expression "fantastic necessity" or "magical necessity" can be better understood through certain ideas expressed by Leśmian in: "Znaczenie pośrednictwa. . . ." He explains that *natura naturata* ("derivative reality"), which only examines in an arrested time those phenomena already created, imposes on the creative processes the equation: "effect = cause." However, due to the unharnessed "creative current," the effects do not entirely correspond to the causes. Something new emerges—something unforeseen, an unknown "X"—which is not included in the cause. The equation is, therefore, altered to: "effect = cause + X," i.e., an equation with one unknown, which is the "magical necessity," an unpredictable, mysterious entity of creative life.

This "magical necessity" has apparently been the subject of scrutiny:

> ". . . for a whole series of philosophers, for more than a century . . . in fact, since Kierkegaard and Schopenhauer—there has been a secret, a revelation, a mystery, which would unveil itself in a magical illumination."

Quotation from the work of Wyndham Lewis, *The Writer and the Absolute*, London, 1952, p. 123.

74. Anthropomorphism, a widely used literary device, has in Leśmian's poetics a deeper meaning. When understood functionally, it is an indispensable means to all human creative processes:

> ". . . the aim of which [Leśmian considers] is not only to perceive nature, but to rule over it and to impose upon it the law of man's creation. . . . In social life . . . anthropomorphism is the most direct, and the healthiest principle. . . . It subjugates any system to man, as the source of this system and as that creative function which requires (for continuous development) a constant change in those conditions of the system which are an obstacle, reducing them to a minimum . . . in order to pass over it towards a creative order."

"Znaczenie pośrednictwa," p. 50.

75. Artur Sandauer, "Filozofia Leśmiana," *Poeci trzech pokoleń*, Warsaw, 1962, p. 21.

76. Leśmian, "Z rozmyślań o Bergsonie," *SL*, p. 41.

77. Sławiński, op. cit., p. 224.

78. Leśmian, "Znaczenie pośrednictwa," *SL*, pp. 64-65.

79. Leśmian, "Z rozmyślań o Bergsonie," *SL*, p. 43.

80. Jan Błoński, "Bergson a program poetycki Leśmiana," *Miesięcznik Literacki*, Warsaw, Rok 111, no. 8/24, 1968, p. 38.

81. Leśmian, "Z rozmyślań o Bergsonie," *SL*, p. 41.

82. Leśmian, "Przemiany rzeczywistości," *UR*, *Listy*, p. 183.

83. Ibid., pp. 183-185.

84. These are philosophical terms, used originally by Johannes Scotus Erigena and Spinoza, and modified by Leśmian to suit his poetic theory. Cf., Leśmian's interview, in which he actually mentions these philosophers as possible influences. Boyé, op. cit., p. 498.

Spinoza was quite influential in the latter part of the nineteenth century on such philosophers as Taine, and later on Bergson. Apparently, the terms adopted by Leśmian from Erigena and Spinoza were popular among some poets at the turn of the century as well.

One example is the young Russian Symbolist poet Aleksandr Dobroliubov, who used these terms as a title of his booklet of poems published in 1895 in St. Petersburg: *Natura naturans. Natura naturata.* Apparently Dobroliubov follows Spinoza's concept of *natura naturans* as the cause of all phenomena which, judging from his poems, is the elemental spirit of music. The same can be attributed to Aleksandr Blok, who, in his antithesis "culture-civilization" considers culture as organized by a primordial entity—"the spirit of music." Like Leśmian, Blok believed that a part of culture—some waste, some entropy—becomes a cliché and is acquired by civilization. This civilization, organized by the collective of man, is for both Blok and Leśmian *natura naturata*, while culture is *natura naturans*. Cf., similar ideas on Blok expressed recently by V. V. Ivanov, Iu. I. Lotman, et al., "Tezisy k semioticheskomu izucheniiu kultur," *Semiotyka i struktura tekstu*, Warsaw, 1973, p. 10.

Much later (in 1925) we come across these terms of Spinoza, used again as a title of a cycle in Mikhail Kuzmin's collection of poems, *Forel' razbivaet lëd.* This cycle of poems, consisting of eight "marginal notes" ("vyveski"), is called "Priroda prirodstvuiushchaia i priroda opriroden-naia." (The Russian translation of *natura naturans, natura naturata.* The active state of *natura naturans* is expressed rather well in the sound of the Russian active participle.)

85. Leśmian, "Znaczenie pośrednictwa," *SL*, p. 46.

86. Ibid., pp. 50-51.

87. Ibid., p. 59. Leśmian's defiance of everyday reality and the domination of the "gray-man" mentality persisted throughout his life.

Publishing his long poem *Eliasz* ("Elijah") in 1929, the poet dedicated it to his lifelong friend Adam Szczerbowski, in the following manner:

> "In the name of our common belief in the victory of art over the prevailing ghost of the 'gray man'."

88. Sławinski, op. cit., p. 225.
89. Ibid., p. 226.
90. Leśmian, "Znaczenie pośrednictwa," *SL*, p. 48.
91. Aleksandr Potebnia, the Ukrainian linguist, was also thinking along these lines when he said that ". . . the word is art, more exactly, poetry." Cf., *Mysl' i iazyk*, Kharkov, 3rd ed., 1926, p. 149. He was also keenly aware of the kinship between poetry and myth. He expressed this in his work, *Iz zapisok po teorii slovesnosti* (chapter on "Myth"), Kharkov, 1905, pp. 397-407, as well as in his discussion of Symbolism in Slavic folk poetry, "O nekotorykh simvolakh v slavianskoi poezii," Kharkov, 1860. For this information I am indebted to Viktor Erlich's book, *Russian Formalism*, The Hague, 1965, pp. 24-26.
92. One of the theories advanced by Vico asserts the poet's right to perceive the world outside the realm of logic, to express himself as primitive man did at the dawn of civilization, i.e., in a language free from the precepts of logic and subject to intuition. Vico considered primitive man a natural poet. This idea is also expressed by Leśmian. The importance of poetic thinking in the evolution of mankind, presented in Vico's work, has been extremely well analyzed by Michał Głowiński in his article: "Leśmian, czyli poeta jako człowiek pierwotny" [Leśmian, or the poet as a primitive man], *Pamiętnik Literacki*, 1964, LV, z. 2.
93. Leśmian, "Znaczenie pośrednictwa," *SL*, p. 47.
94. Ibid.
95. Leśmian, "Przemiany rzeczywistości," *UR*, *Listy*, p. 182.
96. Herder expressed the basic ideas concerning poetry and language in such works as: "Über die neue deutsche Literatur," *Erste Sammlung von Fragmenten* (1767-1768), and *Abhandlung über den Ursprung der Sprache* (1770).
97. Numerous critics have quite often pointed out the elements of original "primordiality" in Leśmian's poetry. However, the first to bring this fact to proper attention was Ostap Ortwin in his article "Bolesław Leśmian: *Łąka*," *Próby przekrojów*, Lvov, 1936.
98. Głowiński, op. cit., p. 397.
99. According to Vladimir Markov this English equivalent of the term *zaum'* has been suggested by Roman Jakobson.
100. *Zaum'* represents a very complex linguistic phenomenon in Russian Futurism, one calling for a separate study. However, for the purpose of this study I found it appropriate to present Leśmian's stand on

the transformation of poetic language in the Symbolist manner, i.e., by showing what it is not.

Leśmian's linguistic practices, although considered extreme in Poland, were conservative when compared with the extreme ones in Russia. In some respects they could be compared to those of Khlebnikov. According to Markov, *zaum'* was used by the Russian Futurists largely inconsistently, except for Khlebnikov and Zdanevich.

> "For Kruchenykh it [zaum'] was a free, but often emotionally expressive, combination of sound, devoid of full meaning; for Khlebnikov, it was the basic meaning expressed in the purest and most direct way."

Vladimir Markov, *Russian Futurism: A History,* Berkeley—Los Angeles, 1968, p. 303.

101. This approach to language would indicate that Leśmian was, in a sense, a forerunner of Russian Formalism; to quote Erlich: op. cit., p. 26:

> The formalist position was that the function of the image in poetry . . . lies, in "making strange" the habitual, by presenting it in a novel light.

102. Głowiński, op. cit., p. 401.

103. Potebnia, *Mysl' i iazyk,* p. 23, p. 149.

104. Aleksandr Potebnia, *Iz lekcii po teorii slovesnosti,* Kharkov, 1894, p. 113.

105. Cf., Hertz-Barwiński, op. cit., pp. 106-111. As early as 1895-1896, he attended lectures on literary criticism given by Professor Chelpanov at the University of Kiev. (Chelpanov's influence on the development and formulation of Leśmian's poetics will be discussed in chapter 4. See also ftnt. 6, about his owning Potebnia's works.)

106. Leśmian, "Z rozmyślań o poezji," *SL,* pp. 76-77. According to Erlich this was how Potebnia conceived language (cf., Erlich, op. cit., p. 25. Cf., also, language as conceived by Jan Baudouin de Courtenay, "Zarys historii językoznawstwa, czyli lingwistyki," in *Poradnik dla samouków,* Warsaw, 1909, pp. 103-105. The views of Baudouin de Courtenay closely resemble those of Potebnia.

107. Erlich, op. cit., p. 47. The extensive studies in comparative literary history of Aleksandr Veselovskii, his preoccupation with the genealogy of poetic language and with the relationship of song to poetic creativity were very influential on the Russian Symbolists of the second generation. His ideas were discussed at length especially in the theoretical works of Andrei Belyi (whose works Leśmian read and whom he knew personally). However, it seems unlikely that while attending lectures on

literary criticism at the University St. Vladimir in Kiev, Leśmian could have avoided a first-hand acquaintance with the works of Russia's foremost authority on comparative literary history and criticism. (For a further discussion of the probable influence of Veselovskii on Leśmian's "formulated poetics," see chapter 4.)

108. Głowiński, op. cit., p. 401.

109. Artur Sandauer, ". . . wobec Leśmiana," *Stanowiska wobec . . .* Krakow, 1963, p. 22. This article, written after Leśmian's death, appeared originally in the *Nowy Dziennik*, Krakow, 1937.

110. Reminiscing about his discussions with Leśmian concerning his views on poetry, Karol Irzykowski writes that they "approximate the views of the formalists." Karol Irzykowski, "Śp. Bolesław Leśmian," *Kurier Poranny*, 1937, no. 309.

111. Leśmian, "Władysław Zaleski: Duszom w locie, [W. Zaleski: To Souls in Flight], "Recenzje i kroniki poetyckie z lat 1910-1913" [Reviews and poetic chronicles for the years 1910-1913], *SL*, pp. 359-360.

112. Boyé, op. cit., p. 497, published originally in *Pion*, Warsaw, 1934, no. 23. (This statement could be an allusion to the philosophy of M. Heidegger, whose work, *Sein und Zeit*, was published in 1927.)

113. Sławiński, op. cit., p. 227

114. Leśmian, "Z rozmyślań o poezji," *SL*, pp. 77-78.

115. Leśmian, "U źródeł rytmu," *SL*, pp. 69-70.

116. Leśmian, "Z rozmyślań o poezji," *SL*, pp. 78-79.

117. Ibid.

118. Julian Przyboś, "Granice poezji," *Linia i gwar*, Krakow, 1959, vol. 2, p. 193. Claude Lévi-Strauss, *La Pensée Sauvage*, Paris, 1962. The first chapter of this book, "La science du concret," contains many remarks about the relationship between art and primitive thought.

119. Ibid., pp. 194-195. ". . . [In Poland] this extreme tendency of setting apart poetic language was expressed earliest by Leśmian."

120. Georges Gusdorf, *La Parole*, Paris, 1956, pp. 10-11.

121. According to Leśmian's friend, Adam Szczerbowski, the poem was written in 1935.

122. Julian Przyboś, "Leśmian po latach," vol. 2, p. 104.

123. Szczerbowski, op. cit., p. 52.

124. Boyé, op. cit., pp. 497-498. When the interviewer commented on the extraordinary words—myths, used by Leśmian in his second volume of poems, *Łąka*—Leśmian replied that it was actually Rimbaud who dreamed about creating some sort of subtle musiclike language. He dreamed about a Promethean poet who would have at his disposal a language capable of speaking straight to the heart, of uttering the ineffable. This, and the attainment of the unknown were the postulate and testament of Rimbaud.

125. Leśmian, "Stanisław Miłaszewski: 'Gest wewnętrzny'," *SL*, p. 320.

126. Leśmian, "U źródeł rytmu," *SL*, p. 71. This same phrase is used

by the poet in the essay, "Przemiany rzeczywistości," *UR*, pp. 183-184.

127. This theory was formulated by Leśmian a number of times in such essays as: "Rytm jako światopogląd" [Rhythm as a World View], "U źródeł rytmu" [At the Sources of Rhythm], and also in large parts of the "Treatise of Poetry."

128. Sławiński, op. cit., p. 227.

129. Leśmian, "Rytm jako światopogląd," *SL*, pp. 66-68.

130. The doctrine of "correspondence" originated with Baudelaire; inspired by Swedenborg, it pointed out the universal analogy of phenomena: ". . . everything—form, movement, quantity, color, scent, equally in the spiritual domain, as well as in nature, is meaningful, interdependent, interchangeable and corresponding to each other. . . ." Baudelaire, "L'Art romantique; Reflexions sur quelques-uns de mes contemporains," *Oeuvres complètes*, Paris, 1922, p. 317.

131. Przyboś, "Leśmian po latach," v. 1, p. 96.

132. Leśmian, "Rytm jako światopogląd," *SL*, p. 68.

133. Ernst Kretschmer, *Medizinische Psychologie*, Stuttgart, Thieme, 1950, p. 91.

134. Vico, *Scienza nuova*, p. 8.

135. Leśmian, "U źródeł rytmu," *SL*, p. 69. It is important to note that the entire argumentation of this "poetic study" refers to folk sources, from which Leśmian also derives the origin of rhythm in language.

136. Both Mallarmé and Valéry expressed the desire "to reclaim from music their own." Cf., Renato Poggioli, *The Poets of Russia, 1890-1930*, Cambridge, 1960, pp. 132-133.

137. The notion that primitive language approximates music because of rhythm was expressed by the French philosopher Condillac, who also pointed out that metrics constitutes the poetic quality of the primeval language. Étienne Condillac, "Essai sur l'origine des connaissances humaines," *Oeuvres de Condillac*, Paris, 1798, Vol. I.

138. Leśmian neither recognized tonic verse, which was formed in Polish poetry after 1900, nor *vers libre*, which played an important role in the poetry of Young Poland. He believed that whereas in Russian versification tonic verse was an innovation, "it was no inventive change for free, in the metrical sense, syllabic verse," cf., *SL*, p. 88.

139. Leśmian, "Z rozmyślań o poezji," *SL*, p. 87.

140. Ibid., p. 86.

141. Ernest Grosse, *Początki sztuki*, Warsaw, 1904, p. 201.

142. Leśmian, "Z rozmyślań o poezji," *SL*, p. 87.

143. Irzykowski, "Śp. B. Leśmian."

144. Cf., Karol W. Zawodziński, *Studia z wersyfikacji pokskiej*, Wrocław, 1954, p. 6:

> "Verse ought to remain verse. For, it constitutes the very first form of the musical element, indispensable in poetry."

For Zawodziński, as for any scholar of versification, rhythm was primarily a linguistic phenomenon, constituting one of the structural factors without which the distinction between poetry and prose is lost. Elsewhere, in "Zarys wersyfikacji polskiej," part I, *Wiadomości o wierszu*, Vilna, 1936, p. 31, Zawodziński, like Leśmian, believes that a poetic work ought to be recited. ". . . For a creative work in verse . . . is only actually realized in recitation."

Ideas about the indispensable role of rhythm were also expressed by Franciszek Siedlecki, a brilliant Polish Formalist, who declared that "the tight organization typical of verse tears the sound-stratum of language out of the amorphous inertia, which is its lot in ordinary speech." Franciszek Siedlecki, "O swobodę wiersza polskiego," *Skamander*, III, 1938, p. 104.

145. In this case Leśmian uses the term "metaphysical," which means direct, anti-intellectual, not differentiated by reason. In other words, primitive man was extremely metaphysical in his thinking.

146. Leśmian, "U źródeł rytmu," *SL*, pp. 71-73. See also p. 71.

> "Even the poorest flower . . . does not develop in disorder but, preceded by a song without words, blossoms forth rhythmically. . . ."

147. Leśmian, "Rytm jako światopogląd," *SL*, p. 67.

148. We find this idea of rhythm as the expression of joyfulness in poetry used in a similar way in the works of other Symbolist poets, e.g., the Frenchman Valéry, who compares it to "the golden coin of dance," and the Russian Viacheslav Ivanov, who calls it *umnoe veselie* ("Intellectual Amusement"). The analogy will be discussed later.

149. Leśmian, "U źródeł rytmu," *SL*, p. 74.

150. Leśmian, "Z rozmyślań o poezji," *SL*, p. 86.

151. Błoński, op. cit., pp. 41-42. There are many examples of this phenomenon in Leśmian's theoretical pronouncements. Perhaps the following is one of the best examples:

> "If a flower were able to record *rhythmically* [italics mine] in suitable words . . . its gradual development from the moment when it first desired to become a flower till the moment when it became one, this seemingly tiny record would be a miraculous poetic creation."

Leśmian, "Z rozmyślań o poezji," *SL*, p. 86.

152. Ludwik Fryde, "Bolesław Leśmian," *Tygodnik Ilustrowany*, Warsaw, 1937, no. 48. Apparently, Fryde considered rhythm to be one of the cognitive premises.

153. Michalski, op. cit.

154. Leśmian, "Z rozmyślań o poezji," *SL*, pp. 80-82. Leśmian sees current literary criticism as a new craft, triumphant over the killing of individuality in the writer. He calls it a new Institution of Depersonification, operating on the Olympus of literature. He compares it to the biological phenomenon called "The King-Rat," described by the natural scientist Bölsche. In a filthy, tight nest twenty rats grow into each other. As a result the individual rat disappears, becoming a part of a powerful Siamese Twenty. This monster "The King-Rat" is, according to Leśmian, a truly contemporary and a most modern creature. It is the adroit, powerful, ever-present Director of a Factory of literary trends, the Judge and Editor of all the publications, the Distributor of fame. His signature appears in the plural (it is not royal, but represents twenty heads).

In another essay, "Znaczenie pośrednictwa," *SL*, pp. 55-58, Leśmian observes that, occasionally, the literary critics magnanimously single out one aspect of an original, great creator which suits political expediency or enriches the national museum. However, on the bronze door looms the inscription: "It is forbidden to touch things directly!" Alluding to critics, he quotes Nietzsche: "It is not enough to have talent! One has to have, in addition, your *permission*, my friends!"

155. Leśmian, "Z rozmyślań o poezji," *SL*, p. 79.

156. Ibid., p. 96. His attitude toward critics was expressed in several essays (cf., footnote 127). However his essay, "Poradnik dla recenzentów literackich" [A Guide for Literary Critics], *SL*, pp. 129-141, assumes a form of parody and satire, written in a seventeenth-century style and similar in composition to the introduction of Gogol"s *Ivan Fedorovich Shponka and his Aunt.* Leśmian expresses the same attitude toward critics in another essay, "Spowiedź dziennikarza" [A Confession of a Journalist], *SL*, pp. 113-122. In both of these essays he uses the pseudonym, Felicjan Kostrzycki.

157. Boyé, op. cit., p. 503.

158. Leśmian, "Pieśni ludowe" ("Folk songs"), *SL*, p. 390.

159. Leśmian, "Edgar Allan Poe," *SL*, pp. 465-466.

160. In renouncing a social system which rests on wealth, reputation and pleasure, Leśmian shows his thorough knowledge of Marxism. In singling out money as the most powerful, independent mediator (cf., "Znaczenie pośrednictwa," *SL*, pp. 63, 84-88), his views come very close to those of Benedict (Baruch) Spinoza, expressed in his *Tractatus de Intellectus Emendatione.* Cf., *The Encyclopedia of Philosophy*, 1967, v. 5, p. 531.

161. Sławiński, op. cit., p. 221.

162. Mieczysław Jastrun, "Od Baudelaire' a do Valery'ego," *Poezja i rzeczywistość*, Warsaw, 1965, p. 291.

163. Zbigniew Bieńkowski, "Szczyty Symbolizmu," *Twórczość*, Warsaw, 1962, no. 8, p. 54.

3: Leśmian's Poetics and the Philosophical Ambience

1. Alfred J. E. Fouillée, *Le mouvement idéaliste et la réaction contre la science positive*, Paris, 1896, p. 5.

2. Thomas Carlyle, *Sartor Resartus*, New York, 1927, p. 179.

3. Karl E. Hartmann, *Philosophie des Unbewussten*, Berlin, 1869.

4. Hugo Friedrich, *Die Struktur der modernen Lyrik*, Hamburg, 1956. The author convincingly argues that modern poetry began with the works of Baudelaire and Rimbaud.

5. Albert Mockel, "Quelques souvenirs sur Stefan George," *Revue d'Allemagne*, Paris, 1928, no. 13-14, p. 94.

6. Charles Morice, *La littérature de tout à l'heure*, Paris, 1889, p. 18.

7. Jan Tuczyński, *Schopenhauer a Młoda Polska*, Gdańsk, 1969, p. 12.

8. Marian Zdziechowski, *Pesymism, romantyzm a podstawy chrzescijańistwa*, Krakow, 1915, II, p. 62.

9. Schopenhauer's last (third) edition of *The World as Will and Idea* (1859), which the philosopher prefaced with an introduction a year prior to his death, was translated by the poet Afanasii Fet as early as 1881. This was the first translation anywhere of the original work. Afanasii Fet, *Artur Schopenhauer: Mir kak volia i predstavlenie*, St. Petersburg, 1881. Later, all Schopenhauer's works were translated into Russian under the supervision of Tolstoy and Iulii I. Aikhenvald. See Tuczyński, op. cit., p. 8.

10. Friedrich Nietzsche, *Thus Spake Zarathustra*, 1883-1884; *Beyond Good and Evil*, 1886; *The Genealogy of Morals*, 1887.

11. In Russia, the influence of Nietzschean doctrines was felt early. The self-styled propagator of a new current in literature, Nikolai Minskii (Vilenkin, N.) was very much impressed by the German philosopher. Renato Poggioli claims that "Minskii was seduced by Nietzsche in the late eighties." Renato Poggioli, *The Poets of Russia*, 1890-1930, Cambridge, Mass., 1960, p. 81.

Minskii presented his interpretation of Nietzsche's ideas in a short treatise *Pri svete sovesti* ("In the Light of Conscience"), published in 1890.

A work on Nietzsche was also written by the literary critic N. K. Mikhailovskii, "Darvinizm i Nitssheanstvo," *Russkoe Bogatstvo*, St. Petersburg, 1898.

However, Nietzsche's greatest admirer was the Russian philosopher Lev Shestov, who fought at this time against the tyranny of reason, which, according to him, had deprived man of heaven. His earliest essays on Nietzsche are *Dobro v uchenii Gr. Tolstogo i F. Nitsshe* ("The Good in the Teachings of Tolstoy and Nietzsche"), published in St. Petersburg in 1900, and *Dostoevskii i Nitsshe: Filosofiia tragedii* ("Dostoevsky and Nietzsche: The Philosophy of Tragedy"), published in St. Petersburg in 1901. Both Nietzsche and Dostoevskii were Shestov's greatest heroes. It is quite possible that Leśmian, who lived in Kiev (Shestov's birthplace and residence) at the time of these publications, could have been acquainted with these works. Certain ideas which Shestov expressed seem to coincide with those of the poet, especially pertaining to religion. According to Berdiaev, Shestov's basic definition of God is that "God represents, first of all, limitless possibilities—this is the basic definition of God." Nikolai Berdiaev, "Osnovnaia ideia filosofii Lva Shestova," introduction to Lev Shestov, *Umozrenie i otkrovenie,* Paris, 1964, p. 6.

12. Bolesław Leśmian, "Ludzie odrodzenia," *SL,* pp. 401-419. In this article he singled out the epoch of the Renaissance as superior, as one that encouraged imagination, originality, and individuality. He drew a sharp contrast with the contemporary spirit, in which individuality and talent are a threat to the average man, to whom conformity is the highest law and represents the greatest security. This view shows the possible influence of Konstantin Leontiev.

13. Friedrich Nietzsche, *Thus Spake Zarathustra,* New York, 1924, p. 52.

14. Leśmian, *UR, Listy,* Kiev, 1900, no. 5, p. 241.

15. Ibid., p. 12.

16. Ibid., Kiev, 1900, no. 4, p. 238.

17. Ibid., p. 239.

18. Nietzsche, *Zarathustra,* p. 180.

19. Leśmian, *UR,* Kiev, 1900, no. 3, p. 20.

20. Leśmian, *UR,* p. 11.

21. Nietzsche, *Zarathustra,* pp. 4, 7, 8, 9.

22. Ibid., p. 37.

23. Leśmian, *UR,* p. 23.

24. Bolesław Leśmian, *Poezje,* edited by Jacek Trznadel, Warsaw, 1965, p. 33. All citations come from this edition.

25. In a mediumistic poem "Pieśń o cierpieniu" ("Song of Suffering"), *UR*—written, according to Leśmian's schoolmate, under the influence of Poe, Maeterlinck, and Nietzsche—the poet complains of a world disintegrating from an excess of suffering and cries out in anguish against a heartless God, "O! mój Boże! bezserdeczny Boże!" Henryk Hertz-Barwiński, "Nasze szkolne czasy," *Wspomnienia o Bolesławie Leśmianie,* Lublin, 1966, p. 107.

26. Leśmian, "Betleem," *Poezje,* p. 395.

27. Nietzsche, *Zarathustra,* p. 34.

28. Leśmian, *UR,* p. 17.

29. Leśmian, *UR,* p. 72.

30. Leśmian, *Poezje,* p. 131.

31. Ibid., p. 31.

32. Ibid., p. 35.

33. The earliest poems of Leśmian cited were definitely an echo of Nietzsche's ideas expressed by Zarathustra: "I love only . . . the undiscovered in the remotest sea, for it I bid my sails seek and seek." Nietzsche, *Zarathustra,* p. 170.

34. Leśmian, *UR*, pp. 22-23. The *voyant* poet (poet as seer) untrammeled by space or time, was a popular theme, owing largely to the influence of Rimbaud.

35. Leśmian, *Poezje*, p. 17.

36. Again Zarathustra's words come to mind: "Descend deeper into pain, than I ever ascended until I reached the blackest flood. . . . Whence spring the highest mountains. . . . They spring from the sea." Nietzsche, *Zarathustra*, p. 220.

37. Ibid., p. 63.

38. Ibid., p. 13.

39. Leśmian, *UR*, p. 15. The disdain, the alienation, felt by the poet for the "rabble" is further confirmed by Hertz-Barwiński, who recalls that the youthful poet composed a poem, each stanza of which ended with: "It is not for you to judge!" H. Hertz-Barwiński, op. cit., p. 112.

40. Leśmian, *UR*, Paris, no. 72, p. 304. The article written by Wacław Berent in 1906, entitled "Źródła i ujścia nietzscheanismu" ("The Sources and Outlets of Nietzscheanism"), was an introduction to his translation of *Thus Spake Zarathustra*, *Chimera*, 1906, IX, 25. Viacheslav Ivanov's article was published in *Vesy* in 1904. The cycle *Oddaleńcy* was written in 1905.

41. Nietzsche, *Zarathustra*, p. 107. The following words of Zarathustra bear witness to the parallelism of the two works: "Ye lonely ones of today who stand apart, ye shall one day be a people; from you who are chosen yourselves, a chosen people shall arise, and from it the beyond-man."

42. Leśmian, *Poezje*, p. 74.

43. Nietzsche, *Zarathustra*, pp. 142, 86.

44. The idea of rejecting the passive gods of antiquity and accepting Dionysus, the god of duality, torn by suffering and passion, and, at the same time, filled with ecstasy and excess of joy, is discussed by Nietzsche in his *Die Geburt der Tragödie aus dem Geiste der Musik* (1872) ("The Birth of Tragedy from the Spirit of Music"). At the turn of the twentieth century, the Dionysian myth, as seen through the prism of Nietzschean impulses, caused a turning point in literary history. For the first time, the base, the dissonant side of antiquity, personified by the mythical Dionysus, attainted literary stature and dignity. This turbulent current, the "Dionysian spirit," sweeping along virtually every poet of that period, proved to be a most effective factor in poetic creation. However, it should be pointed out that the Dionysian current represented an exceptionally complex phenomenon in literary aesthetics. It gave rise to different factions and different aspects of it were adopted by various generations. Thus, the early phase of Modernism saw in the Nietzschean myth of Dionysus a natural justification for writing lyrics of an elemental nature, uncontrolled by intellect, expressing intoxication with life in all its manifestations (ranging from the aesthetics of dance and laughter to brutality). Dionysian excesses appealed to the Decadent poets and suited

well their disdain for the "rabble" and their notion about their own exalted role. The Dionysian myth represented in Nietzsche's early works conveying a profound and important message, was almost completely ignored by the majority of the poets at the turn of the century.

45. Nietzsche, *Zarathustra*, pp. 334-335.

46. Ibid., pp. 50, 239, 335, 294. The idea of the "passive gods" is discussed by Nietzsche in his *Die Geburt der Tragödie.*

47. Leśmian, *Poezje*, p. 61.

48. Ibid., pp. 76-77.

49. Nietzsche, *Zarathustra*, p. 2.

50. Leśmian, *Poezje*, p. 70.

51. B. V. Mikhailovskii, *Russkaia literatura XX veka*, Moscow, 1939, p. 67. "Satanism," a characteristic motif for Russian Decadents, indicates, according to Mikhailovskii, their close relationship to the Western representatives of Decadent art, e.g., Charles Baudelaire, Cornelis Huysmans, Villiers de L'Isle-Adam, Paul Verlaine, *et al.*

52. Leśmian, *Poezje*, p. 75.

53. Ibid., p. 87. Wacław Kubacki sees in this panther a stylization of the Hindu destructive force of Shiva. "Komentarz do Leśmiana" *Lata terminowania*, Krakow, 1963, p. 358.

54. Nietzsche, *Zarathustra*, p. 359.

55. Nietzsche, *Jenseits von Gut und Böse: Was ist vornehm, Gesammelte Werke*, Munich, 1922, p. 223.

56. Leśmian, *UR*, *Listy*, Paris, no. 72, p. 304. There is further proof that Leśmian considered the theme of the Superman a temporary, misguiding influence. In 1912, the poet expressed his doubts about including this cycle in *Sad rozstajny:* ". . . it seems that the *Oddaleńcy* does not fit into this volume." Ibid., Paris, no. 84, p. 314.

57. Nietzsche, *Zarathustra*, p. 343. Leśmian's interest in man is unlike that of Zarathustra. Admiring the sea of men for its variety, Zarathustra throws out his golden fishing rod, exclaiming: "Open, o thou abyss of men!" He wants to force the human fish "to come up to my height, the most many coloured abyss groundlings, unto the most malicious one of all catchers of human flesh." Unlike the poet, the wise man has contempt for man, unless man rises to the level of Superman.

58. Leśmian, *Poezje*, p. 64.

59. Jacek Trznadel, *Twórczość Leśmiana*, Warsaw, 1964, referring to it as "theism," interprets Leśmian's relationship to God by means of concepts characteristic of Existentialism, relating mainly to Christianity either by opposing it or referring to it. Leśmian's God, according to the poet's monographer, is, metaphorically speaking, "a God of philosophers," yet at the same time, he is the expression of a "cultural myth," or a "cultural designate." The latter interpretation is misleading, for in Leśmian's aesthetics it would belong to the accursed realm of "mediation" of *natura naturata*. Trznadel devotes considerable attention to the subject. (Cf., pp. 265-281).

Ostap Ortwin called Leśmian a protozoan, pagan, primitive man, who had not yet reached the stage of the need for a godhead. He represents an atavistic epoch, when man was not yet man, and God not yet God.

> "Dreaming already about each other, still related and resembling each other, as two brotherly mists—thrown heavenward into infinity, they did not know yet what is human and what is divine, and which of them will be given the chance to take up eternal residence in heaven."

Ostap Ortwin, *Próby przekrojów, Recenzja z Łąki,* Lvov, 1936, p. 221. The quotation is a slightly changed translation of part of Leśmian's poem "Do śpiewaka," *Łąka,* p. 179.

Czesław Miłosz, in *The History of Polish Literature,* London, 1969, p. 348, calls Leśmian a born worshipper in need of God—a God who depends, however, on the latter for his existence. This interpretation seems to be partially true—insofar as the God is concerned. As for Leśmian, perhaps Miłosz's final conclusion can be applied to his last period of creativity, namely, that Leśmian—like Yeats—struggled with the dilemma of agnosticism.

60. The first one to point to this was Adam Szczerbowski in his study of Leśmian's work, *Bolesław Leśmian,* Warsaw-Zamość, 1938, VI, 10, 27. He notes that the cycle *Zielona godzina* is the first meeting of the poet with the soul of the world, with nature, which will continue in *Łąka.* God cannot be distinguished from nature, which symbolizes the eternal, limitless, unknown absolute of Brahma.

> "The meeting time of the poet-waverer . . . with the soul of nature is the *green hour.* . . . It is an exit outside time and space, outside human thought. . . . This pantheism . . . of Leśmian has its origin in fairy-tales, myths . . . of various times and various Slavic and Asian people. . . . [E]nriched by the poet's fantasy, it is extremely original in character (p. 27)."

61. Leśmian, "Znaczenie pośrednictwa w metafizyce życia zbiorowego," *SL,* p. 48.

62. Ortwin, op. cit., p. 222.

63. Leśmian, *Poezje,* p. 34.

64. In the introduction to his translation of *Thus Spake Zarathustra,* op. cit., p. 133, Berent speaks of the easy access to the treasures of human spirit. He calls it a privilege of modern man. He refers to the interest in these treasures as to ". . . a true hunger of the contemporary spirit. . . . This necessity, which sometimes exceeds fatally the creative mastery of control, is actually a symptom and an indication of the ones which think and feel today more profoundly." Elsewhere in "Tredecim:

Rozstrojowcy i zamętowcy," *Chimera*, 1906, VI, 17, p. 229, Berent, realizing that this hunger for knowledge and this appetite for new spiritual experiences far exceed the capacity of the digestive system of most people, expresses concern: "All that liberates our spirit, without giving us the self-control, is injurious."

65. Leśmian, *Poezje*, p. 241.

66. Maria Podraza-Kwiatkowska, "Leśmianowy czyn," *Ruch Literacki*, Krakow, 1964, z. 4, p. 266. The Dionysian dance and laughter quite often represent the very opposite of the excess of happiness and rapture. The dance, in particular, seldom materializes into a full form. It is rather a hobbling along, erratic skipping or jumping caused by the physical deformity of the dancer. Cf., the ballad "Żołnierz" ("The Soldier"). This kind of dance corresponds more closely to the *bylejakość* slapdash manner used in practically every aspect of Leśmian's aesthetics which had a philosophical connotation.

67. Leśmian, *UR*, *Listy*, no. 5, p. 241. In 1900, the poet admits his poor knowledge of French.

68. Benedict (Baruch) Spinoza, *The Encyclopedia of Philosophy*, New York, 1967, p. 533.

69. Ibid.

70. Edward Boyé, "Dialogi akademickie—W niepojętej zielonośći," *SL*, Warsaw, 1959, p. 498. Leśmian discusses Spinoza with the author.

71. Ibid.

72. Leśmian, "Z rozmyślań o Bergsonie," *SL*, p. 36.

73. Leśmian, *Poezje*, p. 38.

74. Miłosz, op. cit., p. 348. This is an idea expressed by Miłosz with regard to Leśmian's relationship to God. The author insists that Leśmian was "a born worshipper, *homo adorans*, in perpetual need of contact with God," with which I could agree only if we take into consideration the fact that for Leśmian God was nature, the universe. This at least was the basis for his specific kind of pantheism.

75. Leśmian, *UR*, *Listy*, Paris, no. 81, p. 311. In the next letter to Przesmycki (p. 312), the poet says that he has arrived at the firm conviction that *The Seeing Flowers* is the only appropriate title, since the whole volume revolves around this theme.

76. Leśmian, *Poezje*, p. 125. Already at this stage we are introduced to "denied existence" resulting from the unfulfilled act of incarnation. This state is expressed by words accentuating negation of phenomena. The act of immersion into the depth of the forest, the act of dehumanization is accompanied by a ceaseless motion and enticement of a very animated nature.

77. Cf., Kazimierz Wyka, *Zarys współczesnej literatury polskiej*, Krakow, 1951, pp. 252-253. The Modernist notion that an entity may be penetrated only by the initiated partially applies to Leśmian, but he definitely was not a neo-Kantian, as implied by Wyka.

78. Leśmian, "Z rozmyślań o Bergsonie," *SL*, p. 38.
79. Ibid., p. 41.
80. Leśmian does not just believe in nature being God; he, as nature's equal partner and as a creator, is himself part of this all-embracing divinity.
81. Michał Głowiński, "Recenzja: Jacek Trznadel, Twórczość Leśmiana," *Pamiętnik Literacki*, LV, z. 2, p. 593. In a poem called "Spowiedź" ("A Confession") the poet—using the lyrical "I"—confesses the reason for his regression to primordiality. The emptiness surrounding him made him realize that he does not know who he is. Taken by nature, a sudden realization overcame him, letting him know who he used to be, where he belonged. He returned to nature, began resembling it, and suddenly God was the Forest yearning for a Flower. . . . Leśmian, *UR*, p. 106.
82. Leśmian, "Znaczenie pośrednictwa," *SL*, p. 49.
83. Ibid.
84. Leśmian, "Artysta i model," *UR*, p. 189.
85. Kazimierz Moszyński, *Kultura ludowa Słowian*, Krakow, 1934, z. 1, 428. Professor Jan B. Bystroń acknowledges this same view in his work *Artyzm pieśni ludowej*, Poznań, 1921, p. 162. Speaking of the folksong, he observes that

> ". . . the limits between the animal and vegetable kingdom and man's world are eradicated; people can communicate with animals and plants, which in turn have an emotional inner life resembling man. . . . The possibility of metamorphosis heightens even more this close relationship of man and nature."

86. Leśmian, *Łąka* ("The Meadow"), *Poezje*, p. 256. In this poem the meadow comes to visit man, saying: "Jeszczem ja w żadnej chacie dotąd nie bywała." ("I have never been in any hut before.") The meadow is wondering whether man and she were born the same way. Ibid., p. 252.
87. Kazimierz Wierzyński, *O Bolesławie Leśmianie*, Warsaw, 1939, p. 22.
88. Miłosz, op. cit., p. 348. He considers that "the existence of man and nature is a function of the existence of God. . . ." It should be assumed that they replace the function of God.
89. Michał Głowiński, "Szkic o Leśmianie," *Twórczość*, Warsaw, 1956, no. 10, pp. 76-77. The author attributes Leśmian's pantheism to the influence of Spinoza: "The poems become . . . dialogues with this mysterious being of nature. . . . God has no religious meaning . . . he is simply a fragment of nature." The philosophical meaning of this dialogue with a God conceived in this manner represents a "symbolist romance with the absolute, understood by the poet in *Zielona godzina* . . . as an indestructible, but also incognizable spirit of nature."

90. Jean Jacques Rousseau, "Lettre sur la Providence," *Vocabulaire technique et critique de la philosophie*, Paris, 1951, p. 1123.

91. This epic is older than *Mahabharata*, VIII-VII B.C. It was translated by Antoni Lange in 1898, following Fauche, whose version he expanded. Cf., also, an article by Bolesław Leśmian, *Ramayana, SL*, p. 400.

92. This was apparently based on the title of a poem by Rimbaud, "Le Bateau ivre" ("The Drunken Boat"), which was popularized by Verlaine. It is part of Rimbaud's autobiographical psychological prose poem, *Une Saison en Enfer* ("A Season in Hell"), published in 1873.

93. Wierzyński, op. cit., p. 15. (Speech delivered at a meeting of the Polish Academy of Literature, where the poet was chosen to occupy the vacancy left after the death of Leśmian.)

Zygfryd Krauze, "Ze wspomnień o Leśmianie," *Wspomnienia o B. L.*, p. 188. Krauze, a friend of Leśmian, points out his deep interest in Hindu philosophy. Krauze assumes that the poet tried to find support of his intuitive experiences in the Upanishad or possibly looked for inspiration in the Hindu epics.

94. Szczerbowski, op. cit., pp. 10, 11. This would still represent the pantheistic stage in Leśmian's poetics.

95. Ibid., p. 10.

96. Leśmian, *Poezje*, p. 35. This peculiar way of perceiving things is certainly not common to man.

97. Szczerbowski, op. cit., p. 26.

98. Adam Mickiewicz, *Dzieła*, Warsaw, 1955, Vol. X, pp. 161-162. In lectures delivered in Paris the Polish bard criticized Derzhavin, who in describing God had resorted to tactics reminiscent of Spinoza. He repeats

> "a hundred times . . . that God never had a beginning and will not have an end; he begins from negations, remaining in the undefined mathematical spheres of time and space."

99. Wacław Kubacki, op. cit., p. 337. The device of "negation" frequently used in Leśmian's poetry has been interpreted by Artur Sandauer with the help of the Hegelian triad. Kubacki polemicizes with this approach, trying to give a comprehensive explanation within the framework of literary history of the origin of "negation," beginning with Plato's *Republic*. In his work *Vom Geiste der hebräischen Poesie*, Herder pointed out that the proverbs and riddles are the manifestations of folk poetry of primitive peoples. He was of the opinion that the entire body of Eastern poetry was in the form of an apologue and fairy tale. Even Hegel considered the riddle a creation of the East, originating in the epoch of transition from unconscious symbolism to conscious expression of experiences. These observations can be found in Hegel's lectures on aesthetics *Vorlesungen über die Aesthetik*, Part 2, chapter 3.

100. *Slovo o polku Igoreve,* edition by D. S. Likhachev, Moscow, 1954, p. 51.

101. Artur Sandauer, "Filozofia Leśmiana," *Poeci trzech pokoleń,* Warsaw, 1962, pp. 7-23. This excellent essay will be discussed later.

102. Kubacki, op. cit., p. 349.

103. Leśmian, *Poezje,* p. 373.

104. Ibid., p. 310.

105. Ibid., p. 311.

106. Ibid.

107. Ibid., pp. 424, 443, 427.

108. Ibid., "W nicość śniąca się droga," ("A road that dreams into nothingness"), p. 398.

109. Ibid., p. 449.

110. Ibid., pp. 429, 465.

111. Ibid., p. 444.

112. Ibid., p. 321.

113. Kubacki, op. cit., p. 359. In the Vedanta philosophy, Mâyâ (Sanskrit matter) represents the veil of Nature which obscures the True (the soul of Atma).

114. Krauze, op. cit., p. 187. Bergson's *Creative Evolution* was Leśmian's favorite book of philosophy. He called it a philosophical poem. He often read aloud passages from Bergson's works, and defended the views of the philosopher regarding the intuitive cognizance of reality. Yet, Krauze could not tell whether the poet's views were formulated under Bergson's influence or whether he only found in Bergson support for his own ideas.

115. While Bergson's *Laughter* was translated into Polish in 1902, *An Introduction to Metaphysics* was translated in 1910, *Creative Evolution* in 1912, and *The Immediate Data of Consciousness* in 1913.

116. Leśmian, *UR, Listy,* Paris no. 90, 1912, p. 324.

117. Leśmian, "U źródeł rytmu," *SL,* p. 70. In this essay the poet says that myth knows no time. It represents a "third existence."

118. Henri Bergson, "An Introduction to Metaphysics," *Philosophy in the Twentieth Century: An Anthology,* New York, 1962, III, pp. 304-305.

119. Henri Bergson, *Creative Evolution,* New York, 1913, p. 321.

120. Bergson, "Introduction to Metaphysics," pp. 325, 317.

121. Jan Błoński, "Bergson a program poetycki Leśmiana," *Miesięcznik Literacki,* Warsaw, no. 8/24, p. 37.

122. Bergson, *Creative Evolution,* pp. 199-200.

123. Leśmian, "Znaczenie pośrednictwa," *SL,* p. 51.

124. Błoński, op. cit., p. 38.

125. Henri Bergson, *The Immediate Data of Consciousness* (*Essai sur les données immédiates de la conscience*), London, 1910, p. 18.

126. Henri Bergson, *L'energie spirituelle. Essais et conferences,* Paris, 1930, p. 49.

127. Bergson, "Introduction to Metaphysics," p. 317.
128. Leśmian, "Z rozmyślań o poezji," *SL*, p. 86.
129. Bergson, *Creative Evolution*, p. 159.
130. Ibid., p. 251.
131. Sandauer, op. cit., p. 20. The phenomenon in Leśmian's poetry, whereby his words or "creations, as the expression of a singular experience or feeling [that] arise and perish together with them," the author calls "momentary mythology."
132. Bergson, "Introduction to Metaphysics," pp. 317, 320, 327.
133. Roman Jakobson, "The Kernel of Comparative Slavic Literature," *Harvard Slavic Studies*, Cambridge, 1953, p. 9.
134. Bergson, *Creative Evolution*, p. 160.
135. Kazimierz Wyka, "Klucz nie zawsze doskonały," *Odrodzenie*, Krakow, 1946, no. 5, p. 6.
136. Bergson, *Creative Evolution*, p. 248.
137. Leśmian, "Z rozmyślań o Bergsonie," *SL*, p. 44.
138. Leśmian, *Poezje*, p. 307.
139. Ibid., p. 95.
140. Bergson, *Creative Evolution*, p. 324.
141. This is reminiscent of Aleksandr Blok's "Bolotnyi popik" ("The Swamp Priestlet") and "Bolotnye cherteniatki" ("The Swamp Devils") from his cycle *Puzyri zemli* ("Bubbles of the Earth"), written during the Russian poet's most pessimistic period.
142. Ludwik Fryde, "Bolesław Leśmian," *Tygodnik Ilustrowany*, 1937, no. 48, p. 8.
143. This cry of anguish can be compared to the one found in Russian literature, especially in the works of Gogol'; *Diary of a Madman* and *The Overcoat*, Dostoevsky; *Crime and Punishment*, *The Double*, *Dream of a Ridiculous Man* and *Notes from the Underground*.
144. Leśmian, *Poezje*, pp. 373, 386.
145. Ibid., p. 157. "Dusiołek" has a folkloric genesis. It is a petty demon believed in by the peasants of the Cracow region. S. Udziela, "Świat nadzmysłowy ludu krakowskiego," *Wisła*, 1900, XIV, p. 399.
146. Kazimierz Wyka, "Czytam Leśmiana," *Łowy na kryteria*, Warsaw, 1965, pp. 250-276. In the Polish language *stwórca*—the creator, and *potwór*—monster, have the same stem, the basis for Leśmian's play on words.
147. Leśmian, *Poezje*, p. 391. This poem was translated into Russian by Boris Pasternak. It was written after the death of Leśmian's beloved sister Alexandra.
148. Ibid., p. 387.
149. Ibid., p. 382.
150. Ibid., p. 394.
151. Ibid., "Srebroń," p. 310.
152. Wyka, "Czytam Leśmiana," p. 256.

153. Leśmian, *Poezje*, p. 293.
154. Ibid., p. 348.
155. Ibid., p. 419.
156. Sandauer, op. cit., p. 23.
157. Jean Jacques Rousseau, op. cit., p. 1123.

4: Leśmian and the Russian Contemporary Scene

1. Bolesław Leśmian, *UR*, *Listy*, Kiev, 1897, no. 1, p. 232.

2. Oleg Maslenikov, *The Frenzied Poets*, Berkeley and Los Angeles, 1952, p. 9. Two articles published in 1884 in the Kievan newspaper *Zaria* ("The Dawn") by these lesser-known writers had the effect of a first bombshell, ushering in a new era of Russian literature.

3. Czesław Miłosz, *The History of Polish Literature*, London, 1969, p. 348.

4. Andrei Belyi [Boris Bugaev], "O granitsakh psikhologii," *Simvolizm*, Moscow, 1910, p. 480. Hereafter this work will be referred to as *S*.

5. Some literary historians may argue that a Polish work of "modern" criticism—Ignacy Matuszewski's *Słowacki i nowa sztuka* (*modernizm*), Warsaw, 1902—might have had an even stronger influence. However, due to its later appearance it probably only reinforced the ideas absorbed by the high-school student Leśmian from the teachings of Chelpanov in the late nineties.

6. Belyi, "Printsip formy v èstetike," reprinted in *S*, pp. 176, 178. In discussing the usage and concept of form and content in art as a representation of an indivisible unit and a canon of aesthetics, the author refers to ideas expressed by Aleksandr Potebnia, without quoting him directly. The author considers form and content only as methodical devices for the study of a given artistic unity which is represented by the *symbol*. Therefore (following Potebnia), Belyi maintains that when speaking about symbolism of a creative work, its form and content are a unit and cannot be considered as two entities of contrasting meaning. In the footnotes (ibid., pp. 524, 527) Belyi further echoes Potebnia's ideas when commenting on poetry capable of transforming "spatial characteristics into temporal, and *vice versa*," via a language that attempts "to express the spatial relationship in a sequence of sound." Therefore "causality (in the narrow sense of the word) does not exist in a poetic myth." The story (*fabula*) in poetry is teleological; i.e., it concerns itself with aim, meaning and the value of the portrayed things, rather than with causes. At the eleventh hour before publication, I discovered that:

> "in his library closet [Leśmian] kept many rare volumes of anthologies of Russian poets published in and outside of Russia. . . .

> There was also . . . a sizeable collection of Russian treatises in the field of literary theory. The works of Aleksandr Potebnia, esteemed even in our days, were there . . . books of his student, Dimitrii Ovsianiko-Kulikovskii, the outstanding literary historian and theoretician, and many other rare volumes of Russian Formalists. The appearance of the books attested that their owner must have read and reread them."

P. G. (Piotr Grzegorczyk), "Jeszcze o Leśmiana wierszach rosyjskich," *Twórczość,* no. 4, 1961, pp. 167-168.

7. Belyi, "Lirika i èksperiment," *S,* pp. 574, 577, 586. The author quotes Potebnia's ideas on poetic language and literary criticism as expressed in *Mysl' i iazyk,* pp. 177-192.

> "Potebnia considers the word as an independent art. Symbolism of language can apparently be called its poeticality. . . . We distinguish in the word and *exterior form,* consisting of *content* objectified by means of sound, and the *inner form,* i.e., the closest etymological meaning expressing the content of the word."

He rejects the idea of the word as an expression of a finalized thought. On the contrary, he sees the word as

> "the expression of a thought only to the extent to which it serves *as a means* of stimulating its creation. . . . The inner form . . . changes and perfects those aggregates of perception which it finds in the soul. . . ."

That is why Potebnia considers "the word and poetry as energy . . . inciting continuous transformation of ready concepts." The word and poetry have this in common, that "in action they are a triad consisting of three indivisible, interrelated elements: form, content, and *inner form* . . . i.e., the symbolistic image."

Potebnia measured the artist's achievement by his capacity to create flexible images which would stimulate the reader to find the most diverse content in a given work of art. He believed that the content actually develops in the mind of the creative reader. Thus, he propagated the Symbolist concept of poetry, laying a firm foundation for the future generation. Belyi concedes that Russian Symbolists would sign their names under the tenets of "the most profound Russian scholar." The same could apply equally to Leśmian, whose ideas seem to be a continuation of Potebnia's. Even in regard to literary criticism, the opinion of the great scholar finds an echo in Belyi and Leśmian, who consider literary criticism as a deadly influence upon the taste of the reading public.

8. Aleksandr Veselovskii, *Istoricheskaia poètika*, 1899, Leningrad, 1940, introduction by Viktor Zhirmunskii, p. 47.

9. Veselovskii, cited in Belyi's *Simvolizm*, Moscow, 1910, p. 619, in his addendum to "Magiia slov."

10. Belyi, "Émblematika smysla," *S*, pp. 49-143. Here the author actually quotes Veselovskii. Therefore, Vedantas (via Veselovskii) can be considered the source for Belyi's system of triads.

11. Jan Brzechwa, "Niebieski wycieruch," *Wspomnienia o B. L.*, p. 85. According to the author, Bal'mont visited Leśmian in Warsaw in 1927.

12. *Literaturnyi arkhiv: materialy po istorii literatury i obshchestvennogo dvizheniia*, edited by K. D. Muratova, vol. 5, M.-L., A. N. SSSR, 1960, p. 171. K. Bal'mont mentions Leśmian's appreciation of his poetry in a letter to Valerii Briusov written March 1907.

13. Konstantin Bal'mont, "Slaviia i Litva," *Souchastie dush: ocherki*, Sofia, 1930, p. 69. Bal'mont considered Leśmian's poem, "Szmer wioseł" ("The Sound of Oars"), from *Sad rozstajny*, a beautiful Christmas gift from a close friend. Bal'mont's translation of this poem into Russian entitled: "Vzmakh vesel," appears in the same article.

14. Maria L. Mazurova, "Podróże i twórczość Bolesława Leśmiana," *Wspomnienia o B. L.*, p. 63. The author, the older daughter of Leśmian, writes about her father's frequent visits with various Russian poets during their stay in Paris. Konstantin Mochul'skii, *Andrei Belyi*, Paris, 1955, p. 97, also writes about Belyi's visit with Bal'mont and the poets mentioned above.

Marie Maline, *Nicolas Gumilev, poète et critique acméiste* (A doctoral thesis presented at the Philological and Slavic Department at the Oriental and Slavic Free University of Bruxelles), Brussels, 1954, p. 7. The author informs us about Gumilev's stay in Paris from 1906 to 1909, where he published a literary review, *Sirius*. It is very likely that Leśmian also met Gumilev during those years, since the Russian poets used to gather frequently at the Bal'monts. Xavery Glinka, "Wspomnienia o Leśmianie," *Kultura*, Paris, 1949, no. 4-5, p. 127. Glinka reminisces that Leśmian often recited Russian poems, especially the poems of his good friend Bal'mont. In the same article, the author mentions that he partook in a soirée in Paris, organized to pay tribute to Bal'mont, and assisted Leśmian in this pleasant task, together with Antoni Lange.

15. Vladimir Markov, "Bal'mont: A Reappraisal," *Slavic Review*, June, 1969, p. 246. Among the poets present were Paul Fort, René Ghil, Gustave Kahn. The last two poets, especially René Ghil, were frequent contributors to the Russian Symbolist journal, *Vesy*. Thus, Leśmian was in close contact with both French and Russian literary circles.

16. Antoni Juniewicz, "Nowe rosyjskie wiersze i listy Leśmiana," *Przegląd Humanistyczny*, Warsaw, 1964, p. 149. The author found Leśmian's name in Briusov's diary from 1901-1903. The information was obtained in the Department of Manuscripts of the Biblioteka im. Lenina,

Briusov, Zapisnye knizhki, "Moja zhizn'," notebook no. 4, p. 386. In one of Briusov's notebooks, Juniewicz found a poem from *Sad rozstajny* written down by Leśmian to commemorate their meeting in 1914. Ibid., p. 386, k. ed: khran. 344, notebook no. 5.

17. Ibid., pp. 147-148. In his letter to Briusov, written August 1907, Leśmian thanks the Russian poet for his invitation to be a contributor and co-worker in *Vesy*, considering it a great honor. He also mentions the drama *Vasilii Buslaev*, and his hopes of having it published and staged with the help of Briusov.

18. Ibid., p. 149; *Apollon*, 1912, no. 5, p. 60.

19. Dmitrij Čiževskij, "Zu den polnisch-russischen literarischen Beziehungen," *Zietschrift für slavische Philologie*, Heidelberg, 1955, Vol. XXIII, no. 2. The second part of the article is devoted to Leśmian, pp. 260-271.

20. *Versdichtung der russischen Symbolisten*, herausgegeben von Johannes Holthusen und Dmitrij Tschizevskij, Wiesbaden, 1959, pp. 113-114.

21. Bolesław Leśmian, "Z rozmyślań o poezji," *SL.*, p. 76.

22. Leśmian, *UR, Listy*, p. 55.

23. Fedor I. Tiutchev, *Izbrannye stikhotvoreniia*, New York, 1952, p. 40.

24. Leśmian, *Poezje*, ed. by Jacek Trznadel, Warsaw, 1965, p. 246. In this poem, as is characteristic for the author, he transforms a known wandering motif of the East to express his creed.

25. Richard A. Gregg, *Fedor Tiutchev: The Evolution of a Poet*, New York and London, 1965, p. 40. The "intensified method" is achieved by mobilizing various linguistic means as well as by the astute observation of natural phenomena observed in Tiutchev and described by Blagoi in "Zhizn' i tvorchestvo Tiutcheva," *Polnoe sobranie stikhotvorenii*, Moscow-Leningrad, 1933, ed. by G. I. Chulkov, I. p. 27.

26. Ibid., p. 88.

27. Julian Tuwim, "W dziesięciolecie śmierci," *Wspomnienia o B. L.*, p. 123.

A. Maksim Gor'kii, "Zametki," *L. N. Tolstoi v vospominaniiakh sovremennikov*, Moscow-Leningrad, 1960, Vol. 2, p. 418. Gor'kii recalls that Tolstoi considered Fet's "Ne znaiu sam, chto budu pet', . . ." ("I don't know myself what I shall sing"), an expression of the "true fold spirit" of poetry. He compared it to the peasant who does not know what he is going to sing, yet out comes a true song, straight from the soul.

28. Włodzimierz Słobodnik, "Pieśni mimowolne," *Wspomnienia o B. L.*, p. 244. The author described Leśmian's moving recitation of Fet's "V lunnom siianii," and speaks of Blok and Esenin as the contemporaries he most admired. (It is very indicative that his predilection was mostly for elemental poets like himself.)

29. Translations of Celtic and Scandinavian folk-poetry by Edward

Porębowicz, *Pieśni ludowe,* were a much used source by the poet.

The fact that Leśmian saw the genesis of Żeromski's *Powieść o Wdałym Walgierzu* in the *byliny* shows his attachment to Russian folklore. Cf., his letter in *UR, Listy,* Paris, 1906, no. 72, p. 303.

30. Andrei Belyi, *Mezhdu dvukh revoliutsii,* Leningrad, 1934, pp. 208, 212. "Simvolizm," *Lug zelenyi: kniga statei,* Moscow, 1910, pp. 24-26. The author expresses the same idea in "Êmblematika smysla," *S,* p. 49. "Symbolistic art of the last decade does not differ . . . from the devices of eternal art. It is a return to the forgotten forms of German Romanticism. It opens to us the East. . . . It is a transfer of characteristics existing before." Cf., also "Nastoiashchee i budushchee russkoi literatury," *Lug zelenyi,* p. 84, *passim.* Hereafter, this work will be referred to as *LZ,* Cf., Viacheslav Ivanov, "Dve stikhii v sovremennom simvolizme," *Po zvezdam,* St. Petersburg, 1909, p. 264. Hereafter this work will be referred to as *PZ.*

31. René Ghil, "Pis'ma o frantsuzskoi poèzii: Tancrède De Visan," *Vesy,* 1905, 3 p. 48. Ghil singles out De Visan; he analyzes his ideology and style and compares him to other poets. Georgette Donchin, *The Influence of French Symbolism on Russian Poetry,* S-Gravenhage, 1958, p. 22. The author mentions the volume of translations from French poets, including De Visan's poetry, published by Skorpio in 1906. All this data mentioned above lead one to believe that De Visan could have influenced Belyi, Ivanov and Leśmian whose articles appeared much later.

32. Tancrède De Visan, *Paysages introspectifs, poèmes, avec un Essai sur le Symbolisme,* Paris, 1904, p. lvii.

33. Ibid., p. lviii.

34. Ibid., p. xxxi.

35. Ibid., p. lix. All these ideas are discussed in detail in the introduction to his later work, *L'Attitude du Lyrisme contemporain,* Paris, 1909.

36. Edward Boyé, "Dialogie akademicke—W niepojętej zieloności," *SL,* p. 502.

37. Nikolai Valentinov, *Two Years with the Symbolists,* Stanford, 1969, p. 48.

38. Ibid., p. 49.

39. D. S. Mirsky, *A History of Russian Literature,* New York, 1966, p. 464. Cf., Maslenikov, op. cit., p. 65.

40. Mochul'skii, op. cit., p. 273. The author quotes Zaitsev's reminiscences about Belyi: "People saw in him a similarity to Prince Myshkin. . . . They were saying that at the university someone hit him in the face and he offered the other cheek."

Valentinov, op. cit., p. 49. The author says that some compared Belyi to Alesha Karamazov, some to Prince Myshkin, and others saw in him a *blazhennyi* ("a blessed one").

Maria Kuncewicz, "Lecture on Bolesław Leśmian," *MS,* 1968, p. 4.

41. Maslenikov, op. cit., p. 217.

42. Cf., Leśmian's essays, "Znaczenie pośrednictwa w metafizyce życia zbiorowego" ("The Importance of Mediation in the Metaphysics of Communal Life"), "Z rozmyślań o poezji" ("Treatise on Poetry"), "Ludzie odrodzenia" ("The People of the Renaissance"), all of which are a critique on "modernity," the last showing the poet's admiration for this epoch.

43. Maslenikov, op. cit.

44. Mochul'skii, op. cit., pp. 60, 62.

45. Andrei Belyi, *Zoloto v lazuri,* Moscow, 1904. Information from Mochul'skii, op. cit., p. 58.

46. Leśmian, *Poezje,* p. 77.

47. Leśmian, *UR, Listy,* Cannes, no. 98, pp. 336-337. He writes that he accumulated fairy tales heard in his childhood in the Ukraine. He wants them to have a prattling, uncontaminated, pure quality. He wants to create a Polish *bylina.* In the subsequent letter (pp. 338-339) describing the characters, he speaks about Gogol'.

48. Maslenikov, op. cit., p. ix. Mochul'skii, op. cit., p. 144. He contends that Russian "poetics" as a discipline owes Belyi its birth.

49. Leśmian, "Z rozmyślań o Bergsonie," *SL.,* p. 38.

50. Belyi, "Magiia slov," *S,* p. 431.

51. Ibid., p. 446.

52. Leśmian, "Z rozmyślań o Bergsonie," p. 37.

53. Belyi, "Émblematika smysla," *S,* p. 130.

54. Aleksandr Blok i Andrei Belyi, "Perepiska," *Letopisi,* Moscow, 1940, Kn. 7-r, p. 10. In the conception of music, possibly the closest to Leśmian was Blok. Like Leśmian, Blok identified musical rhythm with culture. (31 March 1919, *Dnevnik A. Bloka,* Leningrad, 1928, p. 31.)

55. Belyi, "Nastoiashchee i budushchee," *LZ.,* p. 59.

56. Leśmian, "Rytm jako światopogląd," *SL.,* p. 67.

57. Belyi, "Magiia slov," *S.,* pp. 435-436.

58. Leśmian, "U źródeł rytmu," *SL.,* p. 70.

59. It can be added that the phonetic and rhythmic patterned elaborations Belyi used in his prose-poetry especially in the third symphony, *The Return* (1905), mirror the Nietzschean idea of "eternal recurrence." This corresponds chronologically to Leśmian's brief enchantment with Nietzsche, as mentioned earlier in the cycle *Oddaleńcy* and particularly in the poem "Śród nocy" in *UR,* p. 13. There is, of course, also an echo of that now threadbare phrase of Goethe's Faust: "Alles Vergängliche ist nur ein Gleichnis."

60. Leśmian, "Znaczenie pośrednictwa," *SL,* p. 64.

61. Georgii P. Fedotov, *Sviatye drevnei Rusi,* New York, 1960, p. 191. The appearance of sainthood, of *iurodivye* dates back to the early Middle Ages. The sainthood of the secular *iurodivye* derived from the masses (peasants), started in the fourteenth century replacing princely sainthood of the early Middle Ages, which was called *Bogumilstvo.*

62. Andrei Belyi, *Stikhotvoreniia i poèmy*, Moscow-Leningrad, 1966, p. 159.

63. Tiutchev, op. cit., p. 229.

64. Belyi, "Émblematika smysla," *S*, pp. 94, 95, 114. In this lengthy article Belyi attempts to arrive at a thesis which he considers a necessary basis for the future aesthetics. His thesis is tied in with the theory of Symbolism as the key to the understanding of the future world. He creates an elaborate system of triads representing creation, religion, and aesthetics. The crowning glory of these triads is the triple unity represented in Symbol, the emblem of unity. In art and aesthetics, this Symbol is an amalgam of form (Apollonian and Dionysian) of the elemental spiritual force (Sofiia-Premudrost') and the masculine image (Lik) which is represented by the Word [Logos]. Belyi's theories are primarily concerned with establishing norms for theurgic art. Elsewhere ("What is a Symbol," *LZ*, p. 184) he says that ". . . the last link in the visible goal of creation is man / . . . *Man is Godlike as a creator* [italics mine]."

For Leśmian man represents the unity of nature and the Creator. His creations supersede God's creations. Cf., poems *Eliasz* ("Elijah"), "W locie" ("In Flight").

65. Belyi, "Simvolizm," *LZ*, p. 22.

66. Ibid., p. 24.

67. The deadening effect of society and science in devaluating creative life is also expressed in Belyi's cycle of poems *Filosoficheskaia grust'*, *Urna*, 1909. His second, *Northern Symphony* (*Heroic*), is filled with satirical remarks about positivistic art aimed especially at Kant. Cf., B. V. Mikhailovskii, *Russkaia literatura XX veka*, Moscow, 1939, p. 234, for similar views on Belyi. Leśmian criticizes the German philosopher and science in "Z rozmyślań o Bergsonie," *passim*.

68. Renato Poggioli, *The Poets of Russia 1890-1930*, Cambridge, 1960, p. 80.

69. Giambattista Vico, *Scienza Nuova*, the first part of Vico's collected works translated into French by A. Doubine, *Principes d'une science nouvelle relative à la nature commune des nations*, Paris, 1953, p. 8. The philosopher looks at poetics as a historiosopher. In his vision of the development of human culture, a poetic period at the end of a century always constitutes the last stage before a new moment arrives, in the ever recurring scheme in the history of poetics.

70. Friedrich Nietzsche, *Die Geburt der Tragödie* (aus dem Geiste der Musik), Munich, 1959, p. 37.

71. Friedrich Nietzsche, *Die Götzendämmerung, Gesammelte Werke*, Munich, 1922, p. 86.

72. Friedrich Nietzsche, *Thus Spake Zarathustra*, New York, 1924, p. 17.

73. Viacheslav Ivanov, "Zavety simvolizma," *Apollon*, 8, 1910, p. 81.
74. Viacheslav Ivanov, "Dve stikhii," *PZ*, p. 248.
75. Ibid., p. 277. Ivanov considered this slogan an "alchemic riddle," capable of establishing "perceiving and discerning in reality a more real reality."
76. Viacheslav Ivanov, "Granitsy iskusstva," *Borozdy i mezhy*, Moscow, 1916, p. 192. Hereafter this work will be referred to as *BM*. The prophet is oriented towards the ascent in a "Dionysian Epiphany," whereas the poet descends via the Apollonian dream, which becomes hell. Leśmian considers the poet a prophet. The Apollonian and Dionysian elements appear under the influence of *Die Geburt der Tragödie*.
77. Ivanov, "Dve stikhii," *PZ*, p. 253.
78. Ibid., p. 283 (cf., p. 269 where Ivanov cites as an example Goethe's "Der Dichtung Schleier aus Hand der Wahrheit," and Novalis's saying, "das absolut Reelle, je poetischer je wahrer.")
79. Ivanov, "Zavety simvolizma," *BM*, p. 11.
80. Viacheslav Ivanov, "O lirike," *PZ*, p. 349.
81. Viacheslav Ivanov, "Predchuvstviia i predvestiia," *PZ*, p. 201.
82. One can see the same loss at the basis of today's troubles: young people, rejecting the stagnation of society and art, revert to a primitive life in communes in an attempt to find their way back to those "inspired moments" of communal creativity which Leśmian calls *natura naturans*. Their aim in this, of course, is to bring social development up to the level of technological development.
83. Viacheslav Ivanov, "O nepriiatii mira," *PZ*, pp. 104-122. This was written after the Revolution of 1905, when Ivanov became the main spokesman for "mystical anarchism." He claimed that without opposition to God there is no mystical life. Thus the "dynamic religiosity," i.e., mysticism has its roots in *bogoborstvo*.
84. Ibid., p. 105.
85. Ibid., p. 104.
86. Leśmian, "U źródeł rytmu," pp. 74-75. Światowid ("Svantovit") was the most prominent deity, the god of gods of the Elbe Slavs later adapted also by neighboring Slavs. Here Światowid represents all religions. *The Mythology of All Races*, Boston, 1918, Vol. III.
87. Ivanov, "O nepriiatii mira," *PZ*, p. 120.
88. Jacek Trznadel, *Twórczość Leśmiana* (*Próba przekroju*), Warsaw, 1964, p. 271.
89. Ivanov, "Dve stikhii," *PZ*, p. 285. The author favors a return of the soul to "K tëmnym korniam bytiia" ("To the dark roots of existence"). According to him, neither folk themes nor the "religious tune of the poet's lyre with [all] his metaphysical aims can by themselves be effective" in changing the human condition. To achieve such a change,

the contemporary human soul must, in Ivanov's opinion, return to a realistic and psychic state in which "the preterpersonal and the pretersensual is tied to the essential, emerging unexpectedly in all its beauty in the desperate moments of a torn consciousness." This state of the human contemporary soul can hardly be prescribed for the masses. It is a state fitting for the esoteric few, especially those infused with the Dionysian spirit, as was, obviously, Ivanov.

90. Ivanov, "O sushchestve tragedii," *BM*, pp. 240-241.

91. Ivanov, "Dve stikhii," *PZ*, p. 285.

92. Ibid.

93. Viacheslav Ivanov, "Predchuvstviia i predvestiia," *PZ*, pp. 196-197.

94. Ibid., p. 218.

95. Viacheslav Ivanov, "O vesëlom remesle i umnom veselii," *PZ*, p. 242.

96. Ivanov, "O nepriiatii mira," *PZ*, p. 119.

97. Vladimir Markov, "On Modern Russian Poetry," preface to *Modern Russian Poetry*, Indianapolis-Kansas City-New York, 1967, p. lviii.

98. Leśmian, *Poezje*, p. 256.

99. Johannes Holthusen, *Studien zur Aesthetic und Poetik des Russischen Symbolismus*, Göttingen, 1957, p. 51. The author considers especially the "garland" sonnets to be the best proof of the triumph of Ivanov's artistic individuality over his lofty theory of *sobornost'* (the "collective creative art"). Holthusen also quotes Sergei Gorodetskii's "Nekotorye techeniia v sovremennoi russkoi poèzii, *Apollon*, I, 1913, p. 47. Gorodetskii's remarks can be considered as a funeral oration over the grave of Ivanov's dreams.

100. Artur Sandauer, "Filozofia Leśmiana," *Poeci trzech pokoleń*, Warsaw, Czytelnik, 1962, p. 23.

101. V. Koroljuk, "Poèziia Boleslava Les'miana v grafike A. E. Goliakhovskoi," *Sovetskoe slavianovedenie*, Izd. "Nauka," 1970, p. 80. The author speaks about Leśmian's ties with Russian literature and culture, his love for the Ukraine and Russian folklore, which proved to be a strong stimulus for his poetic creation. "Khudozhestvennaia Literatura" is preparing for publication a volume of Leśmian's poetry in translation. Each of the volumes will be embellised with an engraving by the artist Goliakhovskaia.

N. A. Bogomolova, "Boleslav Les'mian," *Istoriia pol'skoi literatury*, Moscow, 1969, T. 2, pp. 240-250. The author's short review of Leśmian's creative work and life represents a moving and accurate interpretation. Excerpts of some poems are given in translation by O. Rumer, L. Martynov, and N. Chukovskii.

102. Leśmian, "Duszom w locie." *SL*, pp. 359-360.

5: Leśmian's Immanent Poetics: Poetic Analysis

1. Maria Podraza-Kwiatkowska, "Leśmianowy czyn," *Ruch Literacki*, Krakow, 1964, no. 5-6, p. 270.
2. Julian Przyboś, "Leśmian jako eseista," *Sens poetycki*, Krakow, 1963, p. 356.
3. Mieczysław Jastrun, "Słowo wstępne do: Bolesława Leśmiana," *Wiersze wybrane*, Warsaw, 1955, p. 2.
4. Bolesław Leśmian, "Władysław Zaleski: Duszom w locie," *Szkice literackie*, Warsaw, 1959, p. 360.
5. Kazimierz Wierzyński, *O Bolesławie Leśmianie*, Warsaw, 1939, p. 20.
6. There is good reason to believe that it is perhaps a later version of the poem "Ze wspomnień dzieciństwa" (*UR*, "From Reminiscences of Childhood," 1901, p. 46) that may have had its origin in the unpublished *Pari-Banu* (1900). Furthermore, "Wspomnienie" of *Łąka*, and "Wspomnienie": "te scieżyny. . . ." ("These Paths. . . .") of *Napój cienisty*, can be considered a sequel to the poem of *UR*, and a link tying Leśmian's earliest work with the last period. It also proves the consistency of his work.
7. Wacław Kubacki, "Komentarz do Leśmiana," *Lata terminowania*, Krakow, 1963, p. 364. The author says further about the poet:

> "If he ever left his Buddhist poetic hermitage, then only in order to become indignant at the people who have nothing better to do than worry and break their heads over the question: 'How to establish an economical existence in non-existence'—"Jak ustalić w niebycie byt ekonomiczny." ("Pejzaż współczesny"—"The Contemporary Paysage.")

8. Adam Szczerbowski, *Bolesław Leśmian*, Warsaw-Zamość, 1938, vol. VI, p. 23. The author was the first to point out that "Gad" is "a free paraphrase of the Scandinavian folk ballad 'Dragon' translated by Porębowicz. . . ." He likewise remarked that the ballad originates from a folk motif. It should be added that Leśmian wrote an enthusiastic review in *Kurier Warszawski* (1909) about the translations of old ballads, especially of Scandinavian origin, translated by Edward Porębowicz.
9. Bolesław Leśmian, *Poezje*, edited by Jacek Trznadel, Warsaw, 1965, p. 151.
10. Ibid., p. 132. Oskar Kolberg, *Dzieła wszystkie, Poznańskie*, Krakow, Uniwersytet Jagielloński, 1884; 1962, vol. VII, p. 217. The author speaks about the cult for these animals who are singled out especially during Christmas festivities.
11. *Poezja Młodej Polski*, edited and with a preface by Mieczysław Jastrun, Wrocław-Warsaw-Krakow, 1967, p. 40.

12. Ibid., p. 299.
13. Bolesław Leśmian, *UR, Listy*, edited by Jacek Trznadel, Warsaw, 1962, p. 8.
14. Ibid., p. 12.
15. Leśmian, *Poezje*, p. 129.
16. Ibid., p. 320.
17. Ibid., p. 173. This motif echoes an old funeral folksong. A similar motif is recorded by Kolberg (in *Lubelskie*, part II, no. 19, p. 91). It is the region where Leśmian lived.
18. Ibid., p. 368.
19. Artur Sandauer, "Filozofia Leśmiana," *Poeci trzech pokoleń*, Warsaw, 1962, p. 20.
20. Leśmian, *Poezje*, p. 38.
21. "Momentalism," or the "philosophy of the moment," as Mikhailovskii calls it, played a very important role in Decadent aesthetics. Briusov (cf., "O iskusstve," [1899]) believed it to be the goal of poetry.

Konstantin Bal'mont sang about the "mimolotnost'," the capture of which was, according to him, the only true achievement of a poet. Like the early Leśmian, he was unable to discuss his own earlier works. Yet the "mythology of the moment" in Leśmian's mature poetry differs completely from Bal'mont's because it does not reflect the fleeting *personal* metamorphosis. B. Mikhailovskii, *Russkaia literatura XX veka*, Moscow, 1939, p. 87.
22. Leśmian, *Poezje*, p. 356.
23. Ibid., p. 7.
24. Leopold Staff, "Wstęp do:" *Bolesław Leśmian, Wybór poezyj*, edited with a preface by Leopold Staff, Warszawa-Łódź-Krakow, 1946, p. 5. This was observed by Leopold Staff as follows: "Everything is independent. There is no hierarchy. God, man, a horse, a birch tree, a shadow, all are phantoms. . . . Everything is extraordinary, everything happens, 'zaocznie' 'in absentia', 'na oślep', precipitately, as though 'in a blink of an eye'."
25. Leśmian, *Poezje*, p. 290.
26. Ibid., p. 342.
27. Ibid., p. 365.
28. Ibid., p. 198.
29. Karol Irzykowski, "Dobre wiersze: Recenzja *Łąki*," *Kurier Lwowski*, 1921, no. 191, p. 7.
30. Jastrun, op. cit., p. 3.
31. Leśmian, *Poezje*, p. 150.
32. Ostap Ortwin, "Recenzja z *Łąki*," *Próby przekrojów*, Lvov, 1936, p. 220.
33. Leśmian, *Poezje*, p. 305. Catachresis was a device frequently used by Russian Symbolists, especially Aleksandr Blok.
34. Ibid., p. 254, verses 16, 142.
35. Ibid., p. 296, verse 16.

36. Ibid., p. 254. Kubacki, op. cit., p. 338. The author writes that the catachresis and oxymoron originated in the riddle, which was used for codifying thoughts, and also had a retarding effect. The play of concepts is acheived by a strange combination of contradictory words. These words were usually of a different, and contradictory, semantic level. "The classic poetics called it an oxymoron. These devices were known in Antiquity and Middle Ages." The Symbolists revived the tradition and used these devices liberally to express the enigmatic and to produce shocking effects. As for Leśmian, he used these figures of speech for the same reason as the Symbolists, and also to evoke the folkloric nature of codifying thoughts.

37. Mikhailovskii, op. cit., p. 251. The author gives numerous examples of the usage and aim of the "extended metaphor" in the aesthetics of the younger Russian Symbolists.

38. Leśmian, *Poezje*, p. 202.

39. Ibid., p. 176.

40. Viktor Zhirmunskii, *Poèziia Aleksandra Bloka*, Petersburg, 1922, p. 42. Kazimierz Czachowski, *Obraz współczesnej literatury polskiej*, Lvov, 1934, Vol. III, pp. 64-68. The author pointed out that Leśmian was influenced by the Russian Imagists in his use of a metaphor "which predominates in his creative work after the year 1918" (p. 65).

41. Sandauer, "Filozofia Leśmiana," p. 19.

42. Leśmian, *Poezje*, p. 75.

43. Ibid., p. 386.

44. Ibid., p. 235 (verse 57).

45. Ibid., p. 381.

46. Ibid., p. 248.

47. Michał Głowiński, "Recenzja: Jacek Trznadel, "Twórczość Leśmiana," *Pamiętnik Literacki*, Wrocław-Warsaw-Krakow, 1964, LV2, no. 4, pp. 588-589.

48. Marian Pankowski, *Leśmian, La révolte d'un poète contre les limites*, Bruxelles, 1967, pp. 170-172. Baroque does not hold a monopoly on the grotesque. Furthermore, the author does not specify what kind of baroque he has in mind, and, lastly, it is hard to agree with the author that Leśmian's humor borders on bad taste. Even if that were the case, it would be intentional, and a *sui generis* "révolte contre les limites" (the "limites" here represent the commonplace, the rational.)

49. Leśmian, *Poezje*, p. 318.

50. Kazimierz Wyka, "Czytam Leśmiana," *Łowy na kryteria*, Warsaw, 1965, pp. 238-250.

51. Henri Bergson, *Laughter*, trans. by C. Breveton and F. Rothwell, London, 1911, p. 69.

52. Ibid., p. 96.

53. Ibid., p. 112.

54. Leśmian, *Poezje*, p. 157.

55. Ibid.

56. Ibid., p. 158.
57. Bergson, op. cit., p. 186.
58. Ibid., p. 118.
59. Leśmian, *Poezje*, p. 158.
60. Ibid., p. 308.
61. Jacek Trznadel, *Twórczość Leśmiana*, Warsaw, 1964, p. 249.
62. Kazimierz Wyka, "Klucz nie zawsze doskonały," *Odrodzenie*, Krakow, 1946, no. 5, p. 6.
63. Karol W. Zawodziński, "Leopold Staff i Bolesław Leśmian," *Wśród poetów*, Krakow, 1964, pp. 230, 231. The author claims that one can either admire Leśmian's lexical inventiveness, or see it as the work of a rhymester hastily "filling the cracks in his excessively ingenious structure, not only in such simple, obvious cases, as 'co mu się śniły wzwyż i wzwyż ("Which in dream came to him higher and higher" [. . . a rhyme needed for 'cisz' 'of silences']), but also in more elaborate passages . . . of other poems: 'on jej piersi, zużytym śmiałkujące czarem, / Ogarnia skrzętnej dłoni przymilnym sucharem' ("Her breast boasting with a worn-out charm, / He embraces with the ingratiating crust of his eager palm")." Further, the author questions the "emotional charge" of Leśmian's "hermetic" symbolism and speaks about the *faux clinquant* of his art.
64. Michał Głowiński, "Słowo umotywowane," *Tygiel, rzecz poetycka*, Łódź, 1961, p. 44.
65. Leśmian, *Poezje*, p. 321.
66. Ibid., "A Contemporary Landscape," p. 359.
67. Głowiński, op. cit., p. 50.
68. Leśmian, *Poezje*, p. 166 (italics mine). This ballad is an excellent example of word formation. It is also an example of an intensification of semantic expression, whereby parts of the body attain a full, autonomous lexical existence. Roman Jakobson, "Poetyka w świetle językoznawstwa," *Pamiętnik Literacki*, 1960, vol. II, p. 471, makes some interesting observations regarding Leśmian's word formation in his analysis of the ballad "Piła":

> "In Leśmian's 'Piła' ['The Saw'] after the protagonist's statement: 'Będę ciebie kochał' ['I will love you']—his demonic partner 'Zazgrzytała z rozkoszy' ['She began to gnash her teeth in rapture'], reviving the lost ties between the related words 'kochać' ['to love'] and 'rozkosz' ['rapture']. . . . In response to his parallel assertion: 'Będę ciebie tak całował' ['I will kiss you thus']—she 'całowała go zębami na dwoje, na troje' ['she kissed him with her teeth into halves, in three parts']. 'Poszarpała go pieszczotą na nierówne części' ['with her caresses she tore him into uneven parts'], aided by a particular kind of an oxymoron [the poet] revives the primeval

meaning of the root 'cał' ['the whole'] in the verb 'całować' ['to kiss'] —in contrast to the adverbial expression 'na dwoje' ['in two'], 'na troje' ['in three'], and 'na nierówne części' ['into uneven parts']."

69. Sandauer, "Filozofia Leśmiana," p. 8. "Bylejakość ("Slapdash manner") is a conscious device, a poetic incarnation of Leśmian's philosophical tenets, an expression of three important concepts. It represents the obsolescence of reality in the onward rush which does not allow for static representations of events. The haphazard manner represents the paradox and absurdity of life. It also approximates the folk expression of phenomena by means of guessing. Confirmation and negation coexist in riddles and other folk genres. This manner finds expression in the lexical strata with the prefix *niedo-* ("not quite"), something not finished *niedopląs* ("not quite a dance") as well as in the maimed and handicapped heroes of his ballads. According to Bogumił Linde nouns with the compound prefix *niedo-*, unlike the Polish, are very prevalent in Russian. Linde gives numerous examples.

70. Leśmian, *Poezje*, p. 179.

71. Note that the initials *S.*, *Ł.*, *N.*, *Dz.*, and *Kl.p.* are abbreviations for the four books of poetry *Sad rozstajny*, *Łąka*, *Napój cienisty*, *Dziejba leśna*, as well as prose: *Klechdy polskie*.

72. Szczerbowski, op. cit., pp. 12-13.

73. Sandauer, "Filozofia Leśmiana," p. 17. Also, Artur Sandauer, "Pośmiertny tryumf Młodej Polski," *Samobójstwo Mitrydatesa*, Warsaw, 1968, p. 29.

74. Henri Bergson, *Creative Evolution*, New York, 1913, p. 281. Podraza-Kwiatkowska, op. cit., p. 271. The author uses the concept of nothingness, as understood by Bergson, as a means of comparing Leśmian with Mallarmé.

75. It should be added that in Leśmian's nominal neologisms there is a marked resemblance to Velimir Khlebnikov. Both poets use truncated nouns, often of archaic and dialect origins. Cf., "sprzęg," "usił," ("Dusiołek") "twardź," "płom," "zdrzem," "brzydź," ("Marsjanie"). In general, there are many linguistic and other similarities between the two poets, too numerous to be discussed in this work, thus requiring a separate study. Such critics as Artur Sandauer, Mieczysław Jastrun and others have pointed out this similarity, in particular with regard to language.

76. Leśmian, *UR*, *Listy*, May, 1921, no. 105, p. 346.

77. Many of the examples used above have been taken from Kajetan Papierkowski, whose work deals with Leśmian's language. Kajetan Papierkowski, *Bolesław Leśmian, Studium Językowe*, Lublin, 1964. This is the only work on Leśmian's language; although it is a laudable work it barely scratches the surface of this complex subject. However, it is very

valuable as a reference pertaining to the origins of respective neologisms, i.e., archaisms, dialects, colloquialisms, as well as "Leśmianisms" without any origin.

78. Julian Przyboś, "Niepowtarzalność Leśmiana," *Życie Literackie*, Krakow: 1962, no. 26.

79. Zbigniew Bieńkowski, "Śmiech Leśmianowego słowa," *Poezja i niepoezja*, Warsaw, 1967, p. 252. Leśmian's desire to create laughing words, parallels that of Velimir Khlebnikov (cf., "Incantation by Laughter").

80. Leśmian, *Poezje*, p. 253, verse 124.

81. Ibid., p. 384, 390.

82. Ibid., p. 370.

83. Ibid., p. 215.

84. Ibid., p. 129.

85. Ibid., p. 179.

86. Ibid., p. 464.

87. Ibid., p. 395.

88. This aspect of Leśmian's poetics is dealt with in detail by Jacek Trznadel, in his chapter "O ludowości" ("On folklore") op. cit., pp. 127-257. Therefore, I shall only deal with this aspect inasmuch as the understanding of the totality of Leśmian's poetic output demands it.

89. Leśmian, *Poezje*, p. 166. This ballad is constructed on a folk motif —popular in the region of Małopolska. "A ghost has, instead of a spine, a saw." Kazimierz Moszyński, *Kultura Ludowa Słowian*, no. 1, p. 621. Quoted from Czesław Zgorzelski, *Ballada polska*, Wrocław-Warsaw-Krakow, 1962, p. 677. ". . . The people demonstrate a ghost with a head covered with yellow hair, set upon a saw."

90. Leśmian, *Poezje*, p. 312.

91. Ibid., pp. 176, 300.

92. Ibid., p. 300.

93. Ibid., p. 162. Note the dialectal words *witak* ("a fence") and *boginiak* ("a ghost-rapist").

94. Ibid., p. 171. The motif of the green jug appears in the Polish folk song in the region of Lublin. Cf., Oskar Kolberg, *Lubelskie*, part II, p. 282, no. 457.

95. Leśmian, *Poezje*, p. 171.

96. Ibid., p. 315.

97. Ibid., p. 367.

98. Jarosław Rymkiewicz, "Genezis z ducha," *Myśli różne o ogrodach*, Warsaw, 1968.

99. Leśmian, *Poezje*, p. 404.

100. In a letter dated August 15, 1974, the poet's daughter, Maria Ludwika Mazurowa, stressed this fact. Leśmian wanted the biographers to pay attention to the origin of the title and the form of the poem.

101. Leśmian, *Poezje*, p. 406.

102. Ibid., pp. 405-406.
103. Ibid., p. 406.
104. Rymkiewicz, op. cit., p. 121.
105. Leśmian, *Poezje,* p. 409.
106. Ibid., p. 284.
107. Ibid., p. 350.
108. Jan Tuczyński, *Schopenhauer a Młoda Polska,* Gdańsk, 1969, p. 206. The author discusses the theme of monotony, love and death, pointing out Schopenhauer's pessimism, especially in its effect on the last stages of Leśmian's creation (cf., "Śmierć Buddy"—"The Death of Buddha") discussed previously.
109. Leśmian, *Poezje,* p. 370.
110. For a comparison of Leśmian's erotics with those of Mickiewicz see the article, Rochelle Stone, "Poezja Leśmiana a romantyzm polski," *Pamiętnik Literacki,* Warsaw, LXIV, 2, 1973.
111. Ibid., p. 213.
112. Ibid., p. 399.
113. Kubacki, op. cit., p. 346. The author paraphrases Mochnacki and points him out as a reference.
114. Leśmian, *Pesni Vasilisy Premudroi, UR, Listy,* p. 78.
115. Leśmian, *Poezje,* p. 39.
116. Ibid., p. 349.
117. Ibid., pp. 179, 339.
118. Kubacki, op. cit., p. 351.
119. Leśmian, *Poezje,* p. 461.
120. Ibid., p. 387.
121. Ibid., p. 389. This poem was translated into Russian by Boris Pasternak.
122. Ibid., p. 374.
123. Ibid., p. 313.
124. Leśmian, *UR, Listy,* p. 74.
125. Leśmian, *Poezje,* p. 443.
126. Michał Głowiński, "Szkic o Leśmianie," *Twórczość,* Warsaw, 1956, no. 10, p. 82.
127. Leśmian, *Poezje,* p. 238.
128. Ibid., p. 128.
129. Ibid., p. 240.
130. Ibid., p. 176.
131. Ibid., p. 213. It should be pointed out that internal parallelism was used to the point of obsession by Baudelaire (who, according to Leśmian, influenced him greatly).

Gonzague de Reynold, *Charles Baudelaire,* Paris and Geneva, 1920, p. 350. The author discusses the reasons for the French poet's predilection for this literary device. Repetitive devices became an outstanding feature of French and Russian Symbolist poetry.

132. Leśmian, *Poezje,* p. 250.
133. Ibid., p. 326.
134. Edward Boyé, "Dialogi akademickie: W niepojętej zieloności" *SL,* p. 499.
135. Michał Głowiński, "Dystychy balladowe," *Z teorii i historii literatury,* Wrocław, 1963, p. 141.
136. Ibid.
137. Leśmian, *Poezje,* pp. 222, 339.
138. Ibid., p. 349.
139. Ibid., p. 375.
140. Ibid., p. 440.
141. Ibid., p. 316.
142. Stefan Lichański, *Cienie i profile: Studia i szkice literackie,* Warsaw, 1967, pp. 281-286, 304-305. The author has given a review of the development of the ballad, including Leśmian's. However, the greatest source regarding the development of ballad genres in Polish literary history is contained in the introduction by Czesław Zgorzelski to his anthology of the Polish ballad, in "Wstęp," *Ballada polska,* Wrocław, 1962, pp. iii-lxxxi.
143. Ibid., p. lxx.
144. Kazimierz Wyka, "Bolesław Leśmian: Dwa utwory," *Liryka polska,* Krakow, 1966, p. 215.
145. Leśmian, *Poezje,* p. 155.
146. Michał Głowiński, "Dystychy balladowe," p. 143. The author points out that the parallelism used in Leśmian's distich often has the same function as it does in a folk song. "It combines phenomena not related to each other into one unit."

> "Cień za cieniem się ugania, a motyla motyl ściga—
> Rozpłakała się w lesie niekochana Jadwiga."
> ("Jadwiga")
>
> "Shadow chases shadow, butterfly pursues butterfly— / In the forest unloved Jadwiga burst into tears."

147. Leśmian, *Poezje,* p. 133.
148. Ibid., p. 83.
149. Ibid., p. 320.
150. Ibid., p. 174. One should also note an overall structural parallelism in this ballad, in which the stanzaic beginning and ending are identical, reminding one of the refrain in a folksong.
151. Ibid., p. 323.
152. Głowiński, "Dystychy balladowe," p. 141.
153. Leśmian, *Poezje,* p. 225.
154. Głowinski, "Dystychy balladowe," p. 155.
155. Leśmian, *Poezje,* p. 303.

156. Ibid., p. 196.
157. Ibid., p. 348.
158. Ibid., p. 394.
159. Ibid., p. 193.
160. Ibid., p. 441.
161. M. Głowiński, A. L. Okopień-Sławińska, *et al.*, *Zarys teorii literatury*, Warsaw, 1967, p. 163.
162. Leśmian, *Poezje*, p. 293.
163. Ibid., p. 250.
164. For stanzaic structure and for analysis see text above. Cf., also chapter 5, ftnt. 100.
165. Leśmian, *Poezje*, p. 235.
166. Julian Przyboś, *Linia i gwar*, Krakow, 1959, Vol. II, p. 92.

Selected Bibliography

The following abbreviations have been used throughout in this bibliography:

P.I.W.	Państwowy Instytut Wydawniczy
SL	Bolesław Leśmian. *Szkice literackie.* Edited by Jacek Trznadel. Warsaw: P.I.W., 1959.
UR, Listy	Bolesław Leśmian. *Utwory rozproszone, Listy.* Edited by Jacek Trznadel. Warsaw: P.I.W., 1962.
Wspomnienia o B L	*Wspomnienia o Bolesławie Leśmianie.* Edited by Zdzisław Jastrzębski. Lublin: Wydawnictwo Lubelskie, 1966.

1. Works by Leśmian Cited in Text

Polish Works

Leśmian, Bolesław [Lesman]. "Artysta i model." *UR, Listy.*

———. *Dziejba leśna.* Ed. by J. Tom. Warsaw: Pod Znakiem Poetów, 1938.

———. "Kilka słów o teatrze." *Złoty Róg*, no. 3, 1913.
———. *Klechdy polskie*. Ed. and introd. by Bronisław Przyłuski. London: Veritas, 1956.
———. *Klechdy polskie*. Warsaw: Instytut Wydawniczy Pax, 1959.
———. *Klechdy sezamowe*. Warsaw: Wyd. Mortkowicz, 1913.
———. *Klechdy sezamowe*. Warsaw: Czytelnik, 1954.
———. "Kwiaty grzechu." *SL*.
———. "Legendy tęsknoty." *UR, Listy*.
———. *Łąka*. Warsaw: Pod Znakiem Poetów, 1920.
———. "Ludzie odrodzenia." *SL*.
———. "Mieczysław Smolarski: 'Pieśni i śpiewy rycerskie'." *SL*.
———. *Napój cienisty*. Warsaw: Pod Znakiem Poetów, 1936.
———. "Pieśni ludowe." *SL*.
———. *E. Allan Poe: Opowieści nadzwyczajne*. Warsaw: Muza, 1913-1914.
———. "Edgar Allan Poe." *SL*.
———. *Poezje*. Ed. by Jacek Trznadel. Warsaw: P.I.W., 1965.
———. "Poradnik dla recenzentów literackich." *UR, Listy*.
———. "Przemiany rzeczywistości." *UR, Listy*.
———. *Przygody Sindbada Żeglarza. Powieść fantastyczna*. Ilustr. by J. Tom. Warsaw: Wyd. Mortkowicz, 1913.
———. *Przygody Sindbada Żeglarza*. Warsaw: Czytelnik, 1950.
———. "Rytm jako światopogląd." *SL*.
———. "Spowiedź dziennikarza." *SL*.
———. "Stanisław Miłaszewski: 'Gest wewnętrzny'." *SL*.
———. *Szkice literackie*. Ed. by Jacek Trznadel. Warsaw: P.I.W., 1959.
———. "To co się stało." *SL*.
———. *Utwory rozproszone, Listy*. Ed. by Jacek Trznadel. Warsaw: P.I.W., 1962.
———. "U źródeł rytmu." *SL*.
———. "Wielki starzec." *SL*.
———. *Wiersze wybrane*. Ed. and introd. by Mieczysław Jastrun. Warsaw: Czytelnik, 1955.
———. *Wybór poezyj*. Ed. and pref. by Leopold Staff. Krakow: Spółdzielnia Wydawnicza Książka, 1946.
———. "Władysław Jabłonowski, Dookoła Sfinksa. Studia o życiu i twórczości narodu rosyjskiego." *Prawda*, no. 8, 1910.
———. "Władysław Zaleski: Duszom w locie." *SL*.
———. "Wpływ Wilde'a na współczesność." *SL*.

———. "Znaczenie pośrednictwa w metafizyce życia zbiorowego." *SL.*
———. "Z rosmyślań o Bergsonie." *SL.*
———. "Z rozmyślań o poezji." *SL.*

Russian Works

Leśmian, Bolesław. "Lunnoe pokhmel'e." *Vesy,* no. 10, 1907, pp. 7-18. Reprinted in *UR, Listy.*
———. "Pesni Vasilisy Premudroi." *Zolotoe Runo,* no. 11-12, 1906, pp. 54-55. Reprinted in *UR, Listy.*
———. "Volny zhivye." *Pereval,* no. 11, 1907.
———. *Drama: Vasilii Buslaev.* Lost ms.

Manuscripts

———. *Bajka o złotym grzebyku; Farsa sceniczna.*
———. *Ręce białej Iseult.*
———. *Satyr i nimfa; ballada.*
———. *Skrzypek opętany; baśń sceniczna.*
———. *Zdziczenie obyczajów pośmiertnych.*
———. *Życie snem* (a feuilleton).

2. Other Works Cited in Text

Afanas'ev, Aleksandr N. *Narodnye russkie skazki.* Ed. and introd. by V. Ia. Propp. 3 vols. Moscow: Gos. Izd. Khudozh. Liter., 1957.
———. *Poeticheskie vozzreniia drevnikh slavian na prirodu.* Vol. III. Moscow. 1865-1869.

Balcerzan, Edward. "Pełno rozwiśleń i udniestrzeń (O Srebroniu Bolesława Leśmiana)." *Poezja,* no. 12, 1967, pp. 55-65.
Ballada Polska. Ed. Cz. Zgorzelski. Wrocław-Warsaw-Krakow: Zakład Narodowy im. Ossolińskich, 1962.
Bal'mont, Konstantin D. *Gornye vershiny: Sbornik statei.* Moscow: Griff, 1904.
———. "Pis'ma k V. S. Miroliubovu: 1894-1907." *Literaturnyi arkhiv: Materialy po istorii literatury i obshchestvennogo*

dvizheniia. Ed. by K. D. Muratova. Moscow-Leningrad: AN SSSR, 1960, V, pp. 142-171.

———. "Slavia i Litva." *Souchastie dush: Ocherki*. Sofia: D'rzhavna pechatnitsa, 1930.

Baudelaire, Charles. "L'Art Romantique." *Oeuvres complètes*. Paris: L. Conrad, 1925.

———. "Réflexions sur quelques-uns de mes contemporains." *Oeuvres complètes*. Paris: L. Conrad, 1925.

Baudoin de Courtenay, Jan. *Zarys historji języka polskiego*. Warsaw: Biblioteka Składnicy, 1922.

Bays, Gwendolyn. *The Orphic Vision: Seer Poets from Novalis to Rimbaud*. Lincoln: University of Nebraska Press, 1964.

Belyi, Andrei [Bugaev]. "Ikh lozung." *Russkie pisateli o literaturnom trude*. Ed. by B. Meilakh. Leningrad: "Sovetskii pisatel'," IV, 1956.

———. *Lug zelenyi: Kniga statei*. Moscow: Al'tsiona, 1910.

———. *Mezhdu dvukh revoliutsii*. Leningrad, 1934.

———. *Simvolizm*. Moscow: Musaget, 1910.

———. *Stikhotvoreniia i poèmy*. Moscow-Leningrad: Biblioteka Poeta, 1966.

———. *Zoloto v lazuri*. Moscow: Skorpion, 1964.

Berdiaev, Nikolai. "Osnovnaia ideia filosofii L'va Shestova." Introd. to Lev Shestov, *Umozrenie i otkrovenie*. Paris: YMCA Press, 1964.

———. *Smysl istorii*. Paris: YMCA Press, 1969.

Berent, Wacław. "Tredecim: Rozstrojowcy i zamętowcy." *Chimera*, VI, no. 17, 1906, p. 299.

Bergson, Henri. *Creative Evolution*. New York: Henry Holt & Co., 1913.

———. "An Introduction to Metaphysics." *Philosophy in the Twentieth Century: An Anthology*. Ed. by W. Barrett. New York: Random House, 1962.

———. *Laughter*. Trans. by C. Breveton and F. Rothwell. London: Macmillan, 1911.

Bieńkowski, Zbigniew. "Rocznica Leśmiana." *Twórczość*, no. 12, 1957.

———. "Śmiech Leśmianowego słowa." *Poezja i niepoezja*. Warsaw: P.I.W., 1967.

———. "Szczyty symbolizmu." *Twórczość*, no. 8, 1962, pp. 47-54.

———. "Wrocławska sesja Leśmiana." *Twórczość*, no. 8, 1962, pp. 158-159.

Blagoi, D. "Zhizn' i tvorchestvo Tiutcheva." *Polnoe sobranie stikhotvorenii.* Ed. by G. I. Chulkov. Vol. I. Moscow-Leningrad, 1933.

Blok, Aleksandr. *Sobranie sochinenii v vos'mi tomakh.* Moscow-Leningrad: Gos. Izd. Khudozh. Lit., 1962.

———. *Zapisnye knizhki 1901-1920.* Moscow: Khudozhestvennaia Literatura, 1965.

———. and Belyi, Andrei. "Perepiska." Moscow: Izd. Gos. Lit. Muzea, Letopisi, 1940.

Błoński, Jan. "Bergson a program poetycki Leśmiana." *Miesięcznik Literacki,* III, no. 8/24, 1968, pp. 31-42.

———. "Poezja Kazimierza Tetmajera." *Życie Literackie,* no. 17, 1959.

Bogomolova, N. A. "Boleslav Les'mian." *Istoriia polskoi literatury,* Vol. II. Moscow: Izd. Nauka, 1969.

Bowra, Cecil M. *The Heritage of Symbolism.* New York: Schocken Books, 1961.

Boyé, Edward. "Dialogi akademickie. W niepojętej zieloności." *SL.*

———. "W niepojętej zieloności." *Pion,* no. 23, 1934, n. p.

Bradley, Andrew Cecil. "Poetry for Poetry's Sake." *Oxford Lectures on Poetry,* Oxford, 1909.

Briusov, Valerii. *Dalekie i blizkie: Stat'i i zametki o russkikh poetakh ot Tiutcheva do nashikh dnei.* Moscow: Skorpion, 1912.

———. *Dnevniki 1891-1910.* Moscow: Izd. M. i S. Sabashnikovykh, 1927.

———. "Kliuchi tain." *Vesy,* no. 1, 1903, pp. 3-21.

———. "Moja zhizn'." *Zapisnye knizhki,* no. 14, 1906 (Biblioteka im. Lenina).

Brzechwa, Jan [Lesman]. "Niebieski wycieruch." *Wspomnienia o B. L.*

Brzozowski, Stanisław [Czepiel, Adam]. "Scherz, Ironie, und tiefere Bedeutung." *Głos,* no. 27, 1904.

———. *Legenda Młodej Polski: Studia o strukturze duszy kulturalnej,* Lvov: B. Połoniecki, 2nd ed., 1910.

Bystroń, Jan Stanisław. *Artyzm pieśni ludowej.* Krakow: Polska Akademia Umiejętności, 1935-1938.

Carlyle, Thomas. *Sartor Resartus.* New York: The Macmillan Co., 1927.

Chiari, J. *Symbolism from Poe to Mallarmé. The Growth of a Myth.* Foreword by T. S. Eliot. London, Rockliff, 1956.

Čiževskij, Dmitrij. "Bolesław Leśmian als russischer Dichter." *Zeitschrift für slavische Philologie*, Heidelberg, Vol. XXIII, 1955, pp. 260-271.

———. *On Romanticism in Slavic Literature.* 'S-Gravenhage: Mouton & Co., 1957.

Chtets i deklamator, stikhi i proza. Ed. by M. P. Denison. Kiev: Tipografia, Petr Barskii, 1909.

Condillac, Étienne B. "Essai sur l'origine des connaissance humaines." *Oeuvres de Condillac.* Paris: C. Houel, 1798.

Czachowski, Kazimierz. *Obraz współczesnej literatury polskiej.* Vol. II. Lvov, 1934.

———. "O poezji Leśmiana." *Czas*, no. 278, 1933.

Daszkiewicz-Czajkowski, Michał. "Leśmian w młodości." *Wspomnienia o B. L.*

Dedecius, Karl. "Z doświadczenia tłumacza." *Poezja*, no. 12, 1967, pp. 66-70.

De Visan, Tancrède. *L'Attitude du lyrisme contemporain.* Paris: Mercure de France, 1911.

———. *Paysages introspectifs, poèmes, avec un Essai sur le Symbolism.* Paris: Mercure de France, 1904.

Dobroliubov, Aleksandr. *Natura Naturans, Natura Naturata.* St. Petersburg: Tetrad' no. 1, 1895.

Donchin, Georgette. *The Influence of French Symbolism on Russian Poetry.* 'S-Gravenhage: Mouton & Co., 1958.

Dworek, T. "Dziejba Lesmanów." *Prosto z Mostu*, no. 1, 1939.

Eliade, Mircea. *Tráite d'histoire des religions.* Paris: Payot, 1949.

Ellis [L. L. Kobylinskii]. *Russkie simvolisty: Konstantin Bal'mont; Valerii Briusov; Andrei Belyi.* Moscow: Musaget, 1910.

Erenburg, Il'ia. [Ehrenburg]. *People and Life, 1891-1912.* Trans. by Anna Bostnek and Yvonne Kapp. New York: Alfred A. Knopf, 1962.

Erlich, Victor. *Russian Formalism.* The Hague: Mouton & Co., 1965.

———. *The Double Image: Concepts of the Poet in Slavic Literature.* Baltimore: The John Hopkins Press, 1964.

Europejskie związki literatury polskiej. Ed. by J. Z. Jakubowski. Warsaw: P.I.W., 1969.

Fedotov, George P. *The Russian Religious Mind.* New York: Harper & Bros., 1960.

———. *Sviatye drevnei Rusi.* New York: Russian Orthodox Foundation, 1960.
Fet, Afanasii A. [Afanasii N. Shenshin]. *Stikhotvoreniia.* Moscow-Leningrad: Malaia seriia, Sovetskii Pisatel', 1969.
Fouillée, Alfred J. *Le Mouvement idéaliste et la réaction contre la science positive.* 2nd ed. Paris: F. Alcan, 1896.
Fryde, Ludwik. "Bolesław Leśmian." *Tygodnik Ilustrowany,* no. 48, 1937.
———. "Klasyk i dwaj romantycy." *Tygodnik Ilustrowany,* no. 12, 1937.

Ghil, René. "Pis'ma o frantsuzskoi poèzii: Tancrède De Visan." *Vesy,* no. 3, 1905, pp. 48-54.
Glinka, Xavery. "Wspomnienie o Leśmianie." *Kultura,* Paris, no. 4-5, 1949.
Głowiński, Michał. "Dystychy balladowe Leśmiana." *Z teorii i historii literatury.* Wrocław: Wydawnictwo Polskiej Akademii Nauk, 1963, pp. 131-155.
Głowiński, Michał. "Leśmian, czyli poeta jako człowiek pierwotny." *Pamiętnik Literacki,* LV, 2, 1964, pp. 385-417.
———. "Maska Dionizosa." *Twórczość,* no. 11, 1961.
———. *Poetyka Tuwima a polska tradycja literacka.* Warsaw: P.I.W., 1962.
———. "Recenzja: Jacek Trznadel, 'Twórczość Leśmiana'." *Pamiętnik Literacki,* LV, 2, 1964, pp. 585-597.
———. "Słowo umotywowane." *Tygiel, Rzecz poetycka.* Łódź: Wydawnictwo Łódzkie, 1961.
———. "Szkic o Leśmianie," *Twórczość,* no. 10, 1956, pp. 72-87.
———. *Julian Tuwim, Wiersze wybrane.* 2nd ed. Wrocław-Warsaw-Krakow: Zakład Narodowy im. Ossolińskich, 1969.
———. Okopień-Sławińska, A. L., and Sławiński, J. *Zarys teorii literatury.* Warsaw: Państwowe Zakłady Wydawnictw Szkolnych, 1967.
Gogol', Nikolai V. *Sobranie khudozhestvennykh proizvedenii v piati tomakh.* Moscow: Izd. AN SSSR, 1959.
Gor'kii, Maksim [Peshkov]. "Zametki." *L. N. Tolstoi v vospominaniiakh sovremennikov.* Vol. II. 2nd ed. Moscow-Leningrad: Gos. Izd. Khudozh. Lit., 1960.
Gorodetskii, Sergei. "Nekotorye techeniia v sovremennoi russkoi poèzii." *Apollon,* I (1913), pp. 47-49.
Górski, Artur (Quasimodo). "Młoda Polska," *Życie,* no. 19, 1898.

Gray, Herbert. Ed. *The Mythology of All Races.* Vol. III, Boston: Marshal Jones Co., 1918.

Gregg, Richard A. *Fedor Tiutchev: The Evolution of a Poet.* New York and London: Columbia University Press, 1965.

Grosse, Ernest. *Die Anfänge der Kunst.* Freiburg: I. B. Mohn, 1894.

———. *Pocrątki sztuki.* Polish trans. of the preceding. Warsaw, 1904.

Grossman, Leonid. *Bor'ba za stil': Opyty po kritike i poètike.* Moscow: Nikitinskie Subbotniki, 1927.

Grzegorczyk, Piotr (P. G.). "Jeszcze o Leśmiana wierszach rosyjskich," *Twórczość,* no. 4, 1961, pp. 167-168.

Gudzii, N. K. "Tiutchev—poèticheskaia kultura russkogo Simvolizma." *Izvestiia po russkomu iazyku i slovesnosti.* Vol. III. Leningrad: AN SSSR, 1930.

Gusdorf, Georges. *La Parole.* Paris: Payot, 1956.

Hanson, Lawrence, and Hanson, Elisabeth. *Verlaine: Fool of God.* New York: Random House, 1957.

Hartmann, Karl E. *Philosophie des Unbewussten.* Berlin: C. Dunker C. Heymons, 1869-1870.

Herder, Johann G. "Abhandlung über den Ursprung der Sprache (1770)." *Sämtliche Werke.* Tübingen: J. G. Cotta, 1805-1820.

———. "Über die neue deutsche Literatur." *Erste Sammlung von Fragmenten* (1767-1768). Tübingen: J. G. Cotta, 1805-1820.

Hertz, Pawel. *Ład i nieład.* Warsaw: P.I.W., 1964.

Hertz-Barwiński, Henryk. "Nasze szkolne czasy." *Wspomnienia o B. L.*

Holthusen, Johannes. *Studien zur Ästhetik und Poetik des Russichen Symbolismus.* Göttingen: Vandenhoeck & Ruprecht, 1957.

Irzykowski, Karol. *Czyn i słowo, Glossy sceptyka.* Lvov, 1913.

———. "Dobre wiersze. Recenzja Łąki." *Kurier Lwowski,* no. 191, 1921.

———. "Śp. Bolesław Leśmian." *Kurier Poranny,* no. 309, 1937.

Ivanov, I. I., Lotman, Iu. I. "Tezisy k semioticheskomu izucheniiu kultur." *Semiotyka i struktura tekstu.* Ed. by M. R. Mayenowa, Warsaw: Ossolineum, 1973.

Ivanov, Viacheslav. *Borozdy i Mezhi.* Moscow: Musaget, 1916.

———. *Po zvëzdam, stat'i i aforizmy.* St. Petersburg: Izd. Ory, 1909.

Jakobson, Roman. "Poetyka w świetle językoznawstwa." *Pamiętnik Literacki*, no. 2, 1960, pp. 431-473.

———. "The Kernel of Comparative Slavic Literature." *Harvard Slavic Studies*. Vol. I. Cambridge: Harvard University Press, 1953.

Jastrun, Mieczysław [Agatstein]. "Na krańcach, czyli o poezji Leśmiana." *Między słowem a milczeniem*. Warsaw: Czytelnik, 1965.

———. "Od Baudelaire'a do Valery'ego." *Poezja i rzeczywistość*. Warsaw: Czytelnik, 1965.

———. *Poezja Młodej Polski*. 3rd ed. Wrocław-Warsaw-Krakow: Zakład Narodowy Im. Ossolińskich, 1967.

———. "Słowo wstępne do: Bolesława Leśmiana." *Wiersze wybrane*. Warsaw: Czytelnik, 1955. Reprinted: "Kilka słów o Leśmianie." *Wizerunki, Szkice Literackie*. Warsaw: P.I.W., 1956.

———. "Zmartwychwstanie Leśmiana." *Nowa Kultura*, no. 5, 1960.

Jastrzębski, Zdzisław. "Zejście z Parnasu." *Wspomnienia o B. L.*

Ji, [Jarosław Iwaszkiewicz]. "Pierwszy zeszyt Czartaka." *Skamander*, no. 17, 1922, n. p.

Juniewicz, Antoni. "Nowe rosyjskie wiersze i listy Leśmiana." *Przegląd Humanistyczny*, no. 1, 1964.

Juszczak, Wojciech. *Wojtkiewicz i nowa sztuka*. Warsaw: P.I.W., 1965.

Karpowicz, Tymoteusz. "Poezja niemożliwa." *Poezja*, no. 12, 1967.

Kasprowicz, Jan. *Dzieła poetyckie, Wydanie zbiorowe*. Ed. by Ludwik Bernacki. Lvov: Nakład Tow. Wydawniczego, 1912.

Khlebnikov, Velimir. *Izbrannye stikhotvoreniia*. Ed. by N. Stepanov. Moscow, 1936.

———. *Sobranie sochinenii*. Introd. by Vladimir Markov. Munich: Wilhelm Fink Verlag, 1968.

Kolberg, Oskar. *Dzieła wszystkie*. Krakow: Uniwersytet Jagielloński, 1884; Polskie Wydawnictwo Muzyczne, 1962.

Koroliuk, V. "Poeziia Boleslava Les'miana v grafike A. E. Goliakhovskoi." *Sovetskoe Slavianovedenie*. Moscow: Izd. Nauka, 1970.

Kozikowski, Edward. "Wspomnienie o B. Leśmianie." *Wspomnienia o B. L.*

Krauze, Zygfryd. "Ze wspomnień o Leśmianie." *Wspomnienia o B. L.*

Kretschmer, Ernst. *Medizinische Psychologie.* Stuttgart: Thieme, 1950.

Kridl, Manfred. *An Anthology of Polish Literature.* New York and London: Columbia University Press, 1964.

———. *A Survey of Polish Literature and Culture.* Ed. by C. H. Van Schooneveld. 'S-Gravenhage: Mouton & Co., 1956.

Krzyżanowski, Julian. *Neoromantyzm polski, 1890-1918.* Wrocław-Warsaw-Krakow: Zakład Narodowy im. Ossolińskich, 1963.

Kubacki, Wacław. "Komentarz do Leśmiana." *Lata terminowania.* Krakow: Wydawnictwo Literackie, 1963.

———. "Studium o Leśmianie." *Lata terminowania.* Krakow: Wydawnictwo Literackie, 1963.

Kuncewicz, Maria. "Lecture on Bolesław Leśmian." Ms., 1964.

Kuzmin, Mikhail, A. "Forel' razbivaet lëd." *Stikhotvoreniia.* Vol. III. Berlin: Petropolis, 1923.

Kwiatkowska-Podraza, Maria. "Leśmianowy czyn." *Ruch Literacki,* no. 5-6, 1964, pp. 259-272.

———. *Wacław Rolicz Lieder.* Warsaw: P.I.W., 1966.

Lange, Antoni, *Literatura okresu Młodej Polski.* Warsaw: Instytut Badań Literackich, 1968.

Lévi-Strauss, Claude. *La Pensée sauvage.* Paris: Plon, 1962.

Lewis, P. Wyndham. *The Writer and the Absolute.* London, Methuen & Co., 1952.

Lichański, Stefan. *Cienie i profile; Studia i szkice literackie.* Warsaw: P.I.W., 1967.

———. "Leśmian—eseista i krytyk." *Nowe książki,* no. 7, 1960.

Ligęza, Lidia. "Klechdy polskie Bolesława Leśmiana na tle folklorystycznym." *Pamiętnik Literacki,* LIX, 1, 1968, pp. 111-147.

Literatura Okresu Młodej Polski. Ed. by K. Wyka, A. Hutnikiewicz, and M. Puchalska. Warsaw: P.I.W., 1968.

Livshits, Benedikt. *Polutoraglazyi strelets.* Leningrad, 1933.

Likhachev, D. S. *Slovo o Polku Igoreve.* Moscow: Detgiz, 1954.

Lossky, Nikolai O. "Philosophical Ideas of Poet-Symbolists." *History of Russian Philosophy.* New York: International University Press, 1951.

Łuczak-Wild, Jeannine. *Die Zeitschrift "Chimera" und die Literatur des polnischen Modernismus.* Lucerne and Frankfurt a/M: Slavica Helvetica, Verlag C. J. Bucher, 1969.

Makovskii, Sergei. *Na Parnase "serebrianogo veka."* Munich: COPE, 1962.

Markiewicz, Henryk. "Młoda Polska i izmy." *Modernizm polski.* Ed. by Kazimierz Wyka, Krakow: Wydawnictwo Literackie, 1968.

Markov, Vladimir. "Bal'mont: A Reappraisal." *Slavic Review,* June, 1969, pp. 225-264.

———. *Russian Futurism: A History.* Berkeley and Los Angeles: University of California Press, 1968.

Maslenikov, Oleg. *The Frenzied Poets.* Berkeley and Los Angeles: University of California Press, 1952.

Matlaw, Ralph E. "The Manifesto of Russian Symbolism." *Slavic and East European Review,* XV (1957).

Matuszewski, Ignacy. *Słowacki i nowa sztuka (Modernism).* Ed. by S. Sandler. Warsaw: P.I.W., 1965.

Mayenowa, Maria. R. "Od Mickiewicza do Leśmiana." *O sztuce czytania wierszy.* Warsaw: Wiedza Powszechna, 1963.

Mazurowa, Maria L. "Podróże i praca twórcza Bolesława Leśmiana." *Wspomnienia o B. L.*

Michalski, Hieronim. "Wizerunek poety." *Pion,* no. 38, 1938.

Mickiewicz, Adam. *Dzieła.* Warsaw: "Czytelnik," 1955.

Mikhailovskii, B. V. *Russkaia literatura XX veka.* Moscow: Gosuchpedizd. Narkomprosa RSFSR, 1939.

Miklaszewski, Krzysztof. "Teoria i praktyka (wokół Leśmianowskiej wizji teatru)." *Ruch Literacki,* XI, no. 1, 1970, pp. 19-30.

Miłosz, Czesław. *Człowiek wśród skorpionów.* Paris: Instytut Literacki, 1962.

———. *The History of Polish Literature.* London: The Macmillan Co., Collier-Macmillan Ltd., 1969.

Mirsky, D. S. *A History of Russian Literature.* New York: Alfred A. Knopf, 1966.

Mochul'skii, Konstantin. *Andrei Belyi.* Paris: YMCA-Press, 1955.

Modern Russian Poetry. Trans. and ed. by Vladimir Markov and Merrill Sparks. Indianapolis-Kansas City-New York: Bobbs-Merrill Co., Inc., 1967.

Morice, Charles. *La Littérature de tout à l'heure.* Paris: Maisonneuve, 1889.

Mortkowicz-Olczakowa, H. "Wspomnienie o Leśmianie." *Bunt Wspomnień.* Warsaw: P.I.W., 1961.

Moszyński, Kazimierz. *Kultura ludowa Słowian.* Krakow: Geberthner, 1929.

Naglerowa, Hermina. "Przyjaciel z innego wymiaru." *Wspomnienia o pisarzach.* London: Oficyna Poetów i Malarzy, 1960.

Napierski, Stefan. "Bolesław Leśmian." *Wiadomości Literackie*, no. 15, 1931.
Nietzsche, Friedrich. *Die Götzendämmerung. Gesammelte Werke*, Vol. XV. Munich: Musarion Verlag, 1922.
———. *Jenseits von Gut und Böse; Was ist vornehm. Gesammelte Werke*. Munich: Musarion Verlag, 1922.
———. *Thus Spake Zarathustra*. Trans. by A. Tille. New York: The Macmillan Co., 1924.

Ortwin, Ostap [O. Katzenellenbogen]. "Bolesław Leśmian: *Łąka*." *Próby Przekrojów*. Lvov: Ministerstwo Wyznań i Oświecenia Publicznego, 1936.

Pankowski, Marian. *Leśmian, La révolte d'un poète contre les limites*. Brussells: Presses Universitaires, 1967.
Papierkowski, Kajetan. *Bolesław Leśmian, Studium językowe*. Lublin: Wydawnictwo Lubelskie, 1964.
P. G. See Piotr Grzegorczyk.
Poe, Edgar Allan. *The Best Known Works of Edgar Allan Poe*. Ed. by Hervey Allen. New York: Blue Ribbon Books, 1927.
Poezja Młodej Polski. Ed. and pref. by Mieczysław Jastrun. Wrocław-Warsaw-Krakow: Zakład Narodowy im. Ossolińskich, 1967.
Poggioli, Renato. *The Poets of Russia, 1890-1930*. Cambridge, Mass.: Harvard University Press, 1960.
Pollak, Seweryn. "Niektóre problemy symbolizmu rosyjskiego a wiersze rosyjskie Leśmiana." *Twórczość*, no. 12, 1962, pp. 69-83.
Pomorska, Krystyna. *Russian Formalist Theory and Its Poetic Ambience*. The Hague-Paris: Mouton & Co., 1968.
Porębowicz, Edward. *Pieśni ludowe*. Warsaw: Ludowa Spółdzielnia Wydawnicza, 1959.
Potebnia, Aleksandr. *Iz lektsii po teorii slovesnosti* (1894). Khar'kov, 1905.
———. *Mysl' i iazyk* (1862). 3rd ed. Khar'kov, 1926.
Prokop, Jan. "Niepochwycień złoty." *Życie Literackie*, no. 26, 1968.
Przesmycki, Zenon [Miriam]. "Wstęp do wyboru pism dramatycznych M. Maeterlincka" (1894). *Polska krytyka literacka (1800-1918)*. Vol. IV, Warsaw, 1959.
———. *Wybór pism krytycznych*. Krakow: Wydawnictwo Literackie, 1967.

Przyboś, Julian. "Czytając Supervielle'a." *Sens poetycki*. Ed. by B. Nowotarski. Krakow: Wydawnictwo Literackie, 1963.
———. "Granice poezji." *Linia i gwar*. Krakow: Wydawnictwo Literackie, 1959.
———. "Leśmian jako eseista." *Sens poetycki*. Ed. by B. Nowotarski. Krakow: Wydawnictwo Literackie, 1963.
———. "Leśmian po latach." *Linia i gwar*. Krakow: Wydawnictwo Literackie, 1959.
———. "Mój Leśmian." *Kamena*, XV, no. 22, 1962.
———. "Nieprzestarzałość Leśmiana." *Życie Literackie*, no. 26, (1962).
———. "Poeci żywiołu Sergiusz Jesienin i Bolesław Leśmian." *Ilustrowany Kurier Codzienny*, no. 7, 1926.
———. "Słowo o Leśmianie." *Poezja*, no. 12, 1967, pp. 11-13.
Przybyszewski, Stanisław. "Confiteor." *Polska krytyka literacka (1800-1918)*. Vol. IV. Warsaw: P.I.W., 1959.
Przyłuski, Bronisław. "Wstęp do B. Leśmiana: *Klechdy polskie*." London: Veritas, 1956.

Reynold, Gonzague de. *Charles Baudelaire*. Paris: Cres, 1920.
Rimbaud, Arthur. *Le Bateau ivre*. Ed. by W. Meyerstein. London: Metcalf & Cooper, Ltd., 1948.
———. *Une Saison en Enfer*. Paris: C. Klincksieck, 1960.
Rousseau, Jean Jacques. "Essai sur l'origine des langues." *Oeuvres complètes*, Vol. X. Frankfurt a/M, A. Sautelet, 1856.
———. "Lettre sur la Providence." *Vocabulaire technique et critique de la philosophie*. Paris: Gallimard, 1951.

Ruskoe narodnoe poeticheskoe tvorchestvo. Ed. by P. G. Bogatyrev. Moscow: Gosuchpedizd. Ministerstva prosveshcheniia, RSFSR.
Rymkiewicz, Jarosław M. "Genezis z ducha." *Myśli różne o ogrodach*. Warsaw: Czytelnik, 1962.

Sandauer, Artur. "Czas oswojony." *Poeci trzech pokoleń*. Warsaw: Czytelnik, 1962.
———. "Filozofia Leśmiana." *Poeci trzech pokoleń*. Warsaw: Czytelnik, 1962.
———. "Poezja twórczych potęg natury." *Polityka*, July 6, 1968.
———. "Pośmiertny tryumf Młodej Polski, czyli o poezji Bolesława Leśmiana." *Samobójstwo Mitrydatesa*. Warsaw: Czytelnik, 1968.

———. "... wobec Leśmiana." *Stanowiska* wobec. . . . Krakow: Wydawnictwo Literacki, 1963.
Schopenhauer, Arthur. *The Art of Literature.* Trans. by T. Bailey Saunders. Ann Arbor: University of Michigan Press, 1960.
Shestov, Lev [Shvartsman]. *Dobro v uchenii Gr. Tolstogo i F. Nitsshe.* St. Petersburg: Shipovnik, 1900.
———. *Filosofiia tragedii.* St. Petersburg: Shipnovik, 1901.
———. *Umozrenie i otkrovenie.* Paris: YMCA-Press, 1964.
Siedlecki, Franciszek. "O swobodę wiersza polskiego." *Skamander,* no. 3, 1938.
Sławiński, Janusz. "Recenzja 'Szkiców literackich' Bolesława Leśmiana." *Pamiętnik Literacki,* no. 1, 1961, pp. 218-231.
Słobodnik, Włodzimierz. "Pieśni mimowolne." *Wspomnienia o B. L.*
Sokolov, Y. M. *Russian Folklore.* Trans. by Catherine R. Smith. New York: The Macmillan Co., 1950.
Spinoza, Benedict [Baruch]. "Tractatus de Intellectus Emendations." *The Encyclopedia of Philosophy,* Vol. V. New York: Macmillan & Free Press, 1967.
Staff, Leopold. "Wstęp." *Bolesław Leśmian: Wybór poezyj.* Łódź-Krakow: Spółdzielnia Wydawnicza Książka, 1946.
Starkie, Enid. *Arthur Rimbaud.* Norfolk, Conn.: New Directions, 1961.
Steiner, George. *Language and Silence: Essays on Language, Literature and the Inhuman.* New York: Atheneum, 1967.
Stepanov, Nikolai. "Tvorchestvo Velimira Khlebnikova." *V. V. Khlebnikov, Sobranie sochinenii,* Vol. I. Munich: Wilhelm Fink Verlag, 1968.
Stern, Anatol. "Powroty Bolesława Leśmiana." *Wspomnienia o B. L.*
Stone, Rochelle. "Leśmian i drugie pokolenie symbolistów rosyjskich," *Pamiętnik Literacki,* LXIII, 2, 1972, pp. 19-50.
———. "Poezja Leśmiana a romantyzm polski," *Pamiętnik Literacki,*" LXIV, 2, 1973, pp. 147-166.
Szczerbowski, Adam. *Bolesław Leśmian.* Warsaw: Książnica Literacka, 1938.

Tiutchev, Fedor I. *Izbrannye stikhotvoreniia.* New York: Izd. Imeni Chekhova, 1952.
Trznadel, Jacek. "Bolesław Leśmian." *Literatura okresu Młodej Polski.* Warsaw: P.I.W., 1968.

———. "Nieznane listy Bolesława Leśmiana." *Poezja*, no. 12, 1967, pp. 3-7.
———. "O listach." *UR, Listy.*
———. "Piłka rzucona w zaświat." *Poezja*, no. 12, 1967, pp. 44-54.
———. *Twórczość* Leśmiana. Warsaw: P.I.W., 1964.
———. "Wstęp do: Szkice Literackie Bolesława Leśmiana." *SL.*
Tsvetaeva, Marina. *Proza.* New York: Izd. Im. Chekhova, 1953.
Tuczyński, Jan. *Schopenhauer a Młoda Polska.* Gdańsk: Wydawnictwo Morskie, 1969.
Tuwim, Julian. "Leśmian. W dziesięciolecie śmierci." *Wspomnienia o. B. L.*

Ubegaun, B. O. *Russian Versification.* Oxford: Clarendon Press, 1956.

Valentinov, N. *Two Years with the Symbolists.* Ed. by Gleb Struck. Stanford: Hoover Institution on War, Revolution and Peace, Stanford University, 1969.
Vengerov, S. A. *Kritiko-biograficheskii slovar' russkikh pisatelei i uchenykh.* Vol. VI. St. Petersburg, 1904.
———. *Russkaia literatura XX veka: 1890-1910.* Vol. II. Moscow: "Mir," 1915.
Verlaine, Paul. "Clair de lune." *Fêtes galantes.* Paris, 1869. Reprinted in *Poésies complètes,* Vol. I. Paris: Editions de la Banderole, 1923-1926.
Versdichtung der russischen Symbolisten. Ed. by Johannes Holthusen and Dmitrij Tschizevskij. Wiesbaden: Otto Harrassowitz, 1959.
Veselovskii, Aleksandr. *Istoricheskaia poètika.* Leningrad: "Khudozhestvennaia Literatura," 1940.
Vico, Giambattista. *The Encyclopedia of Philosophy,* Vol. V. New York: Macmillan and Free Press, 1967.
———. *Principes d'une science nouvelle relative a la nature commune des nations.* Trans. by A. Doubine. *Scienza Nuova, Collected Works.* Paris, Editions Nagel, 1953.
———. *The New Science,* tr. by G. Bergin and M. A. Fish, New York: Ithaca, 1948.

Wierzyński, Kazimierz. *O Bolesławie Leśmianie.* Warsaw: Towarzystwo Wydawnicze, 1939.

Wspomnienia o Bolesławie Leśmianie. Ed. by Zdzisław Jastrzębski. Lublin: Wydawnictwo Lubelskie, 1966.

Wyganowski, Wojciech. "O Bolesława Leśmiana." *Wiadomości Literackie*, no. 8, 1931.

Wyka, Kazimierz. "Bolesław Leśmian. Dwa utwory." *Łowy na kryteria*. Warsaw: Czytelnik, 1965.

———. "Czytam Leśmiana." *Łowy na kryteria*. Warsaw: Czytelnik, 1965.

———. "Klucz nie zawsze doskonały." *Odrodzenie*, no. 5, 1946.

———. *Modernizm polski*. Krakow: Wydawnictwo Literackie, 1968.

———. "O czytaniu i rozumieniu współczesnej poezji." *Polonistyka*, no. 6, 1959.

Zawodziński, Karol Wiktor. *Studia z wersyfikacji polskiej*. Wrocław: Zakład im. Ossolińskich, 1954.

———. *Wśród poetów*. Krakow: Wydawnictwo Literackie, 1964.

Zdziechowski, Marian. "Pesymism, romantyzm a podstawy Chrześcijaństwa." *Zeitschrift für Philologische Forschung*, no. 3, 1960.

Zgorzelski, Czesław. "Wstęp do." *Ballada polska*. Wrocław: Zakład Narodowy im. Ossolińskich, 1962.

Zhirmunskii, Viktor M. "Poèziia A. Bloka." *Melodika stikha*. St. Petersburg: El'zevir, 1922.

Index